THE TELEVISION HISTORY BOOK

THE TELEVISION HISTORY BOOK

Edited by
Michele Hilmes

Associate Editor
Jason Jacobs

 Publishing

First published in 2003 by the
BRITISH FILM INSTITUTE
21 Stephen Street, London W1T 1LN

The British Film Institute is the UK national agency with responsibility for
encouraging the arts of film and television and conserving them in the
national interest.

Cover design: Squid Inc.
Cover image: Rediffusion camera technicians, UK, 1960s.

Set by Fakenham Photosetting, Norfolk
Printed in the UK by St Edmundsbury Press, Bury St Edmunds, Suffolk

British Cataloguing-in-Publication data
A catalogue record for this book is available from the British Library

ISBN 0–85170–988–5 (pbk)
ISBN 0–85170–987–7 (hbk)

Contents

(Grey box case studies are indicated in brackets)

PROGRAMMING: NEW VENUES, NEW FORMS

AUDIENCES

Preface

MICHELE HILMES

What does it mean to write, or read, television history? Both television and history are slippery objects of study: specific yet all-encompassing, pervasive yet elusive, sometimes seeming entirely 'natural' and transparent, but often highly selective and always constructed.

The word 'history' itself, in English, elides two separate concepts both crucial to understanding what it is that history does: history means both 'the past' – as in all the events occurring before the present moment in the course of real-life events – and 'historiography' or 'writing about the past', as in the sense of published or accepted narratives of such events (Jenkins, 1991). History as we know it necessarily combines both of these elements. We cannot get at the past except through narratives or accounts of some sort, and even the historians who construct these histories must rely on some kinds of preserved traces of the past, themselves usually constructed or written in some way. Those events that fail to leave records of the traditional or acceptable sort tend to be 'silenced' and dropped from history, as minority groups, women, and less authorised forms of cultural expression – e.g., quiz shows as opposed to news – have found to their peril (Trouillot, 1995).

If we insert television into this mix of elements, the picture becomes even more complicated. Television often serves both as our window onto the past and as an artifact of past events: are its programmes, images, and representations to be treated as historical evidence, as transparent (or semi-transparent) traces of the past? Do the paranoid sci-fi dramas of the 1990s, for instance, reflect something salient about our culture during that period? If so, then television history becomes a kind of social history, less important in itself than for the social trends it channels.

Or must television texts be understood as themselves constructed, not merely by social forces working anonymously underneath everything, but by specific conditions, regulations, and imperatives in the television industry, its social and institutional environment, and the uses made of it by the viewing public? Does *The X-Files*, for example, say more about the industrial circumstances of US television at a certain point in time than it does about some kind of national or global *Zeitgeist*?

At this point yet another complicating factor probably arises in the reader's mind: what about the conditions under which television is used, experienced, consumed? Is the history of *The X-Files* different when it is shown on Australian television than when it first appears on US network schedules? Would its appearance on the public network ABC (for example) rather than a commercial channel affect its reception, and thus its history as a cultural artifact? How do the various understandings that global audiences bring to a television text change its history, and further, if those understandings become a part of other aspects of social life – the activities of fan groups, for example, or the conspiracy theories of paranormal organisations, or concerns about the 'Americanisation' of world culture introduced into the negotiations of the European Union – how can these 'histories' be discussed in a volume such as this, devoted to television history?

Finally, when does history end? Or begin? In organising this particular volume, it seemed transparently necessary to acknowledge something of television's roots in radio broadcasting, if only briefly. But why start there – couldn't one go back to vaudeville, serialised fiction, and the history of the telegraph? And even more pressing for this particular task, when does 'history' stop and the 'current situation' take over? This editor had to be particularly careful not to step on the toes of other volumes in this series, trespassing out of the 'past' and into the 'present' in areas of industry study, genre development, and theoretical issues. Yet the present becomes the past even as you are reading these words, so that everything that we can write about is in fact history, inevitably. Few scholarly analyses divorce themselves from the development of the phenomena they study, so most critical works involve history of some sort. What differentiates a volume on 'television history' from anything else written on the subject of television?

None of these questions can be answered; they are part of the perilous task of writing history. But they can be acknowledged, so that the decisions and selections that underlie every task of historiography are revealed for the motivated choices that they are: inscribed *onto* history, not dictated by the past 'itself'. This volume reveals several such choices immediately. First, it focuses primarily on the television histories of Great Britain and the United States with glances aside at other countries' experience, though staying primarily within the category of English-speaking nations. Most of its contributors are British, North American, or Australian, having been trained in the universities of those countries. This focus is perhaps partially justified by the interests of the British Film Institute, who initiated and publish the volume, but it may also reflect some salient characteristics of world broadcasting history itself, namely the dominance of Great Britain and the United States in television production and distribution, and the vital influence they have had even on very distant and different cultural traditions. However, it also leaves much -- very much – out, including the television histories of other geographical or linguistic groupings, such as Spanish-language television, other European systems, and the huge impact of such Asian countries as India, Taiwan, and China (particularly Hong Kong) on world broadcasting and film (for a broader scope, yet still dominated by British and American history, see Smith, 1998).

Second, it was this editor's decision to divide television history into several different sections and recurring categories. As befits a 'history', most sections are arranged in chronological progression from the more distant past to the more recent. Grey boxes form part of most articles, and bring forward a specific focus – on an event, programme, individual, or case study – that illuminates the material in the larger piece. The first section, technology, concentrates on the history of the electronic instruments and devices that shaped and defined 'television', placed within their social and cultural context. The second section traces the growth of television institutions and policies in both Great Britain and the United States, focusing on industry structures and economics, laws and regulation, social and political context, and generally the infrastructure of television broadcasting over the twentieth century. It is divided into two parts, the first reflecting the institutional origins of the two contrasting systems and the establishment of television on radio's roots. The second part traces the many institutional conflicts, changes, and moments of relative stability as television matures into a national and, increasingly, international medium. Next comes a focus on programming, examining historical continuities and changes that span the decades of television's existence in both the US and the UK. Here a division between television's past decades, from the 1950s through the 1980s, highlights the development of TV in its role as the nation's public sphere, while the following section traces programme innovations resulting from the globalisation of television in the 1990s and beyond. The final section on audiences introduces the indispensable component of television without which all else would be meaningless, but which is particularly hard to discuss. Primarily this section traces the history of ways that audiences have been constructed by those in industry, government and academics, since here, especially, an actual 'history' of audiences would quickly blur into general social history.

However, even within the confines of these fairly arbitrary divisions, what unifies this volume – besides its focus on chronological development and change over time – is the perspective brought to each piece by the individual contributors. All of them are significant scholars in the current field of media studies, and all recognise the unique place that television holds in twentieth, and now twenty-first, century social life. It is a ubiquitous and central force in political, social, cultural and individual experience around the globe, and it cannot easily be separated from the larger events that surround it. Thus this volume seeks to take a cultural approach to television history, envisioning it not as merely a set of technologies or practices or institutions, but all of these things embedded in a larger matrix of experience, use and identity. It should provide more than just a handy and much-needed reference volume, but also stand as a marker for just how far television studies has come, despite its continuing status as a rank upstart in the fields of academe. I hope that it will inspire more cross-cultural, transnational work along these lines, as well as provoke some re-thinking of the ways we construct both television and history.

REFERENCES

Jenkins, Keith (1991), *Re-thinking History*, London: Routledge.

Smith, Anthony (ed.) (1998), *Television: An International History*, 2nd edition, Oxford and New York: Oxford University Press.

Trouillot, Michel-Rolph (1995), *Silencing the Past: Power and the Production of History*, Boston: Beacon Press.

ACKNOWLEDGMENTS

This book would not exist but for the vision and efforts of Andrew Lockett of the BFI, who commissioned it, and Ann Simmonds, who made it all come together. Jason Jacobs, the associate editor, not only played an absolutely vital role in identifying contributors and persuading them to write for the project, but also wrote several key essays himself. I am especially grateful to all our contributors, whose knowledge and scholarly generosity makes the book what it is: a unique compilation of irreplaceable information on the history of this much-discussed medium. I learned enormously in the process of editing this volume, and am pleased to bring the work of so many fine scholars together. Thank you all.

Notes on Contributors

Aniko Bodroghkozy is an Assistant Professor in the Media Studies Program at the University of Virginia. She is the author of *Groove Tube: Sixties Television and the Youth Rebellion* (Duke University Press, 2001). She has also published articles on film and television in the 1960s and early 70s in *Cinema Journal, Television and New Media* and *Critical Studies in Mass Communication*. She is currently working on a book about US television, race relations and audiences during the civil rights era titled *Negotiating Civil Rights in Prime Time*.

Clare Bratten teaches media studies at Middle Tennessee State University with a research emphasis on the cultural and social context of new media. Publications include 'Shore-ing up the Fifties: Constructions of Dinah Shore', in *Small Screens, Big Ideas: Television in the 1950s* (I. B. Tauris, 2001), 'Shoot Out at the Gender Corral: Annie Oakley Deconstructs Gender', *Children's Literature Association Quarterly*, Spring 1997, vol. 22, no. 1, and articles for the *Encyclopedia of Advertising* (Fitzroy Dearborn, 2002) and *Encyclopedia of Radio* (Fitzroy Dearborn, 2002).

Glen Creeber is a Senior Lecturer in Film and Television in the School of Theatre, Film and Television at the University of Wales, Aberystwyth. He is author of *Dennis Potter: Between Two Worlds, A Critical Reassessment* (Macmillan, 1998) and editor of *The Television Genre Book* (BFI, 2001). He is currently researching *Serial Fictions: Television Drama in the Age of the Mini-Series* (BFI), is Reviews Editor for the *International Journal of Cultural Studies* and his article 'Hideously White: British Television, Globalisation and National Identity' is due to be published in the journal *Television and New Media*.

Michael Curtin is Professor of Communication Arts at the University of Wisconsin-Madison. His books include *Redeeming the Wasteland: Television Documentary and Cold War Politics* (Rutgers, 1995), *Making and Selling Culture* (co-editor; Wesleyan, 1996) and *The Revolution Wasn't Televised: Sixties Television and Social Conflict* (co-editor; Routledge, 1997). He is currently writing a book about the globalisation of Chinese film and television and, with Paul McDonald, co-editing a book series for the British Film Institute called 'International Screen Industries'.

John Ellis is Professor of Media Arts at Royal Holloway University of London. His books include *Seeing Things* (I. B. Tauris, 2000) and *Visible Fictions* (Routledge, 1982). Between 1982 and 1999 he ran the independent television company, Large Door Productions, making documentaries for Channel Four and BBC2.

Jane Feuer is Professor of English at the University of Pittsburgh. She is the author of *The Hollywood Musical* (IUP, 1993), *Seeing Through the Eighties: Television and Reganism* (BFI, 1995) and the co-author of *MTM: Quality Television* (BFI, 1984).

Sylvia Harvey is Professor of Broadcasting Policy at Sheffield Hallam University and Principal Associate Director of the AHRB Centre for British Film and Television Studies. She is the author of *May '68 and Film Culture* (BFI, 1978) and has published widely on media policy, broadcasting regulation, independent film and Channel Four. She co-edited *Enterprise and Heritage: Cross Currents of National Culture, The Regions, the Nations and the BBC* (Routledge, 1991) and *Television Times* (Arnold, 1996). She is a founder member of the Sheffield International Documentary Festival.

David Hendy is Senior Lecturer in Radio and a member of the Communication and Media Research Institute at the University of Westminster, London. He is the author of *Radio in the Global Age* (Polity Press, 2000), and is currently researching and writing a social and cultural history of BBC Radio Four for Oxford University Press. He was a producer in BBC Radio between 1987 and 1993.

Michele Hilmes is Professor of Media and Cultural Studies at the University of Wisconsin–Madison and Director of the Wisconsin Center for Film and Theater Research. She is the author of several books on broadcasting history, including *Radio Voices: American Broadcasting 1922–1952* (University of Minnesota Press, 1997) and *Only Connect: A Cultural History of Broadcasting in the United States* (Wadsworth/Thomson Learning, 2002). She is co-editor, with Jason Loviglo, of *The Radio Reader: Essays in the Cultural History of Broadcasting* (Routledge, 2002).

Jason Jacobs is Senior Lecturer in the School of Film, Media and Cultural Studies, Griffith University, Brisbane. His publications include *The Intimate Screen: Early British Television Drama* (Oxford University Press, 2000) and *Body Trauma TV: The New Hospital Dramas* (BFI, 2003). He is currently researching a comparative history of television drama in Britain, America and Australia.

Ros Jennings is Director of Research in Arts and Humanities at the University of Gloucestershire. She has published on a range of television and film topics and is currently finishing projects on Australian television and the history of the female television protagonist.

Elana Levine is an Assistant Professor in the Department of Journalism and Mass Communication at the University of Wisconsin, Milwaukee. Her work has appeared in *Critical Studies in Media Communication, Studies in Latin American Popular Culture* and *The Velvet Light Trap*. She is currently working on a book titled *Wallowing in Sex: Television and Everyday Life in the 1970s*.

Justin Lewis is Professor of Communication and Cultural Industries at the University of Wales, Cardiff. He has written several books about media and culture. His particular interests are media influence, cultural policy and the ideological role of media in contemporary societies. His most recent book, *Constructing Public Opinion: How Elites Do What They Like and Why We Seem to Go Along with It*, is an analysis of the media and public opinion, published by Columbia University Press (2001).

Daniel Marcus is Assistant Professor in the Department of Communication at Wayne State University in Detroit. He has published articles on documentary, docudrama and alternative media. Before entering academia, he worked on a variety of alternative media projects, including Paper Tiger Television and Deep Dish Television.

Allison McCracken is Assistant Professor of American Studies at De Paul University in Chicago. She has published articles on radio, film, popular music and television (including *Buffy*), and her book *Real Men Don't Sing: Crooning and American Culture 1928–1933* is forthcoming.

Jamie Medhurst is Lecturer in Film and Television Studies at the University of Wales, Aberystwyth. His areas of teaching and research interest include broadcasting history, television and cultural theory, and documentary film history.

He has presented papers and published on the history of commercial television in Wales and is a contributor to the forthcoming *Encyclopedia of Documentary Film* to be published by Fitzroy Dearborn in 2003.

Eileen R. Meehan is Lemuel Heidel Brown Chair in Media and Political Economy in the Manship School of Mass Communications at Louisiana State University. She has been honoured with the Dallas Smythe Award by the Union for Democratic Communication and the Garry Carruthers Chair in Honors at the University of New Mexico, 2002–3. She is co-editor with Ellen Riordan of *Sex and Money: Feminism and Political Economy in Media Studies* (University of Minnesota Press, 2002) and with Janet Wasko and Mark Phillips of *Dazzled by Disney? The Global Disney Audiences Project* (Leicester University Press, 2001).

Jason Mittell is Assistant Professor of American Civilization and Film & Media Culture at Middlebury College. His essays have appeared in *Cinema Journal, The Velvet Light Trap, Television and New Media, Film History, Journal of Popular Film & Television* and a number of anthologies. His book, *Genre and Television: From Cartoons to Cop Shows in American Culture* will be published by Routledge in 2004.

Albert Moran is Senior Lecturer in the School of Film, Media and Cultural Studies, Griffith University, Brisbane. He is the editor of *Film Policy: International, National, and Regional Perspectives* (Routledge, 1996) and the author of *Projecting Australia* (Currency Press, 1991) and *Copycat TV: Globalisation, Program Formats and Cultural Identity* (University of Luton Press, 1998)

Rachel Moseley is Lecturer in Film and Television Studies at the University of Warwick. She has published on a range of popular film and television, and is the author of *Growing up with Audrey Hepburn: Text, Audience, Resonance* (Manchester University Press, 2002). She is currently researching teen film and television.

Matthew Murray received his PhD in Communication Arts from the University of Wisconsin-Madison and is currently a Digital Media Producer at the University of Illinois, Chicago. He has published articles on broadcasting history and cultural issues in a variety of journals and anthologies, including *Critical Studies in Mass Communications, Convergence, Society and Space* and *Small Screen, Big Ideas: Television in the 1950s* (ed. Janet Thumim, I. B. Tauris).

Tom O'Malley is Principal Lecturer in Media Studies at the University of Glamorgan. He is co-editor of the journal *Media History*. He publishes on media history and policy. His books include *Closedown? The BBC and Government Broadcasting Policy 1979–92* (Pluto, 1994) and, with Clive Soley, *Regulating the Press* (Pluto, 2000).

Tim O'Sullivan is Professor and Head of Department of Media and Cultural Production at De Montfort University, Leicester. He has written on aspects of historical film, radio, advertising and television and is currently completing a study of British television and the home in the 1950s.

Lisa Parks is Associate Professor of Film Studies at the University of California, Santa Barbara. She is the author of *Cultures in Orbit: Satellites and Television* (Duke University Press, 2003), and co-editor of *Planet TV: A Global Television Reader* (New York University Press, 2003) and *Red Noise: Buffy the Vampire Slayer and Television Studies* (Duke University Press, forthcoming). She has also published essays in *Screen*, *Television and New Media*, *Convergence* and *Social Identities*.

Alisa Perren is a Doctoral Candidate in the Department of Radio-Television-Film at the University of Texas, Austin. Her primary research interests are in media industry studies, US film and television history and the development of niche markets in contemporary Hollywood.

Willard D. Rowland, Jr is President and General Manager of Colorado Public Television, KBDI-TV/12 in Denver, Colorado. He is also Professor and the former Dean of the School of Journalism and Mass Communication at the University of Colorado. His teaching and research focus on media history and policy, the TV violence debates, public broadcasting and the history of communication studies.

Helen Wheatley is a Graduate Teaching Assistant in the Department of Film and Television Studies at the University of Warwick, where she is currently researching a PhD on Gothic television. She has published articles on real crime television in Britain in the 1990s and Gothic anthology series of the 1960s. Her current research interests also include the history and aesthetics of natural history television.

Brian Winston is an active journalist, documentary film-maker and writer. He is the Dean of Media & Humanities at the University of Lincoln and worked as a producer/director at Granada Television and BBC TV. In 1985 he won a US prime time Emmy for documentary script writing (for WNET New York). His eleventh book, *Lies, Damn Lies and Documentaries*, was published by the BFI in October 2000. His ninth, *Media Technology and Society*, was voted the best book of 1998 by the American Association for History and Computing.

INTRODUCTION

TV Nations

Television may have become our leading global medium but its history is deeply bound up in the identities of nations. Despite the ability of electromagnetic waves to defy lines on the map and to cross large distances more efficiently and cheaply than any previous medium, broadcasting as a social technology was captured and confined by national interests from its very earliest years. Born in the struggles of World War I, radio promised capacities too valuable to military, political and economic powers to be left to develop on its own. In Great Britain and in the United States, as in most other countries, national governments assumed a greater degree of control over the establishment and development of broadcasting than they dared for any other medium of communication, in the interests of social order, political control and preservation of central cultural and economic hierarchies. First radio, then television, was defined by such states as a uniquely *national* medium, confined to the borders of the nation (whether or not it might sometimes exceed them physically) and meant to construct and address a national public (Scannell and Cardiff, 1986; Hilmes, 1997).

In most countries, including Great Britain, the state itself took a strong hand in setting up basic structures, including public ownership and funding, with a fairly high level of governmental direction through public policy. In the United States, broadcasting developed as a privately owned, commercial enterprise that nevertheless relied on a higher degree of state regulation and oversight than any other US medium before or since, despite the existence of free speech protections in the US Constitution. Other nations, such as Australia, Canada and Mexico, attempted to integrate private and public systems. Yet across the board, the task of national unification, definition and dissemination of a national culture and defence against the inroads of other nations remained central to broadcasting's mission.

Correspondingly, most histories of broadcasting have stayed within national boundaries. Comparative studies have been few, and largely confined to discussion of structures, laws and economics. The tricky business of comparative *cultural* studies of the media remains largely unexplored, with a few key exceptions (see Ang, 1985; Camporesi, 2000; Lacey, 2002; Miller, 2000).

The last twenty years, however, have seen a breakdown of television's essential nationality, encouraged by new technologies such as cable, satellites and the Internet, but also fuelled by the expansion of the global economy and the movement of peoples around the globe. This new state of globalisation, often adamantly resisted by national broadcasting institutions, has somewhat ironically brought about a recognition of just how narrowly national the history of television has been. This volume is one of the few to specifically engage in a cultural history that cuts across national boundaries, yet it must still acknowledge the fundamental separateness of television's history in Great Britain and the United States. A critical mass of scholars has not yet been trained who could write a history of either television institutions or programmes during a particular period across national boundaries, though their numbers are growing (see, for instance, Smith, 1998; Scriven and Lecomte, 1999; Hendy, 2000). It is my hope that this volume will contribute to such a transnational approach.

Yet television's 'nationalness' goes even further: most nations have essentially defined their task not only as promoting their own culture but as actively resisting and excluding those cultures or cultural influences considered alien – in particular, alien *popular* cultures. Attempts to ward off the inroads of non-national broadcasters form a part of most countries' histories, from the BBC's resentment of offshore radio stations Radio Luxembourg and Radio Normandie before World War II, to the US's discouragement of so-called 'border blasters' located over the Mexican border, to Canada's establishment of the Canadian Broadcasting Corporation to resist cross-border broadcasting from the US, even to the basic requirement of licensing of station operators (usually excluding non-nationals) and the prosecution of pirate broadcasters in nations all over the world. On a cultural level, one of the recurring elements of television history has been resistance to incorporating the popular cultural products of other nations, notably those of the US, into national broadcasting systems (see Collins, 1999; Camporesi, 2000; Vipond, 1992). This is much less true for those elements of culture considered 'high' or 'legitimate', such as classical music, literature, drama or 'authentic' folk forms. At times international exchange of this sort of cultural product has even been regarded as desirable and as part of broadcasting's public service mission.

On a deeper level, the history of broadcasting is as much about *establishing and maintaining differences* between national cultures and systems as it is about recognising or disseminating an integrated, pre-existing cultural whole. Broadcasting has played a significant role in creating and defining national identity in the twentieth century, at least partially through resistance to, and differentiation from, not only those non-authorised aspects of the national culture (as witnessed by the history of suppression of African-American broadcasting in the US, or of working-class culture in the Reithian BBC, or the denigration of women's programmes everywhere) but also from the influences of other nations. One of the most influential sets of differentiations and oppositions in the history of world broadcasting has been that between the US and Great Britain, even though (or perhaps because) they share so many cultural elements in common. Both entered early onto the broadcasting stage, originating important technological and institutional developments that influenced nations across the globe. The commercial, privately owned broadcasting system of the United States, and the public service system of the BBC originated in Great Britain, served as models and basic paradigms for other nations as they grappled with early decisions about the new medium.

Yet, for complex historical reasons, these two nations defined and defended their national broadcasting systems largely in opposition to each other. The BBC's state-chartered, publicly funded system structured itself as specifically non-commercial and non-popular, in distinct and frequently articulated contrast to its American counterpart. The American commercial system, with its penchant for the popular, contrasted itself pointedly against the 'government monopoly' of the BBC and its advocacy of cultural uplift and education. From the earliest evocations of 'American chaos' inscribed in the founding documents of the BBC, to debates over 'Americanisation' of radio and television programming throughout the decades, the public service system in Great Britain as in other countries sought to avoid not only US domination of media production but its 'vulgar' cultural influence as well, by carefully regulating and restricting the commercialisation of television, well into the 1990s. In the United States, constant warnings against the slippery slope of 'government control', as represented by the BBC, aided commercial broadcasters in defending their profitable

franchises against attempts to assert the public interest – from the debates over establishment of the Communication Act of 1934, to the establishment of the 'classic network system' in the 1950s, to the disappearance of the Fairness Doctrine in 1989 (Hilmes, 2003).

Yet in the midst of recurrent outbursts of finger-pointing and blame, much mutual study, cross-influence and cultural borrowing shaped programming and institutional structures in both countries. It is no coincidence that US public television has been so heavily dependent on British production, nor that some of commercial television's most critically acclaimed popular shows have been based on British models. American commercial broadcasters have drawn upon the cultural ideals of British public service broadcasting as well, when it suited them to do so to preserve their hegemony, from the 'sustaining programmes' (non-commercial, public service programmes produced by the networks themselves) of the 1930s to the eminence in the 1980s and 90s of 'producer/auteurs' along the British model. In Great Britain, even as 'Americanisation' was deplored on one hand, British commercial broadcasting made much use of US television series in the 1950s and 60s to win its early victory over the still-stuffy BBC, as did a later, more popularised BBC, and US models have influenced programming ever since. Not least, a kind of 'resistant hybridity' with American popular culture worked to encourage the gradual acceptance of more intrinsically 'British' popular performers and genres, from the BBC's insistence on airing only British jazz musicians in the 1940s to the outburst of 'laddish' comedy in the 1980s.

Now, as the national systems of control established in the early decades of the last century are breaking down under the forces of deregulation, globalisation and new technology, we might re-examine this public service versus commercial, British versus US dichotomy, so influential around the world, and turn our attention instead to the questions raised by their mutual opposition. Why is national identity so much more central in the operations of broadcast culture than it is in print, music, art or film? Does the popular have to be commercial, does quality have to be non-commercial or is this dichotomy a destructive red herring, the result of historical battles whose social and political roots lie far in the past but whose effects linger? Is globalisation necessarily synonymous with Americanisation, or has the emergence of a global popular culture transcended such nationalising categories, and revealed the local hierarchies that work to repress popular cultural hybridity? These are the questions that a comparative historical study can engender, so that we might think outside existing frameworks as we face a radically different future. The essays in this volume, by presenting this contested but mutually constructive history side by side, will, it is hoped, allow the next generation of scholars to address these vital issues.

Michele Hilmes

RECOMMENDED READING

Branston, Gill (1998) 'Histories of British Television', in Christine Geraghty and David Lusted (eds), *The Television Studies Book*, London: Arnold.

Camporesi, Valeria (2000), *Mass Culture and National Traditions: The BBC and American Broadcasting, 1922–1954*, Fucecchio, Italy: European Press Academic Publishing.

Smith, Anthony (ed.) (1998), *Television: An International History,* 2nd edition, Oxford and New York: Oxford University Press.

TECHNOLOGIES

Introduction

Television's history is deeply bound up with the history of technological development in the twentieth century and into the twenty-first. Indeed, its innovations, refinements, conflicts and changes as a medium can hardly be separated from the concurrent inventions, adaptations and revolutions in technology that made first radio, then television, and now the new digital media possible. Yet television's history cannot be reduced to the history of its parts. The essays in this section trace the development of important underlying technologies, from radio's astonishing feat of sending voices and music into the air, through the battles over adding image to sound, and the subsequent technologies that affected the medium's reach, penetration and capacities, up to the current transformations of digital technology and the Internet. But they all add another dimension that keeps this history from falling into the 'technological determinism' trap identified by cultural historian Raymond Williams: the recognition that technology itself does not develop separately from the culture that surrounds it, and that at every step of the process of technological innovation, cultural pressures and demands shape both the technology itself and the uses to which it is put. The development of radio begins this history, not simply as a tale of tubes and circuits but as a process deeply embedded in the needs and desires of nations in the early twentieth century. Radio's emergent technology, closely linked to the processes by which nations determined radio's structures, uses and expressions, set the basic terms under which television would be introduced a few decades later. A grey box on the invention of the soap opera, or serial drama form, demonstrates clearly how broadcasting became a central 'technology of culture' in both the US and the UK, drawing on established forms while adapting them to the technological, institutional and social possibilities of the new medium, and introducing cultural controversies that would persist throughout the century. Television technology emerged over the twentieth century in a transnational setting, reflecting not only the 'march of science', from Nipkow to Zworykin to RCA, but also the conflicts that both stimulated television development and held it to certain paths. Not just inventors working in labs, but politics, social struggles and regulatory decisions worked to shape television as we know it, and led to the controversy over television transmission standards now operating in the debate over high-definition television.

Next, cable, satellite and digital media are examined in terms of the ways in which these technologies, all developed with little thought of their specific applications for television in mind, both responded to tensions in the industry and institutions of television and themselves brought about unanticipated, though profound, changes. The grey box introduces the issue of intellectual property, always an important leitmotif running through the history of broadcasting, but brought into new prominence by the introduction of digital media. And finally, the history of Internet development demonstrates again the heady mixture of national politics, institutional pressures and the occasional intrusion of pure serendipity that produced the technology that has changed many of our basic understandings of information and of media at the beginning of this new century.

Michele Hilmes

Television's Prehistory: Radio

Television is visual. Radio is aural. This stark polarity is true, but profoundly misleading. It gets in the way of a proper understanding of television's past. It blinds us to the many things that hold these two media together – not least that radio's history between the 1920s and the early 1950s established very many of the defining structures and practices of the television era. It was radio that turned a pre-existing technology – the transmission of messages to distant receivers without wires – into a social phenomenon that we call broadcasting.

Not that broadcasting had been a long sought-for activity. Wireless *telegraphy* had been anticipated since the 1860s by the successive work of James Clark Maxwell, Thomas Edison and Heinrich Hertz into electromagnetic waves and electrical currents; Oliver Lodge had sent Morse code messages over the electromagnetic spectrum by 1894; and Guglielmo Marconi had famously succeeded in getting a signal to cross the Atlantic in 1901, proving that the curvature of the earth was no obstacle to the radio wave. But the first application of such technology was seen in strictly limited terms: a way of sending messages from one person to another. The fact that a large number of other people might also be able to catch the signal was seen as a definite disadvantage, particularly by the military authorities that first took a keen interest. Even when the Canadian Reginald Fessenden first used radio waves to carry an actual human voice through the atmosphere, with his Christmas Eve broadcast to several ships off the Massachusetts coast in 1906, the adoption of the phrase 'wireless *telephony*' to describe the achievement is a measure of the limited vision of its potential.

Finding the 'leaky' nature of the radio signal to be an advantage rather than a weakness was a slow and uneven process. The post-World War I craze for 'listening-in' with cumbersome and inelegant receiving equipment in garages, sheds or lofts was largely a phenomenon of men and boys – often more interested in the technology itself than whatever might be heard through the crackle of the ether. Much of what they could hear was, in any case, likely to consist of interminable incantations of 'call-signs'. But the numbers involved alerted more prescient observers to the opportunities that broadcast telephony might offer the entrepreneur. If only receivers could become household utilities like record players, thought one employee of the American Marconi Company, David Sarnoff, the transmission of some form of regular entertainment and information might provide an enormous stimulus to the sale of receivers:

> The receiver can be designed in the form of a simple 'Radio Music Box' and arranged for several different wavelengths, which would be changeable with the throwing of a single switch or pressing of a single button . . . The box can be placed in the parlor or living room, the switch set accordingly and the transmitted music received . . . This proposition would be especially interesting to farmers and others living in outlying districts removed from cities. By the purchase of a 'Radio Music Box' they could enjoy concerts, lectures, music, recitals, etc., which may be going on in the nearest city. (Quoted in Crisell, 1997, p. 12)

Crucially, such rhetoric tapped right into the social milieu of the post-war era. It recognised some of the consequences of a newly industrialised and mass democratic society. Universal suffrage was coming into being, but the public sphere of political debate had always been a strictly invitation-only affair. There was fear too about social division,

Making the nation 'as one man' – John Reith
(Copyright © Hulton Deutsch Collection)

compounded in the early 1930s by the traumatic consequences of recession. America was experiencing new waves of mass immigration, which further muddied any attempt to define national identity. In Britain class divisions were painfully obvious; the mass of new voters were unable to experience most of the pleasures and reassurances of national cultural life. So when John Reith took charge of the cartel of radio set manufacturers set up in 1922, and known as the British Broadcasting Company, he could see that broadcasting was a chance to do something more than sell a new consumer good. Since it was, in principle, available to everyone, radio 'equalised' public life: it gave common access to events and entertainments that only a tiny minority had hitherto been privileged to enjoy. Imbued with a sense of moral purpose and social duty, Reith saw in the BBC the means, not just to plug an information gap but also to provide cultural 'uplift' for the lumpen masses and to make the nation 'as one man'. The transmission, simultaneously, to many millions of people, of the Christmas Day royal broadcasts, or the earliest commentaries on national sporting events, soon defined broadcasting as *the* tool of social inclusion and of expanded horizons of experience. In America, similarly, coverage of the deepening crisis in Europe in 1938 saw over two-thirds of those Americans polled claim radio as their preferred news source (Scannell, 1990, pp. 129–30).

By then, people on both sides of the Atlantic had taken to radio with astonishing enthusiasm. Radio occupied the living rooms of fast-expanding suburbia, and was a taken-for-granted part of domestic life. Very nearly three-quarters of British households had a set. Though many would be tuned to new European commercial stations like Radio Luxembourg – especially during the austere broadcasting hours of the Reithian Sabbath – a majority of the country's adult population would be tuning in to the National Programme's main evening news. In America, 40 million people across the States were tuning in to *Amos 'n' Andy* at its height. Programme-makers were experimenting with the medium – and, slowly and sometimes awkwardly, solving the problem of how to entertain and inform a distant and unseen audience. Before radio, comedians had been used to performing before a co-present and responsive audience; politicians had known only how to declaim at public meetings and speeches. The domestic setting of radio created new standards. The microphone, as the BBC's Hilda Matheson realised, had 'a curious knack of showing what is real and unreal . . . what is sincere and what is an appeal to the gallery' (quoted in Scannell, 1990, p. 162). Talk on the BBC was still very much scripted and rehearsed, but it was increasingly scripted so as to at least *sound* natural to the listener at home: intimate, personal, and informal – in other words, pretty much how people expected to be talked to in their own living room.

Similarly, the 'crooning' of entertainers such as Bing Crosby, though viewed with distaste by many at the BBC, also saw in the microphone a medium of intimacy. The simple re-broadcasting of live stage shows came to be displaced by new forms of 'radiogenic' variety, comedy, drama-serial and chat-show. American radio set the pace with shows like *Burns and Allen* and *The Bob Hope Show*; the BBC followed with its own hits, like *In Town Tonight* and *Band Waggon*. Even news programming came to be structured according to dramatic values. The importance of running orders and eye-witness reports was recognised by the BBC's Head of Talks, Charles Siepmann, as an effort to provide 'a minor drama of events, to give the recital of the disjointed and apparently irrelevant happenings of the day the elements of a story, a flow, a sequence, a dramatic setting' (quoted in Scannell, 1990, p. 107). The monotone of monologue was increasingly relieved by introducing more voices – even sometimes those of 'ordinary' people who could speak from experience – and the clash of opinion came to be represented through the evolution of 'discussions', interviews and 'magazine' programmes. The steady introduction of lighter and more portable recording equipment – cumbersome trucks carrying wax-cylinders

giving way slowly to forms of magnetic tape developed in Germany – allowed the 'actuality' of people in their real settings to be heard. Through radio, the contemporary world became more real and vivid.

In all this, the BBC frequently sniped at American programming techniques but, reluctantly, it slowly recognised the future over the horizon: 'In that country the "So-and-So Hour" of which the label at first conveyed nothing but the advertiser's name came to mean a specific kind of entertainment associated with that name to which people turned regularly' (*BBC Annual*, 1936, p. 58).

This wasn't just about adopting American standards of polish and pace, but about regularity and continuity. Across music, entertainment and news, programmes were being made that had a sufficiently recognisable structure and style to allow for the pleasures of hearing new material *and* of anticipating the reassuringly predictable. A show's 'format', and its *scheduling* to ensure it recurred at a predictable time each week, allowed for the cumulative pleasures of broadcasting, in which loyal audiences shared 'in'-jokes and a sense of belonging to the listening community. 'Serial production' of radio programmes thus solved two central tasks of broadcasting: how to ensure an endless supply of material cheaply and efficiently, and how to provide material that fitted with the rhythms of domestic life. Once solved, radio achieved a sort of 'golden age', a flowering of styles and programmes that collectively became a taken-for-granted part of everyday life for millions. Soon, these practices would become the backbone of television.

This shared sense of national culture could not have been achieved, though, without a relentless and stifling centralisation of production. Networks of high-quality telephone cabling and chains of transmitters allowed programme material to be distributed between individual stations. In the United States, this enabled hundreds of local and independent stations to fall under the logic of cheap production and hugely expanded advertising markets: they started to take more and more material from major production bases in New York, Chicago and Hollywood run by the big advertising agencies – agencies which naturally preferred to reach as wide an audience as possible. Independent local broadcasting, some of it truly public in style and ethos, was irrevocably marginalised after the creation of the National Broadcasting Company (NBC) in 1926 and the Columbia Broadcasting System (CBS) two years later. Though never officially sanctioned, commercial network broadcasting became the *de facto* 'American system' (Hilmes, 1997, p. 22). In Britain, Reith saw a 'top-down' approach to broadcasting as the most effective way of ensuring that programme output fitted his concept of public service, in which the standards and values of metropolitan culture were taken to be self-evidently better than anything in the rest of the country. Stations in Manchester and Birmingham soon learned to defer to London's 'head office', and by 1930 local radio had vanished – replaced by the National programme from London and the Regional programme produced from five centres across England and Scotland. Each programme had to contribute towards the overall objectives of the BBC, and a unity of tone was a central concern: programme-makers learned to recognise 'what goes and what does not'; orthodoxy was established in production techniques.

There was then, as Scannell notes, a gradual process of broadcasters learning 'what their business as broadcasters was' – discovering how to make programmes broadly uplifting in tone that also somehow 'worked' for a distant audience of individuals with diverse tastes. By 1939 'the lineaments of a common culture of broadcasting had begun to emerge' (1990, pp. 17–19). But something was lost, too. The informality of the pioneering days was replaced by a studied formality, a unified conception of culture and manners, and a new 'professionalism' that excluded many styles of broadcasting and individual voices. The BBC remained uncomfortable with working-class accents, particularly if they came with a dose of subversive politics. And despite the BBC's recurrent efforts to carve out its own news service through the late 1920s and 30s, and the innovative social documentaries and talks by pioneers such as Olive Shapley and Hilda Matheson, the BBC had – even by the time of the General Strike in 1926 – become too close to the political centre of British life to resist entirely censorship and interference, or to recognise for itself that the public interest did not necessarily coincide with that of the government of the day. This recognition would come, not least because the increasingly scientific art of audience research soon confronted BBC planners with the reality of just how out of touch they were with popular taste. In the meantime, though, the relative freedom of American networks to report on topical matters of controversy was seen with some envy. Yet in America, too, the centralisation of broadcasting had brought plenty of exclusions: radio shows like *Amos 'n' Andy* perpetuated a longstanding 'minstrel' tradition that demeaned millions of black Americans.

Centralisation and networking had, then, brought a certain uniformity of tone in which aspirations for a 'common culture' of broadcasting were often realised as little more than a broadly acceptable average of tastes and styles. Broadcasting was established as something exciting, but also as something strikingly mundane, continuously produced, bureaucratically directed, generally 'realist' in tone, and middlebrow in feel. Yet the centre could not hold. In America, broadcasters demarcated more and more between the undemanding soaps and chat-shows of the daytime audience of 'impressionable' housewives, and the classier shows transmitted for the more masculine (and therefore 'more discerning') 'prime-time' audience. In the BBC, music programmers failed to convince a public drawn to dance bands and crooning of the virtues of chamber music and modernist masterpieces. Increasingly, the Reithian desire to surprise the listener had to be tempered with the realisation that listeners might not put up with being offered only what was good for them rather than what they wanted: competing styles and values had, sometimes, to be kept apart on the schedules. Hierarchies of taste were reinforced by radio rather more often than they were dissolved. When the technology of FM broadcasting was eventually adopted, and the spectrum available to broadcasting was expanded, the fragmentation of the radio audience across several competing channels, each serving a somewhat different part of the listenership, became inevitable. In that too, radio presaged the path of television – the medium that had already robbed it of its broad and mixed mainstream audience.

David Hendy

RECOMMENDED READING

Crisell, Andrew (1994), *Understanding Radio*, London and New York: Routledge.

Douglas, Susan (1999), *Listening in: Radio and the American Imagination*, New York and Toronto: Random House.

Hendy, David (2000), *Radio in the Global Age*, Cambridge and Malden: Polity.

Hilmes, Michele and Loviglio, Jason (eds) (2002), *Radio Reader: Essays in the Cultural History of Radio*, New York and London: Routledge.

THE ORIGINS OF THE SOAP OPERA

It is in the radio 'soap opera' that we see most clearly the first application of mass production techniques to simple recording practice, the beginnings of a broadcast form which embodied not the free expression of the single creative artist but the application of industrial methods – assembly lines, routines, fast throughput and so on. Though the 'soap' had its origins in the serialised stories of the newspapers, it was through radio, then, that one of television's staples first established itself, not just as a distinctive programme style, but also as a production routine sufficiently mechanised for the unceasing demands of broadcasting.

In American serials of the 1930s, like *Easy Aces*, *The Romance of Helen Trent* and *Ma Perkins*, the pattern is largely set. A medium listened to domestically seemed to demand a programme with a domestic setting of its own, where family life was the main concern. And just as women were at the centre of the daytime audience – and in control of the domestic purse-strings that advertisers wished to prise open – so, too, were women (or, at least, women of a certain kind) placed at the centre of the soap's actions, confronting issues of love and relationships, home and hearth. The drama was open-ended – it had to be to sustain characters and plot-lines across months and years – and generally returned for fifteen minutes at the same time each day, five or more days a week, creating a sense that the fictional lives of the soap occupied the same time-line of existence as the listener at home.

The BBC pioneered its own engagement with the domestic serial drama through comedy series such as *The Plums* (BBC, 1937–?), about a northern working-class family described in *Radio Times* as being 'anyone and everyone'. Such series saw the creation of stock characters, allowing listeners 'to participate in the comedy by anticipating the characters' reaction to a new situation' (Scannell, 1996, p. 250). The BBC would introduce its first attempt at soap opera in 1940 with *Front Line Family*, produced especially for the North American Service as wartime propaganda aimed at the US and Canada, though kept carefully off home airwaves until 1945, when it debuted on the Light network as *The English Family Robinson*. It would be followed by *Mrs Dale's Diary* (BBC, 1947–57). The soap form was most fully realised on BBC radio, however, by *The Archers*, launched in 1951, and running ever since. Some 9 million tuned in each day to *The Archers* by 1953 (Briggs, p. 99).

By the mid-1940s, there were already more than sixty network and local serials in the United States. The sheer quantity of script needed to keep such open-ended dramas on the air led to a more and more mechanised production process. In

BBC radio's *the Archers*: running from 1951 to the present!

America, Frank and Anne Hummert embodied the assembly-line approach. Major plot-lines were sketched out and sent to stables of largely anonymous sub-writers in 'mills' or 'factories' who would flesh out the action and dialogue. Actors would work in studios to record several episodes in one session. As Hilmes observes, volume and consistency were essential (1997, pp. 166–70).

But with success came criticism. There had been serial dramas for the prime-time evening audiences of American radio, but the daytime hours had a reputation for undemanding fare – a reputation that the soaps both played into and suffered from in turn. They were melodramatic and frequently banal. They were damned, alternately, for being too trivial in their concern for the mundane and the domestic, or for being too controversial whenever they dared to tackle broader issues of public controversy, such as illegitimacy or racial inequalities. And, of course, as assembly-line products, they were the antithesis of the traditional concept of Art as the creation of a single – and free – mind. These associations would delay the adaptation of the soap opera form to television. In the US, the first daily daytime television serial did not appear until 1951, and not until the early 1960s would soaps become a daytime TV staple, with more than ten serials running on three networks daily. And despite the anomaly of *Peyton Place* (ABC, 1964–9) and the outbreak of such weekly prime-time soaps as *Dallas* (CBS, 1978–91), *Dynasty* (ABC, 1981–9), and *Knots*

Landing (CBS, 1979–93), the daily serial drama is still excluded from the evening hours. In Britain, it took commercial television to debut the first long-running serial, *Coronation Street*, in 1960 (Granada, 1960–). Other twice-or-more weekly serials followed, such as *Emmerdale Farm*, which debuted on ITV in 1978, and *Brookside*, first appearing on Channel Four in 1982. Though series such as *Compact* (BBC, 1962), a drama featuring female central characters set in the offices of a women's magazine, might have served some of the same purposes, not until 1985 would the BBC itself launch its long-running early evening serial *EastEnders*.

David Hendy

The Development of Television

The technology of television is grounded in the physical phenomena of variable resistance to electricity, photoemission and fluorescence. Its development and application, however, are bound up in the politics of national differentiation, industrial competition and regulation. All of these factors influenced the evolution of television technology.

The ability of a substance to conduct or resist an electrical current can be varied in some instances by changing the physical conditions affecting it. For example, the pressure of a sound wave will alter the resistance of carbon. If an electric current is passed though the carbon as it is subjected to changes of pressure, an analogue of the pattern of the changes will be produced as a pattern in the waveform of the electrical current.

In 1878, variable resistance was exploited to produce the first viable telephone. Almost immediately, it was suggested that the same principle could work with images using a camera with a substance that exhibited variable resistance when subjected to different light intensities. If the substance was also photoemissive, giving off light when stimulated by an electric current, it was possible that it could in some way reconvert the signal and so reproduce the original picture.

In 1873, the engineers laying what was to be the first successful transatlantic telegraph cable had reported that a metal, selenium, exhibited exactly such variable resistance to light and in 1884, Paul Nipkow patented the use of a selenium block as the heart of what he called an 'electric telescope' (Garratt and Mumford, 1952, pp. 25–6; Hubbel, 1942, p. 65). Nipkow suggested a camera with a spinning disc mounted between the lens and the selenium to transform the light into a modulated electrical wave. The disc would be pierced by a spiral of holes so the light coming through the lens would be broken up into a pattern. The electrical current passing through the selenium would then produce a waveform analogous to this pattern in the same way the carbon in the mouthpiece of a telephone 'transduced' sound pressure waves to modulate an electrical current.

Nipkow's device did not work, but that was primarily because the selenium was insufficiently sensitive to light. Moreover, his plans for reproducing the picture were extremely tentative as they had to be before the introduction of the photoemissive cathode ray tube (CRT) in 1897. Nevertheless, as the principle Nipkow had outlined for the camera was perfectly viable, other researchers using potassium, a metal with greater sensitivity to light, began a decades-long series of experiments with spinning discs. Eventually, transmitting to CRTs, precision-engineered discs encased in glass vacuums spinning at as much as 6,000 revolutions per minute, produced mechanically scanned images, nearly matching the image quality of contemporary 1930s' 16mm film; that is, 400 or more lines of horizontal resolution.

Progress from Nipkow to this point in the mid-1930s had been slow not only, or not even primarily, because of technological understanding. After the CRT, no new knowledge was either created or deployed; nor was it needed. The real barrier to progress, at least up to World War I if not beyond, was not the viability of the system as much as a lack of any clear sense of its potential purposes.

In the nineteenth century, no uses for Nipkow's 'electric telescope' were determined, in contrast to, say, radio of which military authorities took considerable notice. Facsimile transmission was a more obvious possible application and, as early as 1881, a system using selenium cells and paper impregnated with potassium iodide was demonstrated. (The potassium turned brown when a current passed through it and in this way an image was built up.) In 1906 a German patent outlined the use of a Nipkow disc and, for the first time, a CRT display for 'the transmission of written material' (Jensen, 1954, p. 174). As late as the 1930s, David Sarnoff, head of RCA and the NBC radio networks, was justifying the facsimile possibilities of telegraphic transmission: 'The ideal way of sending messages is to hold up a printed sheet that will be immediately reproduced at the other end' (Waldrop and Borkin, 1938, p. 74). For him the device was not so much radio with pictures as it was a tool for breaking up Bell's telephone monopoly. But, as the first suggestion for a selenium 'telectroscope' in 1879 had put it, 'fugitive pictures', not permanent copies, would be produced – not much use in a world that had been able to send telegraph faxes from and to paper since the 1840s.

Yet there surely had to be some viable use for the spinning discs. At the outset, that is after the introduction of the 'speaking telephone', some intuited that this might be a videophone. A *Punch* cartoon of 1879 imagined a 'telephonoscope', a picture telephone with a screen as wide as a mantelshelf. In 1927, a team at Bell Labs demonstrated, over 250 miles by wire and twenty-two miles by radio, a mechanically scanned videophone of more manageable proportions, a screen a mere 2 x 2½ inches (5 x 6 cm). By the early 1930s they increased both resolution (to seventy-two lines) and the screen size and had also introduced colour. A two-way interactive system was established in Manhattan. In 1938, the Germans built a videophone link between Berlin and Nuremberg using discs to produce a 180-line picture. Despite oft-repeated promises videophones never caught on – and still haven't.

Nipkow's electric telescope was first described as 'television' in a patent of 1900. In 1908, a senior electrical engineer, Alan Campbell Swinton, had dismissed all experiments with spinning discs to outline the essentials of the television system that was eventually brought to market in the mid-twentieth century. He had suggested that, instead of variants on the disc, an effective television system should be entirely electronic using 'two beams of kathode [*sic*] rays (one at the transmitting and one at the receiving station) synchronously deflected by the varying fields of two electromagnets' (Garratt and Mumford, 1952, p. 31). Magnets and cathode ray tubes in the camera as well as the receiver were to be the answer as Boris Rozing, a scientist in the St Petersburg Institute of Technology, demonstrated in 1911, when he transmitted black and white bars to a screen, for the first time using a CRT both for display and as a pick-up tube in the camera. However, despite this demonstration, a real social purpose had yet to manifest itself and the technology continued to languish. Apparently nobody thought about entertainment. This was not surprising in the 1880s and 90s, before the advent of motion pictures and with the most sophisticated lantern shows only capable of a few seconds of an animated movement. Even after the theatre became organised with industrial efficiency at the turn of the twentieth century, the *home* delivery of entertainment

was still not an obvious objective. For one thing, the habitations of the urban masses were a long way from being the potential site of leisure activities of any kind.

Radio was being similarly frustrated. In the first decade of the twentieth century, a major perceived problem was the security of the radio signal. It was a decade from the first clear demonstrations of wireless telegraphy to the transmission of a voice in 1906. But it took another thirteen years to the first broadcast – and only four of these were taken up by war. It required a post-World War I conceptual leap to turn radio's disadvantage – that anybody could hear it – into its point as an entertainment medium. This was the 'invention' that finally focused television researchers such as C. F. Jenkins, once a pioneer of the movie projector, on the idea of home entertainment. Specifically, Jenkins' objective was the home delivery of movies – although, it must be said that even he initially had a fax application in mind, the transmission of metrological maps for the US Navy.

By 1927 mechanical scanning had advanced enough for General Electric to obtain an experimental licence, while in Britain the independent entrepreneur John Logie Baird, whose mechanical system was then only producing thirty or so lines, was nevertheless already trying to sell 'televisors' to the public. These systems were getting better until, in 1936, Baird's German opposite number, Fernseh, created the best of these machines, exploiting the advantage that mechanical scanning then had with direct illumination of the sort to be found in telecine (film projector/television camera) devices. Fernseh constructed a film camera with an attached developing tank to produce a photographic image in under a minute. This was the machine which then scanned the film frame mechanically at 6,000 rpm to produce 440 lines on the CRT display (Gibas, 1936, p. 741).

Cameras with CRT pick-up tubes were based on a far more complex theoretical concept and, since the only technologists potentially capable of refining them were busy with radio, the very success of that medium in the 1920s acted to suppress concentrated research into all-electronic television. In 1924 Campbell Swinton had said: 'If we could only get one of the big research laboratories, like that of the G.E.C. or of the Western Electric Company – one of those people who have large skilled staffs and any amount of money to engage on the business – I believe they would solve a thing like this in six months and make a reasonable job of it' (Jensen, 1954, p. 176). In the event, another twelve years were to pass.

The last lap began in earnest in 1929 when Manfred von Ardenne demonstrated a sixty-line electronically scanned image, not just bars. In 1932 a team lead by Rozing's pupil

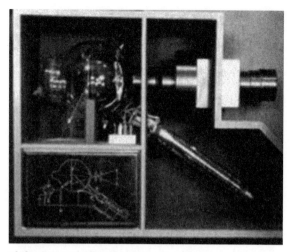

Vladymir Zworykin's *Iconoscope* camera (1932)

Vladymir Zworykin, working for RCA, produced the *Iconoscope* camera whose 240 lines of resolution matched the best of the mechanically scanned systems then available. Nevertheless it was rather 'noisy', displaying interference in the image, and the superiority of the electronic solution over the mechanical was still not clearly demonstrated. It was a sister team to Zworykin's at EMI, led by Isadore Schoenberg who had been another of Rozing's students, which worked out how to control the secondary cathode emissions, the major source of the noise. An individual researcher, Philo T. Farnsworth, initially backed by Philco Corp., contributed an effective method for amplifying the signal within the tube. By 1936 RCA and its British (EMI) and German (Telefunken) partners had a fully practical, entirely electronic system to hand.

But the spinning disc entrepreneurs were not ready to give up mechanical scanning. For example, Baird, an early master of public relations (or 'publicity stunts' as they were then called), had been fuelling an appetite for television long before there were watchable images. Nevertheless, such PR, in effect, forced the 1936 public run-offs between the mechanical and fully electronic solutions in Britain and Germany. The result, in Britain at least, was an unambiguous victory for the fully electronic system. Despite this, although the system existed 'in the metal' by 1936, it was still to be two decades or more before the medium became 'the shining centre of the home' (Boddy, 1990). (Again, only five years of this delay can be blamed on war.)

Germany in 1936 and Britain in 1937 had established television services, using in essence RCA's technology, but neither the Berlin Olympics nor the Coronation of Edward VIII produced much public take-up. In Germany there was a Nazi hesitancy to sell *Volksfernsehen* for home use lest the

Führer was mocked in private, but even in democratic Britain only 20,000 sets were sold prior to the outbreak of war in 1939 (Uricchio, 1990, p. 115; Briggs, 1961, p. 583). One reason was that exactly a decade of hype about barely visible pictures on miniscule screens had deterred potential buyers. Another was that television was the responsibility of radio broadcasters who were just as likely to see the new medium as a threat as they were to push for it as an opportunity.

This conflict of interest was most vivid in the United States where RCA, one radio company among many, threatened all its rivals because it owned the central patents for the triumphant electronic television system. The Federal Communications Commission (FCC), which had already spent decades grappling with the phone company's monopoly, needed little pressure from the rest of the radio industry to frustrate RCA's monopolistic television plans. The commission refused to license a commercial service, persisting in treating the technology as 'experimental' when, as the two European services showed, it was, quite obviously, no longer any such thing. Only five years after the defeat in Europe of the mechanically scanned system did the Americans achieve a *modus vivendi*. In late 1941, a National Television Standards Committee (NTSC) eventually agreed a standard for television that, except for a decision about using FM for the audio part of the signal and an increase to 525 lines, almost exactly matched what RCA had been proposing at the outset in 1936. What had changed were the terms for exploiting the patents. RCA were forced to share in return for the removal of its system's 'experimental' designation (Fink, 1945).

However, within months of this decision the United States was drawn into World War II and the full introduction of the service was further delayed. (The BBC also stopped transmissions but the Nazis continued with programming throughout the hostilities.) After the war, official American opinion saw television both as a consumer item and as a medium for advertising other consumer items, a vital engine for post-war recovery. Yet there were still issues to be resolved before the medium could be fully diffused, notably the need for television to come to terms with the film industry in Hollywood, matching the pre-war arrangements with non-RCA radio interests. This further accommodation was worked out with Hollywood between 1948 and 1952, the period of the so-called 'freeze'.

Following an initial post-war licensing flurry, by 1948 there were four networks, fifty-two stations and nearly a million sets in twenty-nine cities. Then the FCC froze all further applications for stations for four years while, ostensibly, problems with overlapping transmission areas were resolved. During this period, whose protracted duration cannot be explained by simple transmission problems, film became part of the new medium. The studios had been well aware of television before the war and indeed in the late 1940s were proposing using it to establish theatre-based large-screen projected networks. Stripped of their cinema chains by an anti-monopoly legal decision, they were also denied this alternative but a lucrative place for them was nevertheless found both in the licensing of their archives and in original production. In 1948, the nascent television schedules were dominated by live variety shows from New York. In 1952, *I Love Lucy*, shot on film, was the biggest hit on the little screen.

After the freeze progress was rapid. The number of TV stations jumped to 573 broadcasting to nearly 33 million receivers. Television was producing 70 per cent of broadcasting advertising revenues. The last significant technical decision on a colour system was also resolved immediately after the 'freeze' in favour of RCA. Three colour-sensitive pick-up tubes in the camera transmitted to a CRT tube coated inside the screen with triads of fluorescents which emitted primary red, green or cyan when stimulated by the electron stream. In 1956 NBC had offered the world's first full-colour, full-time schedule. By 1960 there were over 650 stations using the VHF waveband to reach 36.5 million homes.

Early TV set

Meanwhile, in post-war Europe black and white television was making slower but equally unstoppable strides. The BBC recommenced its television transmissions in 1946 and by the end of 1952 there were 3 million receivers in the UK; the BBC had completed its network of major transmitters which covered 78 per cent of the population. Having secured the transformation of the state broadcaster from radio to television, a competitive commercial TV service was licensed in 1954. The original London Standard of 404 lines was abandoned in 1960 to mark the start of the BBC's second network in favour of a 625 black and white compatible colour standard of German origin (Phase Alternate Line – PAL). Germany's own system had also been expanding, its northern network being completed by 1952. That year, Italy began a five-year plan to cover the nation. The French, using 819 lines (which was at the limit of what the internationally agreed TV bandwidth could accommodate), added Lille to Paris and started work on three other transmitters. In Canada, CBC began programming.

The rest of the world followed, Japan, Canada and South America adopting the US 525/NTSC colour standard while the Middle East followed the European 625/PAL system, as did the British Commonwealth, Canada apart. The French variant, including its own colour system, was adopted by the Soviet Empire including Cuba and its own ex-colonies. By 1970 there were 231 million sets in the world (37 per cent in the USA) and the system laid down a decade earlier was stable. It was to be so for another thirty years and more.

Brian Winston

RECOMMENDED READING

Boddy, William (1990), *Fifties Television: The Industry and Its Critics*, Urbana: University of Illinois Press.

Shiers, George (ed.) (1977), *The Technical Development of Television*, New York: Arno.

Winston, Brian (1998), *Media, Technology and Society*, London: Routledge.

HIGH DEFINITION TELEVISION: 1969–90

No attempts to revise the TV signal were made prior to 1969. In that year, the research laboratory of the Japanese state broadcaster, NHK, began working on a widescreen television standard to match the definition of 35mm film (that is, 1,000-plus lines of horizontal definition). There was no intrinsic difficulty in this except that such a signal would take up a far greater bandwidth than the established NTSC 525/60 cycle. But NHK's domestic agenda was not constrained by compatibility. Modelled on the BBC to depend on licence fees, it had established, with the introduction respectively of colour and teletext, that it would offer new services to justify any increase in fee. High definition would fulfil this purpose even if the entire production and transmission system as well as every set needed to be replaced. By 1972, the new standard of 1,125 lines and a 16:9 aspect-ratio, based on the old NTSC signal but using five times its bandwidth, was in place. In 1979, NHK successfully tested satellite transmission of 1,125/60 in the gigahertz (GHz) band (above UHF) and two years later Japanese manufacturers, notably Sony, rolled out what was supposed to be the second generation of television.

Although many engineers, by nature 'early adopters', were impressed with the technology, many more were wary of handing over to the Japanese a dominance over their television standards which, after all, had been elaborately created exactly to avoid any hint of monopoly. The Japanese themselves were confused as to their ultimate ambition for HDTV. NHK claimed it would be the new world standard while Sony, for example, saw it rather as a technology which would substitute for 35mm motion picture film and thus revolutionise the cinema, leaving the old home TV standards, and the upheaval required to change them, well alone.

At their meeting in Algiers in 1983, the world's TV engineers mandated a search for a worldwide HDTV standard, obviously giving NHK and its industrial partners a real chance at establishing a market; but three years later, in Dubrovnik, they thought again. Doubts about the system's adaptability to European 625/50 cycle PAL, its real technical advantages and, most of all, its fundamental incompatibility with existing television had grown sufficiently for 1,125/60 HDTV to be effectively buried. NHK's need for a new service to justify increasing its licensing fee was just not matched by any comparable demands elsewhere. Criticism of television had always been about its content and 1,125/60 did nothing about that.

On the other hand, the whole episode did open up the question of a new standard but, as became ever clearer in the 1980s, this would not be analogue-based as NHK's 1,125/60 had been. Digital modulation, which had been first demonstrated in 1938, was now possible for television because computing power could be used to compress its bandwidth requirements into a manageable size. Researchers, including the 1,125/60 team at NHK, began exploring digital and, had the neo-liberal economics not allowed for a plethora of possibly incompatible digital standards in the context of a governmental unwillingness to hold the ring, the changeover would perhaps by now be well under way. Instead, at the turn of the twenty-first century, old analogue sets are being replaced by 'fake' widescreen analogue ones and a new world standard, or even national digital standards, remain elusive.

Brian Winston

Cable, Satellite and the Challenge of Digital Media

From its inception, radio and then television broadcasting developed in deeply nationalist contexts, guided by the twentieth-century imperatives of national definition, unification and defence. Carefully kept from crossing national lines, crafted to address only its own citizens and no others, shaped and regulated by national governments, broadcasting history – and histories – reflect this nationalist bias. Cable, though in many ways a far more localised medium than broadcasting, was able to break through the limitations enforced by regulated broadcasting systems and eventually open up the national media universe. When linked with satellite transmission in the late 1970s, television's channel capacity soared, along with its ability to escape the defining constructs of nation. The rise of digital media heightened and accelerated this trend.

The basic technological premise of cable is simple: a 'headend' receives signals via satellite, microwave, or broadcast antennae; they are ordered into channels and often into 'tiers' of service, then passed through a system of coaxial cables and amplifiers down to the receiving sets in subscribers' homes. Usually one or two tiers of 'basic' service can be had for a relatively small amount per month; more channels can be added for additional fees, including 'premium' or 'pay' channels, such as HBO (Home Box Office) and Showtime, that cost extra due to their lack of advertising. Pay-per-view or subscription channels offer the ability to order films or special events, such as sports, for an additional per-program fee which allows the subscriber to 'unscramble' the electronically encoded signal.

In the late 1940s, a few remote or mountain-locked localities in the US, unable to receive television signals, began to set up high-ground antennae and run wires down into homes and businesses below, charging subscribers a dollar or two a month to pick up signals available from nearby cities. In Britain and other countries where television began as a state-sponsored public service monopoly, great effort was expended to ensure that broadcast reception was available nationwide from the beginning. Competition with state broadcasters was not allowed. In areas where reception difficulties abounded – within large apartment buildings in major cities, or in mountainous areas – cable was used primarily as a retransmission device from the early 1950s on. But until satellite transmission promised an outside source of programming, cable was limited in most public service-based systems to retransmitting the two or three state services available. Few incentives for expansion existed. In some countries, however, particularly Belgium, Luxembourg, Switzerland and the Netherlands, cable was used more extensively to relay multiple public service stations into areas outside their reach (Humphreys, 1996, pp. 164–5). In Canada, with its mix of public and commercial broadcasting, cable expanded much more rapidly, mostly as a vehicle for bringing American programming into Canadian homes, via microwave (Rutherford, 1990, pp. 137–40).

Opposed by broadcasters and regulators, limited at first to twelve or fewer channels, faced by high system construction costs, cable might have remained forever a secondary medium were it not for two technological developments of the late 1970s: satellite broadcasting and fibre optics. In 1975 Time Inc.'s subsidiary HBO launched the first service to take advantage of satellite distribution of unique, film-based programming to local cable franchises nationwide. Leasing a commercial satellite transponder and using it to beam its signal across the satellite footprint, HBO was only the first of cable's rapidly expanding specialised services that began to find a niche. Simultaneously, fibre optic technology – sending data through bundled glass fibres in place of the old copper wire – allowed cable systems to expand their channel capacity exponentially in the 1980s. Now cable came into its own. Atlanta station owner Ted Turner beamed his WTBS, with its exclusive franchise over the Atlanta Braves baseball team (also owned by Turner) up onto a satellite transponder, founding the first cable 'superstation' (see Hilmes, 'US Television in the Multichannel Age', in this volume).

Cable expanded across the globe. Canada's subscription rates had exceeded 80 per cent by the early 1990s (Collins and Murroni, 1996, pp. 45–6). In Europe, as a wave of privatisation and commercialisation transformed the public service environment, cable was envisioned as playing a key role in the new telecommunications infrastructure. It could be used to open up limited national systems to the new, combined public and commercial multichannel service now prevalent in most countries. By 1992, cable reached as many as 92 per cent of TV homes in Belgium and 87 per cent in the Netherlands, with most nations above the 30 per cent mark. Only France and Great Britain resisted the trend. Both had attempted to launch cable services; both had run into unforeseen difficulties resulting from a late start, cumbersome regulatory restrictions, and the unexpected rise of direct satellite competition (Humphreys, 1996, p. 165).

By the mid-1980s satellite broadcasting and cable had become deeply intertwined. Cable as we know it could not exist without the national and international distribution that satellites make possible. On the other hand, as direct broadcast satellite (DBS) becomes a medium in its own right, it promises the first real competition to cable television services. Both media depend on the vital technology of the geostationary satellite.

An Olympus I thermal model satellite

The first satellites used for communication purposes were launched in the early 1960s by US telecommunications companies such as AT&T, Hughes and RCA. COMSAT (the Communications Satellite Corporation) was formed in the US in 1962 with the encouragement and participation of the US government, much as RCA had been formed earlier, to co-ordinate American satellite development, investment and use. In 1964 INTELSAT (the International Telecommunications Satellite Organisation) brought together a consortium of countries to serve a similar purpose for international satellite operation; at first managed by COMSAT, it became an independent corporation in 1973, with shares owned by its member nations, which number over a hundred (the US, through COMSAT, owns 25 per cent).

At first, satellites orbited around the earth at speeds faster than the earth's own rotation; this meant that they had to be tracked as they moved across the sky by large arrays of receiving dishes. But the development of the geostationary, or synchronous, satellites in 1974 meant that now satellites could be launched into orbit in the exact spot – 22,300 miles above the equator – that allowed them to remain stationary in relation to the rotation of the earth. A dish could be set to receive the continuous signal of one satellite in one particular place in the sky, and never be moved. This made distribution and reception of satellite signals much more regular and reliable. Early satellites transmitted back to earth on the C-band, between 4 and 6 gigahertz and required enormous, bulky dishes for reception; more recent ones operate on the higher frequency Ku-band, between 11 and 14 GHz, and enable the use of tiny, pizza-size receiving dishes. Most satellites contain twenty-four transponders, or individual channel transmitters, though today's technology allows each transponder to be split to handle two or more separate signals.

The half-hemisphere-sized footprint of the typical satellite signal began radically to change the rules of the national media game. Because in the early stages of satellite television transmission dishes were so large and expensive to install, most satellite reception was done through cable channels: cable systems provided the middleman between service providers and the home audience. This fact alone helped to slow the development of cable in some European countries, such as France and Great Britain, since so much of the early television material available via satellite consisted of US-based entertainment and news programming. State broadcasters and agencies (particularly those who already produced the bulk of programmes viewed in their home countries) saw no need to invest public money to bring American programming to their national audiences, and would-be commercial providers needed government permission to operate, usually meeting with opposition from state broadcasting interests. However, in more heavily cabled countries the importation of distant signals via satellite, both from the US and from other European broadcasting systems, became a widespread practice.

In the US, DBS – sending satellite signals directly to receivers in people's homes – became a small but thriving industry in the 1980s. By the mid-1990s, with the deregulation of cable television and with most local franchises remaining monopolies in their areas, dissatisfaction with rising subscription rates, limitations on channels carried, and the kind of less-than-perfect service that monopolies tend to provide, began to encourage DBS ownership. Yet in an already commercial and fairly diverse environment, DBS presented simply one more option for delivery of the same kinds of entertainment, news and speciality channels that American audiences have regarded as normal since the 1980s.

In Europe and across the globe, however, the impact of satellite broadcasting has been profound. Coming at a time in the late 1980s when deregulation and commercialisation of broadcasting systems was taking place in most countries, as one author puts it, 'the rapid expansion of satellite channels had a tremendous impact. It removed, effectively, all practical constraints on the prompt development of private commercial channels' (Humphreys, p. 169). The first commercial satellite to debut in Europe was the Astra satellite operated out of Luxembourg, launched in 1988 with sixteen channels. In Great Britain the Independent Broadcasting Authority in 1986 authorised British Sky Broadcasting, a consortium composed mostly of UK commercial TV providers, to introduce satellite television to Britain in a regulated, public service context. However, its launch was delayed until 1990; in 1989 Rupert Murdoch's Sky Channel debuted, broadcasting from the Astra satellite, outside of British regulatory control (see O'Malley, 'Satellites, Cable and New Channels in the UK', in this volume). By 1991 Murdoch had bought out the struggling operation and renamed it BSkyB (see Jennings, 'Satellite and Cable Programmes in the UK', in this volume).

By 1991 a host of pan-European satellite services were on offer: twenty-one English-language services, ten German, eleven French and twenty-nine others. Some of the most popular channels were Sky One, Eurosport, MTV, CNN, Euronews, Canal Plus and the TNT Cartoon Network. In Quebec, satellite channels became an important source of French-language programming. According to *The Economist*, 'Digital technology has transformed the economics of multi-channel television, enabling independent operators to cater to market niches, and the big pay-TV companies to offer hundreds of channels' (2001). Movie channels account for a substantial proportion of satellite-distributed digital fare, especially in their 'nearly-on-demand' manifestations, where staggered fifteen-minute showtimes allow almost continuous availability of individual films. By 2001, digital pay television channels, delivered either by DBS or cable, had reached 44 per cent of UK households and accounted for 20 per cent of all television viewing.

The flexibility, user-friendliness and new creative possibilities that digital media bring to television in the early twenty-first century have been preceded by a number of technologies designed to take media production and use in the same direction since the 1980s. The advent of videotape as an analogue recording technology, pioneered in the 1960s and becoming widespread in news and sports production by the 1970s, led to increasing refinements that brought inexpensive, reliable home video recorders and cameras using half-inch videotape into households around the world in the mid-1980s. By the early 1990s the viewing of films on television at home, along with home taping of TV programmes, had become so widespread that Hollywood studios and networks alike began to adapt their business practices to accommodate this new market. After initially seeking to halt the spread of VCR technology on grounds of copyright infringement in the Universal versus Sony case, studios began to release to video 'sell-through' by 1985 via new in-house video distribution divisions (Austin, 1990). Later, they invested in video rental chains like Blockbuster and Movie Gallery. The A. C. Nielsen company began to account for videotaped viewing of programmes, or 'time-shifting', in the mid-1980s as well, and networks built this data into their programming decisions.

The growing programme choices on cable and satellite channels made VCR ownership virtually a necessity by the early 1990s. Pirate recordings of television shows and films, as well as music, began to circulate around the world, especially in countries outside the reach of US and European copyright law. Here we see an increasingly common pattern being established: as technologies promise to tip the balance of control over distribution and use of media products towards consumers, media corporations attempt to win back control by curtailing fair-use rights and practices even more severely than before: pre-emptive backlash. Though the threat of videotape recording was resolved in favour of the consumer (despite studio and recording company desires to ban, or at least tax, the sale of VCRs and/or blank audio- and videotapes), the matter

would not rest there for long. The legal precedent for fair use established in Universal versus Sony would be challenged not only in the courts but in Congress.

Meanwhile, newly affordable and user-friendly home computers began to bring a digital medium into people's homes. The term digital simply means that information is broken down into a series of ones and zeros and put into a form that can be easily manipulated by the microchips that lie at the heart of every digital device. Though the earliest digital media could only handle the simplest kinds of input – numbers or letters typed in with a keyboard or from punchcards – by the early 1990s it became possible to convert more complex data – pictures, graphics, music, sounds – into digital formats. But for the most part this was happening in discrete, specialised environments: the video editing suite, the design departments of architectural and engineering firms, the sound studios of recording companies, the production facilities of print media companies. However, by the end of the 1990s, the amazingly rapid growth of the Internet and the World Wide Web quickly broke down the barriers between applications and brought such capacities into the home of everyday users of media as well as into the hands of producers of video and audio producers. The new possibilities opened up by digital media in terms of production, distribution and recording/playback promise to completely reorganise media institutions as we know them. They have also spurred a series of challenges to existing copyright law that, paradoxically, may end by more tightly restricting 'fair-use' provisions, in the face of the infinitely expanding field of possibilities, than at any previous time in history (Vaidhyanathan, 2001).

It is particularly in terms of distribution that television's traditional means of transmission are presently being transformed. Over the air (OTA) television remains just on the cusp of digital distribution. In the US, television stations were required by the terms of the Telecommunications Act of 1996 to begin digital broadcasting in 2002, and will be forced to convert entirely to digital within the next ten years, despite the low numbers of consumers who have opted to purchase a digital-ready TV set as of 2003. Whether this means high definition television in every home, or splitting each existing channel into several different ones, remains in dispute (see Grey Box: Protectionism, Deregulation and the Telecommunications Act of 1996). One of the primary stumbling blocks is cable. With 85 per cent of US TV viewers getting their programmes via cable, cable companies are rapidly expanding into digital transmission. This allows them to not only offer more channels, but more services as well, such as interactive programme guides, pay per view and more complicated and personalised packages of service (allowing higher subscription fees, as well). However, broadcasters' conversion to digital presents several problems. If OTA stations opt for the high definition option – carrying high definition programming on their existing signal – cable operators will be required to devote more of their bandwidth to each station under the must-carry rules. If broadcasters, on the other hand, choose to multiplex – split their signal into six or more lower-quality channels – cable operators believe that they should have no obligation to carry the extra channels on their valuable cable line-up. This could make multiplexed channels all but unreceivable by the US public, and significantly complicates the situation for adaptation of digital television. However, signs in 2002 point to an increased rate of purchase of digital-ready television sets, more towards 'home theatre' uses based on DVDs and satellite reception than with an eye to traditional OTA programming.

Other nations have already begun significant digital broadcasting operations. In Japan, NHK has provided an all-digital, high definition, over-the-air service since 1999. In 2002, Britain announced that it was now the 'world's first fully digital TV nation' with the launch of its Freeview service, available to 75 per cent of the British public with the purchase of a set-top box. Over thirty channels were included in the over-the-air digital service, among them all the standard BBC and ITV channels plus special digital-only services like CBeebies (a children's channel), the BBC World News and assorted satellite channels. For most nations, satellite television is the main platform for digital television, and subscriber numbers are growing.

Michele Hilmes

RECOMMENDED READING

Collins, Richard and Murroni, Cristina (1996), *New Media, New Policies*, Cambridge: Polity.

Harries, Dan (ed.) (2002), *The New Media Book*, London: BFI.

Humphreys, Peter J. (1996), *Mass Media and Media Policy in Western Europe*, Manchester: Manchester University Press.

Parsons, Patrick R. and Frieden, Robert M. (1998), *The Cable and Satellite Television Industries*, Boston: Allyn and Bacon.

Vaidhyanathan, Siva (2001), *Copyrights and Copywrongs: The Rise of Intellectual Property and How It Threatens Creativity*, New York: New York University Press.

DIGITAL DISTRIBUTION, INTELLECTUAL PROPERTY AND THE END OF TV AS WE KNOW IT?

The most potentially revolutionary aspect of digital technology is the fact that it has enabled the faster and more perfect transmission of both live and recorded media – whether via broadband, satellite, web, or over-the-air – to the point that the basic distinction between distribution and recording has begun to break down. Essentially, except for a small subset of examples such as digital broadcasting – still in its rudimentary stages in most countries – and audio streaming over the Internet, to transmit a digital work is automatically to make a copy of it. Even with streaming distribution increasingly sophisticated copies can be captured, with far less degradation of image or sound than possible with analogue media. Once a digital text has been downloaded onto a recording device – whether a microchip, a hard drive or a digital recording medium – it can be easily redistributed, sent on to a nearly infinite number of subsequent users, with no degradation of content.

So far, three kinds of digital recording devices or practices have made an impact on audiences and industries around the world: DVDs (and related formats), Internet file sharing, and smart VCRs like TiVo and Replay TV. DVDs have already begun to threaten the status of videotape as the dominant medium for movies in the home, and a significant number of television programmes are now being released on DVD as well. The much larger storage capacity of a digital disc over an analogue tape not only slims the package to be stored on a shelf, but allows much more content to be stored – and in a medium that is fully searchable and easier to access. DVD releases typically contain significant amounts of new material, from scenes cut from the theatrical film to interviews with director and stars to critical reviews to photographs to voiceover commentary, not to mention multiple-language versions, all on one small disc.

And what if one could share a perfect digital recording purchased at the video store with all one's friends, instantly and at very little cost? This is exactly the threat of Internet file-sharing software. First felt in the field of music, whose easier downloadability sparked first the MP3, then the Napster controversy in 2000, file sharing shows no signs of abating as Internet connections become ever faster. The very companies, such as AOL Time Warner, who are banking most heavily on the spread of broadband connections into every home also fear most intensely the uses to which these connections can be put in terms of spreading their video and audio products widely from user to user, bypassing the traditional and profit-making middleman. Though several studios launched their own web-based, pay-per-view services in 2002 – thus attempting to head off the impasse faced a few years before by their recording label subsidiaries – it is still unclear as to whether users can be persuaded to rein in a use of the Internet medium that seems supremely well adapted to its technology and its prevailing ethos.

Finally, it is the prospect of the above combined in some version of 'smart VCR' technology such as TiVo and Replay TV that has the traditional television business most worried in the early years of the twenty-first century. Basically a digital video recorder that downloads films and television programmes onto a hard drive (with up to sixty hours' capacity), smart VCRs can also search for programming by keyword with data downloaded via a telephone connection overnight. The user pays a $10–15 monthly fee for this service – basically an online video directory – with programming delivered through whatever means the user chooses separately: cable, satellite, or OTA. One simple command – such as 'Buffy' – could automatically capture for the home viewer every episode of *Buffy the Vampire Slayer* aired over a four-week period. However, it is not the time-shifting capacity that most threatens networks and producers – though we might ask how much the traditional schedule-building skills and strategies of programmers will count in the new personalised-menu TV age – but the ability of viewers to completely skip over advertising. Essentially, smart VCRs record a programme as it is being viewed; the user can pause the programme to answer the telephone or get a snack, then come back and view the programme interrupted, effectively in a slight time-delayed version. This automatic recording allows for easy ad-zapping; some versions will automatically cut out the ads based on electronic cues.

Taken together, these new technological capabilities threaten existing industry players in many ways, all related to the bottom line. Smart VCRs challenge commercial television's economic base in advertising, creating the prospect of a return to integrated advertising – ads embedded in the programmes, as in the early days of radio and TV and as in product placement – with perhaps the addition of direct marketing to viewers through online integration of ordering services. The WB network, owned by Warner Bros. whose position in the music recording industry looms large, has already begun to list music played during its TV programmes, all by Warner artists, after each show, along with information on how to order. They also bring into questions the whole basic *raison d'être* of the concept of network, if programmes become essentially part of an online library, downloadable and viewable at any time for a separate fee per play. File sharing might allow programmes so downloaded to be distributed off the books to an infinite number of non-paying users, threatening not only networks and studios but individual artists, and if such products are then recorded in perfect-quality versions on CDs, DVDs or Digital Audio Tape (DAT), each user has the potential of becoming a one-man or -woman distribution network themselves.

Such nightmare (for the industry) or dream (for the user) visions have prompted some of the most far-reaching changes in copyright law in the US since the 1920s. The Digital Millennium Copyright Act of 1998 contained stipulations never before considered to be in the realm of intellectual property law. It mandated that, no matter what the legal status of digitally recorded material played on them, it is illegal to attempt to circumvent the copyright protection devices built into digital recorders, players and products. Even discussing evasion of such technologies, or sharing such information, is prohibited. And to prevent control over such material from falling into the public domain, the Sonny Bono Copyright Term Extension Act of that same year added, retroactively, twenty years onto the existing period of copyright protection, bringing individual protection to the life of the author plus seventy years, and industry products ('works for hire') ninety-five years from the date of publication or 125 from creation, whichever is shorter. This was prompted in particular by the Walt Disney Corporation, whose early Mickey Mouse prototype, Steamboat Willy, was just about to fall into the public domain. Many have mentioned the hypocrisy here of a company like Disney, which has 'for decades shamelessly plundered the works of everyone from Homer to Hans Christian Anderson' (Plummer, 2002) – all, of course, in the public domain – now seeking a permanent (in their proposed version) right to all products issuing from the studio (Plummer, 2002). Taken together, these two initiatives more than compensate for the increased flexibility and user control offered by digital media by magnifying legal restrictions surrounding their use, cutting deeply into current fair use and public domain territory.

Michele Hilmes

The Internet: From Cold War to Commercialisation

The Internet has emerged as one of the fastest-growing media in the history of modern communications. Although it has not reached the penetration of radio throughout the world, the rate of its adoption has even outstripped the pace of radio in its earliest days. As television slowly goes digital, its full convergence with the computer-based Internet remains only a matter of time.

Inevitably a technology as vast as the Internet has been constructed subject to social, political and economic influences and is also the result of the convergence of many varying technologies, personalities and pragmatic needs. One likely starting point, however, would be the advent of the computer since the Internet could not have come into being without computer technology. Computers began simply as 'digital calculators', and the earliest computers were used during World War II to help calculate accurate targets for anti-aircraft guns and to draw up navigational tables. Computer development not only produced the technology but also spawned a cadre of scientists in Europe and in North America whose attention was devoted to solving the problems of computing – an environment essential for the development of the Internet.

However, the Internet's development is most securely linked to work begun in the Cold War US 'military industrial complex' of the 1960s – specifically located in the Defense Department's Advanced Research Projects Agency (ARPA) (Schrage, 1983). In 1958, one year after the Russians launched Sputnik, ARPA was formed by President Dwight D. Eisenhower to develop US space and missile capabilities. Later it directed its research towards the military's new interest in behavioural science and the need of the Air Force to find a home for a computer time-sharing project. Scientist J. C. R. Licklider was recruited by the Defense Department in 1962 to lead these two initiatives, although his primary interest centred more around interactive computing (Naughton, 2000, p. 67). That same year, Licklider wrote a series of memos envisioning computer nodes that could pass messages along many different pathways simultaneously, a 'Galactic Network' of computers linked together (Zakon). The agency began to build a network of time-sharing computers linking labs and universities working with ARPA.

ARPA enjoyed a wealth of funding, given its Defense Department agency status, but research was not necessarily conducted along solely military lines. While many histories suggest that the original mandate driving the origins of the Internet was to construct a network that would withstand a nuclear war, others argue that it was more likely the desire to overcome the problem of computer incompatibility. (Naughton, 2000, p. 85) At the time, computers built by competing manufacturers relied upon proprietary languages that could not talk to the computers of other manufacturers. US government agencies were required to purchase computers based on a system of bids on the open market, resulting in many different types of computing systems with unco-ordinated capabilities. The idea of developing a common compatible computer protocol arose out of this problematic mismatch; agencies needed to be able to share information.

Furthermore, when early computer hosts were networked together, it was by direct wired links, physically joining peripheral work stations and processors to each other. Distance, expense and the sheer number of cables required made reliance on a single centralised host impossible, or at least extremely awkward. The structure of the ARPANET emerged as an idea for a distributed network that consisted of smaller hosts so that traffic could easily be routed around any disruption in the network. This concept of distributed networking was the brainchild of Paul Baran of the Rand Corporation, a think-tank founded in 1946 to support US nuclear planners (Naughton, 2000, p. 98). Such a network also allowed routing the information through packet switching, a concept proposed by Baran and developed by British scientist Derek Davies at the National Physical Laboratory (Naughton, 2000, p. 127). Lawrence G. Roberts, a researcher at MIT, joined the Defense Advanced Research Projects Agency (DARPA) and began to implement the ARPANET network.

Vinton Cerf and Leonard Kleinrock at the University of California at Los Angeles (UCLA) developed a Network Control Protocol (NCP) to transfer data that allowed communications between four different hosts running on the early ARPANET network. In 1969 those nodes were located at SRI (in Stanford), UCLA, the University of California at Santa Barbara and the University of Utah. As more interest and more hosts were added to ARPANET, it became evident that the network would require not only packet switching but also a new protocol to allow communication between different networks. With packet switching, small packets of data, each carrying a separate address header, were flooded across the many nodes and varying routes of the network. The receiving computer would then reassemble the packets in the order specified by the address header. Such a system allowed for redundancy and more efficient use of the transmission lines between nodes. Robert E. Kahn and Cerf were among those who worked to develop a new protocol that could cope with varying sources, solve transmission problems, allow a more open architecture and, eventually, provide a computer 'handshake' that would enable different computer networks to communicate. Transmission Control Protocol (TCP) and Internet Protocol (IP) were developed in 1974 to meet this need. This protocol allowed ARPANET to grow from a network to a 'network of networks', which is what would transform ARPANET into the Internet. Eventually TCP/IP was integrated as a standard part of the Unix operating system – the computer language and operating system of most of the computers that composed the Internet (Berners-Lee, 1999, p. 17).

ARPANET emerged as a co-operative and expanding academic–government alliance comprised of universities, military networks and corporations under military contracts. While the goals of sharing scientific knowledge were the primary motivation for the development of ARPANET, individual tinkering on the part of scientists propelled the development of other features that were at first viewed as irrelevant or ancillary. Among the most important of these was e-mail – an unanticipated capability that became the 'killer application' and soon accounted for more than 75 per cent of the traffic on ARPANET, according to one estimate. Online mail existed on time-shared systems, but in 1971 the first e-mail that linked two separate machines was designed by Ray Tomlinson, who also came up with the @ sign to separate the user name from the computer domain name (Zakon). An improved version of e-mail was integrated into ARPANET in 1972. Not only was e-mail the application that dominated the network, but it was also the facility that allowed the resource to be used for matters as frivolous as games, grudges and grocery lists.

The development of personal computers in the late 1970s and the advent of Unix facilitated the creation of 'a poor man's ARPANET' outside the network (Naughton, 2000, p. 171). AT&T (American Telephone and Telegraph Corporation) gave away its program language, Unix, to universities because of regulations that forbade it from entering into the computing market. Because Unix had an open source code that could be modified, licensees of the system communicated regularly about malfunctions and bugs to be fixed. Eventually, a program that automatically updated the software of Unix users over phone lines was developed and with it came the communications link that quickly was used for other purposes. One of the applications that grew upon the Unix environment was Usenet – a program that allowed computer users to virtually access articles and postings under various discussion topics

organised by hierarchies. Individuals could post their own work, musings or invective on virtually any topic. The top-down control of the network began to be contested as more newsgroups challenged the social mores of administrators. Users began to launch irreverent and at times scathing text-based 'flame' wars (Dery, 1994). Additionally, a program, Fidonet, created a network of bulletin boards accessible to PC-owners. With the use of communications freeware such as XMODEM, an individual could use a PC and telephone line to link into other computers outside ARPANET to access a messaging system that became known as the bulletin board system (BBS). The bulletin board system would eventually become linked to the Internet. Users also began to play with the technology and create text-based virtual communities and gaming environments known as multi-user domains (MUDs) and MOOs (MUD-object-oriented) wherein participants could build an on-screen persona that allowed them to playfully explore issues of identity, gender, sexuality and the social contract.

As more and more institutions and university nodes linked to the original ARPANET, the Defense Advanced Research Projects Agency began to worry about security breaches into its network. In 1983, DARPA announced it was splitting its networked computers off into MILnet – a network for military communications only. ARPANET, which had grown to more than 1,000 nodes by 1984, would continue to remain focused on computer networking research. The supervision and provision of a backbone network for ARPANET was handed over to the National Science Foundation Network (NSFNET) which stipulated that commercial, non-research entities could not be a part of the NSF-supported network. Still the network grew to 300,000 nodes by 1990. In that year the network, now known as the Internet, dwarfed and subsumed the entity known as ARPANET.

Companies began to explore the commercial potential of the Internet. In 1987, the first commercial network, UUNET, was launched, although it wasn't until 1991 that the NSF allowed commercial entities access to its backbone network and opened the Internet to public access. Critical to commercial success, however, was the development of a more consumer-friendly interface. For example, with the network growing exponentially, finding sources and databases became a daunting task. In 1989, McGill University in Montreal developed the first Internet indexing system, called 'Archie' (Griffiths, 2001; Zakon). More sophisticated 'search engines' developed – a term used to describe both a computer-programmed 'crawler' that sifts through data for specific terms that may appear anywhere on a web page, or a human-constructed directory wherein a team of people categorises web content based on descriptions of content.

Tim Berners-Lee, a physicist working at CERN, the Swiss-based centre for the European Particle Physics Laboratory, combined an idea he had developed to produce a system of linked knowledge and hypertext capabilities to create the graphical, interface of the World Wide Web that came to be known by its 'www' in the address line of the URL (uniform resource locator). HTTP (hypertext transfer protocol) and HTML (hypertext markup language) became both the address and programming language of the web (Berners-Lee, 1999, p. 68). The development of the World Wide Web transformed the human–computer interface of the Internet from the mysteries of Unix code commands to a consumer-friendly environment as easy as point and click. In 1993, CERN released its rights to royalties on the protocol developed by Berners-Lee and associates and it quickly became the standard.

One concern was the lack of point and click browsers. A few early ones such as Erwise, Viola and Midas were available by 1992. Marc Andreesen, at the National Center for Supercomputing Applications (NCSA) at the University of Illinois at Urbana-Champaign, developed Mosaic, a popular early browser that used colourful graphics. Andreesen left NCSA and with partners developed a rival browser product, Netscape, in 1994 that was given away for free initially (Berners-Lee, 1999, p. 82). That same year, Bill Gates of Microsoft announced his company would develop a competing free browser, which would become Microsoft Explorer. Now the Internet came into its own, at least in developed nations with access to technology, interconnection and a ready supply of electricity; 80 per cent of the world's population remains less well equipped.

Though television has not fully merged with Internet applications as of 2003, clearly the two media are approaching each other experimentally. In the United States, commercial networks have developed special web-enhanced versions of specific programmes and of genres, such as ABC's special 'Drew Cam' episode of *The Drew Carey Show* in November 1999, for which the actor's fictitious character installed a video camera in his house that broadcast to a website, providing Internet-linked viewers with gags and cameo appearances that the show's traditional audience could not see. Sports has been a particularly avid adaptor of extras the web can provide, with channels like ESPN maintaining an active web presence linked to sports broadcasts and ancillary information. All over the world, network and programme-based websites provide scheduling, episode and various kinds of information to their audiences, and those audiences have not been slow to respond with 'fan-sites' of their own. In a few cases these sites became the targets of network wrath, as fans began to circulate their own video clips, audio segments and transcripts of the show, to the industry's cries of copyright violation.

On a larger scale, mergers such as that of the US-based firm Time Warner with Internet-based AOL, to form AOL Time Warner in 2000, became increasingly common. The increasing convergence between Internet service providers and broadband carriers means that it is becoming easier to download large video files on the web – and also to share them with other users. From Hollywood to Bombay to Hong Kong, film studios and television producers are worrying over unauthorised copying and distribution of their digitised work. Digital television will provide an even greater capacity for interactivity between provider and audience, and as 'smart VCRs' like TiVo and Replay TV begin to eat into traditional advertising revenues with 'ad zapping' capacities, many predict that commercial television providers will begin to market directly through screen/Internet interfaces: just click on products you see on the screen and order them for yourself at home. Conversely, some advertisers, such as BMW, have now determined that their video advertising campaigns reach their audience best on the web. The possibilities for the convergence of the Internet with traditional television are infinite, and we have only begun to glimpse their true dimensions. Who can doubt that by 2020 – to name a conservatively distant date – the parameters of what we think of as 'television' will have changed almost beyond recognition?

Clare Bratten

RECOMMENDED READING

Berners-Lee, Tim (1999), *Weaving the Web: The Original Design and Ultimate Destiny of the World Wide Web by Its Inventor*, New York: HarperBusiness.

Dery, Mark (ed.) (1994), *Flame Wars: The Discourse of Cyberculture*, Durham: Duke University Press.

Naughton, John (2001) *Brief History of the Future: From Radio Days to Internet Years in a Lifetime*, Woodstock, New York: The Overlook Press.

Robins, Kevin and Webster, Frank (1999), *Times of the Technoculture:. From the Information Society to the Virtual Life*, New York: Routledge.

Stone, Allucquere Rosanne (1995), *The War of Desire and Technology at the Close of the Mechanical Age*, Cambridge: The MIT Press.

Turkle, Sherry (1995) *Life on the Screen: Identity in the Age of the Internet*, New York: Simon & Schuster.

INSTITUTIONS: FROM ORIGINS TO STABILITY

Introduction

This section begins with the origins of the BBC and of the commercial network system of the United States, going back to the 1920s when crucial structural decisions were made, in essays that make comparisons and draw distinctions between two of the world's most influential broadcasting nations: the state-chartered, public service monopoly of the BBC and the hybrid commercial/public interest system of the US. Television built on the roots put down in radio. The BBC initiated an experimental television service before the war, halted by wartime exigencies. As the post-war BBC rapidly learned the rules of a new game, a debate began to rage in Britain about how best to organise and finance this new service, leading to the introduction of the Independent Television service, Britain's first experiment with commercial broadcasting, in 1955. ITV's immediate success with audiences would issue a significant challenge to longstanding public service philosophy. In the US, the former radio networks retained their dominant position in television via favourable regulatory decisions, and NBC, CBS and ABC transferred the sponsorship system of network radio to the new medium. However, ABC, as the newest and weakest of three major networks, led in the gradual undermining of the basic 'public interest' compromise that had guided network operations since the 1920s, concentrating on ratings points and the newly identified 'youth' audience as its programmes challenged former 'quality' mandates.

By the late 1950s both systems faced challenge and change – in Britain brought about by competition from ITV and pressures for regional broadcasting, in the US by the aftermath of the 'quiz show scandal' which effectively ended the sponsorship system. In Britain, the rise of a more populist programming philosophy, including the strategic use of American programmes on both the BBC and ITV, resulted in charges of 'trivialisation' and pandering in the Pilkington Report of 1962 and brought about the introduction of a second, more 'serious,' BBC television service in 1964. A three-network system stabilised, ushering in an era of standardisation and popularisation amid increased debate. Yet by 1977, the year of the Annan Report, the pendulum had swung back in the other direction, and public service goals were reaffirmed in a way that would affect the

creation of a fourth channel in the 1980s. In the US, the 1960s ushered in the 'classic network system' era, a period of unprecedented network control over programme production, scheduling and profits with increasingly perfunctory nods to the public interest. A three-network oligopoly introduced the 'magazine' system of spot advertising, locked its affiliates into tight agreements, and increasingly turned to Hollywood for the filmed comedies, action/adventures shows and Westerns that dominated the schedule. Standardisation of network practices led to homogenization of programming under the 'genre cycle' of innovation, imitation and saturation, until changing regulations and competition from cable television began to mount a challenge in the early 1980s.

Michele Hilmes

The Origins of Public Service Broadcasting

The origins of public service broadcasting date back to a time in Britain when radio still ruled the airwaves. In the years immediately after World War I the medium had grown at an astonishing rate. In America a large number of different and competing radio stations were set up, primarily financed by advertising revenue. However, the British establishment regarded the US style of broadcasting as nothing short of chaotic and advertising was generally looked down upon as both vulgar and intrusive. According to Andrew Crisell, the British government was 'loath to follow the early lead of America, where insufficient restriction had resulted in a kind of aerial anarchy: too many stations crowded the waveband, some on pirated frequencies and some using stronger signals to drown out their rivals' (Crisell, 1997, p. 13).

In an attempt to avoid such a seemingly chaotic and commercialised system travelling across the Atlantic, in 1922 the British government licensed a number of major radio manufacturers to form a *single* cartel that they called the British Broadcasting Company (BBC). Licensed to broadcast by the Post Office it was run as a monopoly and was financed by an annual licence fee paid by radio set owners (originally ten shillings). This belief in public taxation (to avoid commercialisation) and a trade monopoly (to keep broadcasting under strict control) was continued in 1927 when the company eventually became an independent national organisation, the British Broadcasting Corporation set up by Royal Charter. Although not *directly* controlled by the state, the future of the BBC ultimately lay in the hands of the government that continued to periodically renew its licence to broadcast and determine the cost of its licence fee – a practice that continues to this day. It was out of this climate of anxiety around broadcasting that the notion of public service broadcasting first emerged, spearheaded by John Charles Walsham Reith (1889–1971), the first Director-General of the British Broadcasting Corporation from 1927 to 1938 (and previously the Managing Director of the British Broadcasting Company from 1923 to 1926). Although originally a civil engineer who knew nothing about broadcasting (and apparently did not even own a receiver), Reith soon earned the trust of the government, particularly for his handling of the 1926 General Strike. Despite politicians like Winston Churchill wanting the airwaves closed down during the crisis, Reith assured the government that the fledgling company would do nothing to threaten the 'national interest'. Indeed, Reith's narrow view of what determined the 'national interest' was generally sympathetic to those in power, allowing the Conservative government to use the airwaves while barring trade union leaders. It was an ideology that can be gleaned from a memorandum Reith circulated in the BBC after the strike. 'Since the BBC was a national institution', he wrote, 'and since the Government in this crisis were acting for the people . . . the BBC was for the Government in this crisis too' (cited by Scannell and Cardiff, 1991, p. 33).

Not surprisingly, many critics (including Labour politicians) disagreed with Reith's handling of the strike. Far from being impartial they declared that the BBC was merely an instrument of *propaganda* for the establishment. As Michael Tracey has put it, 'There is no doubt from reading through the various memos and numerous expressions of intent that the BBC's coverage was specifically aimed towards a particular end, which was the defeat of the strike' (Tracey, 2000, p. 42). Some suggested that few in the company even understood the causes of the struggle. Indeed, according to Asa Briggs, 'the straight facts of working-class life were not well known to most members of the early BBC' (Briggs, 1961, p. 374). Later that same year Reith accepted a knighthood.

John Reith was the son of a Scottish Free Church minister and this strict religious (Calvinist) background clearly influenced his paternalistic and almost 'missionary' con-

ception of broadcasting. Echoing the English essayist Matthew Arnold's (1822–88) definition of culture as 'the best that has been thought and written in the world', Reith argued that 'Broadcasting is a servant of culture' (Reith, 1924, p. 217) and should therefore act as its moral guardian. The title of Arnold's most famous collection of essays *Culture and Anarchy* (1869) aptly sums up the Reithian belief in 'civilising' the masses so that the threat of social chaos (as demonstrated in the General Strike) could be avoided. As a result, he argued that the BBC's freedom from commercial interests should allow it to pursue higher social and moral ideals. This high-minded notion of public service broadcasting (building what Krishan Kumar refers to as a 'cultural church' [MacCabe and Stewart, 1986, p. 47]) was one that aimed to provide a religious, moral and educative force to the nation as a whole – a remit not only to 'entertain' but also to 'inform' and 'educate' as well. As Roger Sales has put it, Reith's 'message for the infant medium of sound broadcasting was that it had to be as morally sound as a church bell. He wanted it to take the high cultural road and educate popular taste rather than merely pander to the lowest common denominator' (Sales, 1986, p. 48). Crucial to this Arnoldian mission of broadcasting was the belief that it could reflect and cement notions of a *national culture* – the BBC intent on becoming 'the voice of the nation'. Quoting King George V's first speech on radio when he opened the British Empire Exhibition, Reith argued that through its transmission of national public events (such as the FA Cup Final, a state funeral or a royal wedding) the BBC would have the effect of 'making the nation as one man' (cited by Scannell, 1990, p. 14). It was with this concept in mind that he defended 'the brute force of monopoly' (Reith, 1949, p. 99) so that a general standard and overall policy could be 'promulgated' throughout the country (see Scannell, 1990, pp. 13–14). In his polemical and trenchant manifesto *Broadcast over Britain* (1924) he provocatively put forward these arguments, making no apologies for the crusading and high moral tone of the BBC's mission. 'It is occasionally indicated to us', he wrote, 'that we are apparently setting out to give the public what we think they need – and not what they want – but few know what they want and very few know what they need' (cited by Briggs, 1961, p. 238). Such a philosophy was unashamedly elitist, reflecting an institution that saw itself as custodian of the nation's moral fibre. By all accounts his own strict management of the BBC and its staff was similarly Victorian in approach, intolerant of such 'lapses in moral conduct' as homosexuality, infidelity or divorce.

When Reith left in 1938 to run Imperial Airwaves, an

airline company, one newspaper congratulated him for 'making the BBC into a national institution as thoroughly typical and representative as the Bank of England – safe, responsible, reliable, the guarantor of the nation's cultural capital' (Scannell and Cardiff, 1991, p. 17). Indeed, 'Radio Reith' had been shaped in his image, an authoritarian, paternalistic and innately highbrow institution that tended to promote the interests and tastes of the *English* upper middle class. Working-class and regional accents were banned and traditional upper-middle-class culture (in the form of opera, classical music, religious services and canonical works of English literature) provided much of its early material. In the era of 'uplift' the BBC announcers talked only in the King's English and endeavoured to pre-serve a distance from their audience. Even when the BBC imported the American craze for *Spelling Bees* (an early quiz show) into the National programme 'it managed to make them sound more like a schoolroom test than fireside fun' (Scannell and Cardiff, 1991, p. 294). As this suggests,

even when more popular tastes and pursuits were provided for, the BBC still reported and conveyed the programmes in an inherently pompous and aloof manner. As Tom Burns has put it:

> BBC culture, like BBC standard English, was not peculiar to itself but an intellectual ambience composed of the values, standards and beliefs of the professional middle-class, especially that part educated at Oxford and Cambridge. Sports, popular music and entertainment which appealed to the lower classes were included in large measure in the programmes, but the manner in which they were purveyed, in the context and the presentation, remained indomitably *upper* middle class; and there was, too, the point that they were only on the menu as ground bait. (Burns, 1977, p. 42)

The BBC's slow shift towards more popular programming began before the war, but the war itself clearly speeded up

American 'import' Bob Hope was brought to a British public

the process. With British troops stationed in France preferring to listen to Radio Fécamp than British radio, the BBC finally began to take the demands of its audience more seriously. When US troops began arriving in Britain it was felt that British radio also needed to keep its new audience entertained. As one BBC producer put it,

> generally speaking the ordinary American does not like the British radio. It is going to be a very hard job to make him like it, but the attempt should be well worth making as it might result in the British listener liking British radio!' (Cited by Scannell and Cardiff, 1986, p. 111)

As a result, a more 'Americanised' (intimate, casual, friendlier) style slowly began to emerge. Even American radio shows were finally imported, bringing entertainers like Bob Hope and Jack Benny to a grateful British public.

Inevitably, the BBC's own programmes gradually became less stuffy and aloof. In particular, it was felt that in order to keep morale high during the war the working class and women needed to be both addressed and represented more by the radio they listened to. When war broke out loudspeakers were quickly installed in factories, transmitting such programmes as *Works Wonders* (which began on 5 October 1940), one of the BBC's first amateur talent

---

BRITISH TELEVISION BEFORE THE WAR

It was into the climate of public service broadcasting that BBC television was first introduced at 3pm on 2 November 1936, the 'first high definition' service in the world (Germany had begun transmitting 180-line pictures a year before). Broadcast from Alexandra Palace ('Ally Pally' as it was to become affectionately known) in north London, it was received only within a radius of forty to 400 miles by approximately 400 households. However, this shortage of viewers (originally no more than a few thousand) was not simply the result of technical limitations, but reflected the relatively high price of a set which ranged from £35–£100 (the price of a small car). Added to this, the picture quality was frequently very dim and lacked definition, not helped by a screen that was no more than eight by ten inches. Competing with radio for a share of the licence fee also meant that the programmes themselves were sometimes surprisingly amateurish; the weekly budget for the whole service was only around £1,000.

Early television audiences were provided with two separate hours of viewing a day, excluding Sundays when – in true Reithian style – programming was shut down altogether. On its opening day viewers were treated to 'a display by champion Alsatians from the Metropolitan and Essex Canine Society's Show' which was followed by 'The *Golden Hind*, a model of Drake's ship made by a bus driver' who described its construction (cited by Wheen, 1985, p. 28). Later Leslie Mitchell introduced the first edition of *Picture Page* that included interviews with a tennis player and an aviator. No doubt partly due to cost, the same short newsreels as those showed at the cinema provided the only news on offer. However, this decision may have also reflected the lack of 'weight' or 'gravity' that television seemed to possess in contrast to radio. This was a period which the broadcasting critic T. C. Worsley called 'the era of radiovision' (cited by Briggs, 1979, p. 7), a time when

television was still rather condescendingly treated as simply 'radio with pictures'.

In terms of its Reithian heritage there was little in this early programming that would have unduly worried the earlier director-general. Viewers were dutifully presented with plays and extracts from Shakespeare, George Bernard Shaw and Jacobean dramatists such as Francis Beaumont and John Fletcher. In terms of broadcasting national events, the new medium seemed uniquely suited to the job, reaching a high point with the coronation procession of George VI in May 1937. Although cameras were not allowed in Westminster Abbey for the coronation itself, it was BBC television's first outside broadcast and attracted between 10,000 and 50,000 viewers. Later that same year the Remembrance Day ceremony and Neville Chamberlain's historic arrival at Heston Airport in Munich were both transmitted. However, because the medium was still generally regarded as an experimental novelty it tended to get away with more 'frivolous' entertainment than radio. Indeed, its affluent upper-middle-class audiences were soon demanding to see West End shows and plays such as Noel Coward's *Hay Fever* and Brandon Thomas's *Charley's Aunt*, which were among some of the first contemporary plays broadcast. Sport, such as the FA Cup Final, the Boat Race, the Wimbledon Tennis Championship and test matches from Lord's Cricket Ground was also proving popular with audiences. However, it was felt that broadcasting should be terminated during the war (apparently in case transmissions aided enemy bombers). During the middle of a *Mickey Mouse* cartoon on 1 September 1939 all British television was abruptly brought to an end. But despite these humble origins, 18,000 to 20,000 sets were sold during the three short years it had been on the air – clearly a suggestion of things to come (see Crisell, 1997, pp. 72–3).

Glen Creeber

shows. *Workers' Playtime* (which began on 31 May 1941) used a similar format but included well-known variety performers, while shows like *Music While You Work* were broadcast twice or three times daily. Perhaps most famous of all was the comedy show *ITMA* (short for *It's That Man Again* – an ironic reference to Hitler). Irreverent, fast and unpredictable it used catchphrases, word play and even elements of surrealism to send up the dreariness and absurdity of the war. Characters such as Mrs Mopp the cleaning woman, Colonel Chinstrap, Funf the German spy and Ali Oop soon became nationally known and helped herald in a new era of more 'populist' programming (see Crisell, 1997, pp. 57–66).

Although the BBC was clearly very heavily censored during the war (for example, the terrible defeat at Dieppe was reported as a military 'model'), it won praise and admiration throughout the world for its wartime coverage. Despite its often high moral tone, many felt that public service broadcasting provided a standard of broadcasting that all should aspire to. As a result, after 1945 the Allied Forces saw to it that the general ethos of the BBC was enforced in many parts of Europe so that public service broadcasting (at least, up until the 1980s) was one of its most dominant forms of broadcasting (see Weymouth and Lamizet, 1996, pp. 1–36). Although the new style of public service broadcasting still wanted to 'improve' its listener, more choice and variation meant that the listener could finally choose to be 'improved' rather than 'having improvement thrust upon her' (Crisell, 1997, p. 63).

Glen Creeber

My thanks to Professor Roger Sales for his inspiring lectures on broadcasting history that I still use and remember today.

RECOMMENDED READING
Buscombe, Edward (ed.) (2000), *British Television: A Reader*, London and New York, Oxford University Press.
Crisell, Andrew (1997), *An Introductory History of British Broadcasting*, London and New York: Routledge.
Scannell, Paddy (1990), 'Public Service Broadcasting: The History of a Concept', in Andrew Goodwin and Garry Whannel (eds), *Understanding Television*, London and New York: Routledge. Also published in Edward Buscombe (ed.) (2000), *British Television: A Reader*, Oxford and New York: Oxford University Press.

The Origins of Commercial Broadcasting in the US

Often, in accounts of radio and television history, the market-driven commercial broadcasting model dominant in the United States is regarded as some kind of naturally pre-existing (chaotic, anarchic, vulgar, unredeemed) condition from which national governments, in the years between the wars, wrested with difficulty a more refined, controlled and responsible mode of public service broadcasting, pioneered by John Reith at the BBC and soon adopted by most European and colonial states. Though many nations allowed some early commercial or amateur stations to operate in the decade of the 1920s, by the mid-1930s most had been closed down and replaced with stations owned by the state and programmed either by the ruling government or its parties, or by an arms-length state-chartered monopoly organisation, as in the case of the BBC, financed by taxes on set purchase or licence fees. Only the US made the decision – by default or by some kind of inherent national failing, it is implied – to allow entrepreneurialism to run amuck in the field of broadcasting, with advertising its main support and mindless entertainment its only mission.

What these generally accepted views fail to take into account, however, is the completely unprecedented degree of federal oversight and control exercised over US radio, then television, in the face of First Amendment constitutional protections afforded to media more generally in the US, and the hybrid public service/commercial medium this compromise produced. Long before the regulatory struggles of the early 1930s, reigning Progressive (educated, upper-middle-class, largely white Anglo-Saxon Protestant social reformist) ideas had worked to limit the 'radical potential' (Winston, 1990) of radio broadcasting, often in conflict with a truly free-market, free-speech approach applied to media such as the press and publishing, and to a lesser extent, film (Goodman and Gring, 2000). The US commercial system, then, resulted not from the untrammelled pursuit of private profits but from a carefully crafted co-operative endeavour by national corporations and federal regulators that reflected some of the same ideas of control and uplift driving public service models, and reinforced some of the same social exclusions and cultural hierarchies. As David Goodman argues: 'American broadcasting before 1945 never was free of civic or national obligations, never was free to be purely commercial in its operation' (Goodman, 2001; see also Benjamin, 2001).

However, limitations on government intervention mandated by the First Amendment, a precedent of private ownership and competition set by other technologies such as the telegraph and telephone, as well as the strongly defended tradition of localism and relatively open access to the airwaves established very early on by radio amateurs, led to an American radio situation far more diverse and uncontrolled than those of most other nations. What may have looked like 'chaos' to others in fact reflects the tension between Progressive control and populist 'marketplace of ideas' diversity, but with the Progressives and their heirs, at least until the 1980s, exercising a considerable influence over radio and television development.

This story begins as early as 1917, when the US government shut down all currently operating amateur stations for the duration of the war: free speech curtailed for reasons of national security. Thousands of pre-war amateurs, along with thousands more trained by the Army Signal Corps (including a significant number of women, who had served as instructors for the men posted overseas), returned to find radio the subject of debate at high levels. Many Americans believed that the government, most likely the Department of the Navy, should be the new home of domestic broadcasting activities; others reviled the amount of government intervention into private life that had occurred during the war and determined that radio should remain in private hands. A compromise was reached in March 1919, when it began to look as though the General Electric Corporation (GE), a leader in radio technology, might sell all rights to the Alexanderson alternator to the British Marconi company, giving Marconi a virtual world monopoly on state-of-the-art radio equipment. The Secretary of the Navy, a young Franklin D. Roosevelt, stepped in to propose that instead GE could count on government leverage to force the American Marconi company to sell its assets to GE and withdraw from the US market, in exchange for key patent rights abroad. Government/corporate co-operation in the arena of radio was born.

In October 1919, GE with the guidance of the federal government formed a subdivision, grandly titled the Radio Corporation of America (RCA). Westinghouse, the AT&T and the United Fruit Company became partners in RCA in 1920. This nationalist organisation brought together the major companies involved in radio research to pool their patents and co-ordinate the development of radio in the US. It was stipulated in RCA's charter that its ownership must be 80 per cent American, that its board of directors must consist entirely of US citizens, and that one member must be a representative of the government (Sterling and Kitross, 1990, p. 53). One of those board members was David Sarnoff, formerly with American Marconi; later, he would be named president of RCA and head the US's first network, NBC, the National Broadcasting Company, arguably the most powerful and influential institution in the history of US radio and television.

This early attempt to exert some kind of national control over broadcasting would have a great effect on the equipment manufacturing business; however, radio broadcasting itself was still a remote enough concept in 1919 that no provisions were made for a national broadcasting service (unlike the situation in 1922, when the British Broadcasting Company debuted). US amateurs' early and extensive involvement in wireless telephony meant that over the next three years, not only the members of RCA but thousands of individuals, non-profit-making organisations, small companies and related media concerns such as newspapers and movie theatres applied for and received licences to broadcast with very little thought of interference or overlap. By 1922 the untrammelled diversity and populism of the airwaves provoked the first major Progressive move to rein it in: the creation of the 'Class B' licence which allowed approved broadcasters to shift their operations to a less crowded part of the spectrum, in exchange for certain promises of 'quality' in performance (Bensman, 1976, pp. 550–1). Most notably, these stipulations included a ban on the playing of recorded music (at least in part a reaction to the social panic over African-American-rooted 'jazz' that had recently swept the country) and a mandated preference for more expensive 'live' performance that would persist into radio's heyday.

RCA itself, plus its constituent partners GE, Westinghouse and AT&T, were among the first to obtain the new licences; meanwhile, amateurs faced increasing restrictions on the content of their broadcasts and would soon be banished to another part of the spectrum completely. Setting an important precedent, government and business, working together, had come up with a way to 'improve' broadcasting and restrict access to 'responsible' parties, without making any actual First-Amendment-infringing rules as to what content radio broadcasting should provide. Class B licences became available by the end of 1922. Though their frequency and name changed in the aftermath of later radio conferences, many of the Class B stations remain on the air today.

However, despite increasing restrictions, the Class A and B distinction also worked to confirm the principle of locally licensed stations, establishing for American radio a firm basis in *localism* rarely found in other nations. Even at the height of network radio, a mid- to large-size US city typically offered anywhere from five to twenty locally operated radio stations, most of them unaffiliated with a network and thus open to a plethora of community-originated, syndicated, ethnic, foreign-language and marginal programming, along with a number of regionally available clear-channel independent stations broadcasting from larger urban centres (see Cohen, 1990; Vaillant, 2002; Doll, 1996). Even network affiliates preserved a high level of local identity and content, responsible for programming much of the broadcast day – not least in the area of news – and able to reject network programmes in favour of their own. This principle of localism would be supported by subsequent legislation, though its scope would be narrowed after 1927.

As the number of licensed broadcasters increased between 1922 and 1925 from thirty to 571 (Sterling and Kitross, 1990, p. 632), with the number of amateurs licensed to broadcast exceeding 15,000, so too did the efforts of the US government to exert some kind of order over what not only European observers but some Americans were beginning to see as 'chaos' (though many others, of course, experienced it as 'free speech', including the vociferous amateur lobby) (Hilmes, 1997). A series of radio conferences called by Secretary of Commerce Herbert Hoover between 1922 and 1925 established some of the basic principles under which broadcasting would continue to operate for the rest of the century. First, the principle of open access to all comers was rejected in favour of restriction based on quality: a few 'quality' broadcasters were better for the nation than many poor or mediocre ones. The objections of the amateurs to this provision had, by 1925, begun to be well outweighed by the interests of businesses that had invested significant sums in radio. Second, this distinction should involve the notion of the 'public interest': a term derived from public utility law and difficult to define, but a standard that all parties should use to decide who would be allowed on the air and who would not (see Mander, 1984; Benjamin, 2001).

Third, neither government nor private interests alone would be allowed to dominate radio; decisions as to quality and public interest would be made by an alliance of the two. Radio would be treated neither like the press, nor like the movies, but instead would be a *regulated* medium, despite potential infringement of First Amendment protections. Finally, advertising was given a tacit 'OK' as a means of support for radio, though a too direct or hard-sell approach would not be regarded favourably; advertising on

Herbert Hoover: his radio conferences in 1922–5 established basic broadcasting principles

the air should display 'good taste'. This meant that, after all debate, the US would not seek government or public funds for broadcasting, the way that most nations had decided, and radio would become a commercial medium in private hands (for further discussion, see Sterling and Kitross, 1990; Sarno, 1976).

The results of these conferences were introduced to Congress as House Resolution 5589 in December 1925, and eventually became the Radio Act of 1927. In their analysis of the roots of this fundamental piece of broadcasting legislation, Mark Goodman and Mark Gring argue that:

> Congress in 1927 never intended for radio to become an unregulated part of the marketplace of ideas . . . what Congress had in mind for the radio industry was a system free of direct government interference, but predicated on continual governmental surveillance. Congress intended radio to be the voice for the dominant values in American culture as those values were understood by the Progressives and by much of middle-class America.
> (Goodman and Gring, 2000, p. 398)

This was accomplished through the 'public interest, convenience and necessity' clause of the new Act, which gave the newly created Federal Radio Commission the authority to make a sweeping reorganisation of licence assignments in its wake. Most immediately, it resulted in 1928's General Order 40 which revoked hundreds of licences and reassigned many more, under a principle of distinguishing 'propaganda' stations – those whose main purpose was to spread their own views or agendas, many of them non-profit-making and run by educational and religious groups – from 'general public service' stations that provided a 'well-rounded program' serving 'the entire listening public within the listening area of the station' – defined generally as commercial stations willing to sell their time to anyone with a programme to air (quoted in McChesney, 1994, p. 27).

This uniquely American definition of 'general public service', completely contrary to the sense of the term as it was used in most other nations, stems from the tension between First Amendment protections and the Progressive desire for social order. Congress could not possibly give a station licence to every single group that might want one for its own purpose. And if they had to choose some groups over others, wouldn't that be undue government tampering with free-speech rights? Since *every* group could not get a licence, then *no* group should be shown unfair preference. Instead of seeming to endorse any number of a random grab-bag of groups who might use their air franchise to proclaim radical, subversive, controversial, dangerous and 'selfish' views (by Progressive lights), such groups could simply buy time on a commercial station like everyone else. The effect of this categorising principle, as McChesney writes, was to drive non-profit-making stations off the air in unprecedented numbers.

For commercial broadcasters, particularly the large radio corporations whose stations received the most favourable assignments, the Act ushered in a period of network-building that still forms the backbone of the US television system today. RCA had already established the National Broadcasting Company (NBC) in 1926; by 1928 it operated two networks, the Red and the Blue, comprising over 52 affiliates; by 1941 that number had increased to 225 (Sterling and Kitross, 1990, p. 634). (The NBC Blue chain would be sold under anti-monopoly rules in 1943 to form ABC, the American Broadcasting Company). The Columbia Broadcasting System (CBS) originated in 1927 but languished until cigar-manufacturing magnate William S. Paley purchased it in 1928; it would become NBC's chief rival and a site of considerable broadcast innovation. By 1941 it possessed 118 affiliates. The battle with the reformers in the early 1930s before passage of the Communications Act of 1934 would challenge the triumphant commercial system, but end by reinforcing the 1927 compromise. And by the time the activist Roosevelt administration of the mid-1930s began its series of investigations and reports that would usher in various reforms, the US government needed the support of the radio networks too much, especially in motivating US intervention in World War II, to provide much more than annoyance.

The tension between profit-making and public service obligations for commercial stations, meanwhile, would have a continuing impact on the shape of US broadcasting and on the kinds of programming that developed. First, it mandated a distinction between 'sustaining' and 'sponsored' programmes. As the 'general public service' mandate plus Depression-era economics motivated networks to turn more and more of their programme innovation and production over to others, notably the advertising agencies of their primary sponsors, the one arena in which networks maintained control was in the production of sustaining programmes – those unsponsored programmes put on in the public interest, defined by Progressive 'quality' mandates as 'serious' culture and public debate. According to David Goodman,

> In its public service programming – in educational programmes designed for the classroom, in the forum discussion programmes which had links to a broader adult education forum movement, in classical music programming aimed at inducting a mass audience into the protocols of appreciation of 'serious' music, in religious broadcasts, in the practical advice that proliferated on home and farm and garden programmes – American radio took on a set of civic and national tasks which elsewhere were the job of government-funded national broadcasters. (Goodman, 2001, p. 2)

This sustaining/sponsored distinction would persist into television, most notably in the resurgence of documentary and the development of network news operations in the 1960s, in the wake of FCC Chair Newton Minow's famous 'vast wasteland' speech, until the advent of the Public Broadcasting Service (PBS) in 1967 (see Curtin, 1995).

Second, the mix of advertising-driven and public service pressures on broadcasters would produce the system of gendered programming unique to US radio and television. Unlike most public service systems, American radio created and maintained a lively and productive sect or of programming for women, much of it written and produced by women, aired exclusively during the daytime hours. Consisting of a mixture of daytime serial dramas ('soap operas') and 'chat'-shows, the highly commercialised, culturally 'low' programmes of the daytime hours responded to the economic imperatives of sponsored radio by directly addressing the important consuming audience of women (a frequently quoted statistic asserted that women purchased more than 85 per cent of all household products) at a time and place on the radio schedule that removed it from the more public and highly scrutinised hours of the evening. Daytime nurtured the careers of many important figures in the history of broadcast innovation, including Irna Phillips, arguably the originator of the daytime serial form; Mary Margaret McBride, originator of the unscripted chat-show; Anne Hummert, who with her husband Frank pioneered the 'mass production' method of radio (and later television) drama; and female journalists barred from night-time news programmes such as Dorothy Thompson, Helen Hiett, Pauline Frederick and many more (see Hilmes, 1997; Halper, 2002). The gendered day/night distinction then freed the night-time hours for more prestigious, less heavily commercialised sponsored and sustaining fare, addressing an audience of more 'serious' (read 'masculine') listeners, thus complying with public service expectations.

Finally, the schizophrenic nature of US broadcasting, split between First Amendment, free-market ideals and protective social goals, would carry over into television. Notably, control over the new medium would pass smoothly into the hands of the radio giants, NBC, CBS and ABC, without much thought of introducing competition or change. Buoyed by their strong co-operation with the military effort during World War II, the major networks would benefit from many regulatory decisions – particularly NBC, with its ties to the military/industrial complex in parent RCA – from favourable frequency assignments, to the 'licence freeze' of 1948 to 1952 that consolidated network power, to decisions over colour television and the intermixing of VHF and UHF frequencies. Though local-

ism would continue to factor heavily in regulatory investigations and reports (most notably the 'Blue Book' of 1947, authored by Charles Siepmann, former Director of Talks at the BBC), regulatory decisions would severely limit the number of independent local television stations, compared to radio, especially during the highly concentrated years of the classic network system (roughly 1960 to 1980). Not until the 1980s, when deregulatory ideology and competition from new technologies would combine to unsettle the Progressive compromise of the 1920s, would US television networks begin to shift towards a more purely commercial system, along with the rest of the world.

Michele Hilmes

RECOMMENDED READING

Benjamin, Louise (2001), *Freedom of the Air and the Public Interest*, Carbondale: Southern Illinois University Press.
McChesney, Robert W. (1994), *Telecommunications, Mass Media, and Democracy*, New York: Oxford.
Sterling, Christopher H. and Kitross, John M. (2001), *Stay Tuned: A History of American Broadcasting*, 3rd edition, New York: Lawrence Erlbaum.

Post-war Television in Britain: BBC and ITV

Whilst sound broadcasting settled down to consolidate its war-time gains, television began again from nowhere and suddenly revealed itself as a power to be reckoned with. Between 1945 and 1950 it passed from being a scientific achievement, a futuristic novelty, into being a successful rival to the older medium as a source of entertainment for the modern home . . . The future had changed hands. The fact was that people wanted to look as well as listen. (Gorham, 1952, p. 234)

Transmission of the nascent BBC 'high definition' television service was abruptly halted days before the outbreak of war in September 1939. When the service recommenced in June 1946, Maurice Gorham had been in post as Head of the Television Service for six months. The official decision to resume television transmissions after the war was, however, the result of a rather shadowy committee of Inquiry, led by Lord Hankey. This had been established in secret in September 1943 and two years later the committee's conclusion that 'television is here to stay' was officially given the green light by the Labour government.

Irna Phillips: daytime serial pioneer

The resultant 405-line BBC service from Alexandra Palace began again on the 7 June 1946 and the broadcast schedule included sound-only news bulletins as well as *The Silence of the Sea*, starring Kenneth More, the first full-length post-war television drama. The following day, with Freddie Grisewood and Richard Dimbleby as commentators, the Television Service covered the Victory Parade with great success. This was the first in a long line of post-war BBC outside broadcasts which aimed to televise significant events for domestic reception and mediate national civic rituals with due television pomp and ceremony (see Chaney, 1983).

However, by March 1947 there were less than 20,000 TV sets capable of operating in the UK – all of them in the London area – and progress was slow in developing transmission to 'the regions' and to a genuinely national audience. In part this was due to delays in developing a national television transmission system. Hankey had recommended a network of six transmitters to service major centres of population but these were yet to be completed in the conditions of post-war austerity. As Gorham was to note, however, there were other crucial factors that inhibited the growth of the television-viewing public in Britain at this time:

> This was not because people did not want television after the war but because they could not get it. There were no sets. There was no such thing as 'sales resistance' in those early years; every dealer had waiting-lists and every set that left the manufacturers found its way into a home, but supply fell far short of demand. (Gorham, 1952, p. 237)

Supply eventually caught up with demand by 1949 when set production reached 1,000 per day and the new combined TV/radio licences were selling at the same pace (see Geddes, 1991). However, British television in the late 1940s and early 1950s faced considerable problems and expansion was slow. This was due to technical, investment and market factors, but there were other related complications. Within the BBC at this stage, television was very much the 'poor relation' of radio. In 1947–8, for instance, £716,666 was allocated to TV while £6.5 million went to the senior, sound services (BBC, 1949). Furthermore, the slow technical expansion of television, its expense, national (non)availability and related domestic acquisition were a focus for some cautionary, if not regressive, voices within the BBC itself (including the director-general, Sir William Haley), which identified TV as *the* threat to sound broadcasting (see Briggs, 1995; Silvey, 1974). From outside the BBC in this period, television also

encountered a period of unease if not outright hostility from bodies like the Newspaper Society, British film producers, exhibitors and distributors, and music hall and theatre managers. The Epsom Grandstand Association refused to have the Derby horse race televised and the Football League and the British Boxing Board of Control also boycotted television coverage. The use of popular music was also an issue at this time due to uncertainty over the acquisition of television rights.

On the single BBC channel at this time, television transmission times remained limited. By the early 1950s, the day began with an hour-long programme in the morning – largely for retailers' demonstration purposes – followed by an hour of afternoon programmes at 3pm, and an evening schedule which started at 8.30pm and ended with the sound only news at 10pm. Outside broadcasts were permitted to extend beyond these times and the BBC coverage of the 1948 London Olympics was an important, early example of the power of televised media sporting events. In the late 1940s the BBC also televised *In Our Garden* (1946), *Cookery* (with Philip Harbern, the 'television chef', 1947), and *Television Newsreel* (modelled on the cinema equivalent, 1948–54). Just before the end of the decade, the Sutton Coldfield transmitter came into service, at that time as the most powerful television transmitter in the world. It extended the television service to millions of new, potential viewers from the south-western borders of the Midlands up to the edges of the northern hinterlands of Lancashire and Yorkshire. The North and Scotland were provided with their own transmitters by 1952. On New Year's Day in January 1950, however, less than four hours of television programmes were broadcast by the BBC on two transmitters to some 340,000 licence

The 1948 London Olympics: an early outside television broadcast

holders. The million mark was reached at the end of 1951, at the point that the regular BBC surveys began to indicate a higher preponderance of lower-income viewers (see Silvey, 1974, pp. 155–9).

The Beveridge Committee was appointed in 1949 with a brief to consider the constitution, control and future development of sound and television broadcasting services in the UK. Beveridge's Liberal politics in fact led him to be highly critical of the BBC and its ethos which he described as: 'beginning with Londonization, going on to secretiveness and self-satisfaction, and ending up with a dangerous sense of mission which became a sense of divine right' (cited in Curran and Seaton, 1988, p. 173). His 1951 report finally recommended – but not unanimously – that the BBC monopoly should continue. It emphatically rejected 'sponsored advertising' (as witnessed in the US). In contrast, 'spot advertising' was preferred as likely to be the *least influential* form of commercial support for television broadcasting and the expansion of television viewing outside London, on a regional basis. Dissenting voices on the committee, in particular the Tory MP Selwyn Lloyd, argued that it was unacceptable for the BBC to continue to hold 'the brute force of monopoly' in the provision of television services. Such views were given official endorsement when, following the defeat of the Labour government in November 1951, the incoming Conservatives rushed out a White Paper advocating 'some element of competition'. This allowed a number of key issues to be successfully exploited by the ensuing campaign for commercial television that led to the launch of Independent Television four years later in September 1955. The political culture of the 1950s was changing with a greater premium on notions of new forms of democratic involvement and expression and consumer choice. Economically, television advertising represented a new outlet for growth and potential in a depressed and constrained market. In this changing environment, the BBC internal management and strategy for television constantly encountered complex tensions with its radio provision. There was also the vexed matter of the BBC commitment to a television service that tended too easily to reproduce a pre-war, Reithian mission with its preoccupations with 'high culture' and moral improvement (see Goldie, 1977). The complacency and conservatism of the BBC at the time was epitomised when Norman Collins, the influential Controller of Television and head of the popular Light programme on radio, resigned his post when the controller of the more highbrow Third programme was appointed over his head as Director of Television. Collins told *The Times*, that he had parted company with the BBC:

because of a clash of principle . . . whether the new medium of TV shall be allowed to develop at this, the most crucial stage of its existence, along its own lines and by its own methods, or whether it shall be merged into the colossus of sound broadcasting. (Cited in Curran and Seaton, 1988, p. 174)

He immediately set about forming important political and industrial alliances and spearheaded the Popular Television Association, which acted as the strategic dynamo for the commercial television lobby. It gained ready support from sponsors in the electronic industries and manufacturers, from advertisers and sections of the press, as well as potential programme producers. They argued that commercial television represented enterprise for industry and 'choice' for viewers – a means of liberating control from the patronising and 'out of touch' constraints of the BBC. Against this, the anti-commercial National Television Committee, led by the Labour MP and BBC broadcaster Christopher Mayhew, included eminent church representatives, educators, moral crusaders and some notable journalists and critics. They sought to preserve the BBC public service monopoly and deeply distrusted commercial competition which, they argued, would pander to the lowest kinds of popular culture, drive out quality, and lower standards.

Norman Collins spearheaded the Popular Television Association

This 'Punch-and-Judy' opposition has remained funda-mental to the development of British television culture and criticism ever since and it has intensified with subsequent technical and institutional developments (see, for instance, Brunsdon, 1996; Corner, 1995).

Between 1952 and 1954, the pro- and the anti- campaigns fought to gain public and parliamentary support for their proposals for the future of BBC television. For many of the public of that early 1950s' generation, however, television began with the Coronation in June 1953. The BBC television outside-broadcast coverage of the event was the most ambitious ever undertaken, beginning at ten in the morning and going on until eleven-thirty that night. Richard Dimbleby commentated throughout what has become widely regarded and celebrated as the first British 'TV event':

> The BBC had never before had so large a domestic audi-ence. The listening audience accounted for 37 per cent and nearly all of them had heard it in their own homes. The viewing audience was 51 per cent, but more than half of them saw the Service in the homes of friends or in public places such as shops, cinemas or pubs. (Silvey, 1974, p. 165)

It is claimed that at least 20 million watched the television coverage and that viewers outstripped listeners for the first time. The event prompted a boom in the sales of television sets and 1953 was the first year in which production of TV sets (selling at about £85 or more) exceeded that of radio units. Although these developments were hailed as a land-mark for BBC TV, they also exacerbated the battle over the monopoly, although as Crisell (1997, p. 80) notes: 'The harder the champions of the BBC argued for the retention of its monopoly, the more priggish and patronising they sounded.'

At its reading in the Lords, the Television Act of 1954 and the commercial television system it ushered in, was greeted by Lord Reith as akin to the introduction into Britain of smallpox, the Black Death and the bubonic plague. Notwithstanding, the Act received Royal Assent in July 1954. Within days, the Independent Television Authority (ITA) held its first meeting, planning for regional franchises and a new style of television service and programming. The ITA regulated commercial television in terms of awarding franchises and controlling the nature and quality of advertising. It also required contractors to adhere to a strong public service remit in their provision of information, education and entertainment programmes that had to be balanced, of suitable quality and variety.

Commercial television opened on 22 September 1955, with an evening programme schedule which included Sir John Barbiroli conducting the Halle Orchestra's perform-ance of Elgar's Cockaigne Overture, a variety show, some professional boxing, a star cabaret and a visit to the ITV gala celebrations. The first TV advertisement to be screened was for Gibbs SR toothpaste. Although untypical, the evening was judged a resounding success. In an attempt to upstage and 'spike' the opening of its commercial competi-tor, the BBC radio soap opera The Archers killed off the principal female character in a stable fire. The first night did, however, give some indications of the commitment to popular variety, celebrity and light entertainment forms that would come to be one of the most visible hallmarks of ITV provision as competition developed through the late 1950s and into the 60s.

For the first few months, ITV could only be received in the London area and reception required a new set and aerial or, at the least, technical adjustments to existing arrangements. Broadcasts began in the Midlands in early 1956 and thereafter expanded quite rapidly to the North, with the main population areas throughout the UK catered for by the early 1960s. These developments in the spread of the network and regional ITV services meant that com-mercial TV was not an overnight success – especially with advertisers – who waited to be convinced by the new initiative. The start-up and operating costs for the network and for franchise holders were substantial and with restric-ted ratings in this period, there were some analysts who predicted that the system would fail through lack of invest-ment and revenue. However, by 1957 the situation began to change; ITV viewers were rising by some 50,000 per week, network arrangements had helped to cut costs and, more importantly, demand for television advertising was out-stripping supply, signalling profitability. At the launch of Scottish Television in August 1957, its major shareholder, the media magnate Roy Thomson, claimed in an ill-advised aside that ownership of a commercial TV franchise was 'like having a licence to print your own money'. Developments in ITV programme schedules succeeded in providing competition and a meaningful alternative to the BBC service. New and innovative formats for news (Independent Television News, 1955–) as well as for comedy, light entertainment and imported American programmes all made their mark and prompted responses from the BBC. While there has been a tendency to overes-timate the immediate impact of ITV on the growth of the TV audience and on the BBC (see Curran and Seaton, 1988, p. 177) by the end of the 1950s the ITV commercial network was winning the battle for ratings and viewers (see

Sendall 1982; 1983). However, the commercial populism of a good deal of their programmes – game shows, celebrities and imported series – continued to be regarded with animosity and anxiety by many influential commentators and critics: 'Commercial television had won the lion's share of the audience, but the BBC retained a moral and cultural superiority' (Crisell, 1997, p. 103).

By the end of 1959, the British television landscape had been transformed. From the very shaky post-war technical restart in 1946, television had been reinvented as a national cultural institution with an established and expanding domestic viewing culture. The BBC and ITV provided almost 10.5 million licence holders with about sixteen hours of programming per day on two channels, available to the vast majority of the UK audience. No longer the sole preserve of the BBC, or exclusive to London with regulated commercial competition established, the 1960s were to start with the appointment of the Pilkington Committee.

GRACE WYNDHAM GOLDIE

Goldie was a pioneer in current affairs and political programming on UK television. News and current affairs programming has since been understood as the site (along with drama) where the early ITV companies had the BBC outclassed; but Goldie worked for the BBC for most of her professional career and much of her current affairs programming was pioneering well before ITV gained a foothold. Born in 1900, the daughter of a civil engineer, she received her education at Bristol and Oxford; when she and her actor husband moved to London in 1934 Goldie began writing radio and television drama reviews for the BBC's weekly comment and review magazine, *The Listener*. Occasionally she visited the BBC's early television studio at Alexandra Palace and watched productions take place, and her critical reviews reflected the technical knowledge that she acquired there as well as a passion for the new medium. In the post-war years Goldie rose quickly in the ranks of BBC production, first as a radio 'talks' producer, then as a producer in the Television Talks Department where she produced significant programmes about international current affairs and politics, such as *Foreign Correspondent*. These programmes were often filmed on location and were the first attempt to showcase the journalistic essay form on television. Goldie recruited ex-politicians such as Aidan Crawley and Woodrow Wyatt as presenters for these shows and in the early 1950s she set up an unofficial current affairs unit, again nurturing the talents of younger male staff Michael Peacock, James Bredin and Geoffrey Johnson Smith, all of whom were to become important television executives in the years to come.

One of her major achievements was to utilise television's potential as a component of the public sphere and to this end she was instrumental in setting up the first television coverage of British general elections (the first in 1950); and in convincing politicians to use television to address the electorate. In this coverage she was concerned that the television cameras would reveal fakery and phoney sentiment and counselled politicians to attempt impromptu rather than (totally) scripted interviews, a topic she addresses in detail in her book *Facing the Nation*. She also was the executive who provided the leadership for the groundbreaking current affairs/arts programmes *Panorama*, *Tonight* and *Monitor* as well as the topical 1960s satirical programme *That Was the Week That Was*.

She was appointed Assistant Head of Talks in 1954, despite the fact that she was more experienced as a television manager than the head, Leonard Miall. According to Miall, 'She had to be totally in charge of whatever activity she was engaged in, which did not make her a natural deputy'(1994, p. 139). Miall's solution was to 'put her in total charge of specific activities, such as arranging the training programmes for new staff'(1994, pp. 135–40). In 1962 she became Head of Television Talks; this was during the early reign of Hugh Carleton Greene as Director-General of the BBC. Greene wanted to promote the BBC as a modern institution, far away from the paternalistic Reithian BBC of the 1920s and 30s with which the BBC was still associated to some extent. With her no-nonsense manner and passion for television over radio, Goldie provided a useful figure in this project and her frequent media interviews promoted her as a career woman who exemplified a changing BBC. She retired from the BBC in 1965 and became an associate member of Nuffield College, Oxford, where she wrote *Facing the Nation* – according to Miall, 'one of the best books about the relationship between television and politics, in which she had played such an important pioneering role'(1994, p. 143); she also gave lectures, made appearances on television and wrote articles about the state of national television. *Facing The Nation: Television and Politics, 1936–1976* is a book which continues to be the most important critical history about that relationship during the 1950s but it is also a personal history and a theorisation of the medium itself as at its best when live and engaged with the public sphere.

Jason Jacobs

Its brief was to appraise the performance of post-1955 competition, to recommend on the future pattern of organisation and to advise on the allocation of a third television channel (BBC2 in fact commenced broadcasting in April 1964). British television had emerged not entirely unscathed from its initial conflicts with radio and the crucial battle between public service and commercial conceptions of its organisation and operation. As a result, by the early 1960s, it was poised for a decade of much greater expansion and innovation in terms of programme hours and formats, more channels, transmitters and an ever-expanding, 'mass' audience.

Tim O'Sullivan

RECOMMENDED READING

Briggs, Asa (1995) *The History of Broadcasting in the United Kingdom Volume V: Competition 1955–1974*, Oxford: Oxford University Press.

Clayton, Ian, Harding, Colin and Lewis, Brian (eds) (1995), *Opening the Box: The Popular Experience of Television*, Bradford: Yorkshire Arts/National Museum of Photography, Film and Television.

Corner, John (ed.) (1991), *Popular Television in Britain: Studies in Cultural History*, London: BFI.

Paulu, Burton (1961), *British Broadcasting in Transition*, London: Macmillan.

Roberts, Graham and Taylor, Philip (eds) (2001), *The Historian, Television and Television History*, Luton: University of Luton Press.

Williams, Raymond (1974), *Television: Technology and Cultural Form*, London: Fontana.

Establishment of the US Television Networks

In structure and operation, the network television system that emerged in the United States after World War II closely resembled the network radio system that preceded it. The commercially driven 'American System' of broadcasting that originated with radio in the 1920s carried over into television in the 1940s. It was a system based around centrally produced, live, single-sponsorship programming. Networks 'owned and operated' stations (O&Os) in key markets and implemented rigid affiliation contracts with local stations elsewhere around the country. Ratings typically determined prime-time line-ups and advertising prices. The National Broadcasting Company (NBC) and the Columbia Broadcasting System (CBS) reigned as the dominant networks. Lackadaisical oversight by the FCC and frequent, unproductive investigations into industry practices by Congress characterised government regulation.

But the transition from radio to television along these lines was not inevitable, natural or smooth. Corporate economic manoeuvres and public policy decisions were crucial to the speed and nature of television's development around a network oligopoly. Furthermore, there were definite winners and losers in the shift to television. As NBC and CBS redirected focus, personnel and finances towards television, their radio operations and AM affiliates were forced to find ways to avoid being completely overshadowed by the new audiovisual medium. The Mutual Broadcasting System – a stalwart of 1930s–40s radio – failed in its network television ventures. Meanwhile, the American Broadcasting Company (ABC), a fledgling radio outfit spawned in the mid-1940s through the court-ordered divestiture of the NBC Blue network, became the leading network by the end of the 1950s in terms of its alternative approach to industrial and programming practices, spurred by its third-place status.

In addition, significant changes in television industry structure and programming procedures overall took place during this period. Live dramas and variety shows originating from New York gave way to sitcoms and action-adventure telefilm series produced in Hollywood. The networks began to develop syndication ventures to supply international television markets and the rising number of unaffiliated independent US stations. And 'participation sponsorship' and spot advertising replaced single sponsorship as the financial basis of network and station income. The television system of 1960 owed its shape and foundations to the legacy of thirty years of network broadcasting, but many of its features had been modified, and many of its participant relations had been reconfigured. Experimentation with television technology had been taking place since the 1920s. Franklin D. Roosevelt's televised presidential address from the World's Fair of 1939 finally inaugurated daily television broadcasting for New Yorkers. This much-heralded advent of television proved premature, however, as the technological and economic development of the medium was put on hold during America's participation in World War II. Following V-E Day, pent-up consumer demand combined with strategic industry operations to stimulate the full commercial exploitation of television over the course of the next decade and a half. While there were only six television stations broadcasting to an estimated 8,000 households in 1946, fifteen years later 579 stations were reaching 89 per cent of the population (Sterling and Kitross, 1990, pp. 633, 658).

But the television boom was not instant or constant. Coast-to-coast television networking did not become a reality until 1951, at which point just over one hundred stations were on the air. US television grew fitfully as a commercial medium for the first half of this period, and then expanded massively and profitably through the mid- to late-1950s.

Television's hesitant growth in the late 1940s and early 1950s was partly due to economic reasons and partly due to regulatory decisions. Compared to radio broadcasting, television programming was very expensive to produce. There was the initial capital investment required to construct studios and install transmitting equipment. Prior to network connections and regular all-day schedules, stations couldn't rely on outside sources for programming – generating content hour after hour was costly. Most advertisers were reluctant to invest heavily in the new medium until television set sales had improved to a point where sponsoring TV was more cost-effective than sponsoring radio shows. Consequently, most early TV stations were owned by the networks or by major market AM radio stations. Revenues garnered from radio broadcasting sustained television during these lean economic times. Nowhere was this more apparent than with the Radio Corporation of America's (RCA) lengthy debt-financing of television networking, equipment development and programming – a long-term investment that realised lucrative returns in the 1950s for the giant electronics firm through its network subsidiary, NBC, and its manufacturing divisions.

Two decisions and one extended period of inactivity by the FCC were fundamental to the formation of US television around the network-dominated American system. The first decision was the *Final Reports* of 1945, in which the commission supported RCA's pleas for an immediate endorsement of television as a mass medium by transferring highly coveted Very High Frequency (VHF) electromagnetic spectrum space away from FM radio to TV. Shortly afterwards, the FCC also officially sanctioned RCA's monochrome television technology and, in the process, rejected CBS's more sophisticated prototype colour TV system. These decisions spurred television set manufacturing. Encouraged by the profits it began to realise from set sales and patent licensing, RCA reinforced its commitment to transforming NBC into the leading television network. The combination of favourable policy, unrestrained consumer demand and massive financial investment (on the back of radio profits) created the cli-

mate to allow television to grow into a commercially viable mass medium in the late 1940s.

Smacking of favouritism to the dubious technological advantages of RCA's system, these early FCC decisions also proved shortsighted. The FCC's licence allocations for VHF television followed a predetermined geographical pattern that effectively limited the number of stations in major markets, such as New York City, where television was more established and demand for station licences was greater. Additionally, as more stations began broadcasting in the set-aside VHF band, signal interference increased, revealing that the FCC's *Final Reports* of 1945 had seriously miscalculated the formula for signal strength distances and frequency separation requirements. In order to investigate these and other technical issues, the FCC issued a television licensing 'freeze' in 1948 – it would continue to accept applications to set up stations but would issue no new construction permits until it had resolved existing technical problems.

The second FCC decision that contributed to the establishment of the network television system was the protracted television station licensing freeze and its termination through the issuance of the *Sixth Report and Order* in 1952. Originally expected to last several months, the freeze actually dragged on for four years. Only the 108 stations that had been licensed prior to the freeze were able to broadcast during these years. A large number of these stations were network O&Os, and the overwhelming majority were network affiliates. The freeze granted them years of artificially uncompetitive service at a crucial time in the medium's development, during which they could maximise revenues and establish reputations with sponsors and audiences. After toying with the idea of moving and enlarging the part of the frequency spectrum set aside for television broadcasting, the FCC pursued a policy of 'intermixture' in its *Sixth Report and Order*. This permitted existing stations to remain on the VHF band, while opening the technologically less attractive Ultra High Frequency (UHF) spectrum space for new applicants.

The lifting of the licensing freeze opened the floodgates to television's commercial expansion, but it also represented a crucial turning point in network–affiliate relations. The network model was economically profitable because it was based on centralised programme production and distribution that benefited big sponsors, dominant networks and large market affiliates. This allowed networks and sponsors to spread the higher costs of television programming across multiple markets. Network coordination of affiliate scheduling made nationwide or regional time-buying easier for advertising agencies.

Affiliates earned higher ratings and better revenues with these big-budget shows and big-name stars than their local station competitors. In fact, network affiliation was often crucial to economic survival in television's early years. In 1955, 86 per cent of all profitable stations were affiliated with either NBC or CBS. Consequently, affiliates complained on occasion about their individual affiliation terms, but openly supported the network system as a guarantor of 'quality' programming

As more stations came on the air following the lifting of the licensing freeze, the big networks were able to use the economic lure of affiliation to extract better terms from local broadcasters in their affiliation contracts. Most nefarious was the 'option time' clause, which required affiliates to clear certain times of their daily schedule (primarily the lucrative prime-time period) for nationally distributed network programming. Network chiefs had defended option time during the radio years as a requirement of local market transmission that was crucial to the economic lifeblood of a live, national broadcasting medium. Network heads used this same defence during the 1950s, pointing to their prestigious live dramas and extravagant 'spectaculars', even as telefilms began increasingly to displace live telecasts as the regular network fare.

Independent stations, the weaker networks and critics within government pointed out that the existing network system restricted external competition and limited programme choices for audiences. Opponents argued that option time contradicted the FCC's supposed commitment to 'localism' in broadcasting and made it very difficult for outside producers and the weaker networks to get their programmes onto the air during the high-ratings periods of the day. Despite several inquiries into the subject, option time was not officially outlawed until the 1960s. The subject was moot by that time anyway: affiliates were generally content to split the revenues accrued from high prime-time ratings with networks and would typically clear that time regardless of the option time clause. The complaints of independent stations, critics and outside producers never coalesced into a viable political or economic force. Following the *Sixth Report and Order*, the FCC entered a period of regulatory inactivity that lasted the remainder of the decade, permitting the major networks to consolidate their industrial dominance. This is not to say that there was total silence on the subject in Washington. Federal investigations into television practices permeated the 1950s. These generally fell into one of two areas: a seemingly uninterrupted stream of overlapping inquiries and hearings into network practices originating from Congress, the FCC and the Justice Department; and more sporadic

Congressional investigations into television programme content (typically questioning the moral impact of 'sophisticated' and violent programming on American homes and youth). The industry was able to divert objections regarding programme content by endorsing a Television Code, listing positive values to be promoted and inappropriate material to be avoided, in 1952. Since self-regulation was most visibly practised at the network level, the networks argued that they could 'improve' programme content with greater control over programming production and distribution. This defence helped to deflect criticisms of network industry practices.

Numerous inquiries raised fundamental questions regarding the oligopolistic control held by the networks and their vertically integrated grip over various facets of the industry. But very little actual policy emerged from these investigations. Network supporters were as numerous (if less vocal) than opponents. Few serious challenges were ever levelled at the *modus operandi* of the American system: network executives successfully argued that they deserved a return on their initial capital investments, that they provided 'free' programming of a quality that surpassed alternative production channels, and that television operations as a whole were successful and continuing to stimulate consumer demand and boost the American economy. The limited competition that existed within the industry was enough to avoid anti-trust action.

The status quo consequently moved from strength to strength. The networks began to wrest programme production away from sponsors, permitting them to adopt scheduling techniques to fit their needs and to increase revenues by selling participation deals with multiple advertisers for single programmes. Seeking to recoup earlier investment costs, the major networks adopted a strictly bottom-line approach to content development in the late 1950s that signalled the end of the 'golden age' of programming experimentation. ABC was most prominent in this strategy, targeting the disposable income of young 'get age' families and teenagers, and forging deals with Hollywood studios for telefilm series featuring sexy leads in sunny, bright, action-adventure narratives. Less invested in older methods of network operations, ABC pushed forward aggressively with this 'bread and butter' approach to the medium. While NBC and CBS publicly criticised their rival for the 'vulgar' results of these tactics, ABC's cost-consciousness and ratings success proved irresistible to its competitors.

By the mid-1950s, ABC's economic status was more secure, but it was still lagging far behind NBC and CBS in terms of profitability and ratings. Ironically, this fledgling

THE 'OTHER' NETWORKS

The television system that developed in the decade after the end of World War II favoured the powerful networks but kept the weaker networks at a commercial and operational disadvantage. Economic factors and regulatory decisions resulted in a three-network system that dominated US television for the next forty years, comprised of NBC, CBS and ABC.

In terms of number of affiliates, however, the largest radio network in the 1930s and 40s had been the Mutual Broadcasting System (MBS). Whereas NBC and CBS operated along a centralised, top-down network model – programmes typically originated from network studios and local affiliates dealt directly with network executives in their New York headquarters or regional offices – MBS was formed as a co-operative venture where local stations would lower overheads by sharing popular home-produced programmes with one another. This decentralised model was less financially lucrative and, despite the large number of affiliates, revenue generation for MBS lagged far behind that of NBC and CBS.

Despite plans to carry over into the new medium, the Mutual Television network never got off the ground. The decentralised MBS model hampered decision-making during the crucial post-war years. Many MBS affiliates were smaller outfits, often serving scattered audiences in rural markets, and could ill afford to venture into the high-investment stakes of

television broadcasting. MBS complaints to the FCC regarding NBC and CBS dominance generally fell on deaf ears. And Mutual was impeded by the operating policies of AT&T, which controlled the coaxial cables that linked markets around the country and formed the technological basis of the network architecture. AT&T was slow to make these connections – particularly to smaller, hinterland markets – and also charged a flat rate for usage that effectively penalised smaller networks that were unable to clear extended periods of the daily schedule with stations in a large number of interconnected markets. Some of the larger MBS affiliates did establish television stations, produced programming and managed to survive as independents. The Mutual Television network never began operations, however.

Other efforts to forge national television networks during these early years were undertaken by Paramount Pictures, Philco and DuMont. Hollywood movie company Paramount had long shown an economic interest in broadcasting. It had attempted an alliance with CBS in 1929, only to lose its share of that network to Depression economics in 1932. The studio established TV stations in Chicago and Los Angeles in the late 1940s, but, sidetracked by internal upheavals in the movie industry and fears of anti-trust action from the government, never expanded these into a full-fledged network. Paramount held a financial stake in DuMont Television, which resulted in the FCC refusing its petitions to control more stations. Hamstrung by these decisions, Paramount focused increasingly on alternative ventures, such as subscription television. Its Chicago and LA stations became ABC O&Os in the 1950s.

Philco and DuMont were primarily television set manufacturers who initially saw station ownership and networking as a means to improve consumer set sales and create a parallel revenue source for when receiver sales plateaued. DuMont's venture into network television was the far more significant of the two. Until its demise in 1955, DuMont vied with ABC for third-place network standing.

What makes DuMont's involvement in the network TV fray more interesting than simply an historical curiosity was its outspoken opposition to the network system dominated by CBS and NBC. Allen DuMont was a well-respected industrialist with a certain amount of political clout on the East Coast. Like ABC, DuMont struggled through the late 1940s and early 1950s, having to make do as the secondary affiliated network with many stations, and thus usually usurped by local affiliates in favour of programming originating from the primary network – NBC or CBS. DuMont executives lambasted the FCC for its prolonged station

Allen DuMont: his US network once vied for third-place ranking

licensing freeze and, even worse, the *Sixth Report and Order*'s 'intermixture' policy – which limited the number of VHF stations to three in many large markets and made business extremely difficult for new UHF stations attempting to compete against VHF affiliates. While it was clearly a self-serving argument, DuMont opined that the FCC should license high-power regional VHF television stations (serving several states): this would improve consumer choice (and permit the commercial viability of perhaps a dozen national networks) by raising the number of channels available to audiences. Ignoring the reality that most broadcasters cleared large chunks of time for network feeds, the FCC rejected DuMont's regional model as contrary to its policy of 'local-ism' in broadcasting. DuMont threw in the towel when the FCC approved a merger between ABC and United Paramount Theaters (UPT), the divested theatre-owning arm of Paramount Studios, in 1953. The merger gave ABC a much-needed cash infusion, allowing it to improve programming and contract relations and tie up the affiliation status of the third station in many mid-size markets. The FCC endorsed the merger as a means to increase ABC's competitiveness with NBC and CBS. DuMont closed its network operations shortly afterwards, grumbling that its own interests had been sacrificed in order to permit ABC to survive.

Matthew Murray

status forced ABC into the lead in terms of programming practices and network policies that other networks would adopt over the next ten years: the turn to Hollywood-based filmed production, the elimination of sustaining 'cultural' programmes, an appeal to youth culture, and overall a definition of good programming as that which garnered highest ratings. The network's historically weak clearance levels with affiliates meant that it was less reliant on live studio productions, and more inclined to pursue recorded means of programme distribution. Existing connections with Hollywood resulted in product orders with the older movie studios – and for cheap telefilm series from Warner Bros. in particular. Since NBC and CBS had cornered established broadcasting talent and traditional corporate advertisers, ABC nurtured previously unknown stars in action-adventure series that appealed to younger audiences and sponsors of brand-oriented consumer products. ABC was forced to undertake riskier projects, such as investing capital in Disneyland and running Disney shows, but this ingratiated it more deeply with youth culture and what were becoming more lucrative weekend, afternoon and early evening portions of the daily schedule. ABC's approach epitomised broader changes taking place in network practices. Having established their reputations and opposed regulatory interventions, NBC and CBS reduced prestige productions and cut costly sustaining shows. Exercising greater control over their programming schedules, they rationalised line-ups and increasingly relied upon ratings as the measure of programme performance. Live programming gave way to quiz shows and Hollywood telefilms, signifying a shift towards a bottom-line mentality. While ABC didn't cause these changes, it did lead the way towards dominant network practice by the early 1960s. The same networks that had dismissed ABC as an upstart network exercising questionable integrity and offering inferior programming were now emulating the more focused, profit-oriented telefilm style. By the end of the 1950s, all three of the major networks were pursuing similar strategies. Management shake-ups at NBC and CBS resulted in the appointment of ex-ABC programming heads. Each network was committed to maximising advertising revenues, and contracted with Hollywood studios for marketable programmes appealing to attractive mass consumer demographics.

Matthew Murray

RECOMMENDED READING

Anderson, Christopher (1994), *Hollywood TV: The Studio System in the Fifties*, Austin: University of Texas Press.

Balio, Tino (ed.) (1990), *Hollywood in the Age of Television*, Boston: Unwin Hyman.

Baughman, James L. (1985), *Television's Guardians: The FCC and the Politics of Programming, 1958–1967*, Knoxville: University of Tennessee Press.

Boddy, William (1990a), *Fifties Television: The Industry and Its Critics*, Urbana: University of Illinois Press.

Schwoch, James (1994), 'A Failed Vision: The Mutual Television Network', *Velvet Light Trap*, 33, Spring, pp. 3–13.

Competition and Change in British Television

The 1960s and 70s were decades of expansion and development for television in the UK. As Jean Seaton states, 'In the 1960s and 1970s television came of age' (Curran and Seaton, 1997, p. 195). The medium became more adventurous and more liberal as the old monopoly of the BBC gave way to what was perceived by many to be a 'cosy duopoly' between the BBC and ITV. By the middle of the 1970s, the broadcasting companies between them employed approximately 40,000 people (Home Office, 1977, p. 434). The 1960s and 70s were also times of increased tension between broadcaster and state (particularly during the 1970s) and were years which witnessed the beginning of the end of the Reithian-driven public service ethos in television. ITV continued to grow in the early 1960s, and the network was completed in 1962 with the granting of a licence to the television station Wales (West and North) that served that geographical area. However, the station has the somewhat dubious distinction of being the only ITV company ever to fold due to financial difficulties, and in 1964, its place was taken by the neighbouring Television Wales and the West (TWW) company. Nevertheless, the commercial and popular success of commercial television was knocked somewhat by the publication of the Pilkington Committee report on broadcasting. The report, which was published in 1962, effectively brought the first era of television broadcasting in Britain to an end and can be considered a milestone in several ways. It was a product of its time in that it reflected concerns relating to the decline of organic working-class culture in Britain as a result of a mass-produced culture. However, it also came dangerously close (as Jean Seaton notes) to despising everything that was popular and entertaining (Curran and Seaton, 1997, p. 179). For some, Pilkington represented the last government-established committee report that held on to the paternalistic, Reithian view of broadcasting. To others, the early 1960s heralded the beginning of a 'golden age' that lasted well into the late 1970s and came to an end only with the arrival of Margaret Thatcher. The period saw a growth in home-produced situation comedy (e.g. *Dad's Army*, *Steptoe and Son*, *The Likely Lads*), the likes of which have not been seen since that time. The period also gave rise to drama strands such as the BBC's *Wednesday Play* (later *Play for Today*) that provided a platform for key television playwrights and directors such as Dennis Potter, Tony Garnett and Ken Loach.

In relation to ITV, the committee called for a change in programming content and outlined plans to make commercial television adhere more stringently to public service principles like its counterpart, the BBC. It also paved the way for tighter powers for the regulatory body, the Independent Television Authority (ITA) in terms of franchise renewals in particular. Concerns had also been raised during the consultation process as to the excessive profits of ITV companies (which were still rising even in the mid-1970s), and so a levy was placed on profits, with money being poured into Exchequer funds.

In recommending that a third terrestrial channel be given to the BBC, and thereby paving the way for the advent of BBC2 in 1964, the Committee castigated those in ITV whose sole motive had been profit at the expense of 'quality' programming and vindicated those, such as Hugh Carleton Greene, director-general of the BBC at the time, who believed that the Corporation was right and that ITV was woefully inadequate in its approach. As he wrote in 1969, 'They [ITV] got what was coming to them' (Greene, 1969, p. 59).

The round of ITV contract renewal that took place in 1963–4 was a considerable 'non-event', in the sense that the existing contractors were given the green light to proceed. The only real sense of occasion derived from the fact that this was the first time that contracts had been awarded or renewed on a UK-wide basis. However, the ITV map remained unchanged, apart from Wales where TWW was granted the right to broadcast to the whole of the country. In this instance the ITA also asked the government to provide a second channel in South Wales so that English viewers and viewers in Wales could get their own 'edition' of the regional service – a move that was welcomed on both sides of the Bristol Channel.

The contract renewal in 1967, however, couldn't have been more different and it signalled a much more radical shake-up of the ITV system. In the greatest shock, TWW lost its contract to the Harlech Consortium. In other parts of the UK, Rediffusion lost out to a new company, Thames, which was to broadcast to the London area on weekdays. The weekend franchise was offered to the fledgling London Weekend Television company. The north of England was carved up with the Lancashire area contract staying in the hands of Granada, and Yorkshire Television catering for the other named area.

With ITV making its mark on the viewing public, much has been written about the changes that took place inside the BBC during the 1960s: the growth of populist programming, a changed mode of address from the deferential Reithian tone to a more accessible and affable one. The

'Golden-Age' comedy: *The Likely Lads*

climax of this trend was exemplified in the birth of satirical comedy shows such as *That Was the Week That Was* and the irreverent, inane and often madcap humour of *Monty Python's Flying Circus*. The BBC also took a large step in the direction of hard-hitting, social issue-driven drama. One such play was Jeremy Sandford's documentary-drama, *Cathy Come Home*, that was broadcast in 1966 under the *Wednesday Play* strand. Under the direction of Ken Loach, and shot in a style so as to provide a strong documentary aesthetic, the play tackled the issue of homelessness. Others directed by Loach, such as Nell Dunn's *Up the Junction*, tackled issues relating to sex and young people, in particular abortion. One line of argument sug-

gests that the changes that took place under the stewardship of Hugh Carleton Greene (as director-general) were a direct response to the competition that the corporation faced in the form of ITV. The commercial network had succeeded in drawing a substantial number of the viewing audience away from the BBC, and its share of the audience grew during the late 1950s and early years of the 1960s. In 1957, for example, it was suggested that ITV had a 79 per cent share of the audience, though this figure has been questioned due to the different methods of measuring the audience (Curran and Seaton, 1997, pp. 166–7). Steadily, with a new, more populist approach towards programming, the BBC's share increased and by the end of the

decade (and into the 1970s) the two broadcasting organisations were on a fairly level pegging.

However, the strategy of 'fighting back' by offering a
fresher tone to the programming was not welcomed uni-
versally. In a letter to Oliver Whitley (chief assistant to the
director-general) in 1964, the former director-general John
Reith made his views on Greene's strategy clear:

> He is . . . in favour of what is a negation of almost all that I
> stood for. He gives the public what it wants . . . It is exactly
> what I utterly repudiated . . . this determining aim and
> objective of giving the public what it wants really is the all-
> important and all-operative factor. (Stuart, 1975, p. 512)

This competition, however, was to result in programming
which was similar on both channels. In a study of programming on both channels in 1965, Raymond Williams
suggested that the competition between the two rivals had
led to output that was similar in format and style: 'A good
deal of programme planning is evidently done with an eye
to the other channel, rather than by any more general criterion' (Williams, 1966, p. 68).

Nevertheless, an alternative argument suggests that the
BBC had already put changes in place prior to the advent of
ITV. For example, the BBC had a substantial proportion of
American-produced programming which was designed to
be popular in its appeal, and was forging links on various
levels with American television companies. In addition, it
needs to be noted that although the BBC's reaction was
slow (showing elements of complacency, even, in the early
years), there was an effort to introduce changes to programming. At the end of 1956, the government allowed the
extension of broadcasting hours, thereby ending what was
known as the 'toddlers truce', the period between 6pm and
7pm where parents could see their children to bed. In 1957,
the BBC filled this slot with the innovative *Tonight* pro-

Social issue drama: *Up the Junction*

gramme which provided a mix of light and serious items,
thereby introducing a new mode of address and challenging the long-held notion that the 'serious' or high-minded
could not be offered alongside the entertaining. There is no
doubt that the BBC were forced to a large degree to
respond to the 'threat' of commercial television's popularity, but the 'myth' that the BBC merely changed its tone
in the 1960s as a knee-jerk reaction to ITV needs to be
questioned.

The period between 1970 and 1980 was, according to
Jeremy Potter, 'a decade of debate with few decisions'
(Potter, 1989, p. vii). It was dominated by two issues: first,
the increased standardisation of programming whereby the
differences between the BBC and ITV were becoming less
prominent; and second, by the debate over the allocation of
the fourth terrestrial channel. Internally, the BBC faced
tensions with the publication of a controversial planning
document in 1969, *Broadcasting in the Seventies*, which
dealt almost exclusively with the radio service.

The pinnacle of the decade came with the publication
of the Report on the Future of Broadcasting in 1977 (the
Annan Report) that marked the end of what many saw as
the 'golden era' of television (roughly 1964–79). Whereas
the Pilkington Report of 1962 had accused ITV of 'trivial-
ising' programming standards and had come down firmly
on the side of the BBC, Annan redefined the role of public
service broadcasting altogether. The focus shifted from the
need for broadcasters to provide moral leadership, enlight-
enment and betterment to that of pluralism: providing a
service and satisfying the needs of the full range of groups
in society. In a clear statement to this effect, the report
noted that 'We do not accept that it is part of the broadcasters' function to act as arbiters of morals or manners, or
set themselves up a social engineers' (Home Office, 1977,
p. 26). The report also complimented ITV on its success,
again, in stark contrast to the views of Pilkington fifteen
years earlier. The report is also notable for its role as a
watershed in the history of the fourth terrestrial channel.
During the 1970s, there emerged an increasing sense of
frustration among programme-makers and the burgeoning
independent production sector at what Sylvia Harvey calls
the 'cultural protectionism' of the BBC–ITV duopoly
(Buscombe, 2000, p. 95). Various calls were made during
the 1970s (in particular by the vociferous ITV companies
themselves) for the fourth channel to be allocated to ITV as
soon as possible. There had been mention of this possibility in Pilkington (possibly as a consolation for the allocation of the third channel to the BBC), but changes in
government precluded such a development. The Labour
government under Harold Wilson, which held office

TELEVISION IN WALES 1960–80

Dr John Davies, historian of the BBC in Wales, has maintained that in Wales (perhaps more than any other country) broadcasting has played a central role, both positive and negative, in the development of the concept of a national community. He argues that 'the entire national debate in Wales, for fifty years and more after 1927, revolved around broadcasting . . . [that] the other concessions to Welsh nationality won in those years were consequent upon the victories in the field of broadcasting' (Davies, 1994, p. 50). This is particularly relevant when one considers the development of broadcasting in Wales in the context of the relationship with London. From the early days of wireless broadcasting, control and power had rested in London, often at the expense of the local and regional voice. The ethos or spirit that governed broadcasting policy at the outset was that the 'best' should be made available to all, and that the 'best' came from London. This resulted in a good deal of antagonism in the British regions, not least in the so-called 'national regions' (though this term has an oxymoronic ring to it!) of Wales, Scotland and Northern Ireland.

This tension was heightened in Wales by virtue of the fact that the country is one of two languages and two cultures. The broadcast media, therefore, are servants of two tongues, and this, more than anything else, has coloured the discourse surrounding the development of television in Wales. As the 1969–70 Annual Report of the BBC's Broadcasting Council for Wales stated, 'The major problem remains: that of serving a country with two languages. The problem continues to be not so much one of providing programmes in two languages but rather one of assessing the needs of Wales as a whole.' The report went on to state that 'there are varying views on the extent to which, for broadcasting purposes, Wales can be considered an entity. Some people, indeed, see Wales as an uneasy alliance of two cultures, two nations, with language as a divisive factor' (Lucas, 1981, p. 215).

The 1960s marked the beginning of the reign of television as a mass medium in Wales. At the start of the decade, around 60 per cent of Welsh households owned a television set, and this had risen to 92 per cent by the end of the 1960s. During this period, the BBC finally wrenched Wales from the 'marriage' with the west of England by creating BBC Wales as a separate, semi-autonomous region. The 1960s also witnessed the growth of commercial television in the country with TWW serving south Wales and the west of England and Teledu Cymru providing a service for north and west Wales. The latter was a short-lived company, and was taken over by TWW in 1964.

The 1970s was a decade of increased pressure on the authorities for a separate television channel for Welsh-language programming. The 1974 Crawford Committee's report on the future of broadcasting, which considered the prospects of a fourth terrestrial channel for the UK, represented a milestone in this respect and highlighted the urgency of the situation. It recommended that 'whatever decision may be reached in the rest of the United Kingdom, it [the fourth channel] should in Wales be allotted as soon as possible to a separate service in which Welsh language programmes should be given priority' (*Report of the Committee on Broadcasting Coverage*, 1974, pp. 41–2). Although the Conservative Party committed themselves to the idea in their 1979 general election manifesto, following their election victory, they announced that plans to establish the channel would not go ahead. This led to angry reactions in Wales, including acts of civil disobedience such as withholding television licence fees, raids on transmitters and the threat of a hunger strike by the then leader of Plaid Cymru, Gwynfor Evans, unless the government adhered to its original promise of a separate channel for Wales. Following one of the very few U-turns of the Thatcher government, S4C (the Welsh Fourth Channel) broadcast for the first time on 1 November 1982.

In many ways the advent of S4C provided an answer to a major point of debate in Welsh society. In terms of the television audience, the 1960s and 70s in Wales were characterised by a polarisation of opinion between those who complained about being deprived of British network programmes because of Welsh-language broadcasts (a complaint which is still adhered to by many though in relation to English-language, Welsh-interest programmes) and those who argued that scant regard was being paid to the need for Welsh-language broadcasting. Speaking at a conference held in Bangor in 1970 to debate the future of broadcasting in Wales, the writer and broadcaster, Emyr Humphreys, claimed that broadcasting as a medium had simply failed to reflect the language and culture of Wales. The birth of S4C, under the terms of the 1980 Broadcasting Act, was an attempt to redress the balance.

Jamie Medhurst

between 1964 and 1970, for example, was not noted for its enthusiasm for private enterprise, commercial television, despite the fact that Wilson himself considered ITV to be more 'working-class' in its tone and approach and more in touch with Labour voters. This dichotomy in terms of commercial television that plagued the Labour Party from the mid-1940s onwards is well documented by Des Freedman (Freedman, 1999).

The dramatic shift came in 1979 with the election of a Conservative government. Although the new government rejected much of what was put forward in the Annan Report, they took on board the establishment of a fourth channel. From this point onwards, the landscape of British broadcasting changed dramatically. There emerged, during the second part of the 1970s and embodied in the broadcasting policies of the 1980s, an ideological challenge to public service broadcasting (which included both the BBC and ITV), and an increasing awareness that television, as other public services, would be exposed to market forces.

In summary, the 1960s and 70s saw the ecology of British broadcasting change considerably. As Kevin Williams notes, it witnessed the transformation of Reith's citizens into Thatcher's consumers (Williams, 1998, p. 172). British broadcasting would never be the same again.

Jamie Medhurst

RECOMMENDED READING

Briggs, Asa (1995), *The History of Broadcasting in the United Kingdom Volume V: Competition 1955–1974*, Oxford: Oxford University Press.

Curran, James and Seaton, Jean (1997), *Power without Responsibility: The Press and Broadcasting in Britain*, 5th edition, London and New York: Routledge.

Davies, John (1994), *Broadcasting and the BBC in Wales*, Cardiff: University of Wales Press.

Medhurst, Jamie (1998), 'The Mass Media in Twentieth-Century Wales', in Philip Henry Jones and Eiluned Rees (eds), *A Nation and Its Books: A History of the Book in Wales*, Aberystwyth: National Library of Wales, pp. 329–40.

The 'Classic Network System' in the US

The 1950s are often called the 'golden age' of television in the US, with prestigious, innovative and popular programming breaking new ground for the fledgling medium. One well-known scholar has suggested that the 1980s and 90s represent US television's 'second golden age', as formal experimentation and sophisticated adult content supplanted the 'vast wasteland' of the 1960s and 70s (Thompson, 1996). While few critics have pointed to the 1960s and 70s as the pinnacle of television programming, this era certainly represents the peak of the television industry's centralised control, efficiency and maximum profits. Known as the 'classic network system', the industry in these two decades saw the full transformation of the standards of its radio ancestry to the television medium, the establishment of stable and fruitful relationships with the film industry and advertisers, and the creation of efficient mechanisms to fill out television schedules to minimise financial risk and maximise network profits. Throughout this era, the central operating structure centred around the 'big three' networks, functioning as a closed oligopoly system. The classic network system thrived by restricting competition and avoiding risk. It was only through the inroads of cable television and upstart networks like Fox that the system began to erode in the 1980s, shifting toward an era of 'narrowcasting' and corporate conglomeration.

The parallels between the network system and Hollywood's film industry are telling. At the peak of its oligopoly control, the film industry thrived through vertical integration – owning the means of production, distribution and exhibition of films – with particular emphasis on maintaining a stranglehold on distribution, the key site of control. Likewise, television networks in the 1960s established their identities primarily as programme distributors, while maintaining an important (and profitable) presence in programme production, especially through news, sports and special-event divisions, and exhibition, in the form of owned and operated affiliate stations (O&Os). The networks realised that their most profitable commodity was control of the programme schedules of the majority of the nation's television stations, which relied on network affiliation to fill the bulk of their broadcasting hours. This, of course, was not a new discovery – after all, NBC, CBS and ABC had been in the business of providing programmes for local affiliates since their inception in the radio era. Yet by the early 1960s, the networks had reconceptualised their roles as programme distributors by renegotiating their relationship to their primary 'clients': advertisers.

Since the early days of network radio, networks had seen themselves as brokers of airtime, selling slots of time on their national schedules to sponsors; what aired in that time was up to the sponsoring company and the advertising agencies that often served as entertainment producers. This 'single-sponsorship' system served networks well, as it placed the difficult, expensive and risky process of devising original programming in the hands of outside producers, guaranteeing fairly uniform income from renting out space in the network schedule regardless of the popularity of any given programme. Even when networks did engage in creating or contracting the external creation of new programmes, these unsponsored 'sustaining' programmes were aired with the intention of attracting a sponsor to latch onto the programme and pay for its airtime. Although this system was quite lucrative and successful for

networks, they began to grow frustrated with the lack of control they had over their own programmes and schedules. If sponsors were buying airtime, they could dictate programme content and strategies much more than networks. More to the economic point, networks found they could not capitalise on successful shows, as the sponsors held the rights to hit shows like *I Love Lucy* (CBS, 1951–7) and *Dragnet* (NBC, 1952–9) – having a top-rated show did not mean more advertising revenue for networks when the sponsors held the programming cards. Thus when an alternative model of sponsorship emerged in the 1950s, networks grew eager to shift their practices.

This new form of sponsorship came from NBC's innovative president, Sylvester 'Pat' Weaver. In trying to expand the reach of the network schedule in the early 1950s, Weaver ventured into the traditionally local realms of early-morning and late-night timeslots, with *The Today Show* in 1952 and *The Tonight Show* in 1954. These shows

Dragnet (NBC, 1952–9): when sponsors 'held the programming cards'

were produced by NBC, not as sustaining shows shopping for a single sponsor, but using a model known both as 'participation' or 'magazine sponsorship'. Like print magazines, these programmes featured multiple sponsors scattered throughout their run, with individual commercial 'spots' sold to a variety of advertisers – a mode of production pioneered on women's daytime radio by innovators like Mary Margaret McBride. It had also formed the backbone of ethnic and foreign-language radio's so-called 'brokerage' system, which had come under attack during the war years. However, NBC took on this model and made it acceptable by removing programme content decisions from individual hands and placing it under network control. In doing so, NBC took on the cost of production without guaranteed sponsorship, though they were able to maximise profits by raising the cost of advertising as ratings increased. By the late 1950s, the economic benefits of this experiment were evident to the networks, as increased control over the distribution of programmes gave networks the ability to maximise profits on successful shows, pull the plug on failing ones and arrange their schedule to promote audience flow between programmes and establish a stronger network identity. Yet old systems are hard to change – magazine sponsorship entered into prime time gradually throughout the late 1950s, but the networks needed an excuse to enforce a major overhaul.

That excuse came in the form of the late-1950s quiz show scandals. As the news broke that producers had rigged popular quiz programmes like *Twenty-One* (NBC, 1956–8) and *The $64,000 Question* (CBS, 1955–8) to create dramatic intrigue, the networks funnelled the public's outrage onto the programme's sponsors. Networks claimed that had they been in charge of producing these shows, such a public deception would never have been allowed; they cast the sponsors in the role of greedy exploiters of audiences, interested more in ratings than the ethics of broadcasting in the public interest. The great effect of these claims – and their ultimate goal – was to fuel governmental and public support of shifting the control of programmes from sponsors to the networks (Boddy, 1990a). This public relations coup, along with the timely end of many of the sponsor-owned hit programmes of the 1950s, led to the rise of magazine sponsorship as the norm for most network programming by the early-1960s – only select holdovers from the 1950s and the sponsor-driven realm of daytime soap operas maintained the single-sponsor system. Of course many advertisers benefited from the rise of magazine sponsorship as well, allowing multiple companies access to sell their products to the audiences of the most popular programmes on the air. The

real victims of this shift were audiences, as it led to the continual expansion of commercials and commercialism in television. It was through this shift in sponsorship that the industry established the central economic exchange that structures commercial television to this day: the use of entertainment to bait audiences to be sold to the highest-bidding advertisers.

Another crucial shift in television's norms from the 1950s allowed for the establishment of the classic network system: the growing acceptance of telefilms instead of live television. In television's early days, live broadcast was considered the only acceptable form for 'respectable' programmes. Telefilms were critically derided as crass and commercial, the provenance of fly-by-night syndicators and recycled Hollywood rejects. But as networks began to incorporate more telefilms, economically entranced by their potential for more polished products suitable for lucrative reruns, filmed programmes in a range of genres from Westerns to sitcoms became the rule rather than the exception. As networks seized the power of programme procurement from sponsors, they realised that their strength was not in the creation of filmed programmes. Thus they established a division between network production of live programmes like news, sports, special events and variety shows, and external production of the dramatic and comedic telefilms that made up the bulk of the prime-time schedule. To provide these telefilms, networks partnered with major Hollywood studios as well as select independent producers; the shift to telefilms effectively dried up the first-run syndication market of the 1950s, meaning that producers only had one viable way to get programmes on the air: on the 'big three' networks.

As the networks took the reins of television's distribution system, they worked to maintain oligopolistic control. Realising that the advertising market was lucrative enough to support all three networks in a closed system, NBC, CBS and even perennial runner-up ABC were invested in maintaining the status quo, working to better each other without disrupting the central functioning of the system. They looked to fill their schedules with shows that offered the 'least objectionable programming' possible – shows that made it on the air promised both to appeal to as many average viewers as possible and to attract a broad range of sponsors to buy commercial time. Thus, shows that featured formal innovations, controversial content, or boundary-pushing ideas were passed over in favour of proven formulas, safe representations and efficient, inexpensive retreads. Networks relied upon established genres, often riding cycles of popularity to generate new hits (see grey box). The power to schedule programmes allowed for clear segmentation of genres and audiences: Saturday morning cartoons for kids, daytime soap operas for house-wives and a steady mix of sitcoms and dramas for the prime-time mass audience. Strategies emerged like block programming (running similar shows together in one night), hammocking (scheduling a weak programme between two established hits) and counter-programming (putting a show that appeals to different audiences at the same time as other networks' hits). With no real outside competition, networks had no reason to take many risks; thus most of the 1960s and 70s was an era of formulaic content and record profits.

The bulk of the networks' decision-making came annually in the form of creating the new season's schedule. Since the 'big three' were the only viable option to get a television programme on the air, producers were beholden to network scheduling strategies. Asserting this control, the networks established a system of programme procurement, still in place today, that shifted most of the risks onto external producers – and placed most of the profit potential in the networks' hands. New ideas for programmes came from either external producers or inside the networks' ranks; particularly promising concepts received funding for a production company to develop a script. Networks then evaluated scripts, often with input from audience market research, and underwrote the production of pilot episodes for a select few. After testing and evaluating pilots, each network placed a small number on their annual fall schedules, ordering a set of episodes from the production company. The paring down process here is drastic – according to one source referring to the early 1980s, a network sifted through 3,000 ideas a year, commissioning only a hundred scripts and twenty-five pilots, ultimately only to add five to ten new shows to their schedules, of which few outlasted their first season (Gitlin, 1985, p. 21). Although this is quite an expensive process, networks actually paid producers far less than the costs to develop scripts, pilots and episodic series, forcing the producers to go into debt to create programmes, a practice known as 'deficit financing'. This system ensured that producers took the bulk of the financial risk for any new programme, as networks were assured of getting some advertising revenue, even for failed shows, while they struck it rich on the occasional hit programme obtained from producers for far less than their real value.

So why did producers risk so much money only to let networks take the bulk of the profits? Because the network system was a closed oligopoly, there was no other viable market for original television programming; thus producers had to take what they could get from the 'big three'.

But there was a pot of gold at the end of the occasional rainbow – if a show beat the odds to become a long-running hit, producers hit the jackpot when they sold their programme as reruns in 'off-network syndication'. This form of speculative gambling required deep pockets in a programme's first four seasons before reaching syndication, so most producers worked within established companies like Hollywood studios and talent agencies to fund production overheads and invest in programme development. Although networks saw profits on most pro-grammes they aired, they grabbed a share of the producer's syndication windfall in the 1960s – arguing that a pro-gramme's network run functioned as subsidised pro-motion for its success in reruns, networks began to insist on ownership interests in new programmes to ensure they received payouts from syndication deals as well. While producers had little other choice in the oligopoly and generally accepted the network's terms, they petitioned the FCC to level the playing field. Eventually, in the early 1970s, the FCC did pass two key rules benefiting producers and limiting network control: the Network Financial and Syndication Rules (known as 'Fin-Syn') prohibited networks from owning syndication rights to externally produced programmes, and the Prime Time Access Rule (PTAR) limited network programming to three hours of prime-time per night (four on Sundays) to ensure more access to the airwaves for original local and first-run syndicated programmes. Though almost a decade of litigation would keep the Fin-Syn rules from taking effect before 1979, these regulations benefited independent producers, like MTM and Lorimar, and syndicators, like King World and Viacom. However, the networks' monetary loss did not truly threaten their oligopolistic control.

While producers could not reduce network control, new threats from alternative distributors ultimately did end the oligopoly of the 'big three' in the 1980s. Cable television, a fringe technology until the 1970s, benefited from deregulation, innovations in audience segmentation, and a library of old films and television programmes to cut into broadcasters' audience share. Rupert Murdoch's Fox Network – the first new US broadcast network since DuMont's demise in 1957 – achieved the unthinkable by challenging the 'big three' at their own game, capturing youth and urban audiences with innovative programming, favourable treatment from the FCC and synergistic partnerships with its production studio. Meanwhile the 'big three' failed to take these threats seriously, leading to a rapid erosion of their control of distribution and share of television audiences. Two other studio-owned networks, UPN and the WB, have followed Fox's lead to challenge

GENRE CYCLES: INNOVATION, IMITATION, SATURATION

One of the primary ways networks manage the risks inherent in scheduling so many television programmes is relying upon proven formulas in the form of television genres, capitalising upon popular trends to predict future hits and establish new forms of programming. We can see throughout the classic network era and beyond a succession of *genre cycles* that flood television schedules for a few seasons before disappearing in a string of cancelled shows. Television historian Michael Curtin has characterised this process in three stages: innovation – imitation – saturation (Curtin, 1995, p. 248). Through an outline of this process, we can see how the classic network system used formulas, recombinant innovations and programme cloning to try to appeal to viewers through a strategy of 'least objectionable programming' that remains important to this day.

To label the first stage of a genre cycle an 'innovation' may be an overstatement – television innovations are often fresh only in their new combinations or revival of old formulas rather than pure originality. Thus, one of the first successful generic cycles – Westerns of the late 1950s – was a simple rein-

The Bionic Woman: 'recombinant culture'

terpretation of a classic film genre for the small screen. Other cycles followed these adaptations from film and other sources – the spy cycle of the 1960s followed the popularity of the James Bond novels and films, while superhero adventures of the mid-1970s were adapted from comic books like *Wonder Woman* (ABC/CBS, 1976–9) and *The Incredible Hulk* (CBS, 1977–82). Even one of the most groundbreaking shows in US television history, *All in the Family* (CBS, 1971–9), was adapted from a British sitcom, *Till Death Us Do Part* (BBC, 1966–75). Media scholar Todd Gitlin characterises another mode of network innovation as 'recombinant culture': combining established genres, shows, or styles together to create a new programme or cycle (Gitlin, 1985, pp. 75–85). Thus, sitcoms crossed with the supernatural led to a cycle of mid-1960s' 'fantasy sitcoms' like *Bewitched* (ABC, 1964–72) and *The Munsters* (CBS, 1964–6); an action-adventure show with beautiful women spurred ABC's 'jiggle' line-up in the mid-1970s with *Charlie's Angels* (ABC, 1976–81) and *The Bionic Woman* (ABC/NBC, 1976–8).

Whenever an innovative show succeeds, networks jump onto the bandwagon through a wave of imitations. Some imitations are direct spin-offs – *Maude* (CBS 1972–8), *Good Times* (CBS, 1974–9) and *The Jeffersons* (CBS, 1975–85) all furthered the socially relevant sitcom cycle by giving characters from *All in the Family*'s universe their own programmes. Other imitations are direct clones designed to copy the original's formula: ABC had a huge hit with *Bewitched* in 1964, so NBC transformed the magical leading woman from a witch to a genie with 1965's *I Dream of Jeannie* (NBC, 1965–70). Clones and spin-offs rarely achieve the original's level of success, as the wave of imitation leads to the third phase of saturation – so many programmes in the generic cycle inhabit the schedule that audiences begin to turn away from the formula. Often imitations are dropped after only a season or two, leaving only the first few established hits of the cycle on the air. Once saturated, network programmers move on to the next new combination or adaptation to find an innovative hit to launch another cycle.

A good example of this process is the cycle of animated sitcoms of the early 1960s (Mittell, 2002). Prior to *The Flintstones*' (ABC, 1960–6) debut, animation was generally found in late-afternoon syndication or occasional Saturday morning programmes. But animation producers Hanna-Barbera had reached adult audiences with syndicated shows like *Huckleberry Hound* (syndicated, 1958–62) and *Quick Draw McGraw* (syndicated, 1959–62) in the late 1950s, so ABC offered them the chance to produce a prime-time cartoon for adults. In classic recombinant fashion, they crossed the sitcom scenario of the classic *Honeymooners* (CBS, 1955–6), set it in the Stone Age, and animated their results into the breakout hit of the 1960 season. Imitations followed in the next few years, with similar Hanna-Barbera sitcoms *The Jetsons* (ABC, 1962–3) and *Top Cat* (ABC, 1961–2), a feline version of *The Phil Silvers Show* (CBS, 1955–9), as well as other prime-time animated offerings *The Alvin Show* (CBS, 1961–2), *Mr. Magoo* (NBC, 1964–5) and *Calvin and the Colonel* (ABC, 1961–2), itself an adaptation of radio and early television ground-breaker *Amos 'n' Andy* (CBS, 1951–3). None of these imitations lasted for more than one season in prime time, as audiences tired of the animated novelty; these shows found further life on Saturday mornings as networks expanded their programming to create a kid-centred block of cartoons. But only *The Flintstones* lasted in prime time, running until 1966 before it too was exiled to Saturday morning. Networks moved on to other cycles, not returning to prime time animation until 1990's *The Simpsons* (Fox, 1990–) launched its own wave of failed imitators. This case demonstrates the network logic of innovation through combination and subsequent imitation to attempt to maximise the popularity of a trend without challenging audiences or risking truly original forms of programming.

Jason Mittell

what is now known as the 'big four', while cable television finally overtook broadcast television in overall ratings in the late-1990s. Yet the networks have adapted to this new media landscape – and further deregulation – by following the leads of cable and Fox, focusing on narrowly defined audience segments, drawing on ownership ties to maximise synergistic profits and investing in cable channels to augment their broadcast presence. While the era of 90 per cent audience shares by the 'big three' are long gone, the television industry is still a closed oligopoly controlled by major companies; consumers and producers may have more channels to choose from, but the lessons and logic of the classic network system still remain in place, as centralised distribution, magazine sponsorship, safe programming and closing off external competition still rule the airwaves.

Jason Mittell

RECOMMENDED READING

Alvey, M. (2000) 'The Independents: Rethinking the Television Studio System', in H. Newcomb (ed.), *Television: The Critical View*, New York: Oxford University Press, pp. 34–51.

Balio, Tino (ed.) (1990) *Hollywood in the Age of Television*, Boston: Unwin Hyman.

Gitlin, Todd (1985) *Inside Prime Time*, New York: Pantheon.

Mittell, Jason (2002), 'The Great Saturday Morning Exile: Scheduling Cartoons on Television's Periphery in the 1960s', in C. Stabile and M. Harrison (eds) *Television Animation: A Reader in Popular Culture*, New York: Routledge.

Spigel, Lynn and Curtin, Michael (eds) (1997) *The Revolution Wasn't Televised: Sixties Television and Social Conflict*, New York: Routledge.

INSTITUTIONS: CONFLICT AND CHANGE

Introduction

By the early 1980s, both the US and Britain stood on the verge of significant change, not only in television institutions but in the basic philosophies behind each system. Debates over the introduction of a fourth network had begun in Britain in the 1970s. The creation of Channel Four in 1982, a unique combination of commercial and public service structures and economics, rested on a redefinition of the public service mission that now included a carefully insulated advertising base, an emphasis on independent production and a recognition of the interests of minority audiences in an atmosphere of diversity and choice. The United States had mobilised to introduce its first publicly funded television channel, the Public Broadcasting Service (PBS), in 1967, under some of the same impulses that had led to the founding of BBC2 in Britain, yet the political and social pressures of the 1970s and 80s challenged PBS's 'education and uplift' goals and led to the establishment of a different kind of public access television on cable as the US rapidly became a 'wired nation'.

By the late 1980s, new technologies such as cable and satellite television had begun to effect major transformations in television institutions across the world. Together with deregulatory, market-based policies they led to the introduction of new channels and services in both Britain and the US. Rupert Murdoch's BSkyB brought a host of mostly imported programming, along with an increasing lock on sports, to satellite subscribers in Britain and Europe, while the expansion of the cable industry in the US led to an explosion of television offerings and new forms of competition. Murdoch would also play a significant role in US television, accomplishing the long-delayed merger of Hollywood and broadcasting interests with the debut of the Fox television network in 1986, followed by the WB (Warner Bros.) and UPN (United Paramount) networks in 1995. The US Telecommunications Act of 1996 would cap this period of expansion and deregulation with provisions for digital television that promised extensive future change, yet still privileged the same cast of industry players.

Michele Hilmes

Channel Four and the Redefining of Public Service Broadcasting

FIGURES IN A LANDSCAPE

In little more than half a century of British television history the creation of new channels has been a slow affair. By 1964 there were just three of them. Two were allocated to the BBC and one – by Act of Parliament in 1954 – to the private sector. Unlike the exclusively licence fee-funded BBC1 and BBC2, the 'Independent Television' service (ITV) provided programmes funded by advertising and therefore interspersed with commercials. This service on the ITV channel was provided by a cluster of regionally based companies, offering at times a single, networked service to the whole country and at times a series of 'opt-out' services carrying material of local interest. After an uncertain start ITV was to become extremely profitable for its constituent companies. Moreover, it provided some welcome programme competition for the BBC, introducing a more inclusive and less elite 'tone' into the world of British television while maintaining the range and quality of programming as a result of a strict regulatory regime and a significant income stream.

The programming and financial 'ecology' of this three-channel television system was finely balanced on a clear separation of funding sources and a cross-party political consensus on the need to maintain quality, diversity and pluralism in programme content. Separation of funding was established as the licence fee – collected from all television-owning households – was allocated exclusively to the BBC, while advertising revenue was tapped to provide an ITV service free at the point of reception to its viewers. It is arguably the case that this separation of funding sources (which diminished the urge to compete) in practice provided favourable conditions for a diverse, pluralistic and well-resourced programming system with corresponding benefits for the public and an organisational and economic framework for the delivery of 'public service'.

The term 'commercial television' was reserved for the one channel that combined the principle of private shareholder investment and profit maximisation with a financial infrastructure that was reliant upon advertising income.

The creation of Channel Four in 1982 was to change this simple separation, and to require a reconsideration of the term 'commercial television'. For, although the Channel Four programmes were to be financed by advertising, the new broadcaster was set up on a 'not-for-profit' basis, operating as a wholly owned subsidiary of the regulatory body, the Independent Broadcasting Authority (IBA). There would be no private investors whose primary interest would be in dividend returns and profit maximisation. This was seen as the most appropriate organisational form for the delivery of a public service remit, offering genuine programme (and not just channel) choice to audiences. However, most viewers – seeing the 'commercials' on the screen – doubtless remained unaware of this curious new hybridity in institutional arrangements.

Judged by twenty-first-century standards, the gap of eighteen years between the creation of BBC2 in 1964 and the appearance of Britain's fourth channel in 1982, may seem a little mysterious. I shall return to this issue shortly. But before plunging back into the third quarter of the twentieth century it may be useful briefly to note some of the bigger and broader shifts in the broadcasting landscape since then. It was only in the last decade of the twentieth century that a combination of technological invention and political policy resulted in an explosion of televisual provision. In the UK the Conservative Broadcasting Act of 1990 provided the enabling legal framework for a plethora of new channels and services. A fifth and final land-based or 'terrestrial' channel (Channel Five) began broadcasting in 1997. But by 1998 there were over 400 licensed cable, satellite and digital providers, with over a hundred additional services licensed in the year 2000 alone (ITC, 2001a, p. 10).

The modest creation of five national channels in fifty years, in a country with a population of just under 60 million people and an estimated total advertising spend of £11 billion, has meant that considerable resources could be targeted at the production of indigenous programmes of a high standard. In the year 2000, over 75 per cent of programmes shown on BBC1, BBC2 and ITV were made in the UK, with the relative newcomers – Channels Four and Five – screening 'home-grown' programmes at a rate of respectively 66 per cent and 55 per cent of their total transmission time (ITC, 2001, pp. 80, 86).

It is, arguably, a combination of the high regulatory standards set, together with a concentrated richness of resourcing that has created one of the peculiarities of British culture, namely, the apparently continuing market dominance of these five terrestrial channels. Thus, by the end of 2001 and a good ten years into the multichannel era the five 'old' channels still attracted, between them, over 80 per cent of all viewing time. In the same year, Channel Four's 10 per cent share of the total audience compared favourably with the twenty Sky channels' combined share of just over 6 per cent (ITC, 2002). With the wisdom of hindsight we can see that some reconsideration is required of earlier assumptions about the significance of a marginalised, 'out on a limb', minority channel (the 'channel bore' and 'channel swore' of the tabloid press attacks on Channel Four in the 1980s) (Isaacs, 1989, p. 51).

From these 'figures in a landscape' which provide us with some of the basic features of British broadcasting in the first half century of its existence, I turn now to a consideration of the more specific ways in which Channel Four was to revive and remodel the public service ethos and mode of production.

THE ORIGINS OF CHANNEL FOUR: A NEW INDUSTRIAL MODEL

In the new millennium it remains to be seen what impact the growth of satellite, digital and Internet services will have upon the old systems of national broadcasting. However, almost regardless of the ways in which new technologies reconfigure patterns of human behaviour, certain constant issues will demand our attention and recognition. These are: the costs of cultural production, the degree of its inventiveness and attractiveness, the preferences of the audience/users and the wisdom or folly of public and business policy considered from a variety of political perspectives. In the UK the emergence of Channel Four presents us with a complex and revealing instance of these key factors at work, pushed onwards by a series of both competing and co-operating interests.

It may be helpful to signal, at this point, one of the key instances of competing interests. Apart from the increasingly intense competition for audiences ('ratings wars'), the significance of new competition for television advertising revenue has already been indicated. In the British broadcasting system, competition took some time to arrive and was, arguably, fairly carefully managed in relationship to public interest criteria. If the BBC had enjoyed around ten years of monopoly in the provision of television services, ITV enjoyed a monopoly in the sale of television airtime ('commercials') for more than twenty-five years. Although, as we shall see, ITV's monopoly was not in fact ended with the advent of Channel Four in 1982 and was to continue for a further ten years, until the end of 1992.

As a result of a complex deal struck by the regulatory body and perhaps only half understood by the politicians, ITV was granted the right to sell the airtime on Channel Four. The IBA was to act as the 'honest broker' passing on an ITV subscription to meet the programme production and running costs of Channel Four. The 'catch' for ITV was that the running costs of the new channel were in excess of the value of its advertising income for the first five years of its existence. It was only in 1987 that for the first time, advertising income exceeded channel expenditure (Channel Four, 1988, p. 18). However, the payments already made by the ITV companies to the IBA, apart from the Channel Four levy, were reorganised in such a way that the financial pain of subsidising a competitor was minimised. And so, while ITV lost its long campaign for an 'ITV2' and for its right to own and programme the new channel, it won the considerable consolation prize of the right to continue to set the price of airtime sales without competitors.

It is arguable that this deal achieved two public interest and public service objectives. First, it allowed Channel Four the space to grow and experiment since ITV did not have an overriding interest in killing off its rival through fierce scheduling competition. The 'big barons' were locked into a method for relatively peaceful coexistence. Second, it found a discreet means of providing a kind of public subsidy to a new and risky initiative in British broadcasting. In practice the IBA made rather lower returns to the government Treasury during the first five years of this experiment and the Prime Minister, Margaret Thatcher, vigorously attached to the principles of the free market and deeply opposed to any extension of the public subsidy system, appeared unaware of the subversively uncompetitive nature of the new funding arrangement.

In addition to the interesting relationship with big brother ITV, a second key element of the new model represented by Channel Four was the introduction of the concept of the 'publisher broadcaster' into British television. As a result of widespread debate within the industry, Channel Four was expected to commission the majority of its programmes from 'out-of-house'; some from the existing ITV companies but a growing proportion from the much smaller and new independent companies which came into existence to service the innovative programming needs of the channel. This new method of production was to be influential throughout UK television and by 1990 all broadcasters (including the BBC) were required to commission up to 25 per cent of their programmes from independent producers.

A NEW CULTURAL MODEL

The cultural significance of Channel Four and the impact that it had upon other channels and upon the range and character of programming within the broader ecology of British broadcasting in the 1980s can be attributed to a number of factors. These include: a vigorously conducted debate among media professionals; a slowly surfacing public dissatisfaction with the blandness, 'safeness' and establishment partiality of television; a government willing to translate some of the principles of this debate into legislation; and a regulatory body committed to identifying the resources to permit the implementation of the principles. The range and volume of the debate and the sounds of special pleading and of corporate concern echoed across what I have previously referred to as the mysteriously long period between the advent of BBC2 (1964) and the birth of Channel Four (1982).

By 1980 thoughts, speeches and memos were ready to be turned into a new institutional reality and three key provisions in the 1980 Broadcasting Act constituted what came to be known as the 'parliamentary remit' for the new channel. Firstly, there was a requirement to ensure that the new service would contain: 'a suitable proportion of matter calculated to appeal to tastes and interests not generally catered for by ITV'. Second, the channel was required to broadcast a 'suitable proportion of programmes . . . of an educational nature'. And, finally, Channel Four should: 'encourage innovation and experiment in the form and content of programmes' (Lambert, 1982, p. 108). It was the last requirement that was to become the most famous with the *Eleventh Hour* broadcasting anti-government and avant-garde material late at night, a new soap opera, *Brookside*, reflecting a social reality considerably less cosy than that of ITV's ratings winner, *Coronation Street*, a *Right to Reply* strand calling television executives and programme makers to account, an hour-long news programme in peak time, investment in a range of imaginative and controversial feature films and a set of documentaries and current affairs programmes that introduced the audience to international issues and made powerful decision-makers sleep a little less easily at night.

In addition, the particular needs of Welsh culture were recognised with the creation of a separately funded Welsh Fourth Channel (Sianel Pedwar Cymru or S4C) (Tomos, 1982). This introduced for the first time into British broadcasting extensive, peak-time transmissions of originally produced fictional and factual material in the Welsh language.

Under the direction of its first Chief Executive, Jeremy Isaacs, the programming philosophy of the channel drew upon the many interventions of earlier commentators:

JEREMY ISAACS – FIRST CHIEF EXECUTIVE OF CHANNEL FOUR (1981–7)

The distinctive character of Channel Four, and the extraordinary and often controversial range of its programming, owed much to the enthusiasm and generosity of spirit of its first chief executive, Jeremy Isaacs. Born in Glasgow in 1932, Isaacs went on to establish a distinguished career in factual and documentary television, working as a producer for Granada, Associated-Rediffusion and the BBC and undertaking wider responsibilities on becoming Director of Programmes at the London ITV company, Thames Television in 1974. As a producer he is perhaps best known for three major documentary series commissioned by different broadcasters, both before and after his time at Channel Four. These were: the twenty-six-part *The World at War* (Thames, 1974), the thirteen-part *Ireland – A Television History* (BBC, 1981) and the twenty-four-part *Cold War* (CNN/BBC, 1998).

In a speech delivered at the Edinburgh Television Festival in 1979 (the first year of Margaret Thatcher's Conservative government) he had argued that any new fourth channel should have at least the following five objectives: to extend the choice available to viewers; to cater for 'substantial minorities presently neglected'; to offer programmes with a 'complete spectrum of political attitude and opinion'; to fulfil 'broad educational purposes'; and to encourage 'worthwhile independent production' (Isaacs, 1989, p. 19). When appointed to lead the new channel in 1981 he set about putting these proposals into effect, finding premises, appointing staff and beginning the process of commissioning programmes.

Thus, in fulfilment of its parliamentary remit, Channel Four embarked upon the energetic pursuit of experiment and innovation in the form and content of programmes, closely monitored by communities both inside and outside the world of broadcasting who were determined to see 'something different' on British television screens. And innovations came not only in the form and content of programmes but also in pushing at the limits of what people had previously thought television was for and could do. Thus, for example, a space was created for an hour-long news programme in peak time but this was deliberately disturbed by what Isaacs referred to as two 'alien elements' (Isaacs, 1989, p. 82). First, a three-minute *Comment* slot was scheduled at the end of the news, and a different person was selected for each night to advance a strongly argued point of view. Second, a full thirty minutes of the news hour was handed over, once a week, to *The Friday*

Shoah: a remarkable scheduling moment

Alternative; this offered a critical interrogation of the news from the point of view of those affected by particular political or industrial decisions. In addition to these initiatives, a weekly *Right to Reply* programme and a regular thirty-minute *Opinions* programme attempted to work against the grain of what Isaacs had called 'a subtle centrist, conformist bias' (Isaacs, 1989, p. 85).

Through these factual programmes as well as through the imaginative, risky and often visually innovative material commissioned for the *Eleventh Hour* and *People to People* slots ('most at risk if Channel Four falters' as Isaacs put it) (Isaacs, 1989, p. 174) a range of new voices, experiences and attitudes entered the world of television. This, together with a sus-

tained programme of investment in the production of feature films and occasional but remarkable scheduling moments (such as the 1987 screening over two nights and without commercial breaks of Claude Lanzmann's nine-hour film about the holocaust: *Shoah*) established a striking identity for the new channel.

As Channel Four enters its twentieth-anniversary year (2002), we may consider the legacy of Isaacs to be the creation of a channel that attained the status of 'event TV' only because it was seriously and often humorously interested in the significance of events, both great and small, outside the world of television.

Sylvia Harvey

hence the interest in reaching out to minorities and in recognising the value of programmes that did not offer easily popular 'light viewing' for majority audiences, or, as the Annan Committee of 1976 put it, the creation of 'a test bed for experiment' to 'symbolise all the vitality, the new initiatives, practices and liberties which could inspire broadcasters' (Home Office, 1977, p. 472). Related views can be found in a 1976 essay from the distinguished commentator, Anthony Smith, arguing for commitment to 'a doctrine of openness rather than to balance, to expression rather than to neutralization' (Harvey, 1994, p. 109). As Isaacs himself had put it, what was wanted was a channel that would genuinely extend choice by including a 'complete spectrum of attitude and opinion . . . that everyone will watch some of the time and no one all the time' (Isaacs, 1989, pp. 19–20).

These views and their accommodation within the world of broadcasting gave rise to a new, sharper and more polemical sense of the meaning of public service within the field of communications. From the vantage point of early 2002, what is striking about the early output and impact of Channel Four is the sheer originality and verve of the work produced, as though a long pent-up stream of unmet need had finally been released. But the uniqueness of the original Channel Four experience should perhaps be seen in the light of its early willingness to take risks, the financial safety net provided by the IBA and the particular conditions generated by the social, political and economic tensions of the Thatcher period. That the then-Prime Minister was passionately committed to radical, free-market reform of a largely non-consensual kind, in conditions of mass unemployment, created an environment in which sharp differences of opinion needed to be expressed and reflected. As the general economic situation improved and

the relatively more consensual governments of John Major and Tony Blair emerged, the role of Channel Four as the lightning conductor of political conflict and social debate diminished.

Moreover, the intensified competition for audiences in a new multichannel world has made the channel more cautious in its commissioning policies. The greater frankness about politics, sex and religion and the greater openness to formal experiment and to an interest in cultural expression and political conflict in other parts of the world, championed by Channel Four, have now either become routine features of the televisual landscape (perhaps especially on BBC2) or been banished into the nether world of topics seen as threatening to life-saving ratings. Thus, while Channel Four continues to provide some of the most stimulating and entertaining television available, the golden age in which its innovative approach transformed that of its competitors, is now passed.

Sylvia Harvey

RECOMMENDED READING

Blanchard, Simon and Morley, David (eds) (1982), *What's This Channel Four?*, London: Comedia.

Docherty, David, Morrison, David E. and Tracey, Michael (1988), *Keeping Faith? Channel Four and Its Audience*, London: John Libbey.

Grade, Michael (1999), *It Seemed Like a Good Idea at the Time*, London: Macmillan.

Harvey, Sylvia (1994) 'Channel 4 Television: From Annan to Grade', in Stuart Hood (ed.), *Behind the Screens. British Broadcasting in the 1990s*, London; Lawrence and Wishart; reprinted in Edward Buscombe (ed.) (2000), *British Television: A Reader*, Oxford and New York: Oxford University Press.

Isaacs, Jeremy (1989), *Storm over Four: A Personal Account*, London: Weidenfeld and Nicholson.

Lambert, Stephen (1982), *Channel Four: Television with a Difference?*, London: BFI.

Public Television and Public Access in the US

In a system as determinedly commercial as American television, public television and public access represent the two major efforts to create programming outside of the strictures of production for profit. Inspired at various times by ideas of education, cultural uplift, giving voice to minority viewpoints and free speech, public television stations and public access channels have arguably constituted a 'public sphere' of discussion and entertainment that has created innovations in programming form and content. Limitations in funding, political pressures and the lack of structures that would foster public participation, however, have hampered both systems to a point at which both seem in perpetual crisis.

Public television has its roots in the National Association of Educational Broadcasters (NAEB), an alliance of primarily college and university radio stations that moved into television in the early 1950s. Federal Communication Commission (FCC) member Frieda Hennock, a strong believer in educational television's potential to provide intellectual and cultural uplift to mass audiences, organised public hearings on non-profit television in 1950, and raised public awareness of its possibilities (Brinson, 1998). The NAEB, along with the Joint Committee on Educational Television, successfully lobbied the FCC to reserve a channel in every significant television market for educational, non-profit use. Throughout the 1950s, supported financially by the Ford Foundation, the two organisations tried to stimulate further interest in educational programming, to little avail. Most of the reserved spaces on the dial went unfilled, due to the prohibitive start-up costs of station management, and a lack of stable funding for ongoing production. The Ford Foundation increased funding in the late 1950s to spur further station development, and, eventually, for programme production. By 1963, five hours of programming per week were being distributed to member stations of National Educational Television (NET), as the loose network of stations was dubbed. Most programming was devoted to public affairs or classroom-type shows.

NET was given a boost by the support of FCC Chair Newton Minow, who was famous for his dissatisfaction with the commercial networks. Minow helped to convince Congress to provide additional funding for educational stations, and was instrumental in setting up a NET affiliate in New York City, which became WNET, the flagship station of the network. NET took another step forward with the premiere of the Public Broadcast Laboratory (PBL) (1967–9), under the aegis of producer Fred Friendly, famous for his work with Edward R. Murrow at CBS in the 1950s. PBL provided new visibility for NET fare, with its investigations of the Black Power movement, the hippie phenomenon and other highly charged issues. PBL opened itself up to non-professionals, and provided significant, untrammelled space for voices rarely heard on commercial networks. NET provoked its greatest controversy with its airing of *Inside North Vietnam* (1968), a documentary originally produced for, but ultimately rejected by, CBS.

Public television advocates worked with the Johnson administration in the creation of the Carnegie Commission on Educational Television. Inspired by the notion that non-commercial television could provide culturally uplifting programming, more open discussion of public affairs, and greater educational opportunities for children and adults, the Carnegie Commission recommended new legislation to provide federal money for increased production, and the establishment of a high-profile, national network connecting the individual public stations around the country. The commission proposed

FCC Chair Newton Minow was famously critical of commercial television

that the system be financed by a sales tax on television sets, providing a stable source of funding outside the purview of Congress and the president. While many Carnegie recommendations found their way into the Public Broadcasting Act of 1967, Washington officials refused to provide independent financing, preferring to tie public television to the annual round of Congressional appropriations. The 1967 Act created a new non-profit body, the Corporation for Public Broadcasting (CPB), to distribute programming and foster interconnection between stations. The CPB board was designed to be bipartisan, appointed by the president and approved by Congress. The CPB in turn created the Public Broadcasting Service (PBS), to serve as a network of stations, whose board membership came from the CPB, producers, individual stations and members of the public. PBS effectively replaced the increasingly controversial NET as the national non-profit network, while NET continued as a source of productions into the 1970s. As noted by Ralph Engelman (1996), the Public Broadcasting Act was a watershed for non-commercial television in the United States, marking a shift in central control of the system from educators and foundation officers to government appointees. The CPB received federal funding, which it distributed to producers for programme creation. Producers were associated with individual stations or independent production centres and companies. PBS handled scheduling and publicity, but each station retained ultimate control of its programme schedule. Programming in the late 1960s and early 1970s often continued the adventurous agenda put forth by NET; public television pioneered formats in dramatic mini-series, business news, public affairs, nature documentaries, children's television and cooking shows, among others. NET itself, now working under the aegis of WNET in New York City, produced *The Great American Dream Machine* (1971–2), a mix of investigative pieces and whimsical satire unlike anything seen before on American television. African-American producers created the public affairs series *Black Journal* (1968–76) and the entertainment show *Soul!* (1970–5). *Sesame Street* (1969–), produced by the Children's Television Workshop, became a pre-school institution.

Public television's willingness to pursue controversial public affairs programming did not go unnoticed by Richard Nixon, elected to the White House in 1968, who held a deep-seated suspicion of the news media. Nixon saw public television as a bastion of East Coast liberalism and critics of his administration, and used his power to veto CPB budgets to pressure the system to move away from political programming. By appointing conservative friends of his administration to the CPB board, Nixon was able to

restructure relations among the institutional players; independent production centres and NET saw CPB support cut for their work, and programme initiation moved more consistently to individual PBS stations, who tended to be conservative, outside the major cities and dependent on local business elites to fund their day-to-day operations. Treatment of public affairs and experimental formats declined, replaced by high-toned cultural programming and imports of British television dramas, both of which appealed to increasingly important corporate contributors to the system. The prime-time emphasis on the high arts and innocuous documentary led PBS to become increasingly associated with a sense of effete cultural snobbery, despite the fact the actual viewership tended to be relatively small but demographically diverse. (PBS generally garnered two shares in most markets.) Funding levels for production, never generous to begin with, began to stagnate, paradoxically placing PBS in the position of the poor cousin of the commercial networks. The lack of a stable, independent, funding base had left public television subject to the vagaries of Washington politics, and to reliance on contributions from the same corporations who supported and influenced commercial television through their advertising budgets.

Public television in the 1980s faced the twin onslaughts of renewed political pressure by Republican administrations and the rise of cable channels. An aggressive strategy by Republicans in the White House and Congress, including repeated threats to end federal funding, led PBS programmes to feature conservative voices more strongly in the news and public affairs programmes that remained on the schedule, many of which began to be produced by private operations also active in commercial television. Cable networks began poaching PBS formats as the basis for entire channels, such as Discovery's programming of science and nature shows and Nickelodeon's children's shows. A&E contracted with the BBC to broadcast many of its crime dramas and documentaries, and Bravo concentrated on arts programmes. PBS entered into a crisis of confidence, a lack of definition as to its mission in the newly multiplicitous television environment. While the system has occasionally produced critical and popular successes, such as Ken Burns' documentary mini-series *The Civil War* (1990), and continues to feature the incisive *Frontline* (1983–) and the free-spirited *POV* (1988–) as two prominent documentary series, PBS has lost both viewers and social impact. It is indicative that the network turned down the chance to air the sequel to *Tales of the City* (1994), a comic mini-series portraying life in countercultural San Francisco that had been one of its greatest

PAPER TIGER TELEVISION

In his essay 'Constituents of a Theory of the Media', Hans Magnus Enzensberger (1974) envisions a communication system that reverses the producer–receiver model of modern broadcasting, by turning every receiver into a producer. *Paper Tiger Television* constitutes one of the foremost examples of public access television's potential to bring Enzensberger's vision to life, by usurping the televisual apparatus to talk back to the cultural industries. The Paper Tiger collective's critiques of print and electronic media, its incursions into cultural politics and its role as catalyst of new networks of production and distribution of alternative media have served as models for the surge in media activism since the early 1980s.

Founded by producer, teacher and activist DeeDee Halleck, Paper Tiger is organised as a predominantly volunteer collective that produces a regular series on Manhattan public access. The *Paper Tiger Television* series (Manhattan public access, 1981–), featuring hosts culled from the ranks of writers, academics and media activists, began by skewering publications such as the *New York Times*, *Vogue* and *Time* with critiques that combined investigation into the economic structures of the information industry with semiotic analysis of media imagery and representations. Informed by Frankfurt School theory and feminism, and inspired by the non-hierarchical, communal ethos of the guerrilla television collectives of the late 1960s, Paper Tiger soon expanded its focus of analysis to television and film productions, the cultural battles of the Reagan era, and the work of producers outside the commercial nexus of mainstream media.

The on-screen provocateurs are abetted by collective members who provide research assistance, production staff and the visual design for each episode. Paper Tiger started with a determinedly low-tech, handmade look, which served to catch the attention of channel surfers by its comic funkiness, while also asserting the viability of everyday television viewers seizing control of cameras, microphones and character generators to become active producers of culture. Self-reflexive strategies, such as showing crew members doing their jobs during live studio shoots and disclosing production budgets in the final credits ('This show cost $42.53'), aimed to demystify television technology and processes, anticipating the camcorder revolution of the 1990s. Over the years, Paper Tiger has expanded its aesthetic strategies to include a greater reliance on post-production editing and camcorder footage, while also expanding its distribution to other access systems, museums and art spaces, and university classrooms.

The collective's outreach efforts resulted in the creation of Deep Dish Television in 1986, the first organisation to provide public access producers with a national distribution system. Working with access producers and programmers from around the country, Deep Dish initially took advantage of the relatively low cost of satellite transponder time to telecast anthologies of video work dealing with contemporary social issues. Eventually, Deep Dish distributed themed series on health care, international video and other topics to hundreds of access stations nationally. One culmination of the two series' networking efforts was the Gulf Crisis Television Project, which telecast ten programmes critical of Bush administration policies during the Persian Gulf War (Deep Dish Television, 1991). Amid the general pro-war frenzy of network news, the project pioneered an immediate alternative media response that was exhibited widely via public access and public television channels, as well as internationally. Paper Tiger, Deep Dish and Gulf Crisis TV demonstrate the potential for counter-programming on political and cultural issues using contemporary technology, organisational savvy and protected spaces for speech not dominated by corporate elites in the American and international media environments.

Daniel Marcus

ratings successes, for fear of offending Congressional Republicans with its gay-friendly themes; the commercial cable network Showtime screened the series instead. Commercial networks and cable channels today often show a greater willingness to exhibit controversial and minority-themed programming than does PBS, inverting the argument that NET, the Carnegie Commission and other advocates of non-profit broadcasting had put forward during its creation.

James Ledbetter (1997) has made the point that while PBS pioneered several new television formats in America, the network never established a new relation to its viewers; it generally shared the attitude of the commercial networks that maintained a strict division between professionals in control of the production and distribution apparatus and viewers watching at home. In the 1960s, some public stations aired programmes that featured elements of community involvement in production, but these faded as the public system became more institutionalised. Despite continued appeals for financial support from viewers, PBS stations have continued to operate as self-perpetuating, closed institutions similar to the foundations that provided much of the early impetus to develop 'public' television. At the same time that Richard Nixon was pressuring PBS to not exercise its freedom of speech, another form of television highlighted the promise that television technology held to create a robust forum for free expression, based on overturning the distinction between producer, exhibitor and viewer. Public access television sought to extend the principles of free speech to electronic media by the creation of production and exhibition facilities open to anyone who wanted to use them.

Public access, or community television, emerged from the experience of Challenge for Change, a project created by the National Film Board of Canada in 1966. Challenge for Change sought to use film, and later video, as an instrument of community dialogue and social change. Challenge for Change producers worked with various communities to document local issues, train residents in basic production techniques and provide a means for subordinated groups to make their voices heard in public debate. In conjunction with former National Film Board employee Red Burns, Challenge for Change veteran George Stoney founded the Alternate Media Center (AMC) at New York University in 1971, and established links to 'guerrilla television' collectives that had grown out of the 1960s' anti-war and civil rights movements. Stoney and Burns promoted the creation of production facilities around the country, staffed by producers who could serve as teachers for community residents who wished to make television.

The development of cable television in the 1970s provided new exhibition opportunities. Most cable systems had unfilled space for channels on their systems; in 1972, the FCC mandated that cable systems in the hundred largest markets each reserve space for three non-commercial access channels, for public, educational and local governmental use. The AMC was instrumental in getting many access centres up and running. The FCC mandate was eventually struck down judicially, but the idea of community television had been established, and many cities required the continuation or creation of access centres and channels in their contracts with cable providers. Typically, cable providers would provide basic financing for a public access studio and skeleton staff; some city governments supplemented the budget with municipal funding. Universities or public school systems often programmed the educational channels, while city governments put city council and school board meetings on government channels. In some localities, the function of the three forms of access were consolidated into one channel.

Public access television has created millions of hours of television produced by individuals, religious groups, community organisations and student groups. Thousands of people have attended low-cost training sessions at access

centres in the operation of television studios and equipment. Because access channels contain no advertising and exist almost exclusively on cable, ratings information has rarely been gathered; the few in-depth studies show a significant viewership in cities with well-developed systems. The growth of community television, however, has been hindered by the hostility of many cable companies, who often see the channels as taking up potentially lucrative space on their system, lacking in professionalism and courting controversy by the relatively untrammelled expression of political and sexual material. (Basic obscenity laws do apply to access programming.) Community television's inveterate localism, while an important precept in the access movement, has also hampered its visibility in the media environment. Because there is no regularised interconnection between access channels, producers have great difficulty in distributing their work beyond their own cities or towns, limiting the impact that their work may have. The amateur ethos of access also restricts the amount of time and resources that producers can put into their productions. Lack of centre resources and the individualised focus of free speech rights in the United States has also led to an inconsistent effort by access centres to foster participation by community groups involved in social change, as originally envisioned by Stoney. Finally, community television's dependence on the cable industry endangers its future, as cable providers try to limit or eliminate their access obligations, and cable's future as an industry is unclear.

Even as the number of active and vibrant access centres has declined in recent years, several production and distribution projects have used access to enter into public discussion, sometimes forging links among producers nationally and internationally (see grey box). The 1999 Seattle protests against the World Trade Organisation became a focal point for alternative media production, which ran on access channels nationally through the distribution service Free Speech TV. Inspired in part by the activity surrounding the WTO protests, independent media centres using video, cable and Internet technology have sprung up in recent years, as the next generation of producers continue the experimentation with new technology and formats set in motion by Challenge for Change.

Daniel Marcus

RECOMMENDED READING

Boyle, Deirdre (1997), *Subject to Change: Guerrilla Television Revisited*, Oxford: Oxford University Press.

Engelman, Ralph (1996), *Public Television and Radio in America: A Political History*, Thousand Oaks: Sage.

Ledbetter, James (1997), *Made Possible by . . .: The Death of Public Broadcasting in the United States*, New York and London: Verso.

Marcus, Daniel (ed.) (1991), *ROAR! The Paper Tiger Guide to Media Activism*, New York: Paper Tiger Television and Wexner Center for the Arts.

Shamberg, Michael and Raindance Corporation (1971), *Guerrilla Television*, New York: Holt, Rinehart and Winston.

Stein, Laura (2001), 'Access Television and Grassroots Political Communication in the United States', in John Downing, *Radical Media: Rebellious Communication and Social Movements*, Thousand Oaks: Sage.

Satellite, Cable and New Channels in the UK

In the 1980s television in the UK took the form of three national channels: BBC1, BBC2 (licence fee-funded) and ITV (funded by advertising). By 2000 the numbers of channels available was in the hundreds. Television in 1980 was delivered by land-based, terrestrial, over the air signals. In 2000 it was still delivered terrestrially, but was also available in digital form via cable and satellite. The speed and significance of this change should be compared with the spread of radio in the 1920s and 30s and TV in the 1950s and 60s, when new technologies embodied in new institutions, the BBC (1926) and ITV (1954), altered significantly the nature of mass communications in the UK (Pegg, 1983, p. 7; Briggs, 1995, p. 1005).

The framework for the introduction of satellite and cable services in the UK was established in the 1980s. Policy was affected by a range of factors, including the influence of multinational corporations on policy, the strong free-market politics of the Conservative governments of Margaret Thatcher (1979–90), the widespread view that the UK's future industrial success lay in developing new technologies, and divisions within and between broadcasters, civil servants and politicians (O'Malley, 1994; Goodwin, 1998).

The UK was awarded five direct broadcast satellite (DBS) channels by the World Administrative Radio Conference in 1977. The election of Margaret Thatcher in 1979 as leader of a Conservative government led to a decade of active policy development in this area. Under Thatcher the traditional principle that broadcasting should be organised primarily as a public service designed to serve the informational, educational and entertainment needs of the UK was replaced by the principle that broadcasting was to be primarily a market-driven industry, with public service increasingly less central (O'Malley, 2001a).

The governments of the 1980s wanted rapid developments in satellite services to boost UK industrial competitiveness, but were unwilling to provide the finance for a UK satellite and insisted on cable services being financed by private investment. In 1981 the Home Secretary William Whitelaw announced that DBS would start in 1986. Although the BBC took the lead, the project proved too costly for the corporation. The BBC and the Independent Broadcasting Authority (IBA) were unable thereafter to build a consortium for the costly venture and the project collapsed in 1985. The IBA then advertised the DBS services. The contract was won by British Satellite Broadcasting (BSB) in December 1986. BSB promised one channel of plays, series and soaps, another of news and another of cartoons and movies (O'Malley 1994, pp. 141–5; Goodwin, 1998, pp. 38–68).

In 1989, the media businessman Rupert Murdoch launched a four-channel Sky service from the Luxembourg-owned Astra satellite before BSB, which launched on cable in March 1990 and on satellite in April. The launch costs of both services, plus the small scale of the market, contributed to financial crises for both operators. The 1990 Broadcasting Act forbade the ownership by one company of both a domestic (BSB) and non-domestic (Sky) satellite service. Nonetheless, without informing the IBA or the Home Secretary, Sky and BSB merged at the end of the year. In the end the IBA had to accept the merger. The company that emerged was BSkyB with News Corporation as the dominant force (ITC, 2001a; Goodwin, 1998, pp. 50–1).

BSkyB became the major provider of satellite TV services in the UK during the 1990s. A framework for the introduction of digital TV was established by the 1996 Broadcasting Act, which led to the rapid expansion of digital services from companies like BSkyB, the ITV companies and the BBC. These were mainly, with the exception of many of the BBC's, commercially funded services, raising revenue from a mix of advertising, subscription and pay-per-view. The first commercial multiplex digital licences were awarded by the ITC in 1997. The Labour governments elected in 1997 and 2001 pursued a strong commitment to commercially driven services (Goodwin 1998, p. 152; ITC, 1999, pp. 10–11).

Cable development was also driven by a market-oriented approach. The 1984 Cable and Broadcasting Act was based on policy developed after 1980. The Hunt report on *Cable Expansion and Broadcasting Policy* (1982) established a framework for commercially driven cable. The Act established a Cable Authority to grant franchises for companies to cable and provide programmes to different geographical areas. (Hollins, 1984; Goodwin, 1998, pp. 59–64; ITC, 2001b).

The initial take-up of cable was slow. This was primarily due to the costs involved in building the system and the lack of suitable programming. By the end of March 1988 only twenty-three franchises had been awarded by the Cable Authority, covering fewer than 2.4 million homes. This was less than 12 per cent of TV homes, and only ten of these were operational. By mid-1988 an influx of investment from North America helped boost the industry. The 1990 Broadcasting Act, as well as placing cable under the ITC, relaxed the rules on non-European Union ownership of cable, and the industry developed in the 1990s in the context of being able to offer both telephony and an alternative means of accessing terrestrial, satellite and digital TV services (Goodwin, 1998, pp. 64–5; ITC, 2001b).

Television spread into UK homes between the 1950s and the 70s. In 1957 7 million out of 15.8 million homes in the UK had a TV. By 1978, of the 20 million homes, 19.5 million had a TV. This near saturation level of ownership remained the case thereafter. In January 2001, of 25 million homes, 24.4 million had a TV (BARB, 2002a). Thus, by the 1990s, the TV set had become a major conduit into UK homes through which businesses could develop new markets.

In 1988 one estimate put the number of individual satellite dishes at 18,000. Sky went on air in 1989 and the company had installed 600,000 dishes by April 1990. By 1991 1.7 million households had satellite. Up to 1990 cable growth was slow. By March 1988 cable systems had been built to pass around 300,000 homes, of which only 45,000 were connected. The arrival of Sky in 1989 improved the number and appeal of channels, which, along with the growth of cable telephone provision boosted the industry (Goodwin, 1998, pp. 49–53, 64–5). During the 1990s the number of homes with satellite and cable TV grew steadily (see Table 1) so that by January 2000, over 7.6 million homes had either satellite or cable services, a rise of 231 per cent since 1992. By 2000, of the 24.2 million homes with a TV in the UK, 31.4 per cent were connected to cable or satellite. In addition, by December 2000 digital TV had spread. BSkyB had achieved the largest take-up of digital pay-television with 4.6 million subscribers, and digital services were available in 6.5 million homes. So, compared to 1980, when there were no satellite or cable channels, the new technologies had made a significant breakthrough into both the industry and people's homes (BARB, 2002a; 2002b; ITC, 2001c).

A key measure of the impact of these changes is their effect on the proportion of total viewing accounted for by a particular channel, a measure known as audience share (DCMS, 1999, p. 43). In 1985 the figures were: BBC1, 36 per cent; BBC2, 11 per cent; ITV, 46 per cent; and Channel Four, 7 per cent. In 2000 the figures were: BBC1, 27.2 per cent; BBC 2, 10.8 per cent; ITV, 29.3 per cent; Channel Four 10.5 per cent; Channel 5, 5.7 per cent; and satellite and cable, 16.6 per cent. (Total of 100.1 per cent as given in BARB, 2002c.) Thus the new services hit the BBC and ITV hardest. Indeed in 2000, in multichannel homes, ITV's share was 29.3 per cent, but in digital only homes it was just 19 per cent. Given that ITV depended on advertising income generated by audience size, this change placed it under severe financial pressure (ITC, 2001c).

The characteristic feature of this change has been an increase in competition for viewer attention and, consequently, in the commercial sector, for revenue. By 1999 the ITC was licensing 244 satellite TV services including sport, films, music, shopping, money, health, cartoons, history and channels of particular interest to different cultural groups. These were in addition to the ITV and cable services it supervised (ITC, 2000, pp. 24–5). Barnett and Seymour have mapped some of the changes in programming consequent on increased competition. Commenting on drama and current affairs in the period 1977–98, they conclude: 'The drive for ratings in peak-time has greatly increased over the last ten years, and appears to be almost as dominant on the BBC and Channel Four as ITV. Especially on ITV ratings targets or guarantees increasingly

Table 1: *The spread of cable and satellite in UK homes, 1992–2000*
(Adapted from BARB, 2002b)

Year (at January)	Homes (thousands)		
	Satellite	Cable	Total
1992	1,893	409	2,302
1993	2,387	625	3,012
1994	2,754	744	3,498
1995	3,060	973	4,033
1996	3,542	1,399	4,941
1997	3,804	1,845	5,649
1998	4,117	2,471	6,588
1999	4,114	2,911	7,126 [*sic*]
2000	4,196	3,352	7,618 [*sic*]

RUPERT MURDOCH

Rupert Murdoch has played a major role in the media industries in the UK since the 1960s, dominating the popular tabloid press, and creating the UK's first major provider of satellite and cable TV in the 1980s and 90s. He has also been an important player in UK politics through the influence wielded by his media properties.

Murdoch was born in Australia in 1931. On the death of his father Keith, he took control of his family's newspaper interests. During the 1950s he built up these interests and established a presence in Australian TV (Shawcross, 1993, pp. 77–94). By 1969 he had purchased the UK Sunday paper, the *News of the World* and the daily, the *Sun*. In the 1970s he switched the *Sun* from a Labour to a Conservative paper, vigorously supporting its leader Margaret Thatcher, who was elected Prime Minister in May 1979. (Curran and Seaton, 1997; pp. 73–4). Under Thatcher his business interests in the UK flourished. In 1981 he bought *The Times* and *The Sunday Times*. He developed interests in the US, buying a controlling interest in 1985 in 20th Century-Fox, the film studio. In the same year, he took citizenship of the US so as to protect and develop his interests there. This allowed him to start up the first new terrestrial television service in the US since the 1950s, the Fox network (Shawcross, 1993, pp. 321–3).

He used his UK papers to launch a sustained attack on the BBC in 1984 and 1985, as part of an attempt to break into UK broadcasting (O'Malley, 1994, pp. 31–46). He launched a major attack on trade unions in the print industry (1986–7), thereby helping to shift the balance of power in the UK newspaper industry in the employers' favour. In 1989 he launched his Sky satellite TV channel, in a pre-emptive strike against BSB, the IBA's contractor. He used his UK newspapers to give 'disproportionate and largely uncritical support' to Sky television in 1989. The two companies merged in 1990 with Murdoch's News Corporation the dominant partner (Curran and Seaton, 1997, pp. 83, 102–5; Briggs and Burke, 2002, p. 295). BSkyB became the dominant provider of UK satellite in the 1990s.

During the 1990s he joined other European publishers in lobbying the UK government for 'Large scale deregulation of national cross-media ownership restrictions' (EPC, 1993, p. 1). By the late 1990s, after twenty years of supporting the Conservatives, Murdoch had switched the *Sun* behind Tony Blair's opposition, 'New Labour Party'. In 1995 Blair had signalled that his desire for press support in the run up to the general election meant he would not take steps in government that would damage Murdoch's interests (Curran and Seaton, 1997, p. 300). The 'New Labour' governments of Tony Blair elected in 1997 and 2001 pursued an agenda of lifting

Rupert Murdoch built a global media empire in forty years

restraints on the commercial expansion of mass communications (O'Malley, 2001b). During the 1990s Murdoch developed satellite interests in Asia. By 2001, News Corporation, of which Murdoch was the managing director, controlled newspapers in the UK, the US and Asia; television in the UK (BSkyB), USA (Fox) and Asia (Star); film studios in the US and Australia; and the book publishers HarperCollins (Briggs and Burke, 2002, p. 256; News Corporation, 2002).

Murdoch built a global media empire in forty years. He combined ruthlessness and poltical acumen. He persuaded politicians in the UK, Australia and the US to deliver favourable conditions for his interests in return for political support in his media outlets. His UK newspapers became marked by a fierce commitment to Conservative politics. His career exemplified the tendencies in the late twentieth century for media ownership to become concentrated and global in reach. It also provoked international concerns about the way in which the cultural and social power of the media could be used by one person to promote his particular economic and political agenda.

Tom O'Malley

dictate programming decisions'. This has led, in drama, to pressure 'for predictable hits' and in current affairs to 'a significant decline . . . in foreign affairs coverage' in favour of more emphasis on 'consumer and ratings friendly subjects' (Barnett and Seymour, 1999, p. 5). While the diversity of news coverage between 1975 and 1999 improved on terrestrial channels, 'there has undoubtedly been a shift in most bulletins towards a more tabloid domestic agenda', in particular there was 'a decline across the board in coverage of political affairs' (Barnett, Seymour and Gaber, 2000, p. 12).

The increase in the number of TV services since 1980 has to be balanced against its effect on the range, quality and depth of programming on offer. Although, in 2000, the ten most-watched programmes on UK TV were from either the BBC or ITV (ITC, 2001c), the continued popularity of these channels remained dependent, arguably, on the fact that only 31.4 per cent of homes were connected to new services. Assuming a continuing upward trend in connections to these services, the historic role of public service television as being at the centre of viewing in the UK is likely to be seriously undermined.

The full consequences for TV in the UK of the arrival of these new technologies are yet to become fully apparent. What is apparent, however, is that in less than twenty years the form, economics and viewing patterns of the UK TV industry have been altered permanently. In the long term the twentieth century now appears to be a period of rapid evolution in the technological, financial and institutional framework of mass electronic communications, an evolution that seems set to accelerate in the twenty-first.

Tom O'Malley

RECOMMENDED READING

Curran, James and Seaton, Jean (1997), *Power without Responsibility: The Press and Broadcasting in Britain*, 5th edition, London and New York: Routledge.

Goodwin, Peter (1998), *Television under the Tories: Broadcasting Policy 1979–1997*, London: BFI.

O'Malley, Tom (1994), *Closedown? The BBC and Government Broadcasting Policy 1979–1992*, London: Pluto Press.

US Television in the Multichannel Age

Contrary to the version of the story told by 1990s' free marketeers, the beginning of the end of the classic network system – the most heavily centralised, vertically integrated, standardised and homogenised period of US network television – was brought about not by deregulation but by regulation. The passage of the Fin-Syn rules in 1971, along with the Prime Time Access Rule (PTAR) in 1970, provided the necessary rebalancing of power among producers and distributors required to open up the landscape of television to more diverse production, representation and control. Though full implementation of Fin-Syn was delayed until 1979 due to a series of court challenges and appeals, its restriction of network production of programmes and ownership of syndication rights led to a rebirth of independent production, which along with PTAR – the return of the first hour of prime time to local station control – gave rise to the boom in first- and second-run syndication that in turn fed the resurgence of independent local stations.

The FCC's Third Report and Order on Cable Television in 1972 also represented a regulatory rather than a deregulatory turn: cable was finally recognised as a legitimate medium in its own right, no longer merely an adjunct or threat to over-the-air (OTA) broadcasters, and brought under the FCC's regulatory aegis. Through imposition of new rules such as must-carry (ensuring that all significantly viewed local stations must be carried on cable systems) and public access channel requirements, the FCC ensured that cable television would be eagerly adopted by local communities and that long-neglected principles of localism would be upheld. It also meant that formerly struggling, often low-powered local independent stations on the UHF band, with refreshed sources of programme supply and now with a position on the cable line-up right next to their bigger competitors, could thrive and grow. Some would become the superstations of cable's expanding service; others would form the backbone of the new studio-owned over-the-air networks that would form in the late 1980s and early 1990s (Fox, United Paramount Network and Warner Bros.).

Taken together, these forces resulted in a radically changed media universe for most Americans. The three-network oligopoly of the classic network system, itself a product of decades of industry-friendly regulation, was brought down by yet more regulation. Though the main supporters and beneficiaries of the new regime might have been Hollywood studios and the nascent cable industry – longtime rivals and opponents of broadcasters – the public exerted an influence in the debates as well, and reaped many benefits, though not as many as might have been possible (Streeter, 1997). As major film studios and Hollywood-based independent producers moved in to fill the void produced by the new rules, broadcasting in the United States went through its first major structural change since the days of radio. The fact that it unfolded during an era of deregulation only points to the necessary prior rebalancing carried out by the activist FCC of the 1960s and 70s.

At the heart of the cable revolution lies a technological innovation that is too often overlooked in histories of American broadcasting: the invention of the geostationary satellite. Satellite transmission turned cable from a local to a national, even global, medium. One of the first commercial concerns to see the possibilities was the upstart company Home Box Office, owned by Time Inc., which in 1978 began using the new technology to beam everything from heavyweight championship fights to uncut recent movies up to its leased satellite transponder, then down to the receiving dishes of cable system headends across the nation (and indeed, the world), and thence to the consumer, for a hefty fee. New cable channels began to spring up at a great rate, from the first superstations (a local station using a satellite to transmit nationwide, such as Ted Turner's WTBS Atlanta, WOR New York, or WGN Chicago), to basic cable channels (advertising-supported services appealing to niche audiences such as CNN [Cable News Network]) USA (an entertainment-based channel owned by several film studios), MTV (music videos and other youth-oriented programming), BET (Black Entertainment Television), ESPN (all sports, all the time), A&E (Arts and Entertainment, specialising in 'quality' drama and movies), the History Channel, Animal Planet, and so on in an amazing array of diverse and competing offerings.

Cable economics differ from broadcasting enough to make such diversity and niche-orientation possible.

Edgy, adult programming: *The Sopranos* (HBO, 1999 –)

Besides revenue from advertising, cable channels receive a fee from each local cable franchise, usually an amount ranging from $0.25 to $1 per subscriber per month. This gives the channels an extra revenue stream to support programming; in addition, the ability of cable to target certain specific groups of desirable consumers – those who play golf, say (the Golf Channel), or children (Nickelodeon), or women (Lifetime), or Spanish speakers (Telemundo, Univision), or those interested in the BBC (BBC America) – sometimes allows it to charge relatively higher cost-per-thousand charges than general service networks. Pay cable channels such as HBO and Showtime eschew advertising altogether in favour of a premium paid directly by the subscriber – usually $10 to $15 per month on top of the basic cable subscription fee – with half of it going to the cable operator and half to the programme provider. This freedom from advertiser support, and the motivated audience it tends to draw, allows such channels to experiment with edgier, more adult programming, as series like *The Sopranos* (HBO, 1999–), *Sex and the City* (HBO, 1999–), *Resurrection Blvd.* (Showtime, 2000–), and *Oz* (HBO, 2000–) demonstrate.

By 1985, almost 50 per cent of homes in the United States subscribed to cable, and the traditional networks were beginning to feel the heat; their share of viewers dropped to 75 per cent from a 1960s' high of over 90 per cent. By 2002, cable's audience had increased to nearly 70 per cent of the public, with over 73 million subscribers. Vertical integration was also on the rise, with the four largest MSOs (multiple systems operators) controlling almost 50 per cent of the market: ATT Broadband, AOL Time Warner, Comcast and Charter. In November 2002 the FCC approved the merger of Comcast and ATT, giving the new company a lock on roughly a third of all cable households (National Cable Television Association, 2002). Most MSOs owned a substantial stake in a number of cable programme services as well. Time Warner Cable, subsidiary of the world's largest media company, owns multiple MTV, HBO and CNN channels, Court TV and Cinemax and has shares in many others. Vertical integration in the cable industry began to resemble that of the classic network system, only more so. By 2001, the average number of channels received in a US household was up to fifty-five, from thirty-nine only eight years previously (Parsons and Frieden, 1998). By 2002, the combined OTA network share had fallen to less than 40 per cent of overall audiences, with cable picking up 60 per cent.

In this kind of environment, given the way that cable and DBS continued to chip away at traditional broadcast audiences, why would anyone choose to debut a new over-the-air network? This was the question asked when Australian media magnate Rupert Murdoch launched his Fox network in 1986, and asked even more loudly in 1995, when two more new networks debuted, UPN (the United Paramount Network) and WB (Warner Bros.). Yet conditions were ripe for the first attempt at a 'fourth network' since DuMont's ignominious demise in 1955. First, independent stations had become more viable than ever, thanks to cable and the newly invigorated syndication market. Second, Murdoch envisioned a sort of mini-network, a cross between a traditional over-the-air operation and a cable channel, that combined something of the national reach of a broadcast net but with the niche appeal of a cablecaster. Third, Murdoch was able to use his influence in Washington not only to get around foreign-ownership rules – though he did have to become a US citizen – but to attain exemptions from Fin-Syn restrictions. And finally, the public recognition and glamour of the Fox name promised to fulfil the cross-promotional and production synergies that Hollywood had always sought in an alliance with the television network business, only to be balked in the past by regulatory barriers set up to protect big broadcasters (Hilmes, 2001). The Fox network finally consummated the marriage of Hollywood and broadcasting that had been postponed since the 1920s. Starting out slowly, with just a few hours of programming on a few nights every week, Fox effectively targeted its desired youthful demographic, particularly young men, notoriously hard to reach by the more mass-minded 'big three' networks. Using the strategy of 'creamskimming' – programming only for the most profitable prime-time hours, and leaving it to affiliates to fill up the rest of the daily schedule – the Fox network introduced an envelope-pushing line-up of popular programmes (see Perren, p. 107) that made an immediate cultural and industrial impact, even if the netlet's profits failed to materialise until the Aaron Spelling-produced series *Beverly Hills 90210* (1990–2000) and its spin-off *Melrose Place* (1992–9) brought in the commercially necessary young female demographic. The network's early attention to African-American audiences with popular programmes like *In Living Color* (1990–4), *Martin* (1992–7) and *Living Single* (1993–8) faded as finances and ratings rose (Zook, 1999). Eliminating the traditional 'station compensation' offered by the 'big three' networks – a percentage of advertising revenue paid to affiliates each month – also helped Fox's bottom line. Though the size of its overall audiences remained relatively small, by 1995 a few Fox programmes began to penetrate the Nielsen top ten, even beating CBS at times, prompting a wave of affiliate defections to the upstart network.

The plans announced by Paramount and Warner Bros. in 1993 for two more networks brought reactions of disbelief and skepticism, yet once again many forces worked in their favour. The FCC was under heavy lobbying pressure in the early 1990s to deregulate ownership restrictions on broadcasters, not least from Hollywood studios, who anticipated a profitable return on their campaign contribution dollars that finally paid off in the Telecommunications Act of 1996 (see grey box). Raising station ownership caps to a new high, deregulation allowed Paramount and Warner Bros. to purchase and operate a significantly higher number of stations across the country than would have been permitted previously. Like Fox, and Disney's acquisition of ABC, they followed the trend towards studio-owned networks, in UPN's case building on its *Star Trek* franchise and in WB's case, on its movie and cartoon library. Reversing the concept of station compensation, the WB actually required affiliates to pay the network a portion of their advertising revenues, a revolution in the commercial television industry, supposedly justified by the much-heightened profits the resonance with Warner Bros. would bring. And fears of scarcity, too, played a part: each new network feared that if they didn't bring the remaining independent stations in the most profitable markets under their own aegis, their competitors would.

By the late 1990s all three new networks were still in operation, though UPN trailed behind its two more successful competitors. Fox had arrived at a position nearly equal to NBC, CBS and ABC in ratings, buoyed by its acquisition of some major sports franchises as well as by programming synergies brought about by in-house production. UPN took over the African-American emphasis dropped by Fox, airing such programmes as *Moesha* (1996–2001), *Homeboys in Outer Space* (1996), *The Parkers* (1999–) and *The Hughleys* (1998–2002) and diversified into wrestling and other testosterone-charged programming aimed at young male audiences, while WB specialised in teen melodrama such as *Buffy the Vampire Slayer* (1997–2002), *Dawson's Creek* (1998–2002), *Felicity* (1998–2002) and *Charmed* (1998–), appealing to women. A growing American Latino/a audience found little inclusion on broadcast networks, but began to capture an increasing share of cable's viewership on Telemundo and Univision.

Meantime, a wave of mergers and acquisitions swept over the television industry. General Electric had added NBC's owner, RCA, to its dominant position in the telecommunications, electronics and defence industries in 1989. Time Inc. merged with Warner Communications in 1989, forming Time Warner Inc., the largest communica-

tions company in the world at that point, only to add Turner Broadcasting to the line-up in 1995, producing Time Warner Turner. This behemoth enlarged even further in 1999, when it combined with digital giant AOL to form AOL Time Warner. Viacom, a multimedia empire, purchased Paramount Pictures in 1994, taking over UPN, then combined this with its acquisition of another network, CBS, in 2001. Disney merged with ABC in 1995, adding it to its inventory of media and other holdings, including sports teams, amusement parks, resorts and retail stores. Though the economic downturn of the new millennium meant that many of these much-vaunted synergistic conglomerations failed to produce much besides huge new levels of debt, the repeal of the Fin-Syn and PTAR rules in the mid-1990s ultimately produced a return to the kind of vertical integration of production, distribution and station ownership seen under the classic network system, only this time with more, and bigger, players.

Under these pressures, some of the most familiar characteristics of US commercial network television began to change. Cable channels began to produce original programming to rival the old networks, not only pay cable channels such as HBO and Showtime, but basic channels like Lifetime (*Any Day Now*, 1998–), USA (*Monk*, 2002–), Comedy Central (*South Park*, 1997–) and A&E (*100 Centre Street*, 2001–). Networks expanded into cable, with NBC's

Dawson's Creek: targeting teens

PROTECTIONISM, DEREGULATION AND THE TELECOMMUNICATIONS ACT OF 1996

The role of the state in US commercial broadcasting has always been a contentious and conflicted one, from its earliest roots in the Radio Act of 1927 up through the battles over the Communications Act of 1934, the primary piece of broadcast legislation until the rewriting of 1996. Operating between the First Amendment protections on free speech so often invoked by recalcitrant broadcasters, and the public service principles adopted from public utility law (and heavily influenced by the example of the BBC), US broadcast regulation has swung in a broad arc between *laissez-faire* market populism and public interest-based federal interventionism rooted in Progressive principles and New Deal ideologies. Yet the close relationship between the industry and its regulators has resulted in a strong tradition of protectionism, often repelling both reform and competition. In the end, the combined forces of industry and regulators work to the advantage of both, and to the permanent disadvantage of the local, the different, the challenging and the non-profitable.

Television debuted in a period of heightened corporate liberalism, promising to continue its wartime level of public service while expanding aggressively as an industry. Dissatisfaction with its performance rose through the 1960s and 70s, prompting the introduction of the Public Broadcasting Service (PBS) and a series of regulatory decisions designed to curb the 'excessive commercialism' of the major networks. Yet by 1980 the regulatory pendulum had swung back again, giving rise to the period of deregulation under President Reagan's FCC Chair Mark Fowler. Fowler proposed a new philosophy for broadcasting, abandoning the old principles of spectrum scarcity, federal oversight of a public resource and fears of television's intrusiveness for new principles of diversity, competition and innovation. Famously, he referred to television as nothing more than 'a toaster with pictures' and proposed auctioning off the spectrum to private corporations to promote better competition (Brown, 1994; Fowler and Brenner, 1982). This did not come to pass, since broadcasters relied upon their protected position on the free airwaves, but Fowler's deregulatory mystique continued on even after he himself had left.

Pressures to reform the 1934 Act had been building since the early 1980s. By the early 1990s they had reached a peak, driven by the onslaught of corporate mergers and acquisitions common to all industries, but particularly by the ongoing force of digital convergence. Regulations placing limits on ownership of radio and television stations, or prohibiting cable companies from owning broadcast properties, seemed like relics of another age when digitisation promised to erase the very distinctions that separated one industry from another. Telecommunications giants showered key politicians with campaign contributions (Shivers and Morris, 1996). The legislation that finally passed both houses in the spring of 1996 contained a curious mixture of industry deregulation and attempts to clamp down on media content, most of the latter obvious sops to the conservative Christian right. Broadcast station ownership caps were raised from 25 per cent to 35 per cent, meaning that a single company could now own stations reaching up to 35 per cent of the population. Caps were eliminated almost entirely for radio. Cross-ownership rules were suspended between telephone and cable, as well as television and radio. The term of a broadcast licence was extended to eight years, and terms crafted that virtually guaranteed automatic renewal. The cable industry was almost completely deregulated. Most industry-favourable of all, an enormous and very valuable chunk of the UHF spectrum was given away for free to existing commercial broadcasters, in return for a promised roll-out of digital television. The Communications Decency Act, the part of the larger bill designed to outlaw 'indecent' content on websites, was struck down almost immediately by the courts. The V-chip legislation (see Rowland, p. 134) passed, to little actual effect. Most remarkably, what one analyst called 'one of the biggest corporate financial coups of the century', the digital TV frequency giveaway, was passed without any restrictions on how these frequencies might be used, other than for 'advanced television services'. The fact that many broadcasters might choose to split their frequency into six or more standard definition channels, selling advertising on each one, rather than provide the high definition service envisioned by legislators, went unnoticed. A later report, authored under the auspices of then-Vice President Al Gore, recommending a series of public service obligations attendant on the gift of frequencies, failed to receive Congressional attention in the swirl of Clinton impeachment proceedings (Advisory Committee, 1998).

Passage of the Act sparked a tsunami of corporate mergers, raising station values to extraordinary heights and creating something of a feeding frenzy among media giants. Consolidations pulled many of the hundreds of 'diverse' new media offerings under the same corporate ownership. And Mark Fowler's initial idea, that commercial broadcasters should pay for use of the airwaves, if not in service then in actual dollars that might even be used to support the public broadcasting system, goes unfulfilled. The last thing that media industries want is actual deregulation, which might undermine their privileged position on the spectrum and in Washington. The Telecommunications Act of 1996 marks a high-point of industry protectionism under another name.

Michele Hilmes

news-related ventures CNBC and MSNBC, ABC's Soap Channel (rerunning network daytime serials) and parent Disney's multiple sports-oriented ESPNs. With most integrated companies having holdings in film production, video distribution, pay cable, network television and theatrical exhibition, the old distribution patterns have begun to erode, blurring the distinctions between film and television, and bringing formerly ancillary businesses like music and recordings ever more firmly under the same big tents. New technologies such as 'smart VCRs' (Replay TV and TiVo) promise to allow viewers to break free of network scheduling – and advertising – just as the Internet provides a new venue for digital piracy, eroding old intellectual property and copyright arrangements.

Attempts to reign in the rampant deregulation of the 1990s, or to counter-balance its effects, have so far proved disappointing. The movement towards low-power radio, introduced specifically to offset conglomeration in that industry, was stalled and minimised by an alliance of commercial and public broadcasters. Public broadcasting faced major budget-cutting challenges in the 1990s, and though it emerged fairly strongly with big plans for digital broadcasting, increasing reliance on corporate underwriting and the marketing of its own products threatens to undercut its public service mission (see Marcus, 1991). It is certain that far more diversity of offerings exists in 2002 than in 1965, but this diversity exhibits its own exclusions and blind spots, and with the increased influence of integrated, global media corporations, the influence of national regulations and national cultures on television seems to be shrinking, even as the size and volume of the media grows.

Michele Hilmes

RECOMMENDED READING

Croteau, David and Hoynes, William (2001) *The Business of Media: Corporate Media and the Public Interest*, Thousand Oaks, CA: Pine Forge Press.

Sterling, Christopher H. and Kitross, John Michael (2001), *Stay Tuned: A History of American Broadcasting*, 3rd edition, New York: Lawrence Erlbaum.

Walker, James and Ferguson, Douglas (1998), *The Broadcast Television Industry*, Boston: Allyn and Bacon.

PROGRAMMING: 1950s–80s

Introduction

The essays in this section provide an overview of the development of television programming, from the early period of experimentation in the 1950s, through the period of institutional standardisation and stability reaching into the 1980s, as change loomed on the horizon. For the BBC, drama represented one of its most successful efforts during the early years of live production from early television headquarters at Alexandra Palace. Gradually the repertoire of television offerings expanded to include serial as well as stand-alone drama, the introduction of filmed programmes, children's programmes, sports and news, with coverage of the Coronation of Queen Elizabeth II in 1953 one of its most significant successes. Newly fledged ITV also produced programmes of critical weight during this early period, including the experimental and critically acclaimed *Armchair Theatre*. American imports became a feature of both services, especially as competition with ITV urged the BBC in a 'solid, safe middle-class' direction. In the US, early offerings focused more heavily on the variety show, carried over from vaudeville via radio, and the comedy serials so popular on radio. Yet this period is also known for its innovations in live anthology drama in such programmes as *Studio One*, the *Kraft Television Theatre* and the *Hallmark Hall of Fame*. By the end of the decade quiz shows had reached their apogee and sparked a revolution in the system of sponsor production, driving the close alliance with Hollywood that would become the mainstay of American television.

From the 1960s into the 80s, ITV in its role as the BBC's first domestic competitor at first took the lead in television innovation, though its penchant for the popular also brought considerable debate. The regional structure of ITV, along with its emphasis on light entertainment, brought local sport, news and entertainment to Britain's audiences, but also led the way in filmed drama series, variety shows, 'infotainment' genres and current affairs programming, and introduced the first long-running television soap, *Coronation Street*. Similarly, in the US, the three-network oligopoly of the classic network system adopted an increasingly ratings-oriented tone, heightened by the emphasis on the developing 'youth audience' of the 1960s and 70s. Shows such as the early music-oriented

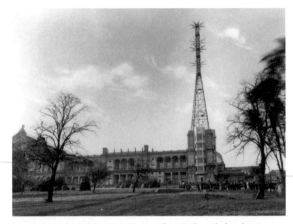

Alexandra Palace Television Tower: the BBC's early headquarters

Shindig and *Hullabaloo* led to more controversial fare in *All in the Family* (an adaptation of the BBC's *Till Death Us Do Part*) and *The Smothers Brothers Comedy Hour*, whose overt embrace of left-wing politics led to its abrupt cancellation by the network in 1969.

The BBC responded to competition in the 1960s with a wave of innovative populism of its own in such programmes as *Z Cars* and *Steptoe and Son*. The renewed emphasis on serious drama, news and public affairs mandated by the Pilkington Report sparked further innovation and led to the production of high-quality comedy and drama with programmes such as *Yes Minister*, *I, Claudius*, and *Pennies from Heaven*, along with successful news and current affairs shows like *Panorama*, *World in Action* and the controversial *Zircon*. By the late 1970s and early 1980s, both television systems faced substantial changes as competition from new technologies moved from relative stability to a period of fragmentation and multiplying offerings. Commercial satellite and cable systems not only competed with the BBC/ITV hegemony but brought a new emphasis on market-driven innovations to the established terrestrial broadcasters. In the US, the same market demands that had responded to the imperatives of the 'youth audience' now identified other demographic groups of interest to advertisers, as cable television promised to bring a new era of 'narrowcasting' to US TV. This resulted in an emphasis on working women and minority representations in such programmes as *The Mary Tyler Moore Show*, *Maude*, *The Jeffersons*, *Good Times* and *Chico and the Man*.

Later programmes reflected the networks' goals of attracting key working women audiences while not alienating the mass audiences on which commercial network success still depended, combining a strong emphasis on sex and violence with feminist messages, most notably in *Charlie's Angels*. Such contradictions pointed the way towards the multichannel revolution that lurked in the wings.

Michele Hilmes

Early Television in Great Britain

Until the late 1950s British television was characterised by the transmission of live programming, most of which was not recorded (and therefore does not survive for viewing): all of it was produced by the BBC, until competition came in the form of the commercial ITV network in 1955. The few programmes that survive demonstrate that the technical limitations of the small BBC studios did not dampen the creative ambitions of the programme-makers.

The BBC Television Service began its regular scheduled broadcasts in November 1936, closing for the duration of the war and starting again in 1946. During this time the vast majority of programmes were transmitted from the two main studios at Alexandra Palace. Working within an organisation that devoted most of its resources to sound broadcasting was to prove problematic for the early television pioneers since their colleagues in radio considered television a luxury item, something that did not fit comfortably with the BBC's public service broadcasting ethos which was based on principles of free universal coverage: television sets were available only to the few who could afford them and the initial range of transmission covered only the London area. In addition, its visual appeal seemed to the 'radio men' to provide opportunities for crude sensationalism and spectacle over their preferred mission of cultural improvement using words and music alone. While the 'radio men' in central London disparaged the novelty of television, those working at Alexandra Palace gained a reputation for their devoted enthusiasm to the new medium.

Policy limitations had the greatest effect on early programming success: in 1935 the Selsdon Committee recommended that the BBC use two television systems, John Logie Baird's mechanical one and EMI-Marconi's cathode ray tube version. The recommendation that rival television systems be used alternately until one or other proved com-patible with the requirements of the new service at Alexandra Palace immediately prevented any standardisation of production practices. Within three months Baird's system proved unworkable and from then on television production continued to improve.

The service was headed by Gerald Cock, the first Director of Television, who believed that television programmes should exploit the medium's ability to 'see at a distance' and should therefore be live and topical (see Jacobs, 1997, pp. 387–8). Cock had worked in outside broadcasts (OB) for BBC radio and his influence can be seen in the number of OBs broadcast in the pre- and post-war years. BBC OB cameras covered various sporting, military and national events and they continued to mount ambitious and popular live coverage in the post-war years, culminating in the expensive and elaborate coverage of the Coronation (see grey box). Although such broadcasts were surely topical they did not constitute a news service: in fact, during the pre-war years BBC television produced no news programmes, instead relying on Movietone newsreels. In 1948 a dedicated film unit was set up to produce in-house newsreels as well as documentaries and travelogues.

Television's ability to image the world as it was living and breathing was rightly seen as a major advantage over other media; however, BBC television was not so far away from the public service broadcasting ethos that Cock did not endorse its principles of 'variety and balance', and he invested a considerable proportion of the small budget in drama, variety (*Cabaret Cruise*, 1939) and magazine programmes (*Picture Page*, 1936–9; 1946–52), as well as *For the Children* (1937–9; 1946–50). There were also topical and educational 'talks' including ones by film-maker Robert Flaherty and cartoonist David Low.

In the early years the schedules were organised around a single main-event programme, either a play or a variety show, or occasionally sports coverage or opera. Weekend evening viewing was devoted to plays, a 'classic' on Sunday night (repeated on Thursday night), a popular play for Saturday and a comedy or thriller for Tuesday night. (The repeat of a play meant just that: the entire cast and technical staff performed the play again in the studio.) Drama played a central role in the schedules and was consistently popular.

Drama in particular was a success story for early BBC television, although its achievements have been overshadowed by the reputation of early ITV drama anthologies such as *Armchair Theatre*. Beginning in 1936 with the transmission of ten- to twenty-minute 'extracts' from current West End plays (using the same actors, costumes and props), the producers gradually gained overall control of

Armchair Theatre (Susannah and a Suicide): original drama at the BBC

the productions, adapting novels, plays or using original material for productions that, by 1938, lasted up to ninety minutes. Although most of the material had a theatrical source, the process of adaptation allowed for experiment and innovation, an evident feature of such plays as *Clive of India, Juno and the Paycock, The Ascent of F6* (all 1938), *The Two Mrs Carrolls* (1947) and *Rope* (1950).

Live drama production was particularly testing for the fledgling service because of the restrictions of studio space, the little time available for camera and actor rehearsals and the necessity to maintain continuity as the actors changed costume and make-up. In order to minimise these problems narratives with relatively few settings and characters were selected for adaptation, and pre-filmed material was often 'inserted' into the live transmission in order to allow for costume and scenery changes, as well as to provide location shots of exteriors, landscapes, etc. Maintaining continuity and structuring the on-screen performance and narrative space into a meaningful order was a hectic time for both production staff and actors, since it required the live mediation of performance, sound and cameras. This mediation is exemplified in D. H. Munro's description of the drama producer at work in the Central Control Room:

> You were transmitting, say, camera 1; your next shot was on camera 2, then from the script which you'd worked out in advance, you could see that you wanted camera 3 set up at a certain angle. So you OKed 2 on the preview monitor and you called out to the vision mixer, 'I want to preview camera 3.' He'd set that up and you'd say 'that's fine. 3, stand-by. I'll be coming over to you later.' There was no great bank of monitors, one for each camera as there is today so that you know everything that is

happening. You only had the transmission monitor and the preview monitor, and in anything complicated the producer was doing a running commentary all the time through his microphone not only to the cameramen on the floor but to his stage manager on the floor and to the vision and sound mixers in the gallery. (Quoted in Norman, 1984, p. 170)

All live programmes involved this fast-paced pressure, and in the years before 1955 the expansion in the schedules to several hours of television per day increased the pressure on programme-makers. Thankfully there was some relief brought by gradual technical improvements and greater investment by the BBC in the future of television. In 1946 engineers enabled the switching between cameras to be achieved in a single cut rather than the pre-war necessity of a slow-dissolve; in 1947 they developed a method for recording television on film permitting for the first time the storage, sale and repeat of pre-recorded television. (Both developments had been available in the US some years before.) New cameras were installed with changeable lens turrets and the ability to zoom. In 1949 the plans for a new Television Centre were announced, with a large television complex of studios, offices and storage space, and in the same year a new transmitter was opened at Sutton Coldfield (servicing the Midlands), followed by others, so that by 1954 BBC television reached the majority of the UK population. Since television was reaching a wider audience and the Television Centre would not be completed for several years, the BBC acquired additional studios at Lime Grove, bought from the Rank Organisation in 1949 and opened in 1950. The total floor space of its five studios was six times that of the studio space at Alexandra Palace. Television training courses were in place by 1951 and in the same year the BBC hired two staff writers Philip Mackie and Nigel Kneale, signalling a willingness to include original material in its schedules.

Kneale was to write some of the most memorable drama of the 1950s such as the three serials, *The Quatermass Experiment* (1953), *Quatermass II* (1955) and *Quatermass and the Pit* (1959) as well as an expensive and elaborate adaptation of George Orwell's novel, *Nineteen Eighty-Four* (1954) directed by Austrian émigré and film-maker Rudolph Cartier, probably the most influential BBC director of the 1950s.

Kneale's *Quatermass* trilogy indicates the growing importance of the serial/series form on television, something that was mostly absent from the pre- and immediate post-war years. In the early 1950s there were adaptations in serial form of *The Warden* (1951), *Pride and Prejudice*

THE CORONATION (BBC, 1953)

The coronation of Elizabeth II on Tuesday, 2 June 1953 was a major national event and also the point where television first demonstrated its abilities as a national medium. A national event was congruent with a television event and in subsequent years such royal and other national 'events' (such as the World Cup Final in 1966) became memorable first of all as television images. Since BBC television had been obscured by the success of BBC radio during World War II, the Coronation coverage became an opportunity for the television engineers and production staff (led by Peter Dimmock), to make their mark institutionally and publicly. As Andrew Crisell argues,

> The coronation usefully symbolizes the point where television surpassed radio as the major mass medium. In itself it prompted a boom in the sales of TV sets, and 1953 was the first year in which more television than radio sets were manufactured. (Crisell, 1997, p. 75)

The 20 million television *viewers* of the live broadcast (56 per cent of the population) numbered far in excess of *listeners* who tuned into the radio coverage: for the first time television had taken a national event and made it the most popular media event, an important sign that 'television was now in the process of becoming the principle instrument of both public information and of national cultural identity' (Corner, 1991, p. 4). Television sets were still expensive and while 8 million watched the Coronation in their own homes, the rest did so on the television sets of their friends, neighbours or extended family, a necessity that further enhanced the sense of a shared national experience.

A year in the planning, it was to be the most elaborate live outside broadcast (OB) to date, with mobile OB units and sixteen cameras positioned outside for the State Procession, and five cameras inside the Abbey for the Coronation Service itself, which was commentated by Richard Dimbleby. The live broadcast lasted from 10.15am to 5.20pm, and two telerecording machines (specially developed for this occasion by the BBC Research Department) recorded the events on 35mm and 16mm film to be broadcast in an edited form that night and sent to Canada, the US and European countries (the other copy was archived unedited).

The televising of the Coronation was a landmark in the growing visibility of television as a national medium rather than a novelty, a luxury or an 'experimental' service for the privileged few. As Paddy Scannell argues,

> If the BBC was, as it claimed to be, a *national* [my italics] institution, such a claim was, as it well knew, to be tried and tested on great national occasions such as a coronation. At the very least the BBC showed that it had the technical resources to do justice to the nature and scale of the day. (1996, p. 84)

The BBC had to make sure the broadcast allowed access to the specialness and magnificence of the event. The planned and elaborate live coverage offered the temporal co-presence between the television audience and the Coronation, inviting an excitement only available through live transmission with its uncertainties and dangers, and the appeal of the 'liveness' of the Coronation broadcast overwhelmed any problems with sound or image quality. Dimbleby's reverent and sometimes emotional commentary seemed to capture a national mood of celebration and appropriate solemnity. But the evident power of television also provoked caution from the political and royal elites since they forbade the BBC to broadcast pictures of the anointing or close-ups of anyone during the ceremony.

Jason Jacobs

(1952) and John Buchan's *The Three Hostages* (1951) as well as original series such as *Dixon of Dock Green* (1955). Serials and series were more economical than one-off dramas (one could use the same sets and costumes each week) and provided a regular identity for certain times in the weekly schedule, something that became essential with the coming of competition in the form of ITV. All were broadcast live until 1954 when pre-filmed programmes such as the US twelve-part cop show *I Am the Law* and *Fabian of Scotland Yard* became common, a trend that was confirmed when the ITV network began its programming with a significant proportion of pre-recorded and imported filmed material.

Apart from drama, many of the television forms and genres familiar to later audiences emerged in these early years. The BBC eventually developed 'BBC Television News' (1954–) during this time, as well as their landmark current affairs programme *Panorama* (1953–). There was also the acclaimed *Watch with Mother* (1950–80) – programmes such as *Andy Pandy* (1950–7) and *The Flowerpot Men* (1952–4) – as well as sports magazines such as *Sportsview* (1954–68), which combined OB broadcasting of matches with commentary and results coverage. *Zooquest* (1954–61) for the first time showcased David Attenborough's engaging persona; popular shows such as the early soap opera *The Grove Family* (1954–7) and the panel game *What's My Line?* (1951–62) proved that the BBC understood and catered for popular tastes before the commercial networks began.

The impact of competition from ITV companies (to which many BBC television production staff migrated in 1955) was nevertheless considerable. As well as US programme imports, such as *I Love Lucy*, the commercial network imported presentational and performance styles from theatrical variety shows, vaudeville and US television. For example, Hughie Green, presenter of the game show *Double Your Money* (ITV/A-R, 1955–68), used what was clearly a US-influenced performance style, that included 'knowing' glances at the camera and the live audience and the gentle ribbing of contestants as well as a variety of slick catchphrases. In drama, Sydney Newman, Canadian producer of *Armchair Theatre* (ITV/ABC TV, 1956–69) recruited directors and writers keen to innovate with original material, beyond what they saw as the static, bourgeois and theatrical drama tradition of the BBC. In a few years BBC television had gone from being the pioneer and innovator of new television forms to the epitome of solid, safe, middle-class values. It was not until the 1960s that they recovered their reputation with programmes that outshone those of the ITV networks.

Jason Jacobs

RECOMMENDED READING

Crisell, Andrew (1997), *An Introductory History of British Broadcasting*, London and New York: Routledge.

Jacobs, Jason (2000), *The Intimate Screen: Early British Television Drama*, Oxford: Oxford University Press.

Norden, Denis (ed.) (1985), *Coming to You Live!: Behind-the-screen Memories of Forties and Fifties Television*, London: Methuen.

Norman, Bruce (1984), *Here's Looking at You*, London: BBC and Royal Television Society.

Vahimagi, Tise (ed.) (1994), *British Television: An Illustrated Guide*, Oxford: Oxford University Press.

Experimental and Live Television in the US

Television was imagined in the 1920s and 30s as a medium for the instant transmission of news, sport and entertainment – a 'radio with eyes'. Before regular scheduled broadcasts became common there was an already rich discursive context of popular ideas about what television would do when it was eventually perfected for sale, ranging from the technical enthusiasms of amateur hobbyists to corporate figures such as NBC's David Sarnoff who proselytised the growth of television in 1936 (Jowett, 1994).

However, the provisional technology of television broadcasting did limit the realisation of these imaginings and most of the early broadcasts in the latter part of the 1920s and 30s were experimental demonstrations. In 1932 NBC had installed a television station in the Empire State building, although it only produced two programmes a week. CBS was also experimenting with television during this period and there were occasional glimpses of creative ambition and aspiration realised, for example in a production in 1937 of *The Three Garridebs* that combined filmed exterior locations with live studio action (Marschall, 1986, p. 21).

It was not until 1946 that television programming began to establish and develop forms that are recognisable today. Sports coverage (such as NBC's live transmission of the Joe Louis–Billy Conn boxing match) could take advantage of simultaneity of events and viewers, although sports organisations soon found that attendance at such events was dropping and swiftly introduced measures to combat it. In 1948 two variety shows were launched, *Texaco Star Theatre* (NBC) with Milton Berle and *Toast of the Town* (later known as *The Ed Sullivan Show*); these provided an opportunity for the television celebrity to emerge in the form of well-known hosts and their guests. The success of this format was confirmed when NBC launched its innovative variety/interview programme *The Tonight Show* in 1954 with Steve Allen, and later Ernie Kovacs (subsequent hosts have been Jack Paar, Johnny Carson and Jay Leno). There were also situation comedies, most of them derived from radio versions of the same name, such as *The Goldbergs* (various, 1949–55) and *Father Knows Best* various, 1954–60), although the transition to a visual medium was problematic for those shows that used race as a central aspect of their comedy (Marc, 1997, pp. 44–5).

Unsurprisingly, these sitcoms tended to engage with issues and narratives relevant to their reception in a domestic setting: marriage, neighbours, housework, chil-

Father Knows Best: sitcom with origins in radio

dren and family. While it is possible to see a vein of conservatism in this subject matter since the social order was rarely challenged, sitcoms like *I Love Lucy* (CBS, 1951–7) could provide rebellious energy:

> The true force of each episode lies not in the indifferent resolution, the half-hearted return to the status quo, but in Lucy's burst of rebellious energy that sends each episode spinning into chaos. Lucy Ricardo's attempts at rebellion are usually sabotaged by her own incompetence, but [Lucille] Ball's virtuosity as a performer perversely undermines the narrative's explicit message, creating a tension which cannot be resolved. Viewed from this perspective, the tranquil status quo that begins and ends each episode is less an act of submission than a sly joke; the chaos in between reveals the folly of ever trying to contain Lucy. (Anderson, 1997, p. 816)

I Love Lucy was a ratings hit, but it was relatively unusual for the early 1950s in that it was pre-recorded on film. Most programming at that time went out live, including dramas, sitcoms, variety and news. 'Liveness' was often seen as a unique quality of television broadcasting and many producers, writers, critics and networks embraced this technological aspect of the medium as definitive of its creative potential.

In an ambition that is related to the work of the video avant-garde during the 1960s, such as that of Nam June Paik, some of the network-produced programmes of the 1950s also investigated the medium in order to define and explore its essential properties. For example, Worthington Miner, the producer of CBS's live drama anthology series *Studio One* recalled that he undertook to explore

> what made television unique, what was its peculiar and most impressive capacity, and I concluded that TV's supreme capacity was as a reporter, that this aspect of the medium must never be forgotten, even when it was operating in as remote an area as dramatic production (Miner, 1985, p. 150)

And Rod Serling, the writer of landmark 1950s live television dramas such as *Patterns* commented in 1957:

> It is unquestionable that in the golden days of live television's ascendancy its filmed counterparts on the West Coast were pretty much uninspired, formulated, hackneyed assembly-line products that could boast fast production and fast profit, but little strain in the creative process. Whatever memorable television moments exist were contributed by live shows. Whatever techniques were developed that were television's own were live techniques. Whatever preoccupation there was with quality and the endless struggle against sponsors dicta, fears and endless interference existed in New York and Chicago not in Los Angeles. (Quoted in Boddy, 1993, pp. 74–5)

However, some scholars have argued that the theorising of live television by programme-makers and critics during the 1950s constituted little more than 'poorly argued essentialist claims' (Boddy, 1993, p. 125), although others have warned that we need to be 'cautious about dismissing so wide a range of early practice and early theorising' (Barr, 1997, p. 52). Nevertheless, it was the case that elevating 'liveness' as a marker of quality had a number of advantages for the industry: 'the live anthology drama was actually a function of a complex aesthetic alliance between network programmers and critics, a defence mechanism against Hollywood film producers, and a symbolic pawn in television's regulatory game with Washington' (Caldwell, 1995, p. 38).

During the 1950s the rivalry between NBC and CBS was often fought out in terms of their prestige live programming and both gained prestige from producing critically acclaimed dramas. At the top were two media forms – the documentary/news magazine and the quality drama. Television news and documentary was still a relatively trivial affair in the late 1940s and early 1950s since the

STUDIO ONE, 'THE HOSPITAL' (CBS, 1953)

John Caldwell has argued that early television drama in the US delighted in putting its technical limitations on display:

> in serious, quality artistic offerings like *Marty*, technical limitations were not only evident, but they became a kind of badge of honour. Poorly diffused pools of light and shadow abound in *Marty*. Focus and depth of field were problems as actors moved in real-time; the sets were clearly inexpensive and minimal; and luminance levels changed noticeably as the actors walk from one side of the set to another. Even those generic forms from the period of 'great' television art – like the live anthology drama from New York – flaunted explicit low-tech and anti-style airs as marks of distinction . . . The whole point . . . was to show how much one could do with so little.' (Caldwell, 1995, pp. 48–9)

It is possible to see this happening in an edition of CBS's *Studio One*, 'The Hospital'. CBS had a strong reputation in quality drama derived from its experimental and innovative track record in radio drama production (e.g. the Mercury Theatre), and during the 1950s *Studio One* was its flagship drama anthology. *Studio One*'s reputation was for technical innovation and visual experimentation in live studio drama – pushing to the limits what could be feasibly achieved in real time in a television studio. 'The Hospital' was an adaptation produced during the 1952 season, and directed by Franklin Schaffner.

Like many subsequent medical dramas 'The Hospital' has multiple narrative strands that are elaborated – the threat of closure, a suicidal doctor, as well as the various ailments and anxieties of patients. The climax of the play occurs when a porter, who appears crazy, shuts off the power supply. Although the content of these strands is quite conventional the means of presentation is not: the transmitted play lasts fifty minutes, though the story-time takes up only eighteen minutes. This is because some scenes are repeated (from different viewpoints), while others elaborate on issues and events only hinted at in earlier acts. Effectively the drama shows the eighteen minutes of narrative from several different viewpoints, each unaware – unlike the audience – of what will happen next. As some scenes are lengthened or modified in the light of what we have seen before we gain a greater understanding of the events from each character's viewpoint. So, we see the power going out in the operating theatre in the first act, but not until the second do we learn that it is a result of the porter's actions and the events that led up to them. The narrative's convolutions are matched by a snaky and low camera style which provides effective coverage and suspense. It also seems to want to mimic the effects of post-production by beginning with a title sequence that appears to freeze-frame the image as the credits come up. In fact, it is clear that the actors in the background, abruptly stopped in their tracks, are attempting to stay very still, returning to motion once the credit caption fades out.

The whole thing would be relatively simple to do on film or tape or with the freedom of editing in post-production. However, as a live drama 'The Hospital' was setting itself a very difficult task. The achievement of a credible drama in these circumstances is underlined by the repeated close-ups of a clock and the commentary of one of the hospital patients who, with head bandaged, declares 'Time? There is no time. Time is only an illusion.'

Jason Jacobs

networks depended on newsreel companies for their film, and with shows such as the early morning *Today* deploying a chimpanzee to augment its visual appeal (Barnouw, 1975, p. 168); this changed with *See It Now* (CBS, 1951–8). It was developed by prestige radio reporter Edward R. Murrow, who transferred the format from his radio magazine show. The show had its own camera crews and correspondents across the world and their material was collated and presented by *See It Now* in often striking ways. Their coverage and analysis of Cold War developments demonstrated a shrewd understanding of the national psychology (for example, they simulated coverage of a nuclear bomb attack on New York, and effectively destroyed the career of Joseph McCarthy in a series of programmes), and *See It Now*

became the model of the news/documentary television form.

Developments in quality drama were not so lasting but it is here that television's 'golden age' of live programming is most frequently identified. Most of the anthology dramas such as *Kraft Television Theatre* (NBC, 1947–), *Hallmark Hall of Fame* (NBC, 1951–79), *Studio One* (CBS, 1948–58), *Philco and Goodyear Television Playhouses* (NBC, 1948–55) began in the late 1940s with adaptations of classic theatre as well as recent Broadway plays, but in the 1950s there was a growing visibility of plays originated for television, culminating in 1953 with the most famous, Paddy Chayefsky's *Marty* (NBC, 1953).

Drama anthologies allowed writers to develop unique

A ratings winner: *The $64,000 Question*

stories each week unlike the episodic series and serials that were perceived as more predictable and formulaic, and in a single evening viewers could choose between several dramas. Rather than engage with social issues, many of the dramatic narratives concerned lonely or alienated characters with ordinary lives. In this thematic bias the live drama was showing its affinity to contemporary US theatre as well as deliberately shunning the glamour of Hollywood which many creative artists working in television and theatre considered to be formulaic, over-glamorous and star-struck. However, there was also a tendency stylistically to emphasise a distance from the theatre, particularly in the excessive display of virtuoso camera movements, or staging the story in what seemed to be 'impossible' situations for live studio production (such as a flooded submarine in *Studio One*'s 'Shakedown Cruise' [CBS, 1955]). Whatever the artistic aspirations of live drama each edition was still transmitted in a commercial environment and writers needed to shape their narratives around commercial breaks every fifteen minutes. (However, truly prestige productions could avoid commercials: the Orson Welles/Peter Brook television adaptation of *King Lear* [CBS, 1953] was sold as 'A specially staged production without commercial interruption'.)

The drama anthologies also provided a training ground

for actors who later would become Hollywood stars, such as Steve McQueen, Marlon Brando and Rod Steiger. Paddy Chayefsky, Rod Serling and Reginald Rose were among the many writers who achieved success at this time; as did directors such as Arthur Penn, Sam Peckinpah, Franklin Schaffner and Robert Altman.

While the quality end of programming provided ammunition for industrial and critical manoeuvres, game shows and variety were ratings winners by the late 1950s, with shows such as *The $64,000 Question* (CBS, 1955–8), although their luminescence was tarnished by the quiz show scandal of 1958. By that time much had changed in the economic and industrial environment, with the majority of network television production moving from New York to Hollywood and the consequent origination of most television shows on film or tape. Live anthology drama began to disappear in the late 1950s with shows like *Playhouse 90* (CBS, 1956–60) shown in both live and taped versions, indicating that the mystique and appeal of live production had vanished. Nevertheless the early period of US television was one where ideas and practices that were central to the later development of programmes in the 1960s and beyond were developed and nurtured.

Jason Jacobs

RECOMMENDED READING

Barr, Charles (1997), ' "They Think It's All Over": The Dramatic Legacy of Live Television', in John Hill and Martin McLoone (eds), *Big Picture, Small Screen: The Relations Between Film and Television*, Luton: University of Luton Press/John Libbey.

Sturcken, Frank (1990), *Live Television: The Golden Age of 1946–1958 in New York*, Jefferson: McFarland.

ITV 1955–89: Populism and Experimentation

The official histories of British broadcasting have depicted the emergence and impact of ITV in rather damning tones, as a chronology of populist programming catering to the lowest common denominator, in which trite or morally dubious programme formats (the quiz show, the variety show, the fast-paced and violent American or 'Americanised' filmed series) feature heavily. This image of ITV has accumulated over the last fifty years, fuelled by the press, critics, spokespersons within the industry and, more often than not, those government bodies established to assess the successes and failures of British broadcasting. However, what narratives such as these belie is the fact that the history of ITV programming is also one of innovation and experimentation, in which areas of broadcasting as diverse as news, current affairs, drama, education and regional programming were radically influenced by the arrival of independent television in Britain.

If the picture of ITV programming offered in television histories and within the public imagination is somewhat biased, it is unsurprising: the history of ITV programming began with a lengthy series of Parliamentary debates (surrounding the findings of the Beveridge Report [1951] and the production of the Television Bill [1954]) in which both the form and content of ITV programmes were discussed before a single programme had been made or broadcast. A typical attack on the content of ITV's broadcast output *in theory* came from Lord Reith in the House of Lords who compared a potential commercial television service to 'dog racing, small pox and the bubonic plague', with much debate offered in Parliament as to whether commercial broadcasting could deliver the 'high quality' and 'proper balance' which the Television Bill promised. While the Tory government resisted urges from the Labour opposition to write a statutory quota of named programming categories into the Television Bill ('religion', 'current affairs', etc.), it established the Independent Television Authority to oversee the contractors and to ensure that an ethos of public service broadcasting was adhered to, requiring programme-makers to produce programmes which would 'inform, educate and entertain'. In addition, the ITA established a number of rules which aimed to keep programming and advertising completely separate, and which attempted to combat a potential 'Americanisation' of British broadcasting and the threat which this posed to Britain's cultural 'superiority' (the wording of the 1954

Television Bill stated that the 'tone and style' of ITV programming should be 'predominantly British'). However, perhaps the most important part of the Bill in relation to the programming of ITV was an amendment to the 'Programme Requirements' section which stated that ITV should produce 'a suitable proportion of matter calculated to appeal specially to the tastes and outlook of persons served by the station'. Clearly, this statement offered the ITV contractors a certain amount of interpretative licence.

When ITV began broadcasting in London in September 1955, and in the rest of the country at various points starting from the following year, its programming was seen in part as a response to a growing desire for democratisation within the socio-political climate of Britain in the 1950s (see Briggs, 1979). What ITV programmes offered, in opposition to the capital-centred BBC, was a socially extended, regionally specific address to viewers throughout the UK, with individual companies producing local programmes as well as providing a range of programming output which could be sold to the other franchise holders and screened nationally. For example, in the first week of broadcasting by ATV and ABC in the Midlands (17–23 February 1956), over 20 per cent of the schedule was taken up by regional programming, which on the first day included boxing from the Embassy Sports Drome in Birmingham, a variety show entitled *Midland Cabaret* broadcast live from the Midland ITV Opening Ball at Birmingham Town Hall, and an *Epilogue* from the Right Reverend Leonard Wilson, Lord Bishop of Birmingham (10.50–10.55pm). These initial broadcasts, while 'special' in the sense that they marked the beginning of the service in the Midlands region, can also be seen as indicative of ITV's commitment to producing locally focused news, sport, entertainment, etc.

However, along with the new regional programmes, ITV in the 1950s would soon become known as the home of light entertainment, offering a number of popular variety spectaculars: typical examples of this variety entertainment are ATV's *Sunday Night at the London Palladium* (1955–67; 1973–4), *Chelsea at Nine* (Granada, 1957–60), and big-money quiz shows like *Take Your Pick* and *Double Your Money*, both made by Associated-Rediffusion between 1955 and 1968. Both light entertainment formats had the benefit of being economical and capable of attracting big audiences, and continued to proliferate in the schedules until the 1960s when the number of quiz shows was capped by the ITA and the variety show became unfashionable. Other 'light entertainment' formats were also developed on ITV in the 1950s; the channel produced a number of popular sitcoms such as *The Army Game*

Imported ITV shows included *Highway Patrol* (1955–9)

(Granada, 1957–61), broke new ground in the 'youth' market with pop shows such as *Cool for Cats* (A-R, 1956–61) and *Oh Boy* (ABC, 1958–9), and developed new forms of 'infotainment' with the introduction of 'admags', early precursors to 'lifestyle' television and home shopping programmes built around characters or presenters discussing the price and quality of a range of commercially available products, such as *Jim's Inn* (A-R, 1957–63) and *About Homes and Gardens* (ATV, 1956). Admags were eventually outlawed by Parliament in 1963, under the recommendation of Postmaster General Reginald Bevins' 'Operation Clean Up' campaign, on the grounds that they came too close to blurring the boundaries between programming and advertising (see Thumim, 2002).

In the field of drama, ITV took full advantage of the new possibility of broadcasting from film and drew on the volume of filmed drama being made in the United States in the 1950s, filling the schedules in the early years of the channel with imported cop shows, such as *Dragnet* (NBC 1955–9, 1967–70) and *Highway Patrol* (Ziv/UA TV, 1955–9) and Westerns, including *Gunsmoke* (CBS, 1955–75) and *Rawhide* (CBS, 1959–66). In addition, British commercial television also produced a number of its own drama series which reflected this American 'cinematic' aesthetic and which could be readily exported to the

The popular Western series: *Rawhide* (1959–66)

United States (see Bakewell and Garnham, 1970). The most successful of these filmed series were Sapphire Films' 'swashbucklers', such as *The Adventures of Robin Hood* (1955–9) (sold to the US for £500,000 before its first broadcast), and *The Buccaneers* (1956–7). However, while it would be incorrect to suggest that the trade between the US and ITV was simply one of import, those programmes that were made for export to North America were often seen to be less than British in 'tone and style', thus inviting claims of cultural colonialism in the early days of ITV drama. In the late 1950s the 'gentleman's agreement' between the ITV franchise holders and the ITA on the scheduling of imported series (no more than seven hours per week) was also circumvented by the 'buying in' of filmed drama from East African colonial production units, high-action dramas which amounted to little more than wildlife photography coupled with rather predictable and racially problematic narratives (e.g. *African Patrol* [Gross-Krasne Prod./Kenya Prod., 1958–9] and *White Hunter* Beaconsfield Prod./ITP, 1958–60]).

Perhaps the most celebrated achievement in British television drama in the 1950s was that of ABC's *Armchair Theatre* (1956–69, Thames 1970–4), especially during the period in which Canadian Sydney Newman acted as series producer (from 1958 until 1962, when he was 'poached' by the BBC as their new Head of Drama). As John Caughie has argued, '*Armchair Theatre's* achievement was to shake loose the metropolitan, theatrical, and patrician codes which had defined the role of television drama in a public service system' (2000, p. 14). During this period Newman encouraged experimentation with the form and content of television drama, and built up a prestigious team of writers (e.g. Alan Plater, Harold Pinter, Rod Serling) and directors (e.g. Dennis Vance, Philip Saville, Ted Kotcheff) who were willing to see the series as more than an extension of filmed or theatrical drama.

ITV also excelled in various areas of factual programming, primarily with the establishment of Independent Television News (ITN) in 1955, a company set up to supply news coverage to all of the regional companies. BBC news, with its immediate heritage in radio broadcasting, was characterised during this period by a heavy emphasis on talk and 'objective' reportage, whereas ITN, unencumbered by a radio background, set out to produce 'telegenic' news which was led by an increasing use of filmed, on-location reporting and the presence, in the studio, of authoritative, journalistic newscasters, offering comment on the day's events (Robin Day, Christopher Chataway, Barbara Mandell). Later, in 1967, ITN made its first extended news bulletin (a move from twelve minutes of news to half an hour) entitled *News at Ten* which deployed the US model of news broadcasting, using two newscasters (a combination of Alastair Burnet, Andrew Gardner, Reginald Bosanquet and George Ffitch), interviews, special reports and features, and the introduction of now-familiar on-screen graphics. This programme can be seen as establishing the form and content of the extended news format that is still prevalent in British broadcasting today.

ITV's current affairs programming also led the way in its field, becoming particularly notable for programmes like the radical and irreverent *What the Papers Say* (Granada, 1956–68, 1970–89) and the hard-line *This Week* (A-R 1956–68, Thames, 1968–92). Later in the 1960s and 70s, *World in Action* (Granada, 1963-) became one of the most highly regarded current affairs programmes on British television, notable for its investigations into scandal and political corruption such as the 1973 episode 'The Friends and Influence of John G. L. Poulson' (30 April), focusing on Poulson, an architect and builder who made a fortune in the North-east by offering bribes to local politicians and businessmen.

Also in the 1950s, the ITV franchise holder for London weekday programming, Associated-Rediffusion, began the first experiments in educational broadcasts on British television, which soon developed into a regular service on both ITV and the BBC; by 1978 ITV programmes were being used in 250,000 teaching sessions per week (Potter, 1990, p. 253). On ITV each company took on responsibility for different areas of the curriculum and service-wide broadcasts ceased advertising during the mid-morning 'schools' slot in the schedule. Later, in the 1970s, ITV branched out into areas of adult education, targeting adult viewers outside of recognised educational programmes (like the Open University, which was serviced by the BBC), offering programmes such as the highly popular *Yoga for Health* (Thames, 1970–1) and *Play Guitar* (Yorkshire, 1975–6).

The greatest impact on ITV's first decade of programming came in the form of the Pilkington Report into British broadcasting (June 1962), as it was extremely critical of commercial television, proposing that ITV completely rethink its public service ethos. While the findings of the report can be contested (particularly in its inclination to equate 'popularity' with 'badness', its refusal to judge commercial television on anything other than Reithian standards of public service broadcasting, and its attention to the complaints made against ITV instead of its many commendations), the contractors did take heed and began to focus on producing serious, 'prestige' programming; as Denis Forman, a key member of the Granada team in the 1960s remembers, ' "Brownie points" became

as important as ratings' (1997, p. 265). The Television Act of 1964 allowed the ITA to mandate 'serious' programmes, and by the late 1960s, all contractors had to carry *News at Ten*, one weekday and one weekend play, and two weekly current affairs programmes (Curran and Seaton [1991] claim that there was a 10 per cent increase in 'serious' ITV programming between 1959 and 1965). In short, the entertainment culture on ITV of the 1950s and early 1960s gave way to a journalistic culture in the later 1960s and 1970s.

The 1960s and 70s can also be seen as an era on ITV in which programme-makers began to respond more ingeniously to the requirements of the medium, particularly to the reception context of television and the need for more parochial or domestic forms of entertainment; ITV's commitment to the soap opera format might be seen as evidence of this response. With the introduction of *Coronation Street* (Granada) in 1960, which remains the most successful and long-running TV soap drama of all time, the company acknowledged the nation's desire to become absorbed in narratives of everyday life within locally specific domestic milieus – a North-west industrial town in the case of *Coronation Street*, a Midlands motel in the low-budget *Crossroads* (ATV, 1964–88, Carlton, 2001–3) and a Yorkshire farming community in *Emmerdale Farm* (Yorkshire, 1972–). Also, during the 1960s and 70s, the theatrical extravagance of *Sunday Night at the London Palladium* and its ilk gave way to televisation of 'pub entertainment' such as *Stars and Garters* (A-R, 1963–6), *The Wheeltappers and Shunters Club* (Granada, 1974–6) and the domestic sitcom, with shows like *Bless This House* (Thames, 1971–6) and the racially offensive Johnny Speight series *Love Thy Neighbour* (Thames, 1972). However, contrary to these forms of 'home-centred' entertainment, ITV in the 1960s also continued to produce high quality, filmed fantasy drama (e.g. *The Avengers* [ABC 1961–9]; *The Prisoner* [Everyman/ATV, 1967–8]) and Gothic/supernatural anthology series (e.g. *Tales of Mystery* [A-R, 1961–3]; *Mystery and Imagination* [ABC, 1966–8, Thames 1968–70]) which challenged the mainly realist aesthetic of television drama in favour of escapism, camp and formal experimentation.

In the 1970s, the deregulation of television schedules in January 1972 meant an increase in advertising revenue for ITV, and consequently an increase in the production of commercial television, both with new soaps (*Emmerdale Farm, General Hospital* [ATV, 1972–9]), and more current affairs/documentaries filling in the gaps in the schedule. While the decade saw the decline of the single play on ITV (112 were screened in 1969–70, thir-

MYSTERY AND IMAGINATION (1966–70)

Mystery and Imagination was an anthology series of adaptations of classic Gothic novels, short stories and plays, produced by Jonathan Alwyn for ABC Television (1966–8), and later by Reginald Collin for Thames (1968–70). The series is a striking example of the way in which anthology drama on ITV, during a time of intense competition, produced innovative, experimental 'teleplays' which responded to the possibilities of television, showcased new production technologies, and challenged the predominance of naturalistic television drama in the 1960s (see Kennedy-Martin, 1964). Indeed, a document produced to accompany ABC's April 1967 franchise application laid our their commitment to the format as a source of challenging, quality entertainment, stating: 'ABC Television has always seen anthology drama as an opportunity for stretching the minds and feelings of peak viewing audiences beyond the narrow confines of variety acts and storytelling.' While some critical attention has been paid to the impact of ABC's *Armchair Theatre* anthology drama series on the development of the dramatic form on television, focusing particularly on the figure of Canadian producer Sydney Newman (see Caughie, 2000; Crisell, 1997), other popular, generically defined anthology series such as *Mystery and Imagination* have received little consideration. This oversight is partly due to the privileging of progressive, social-realist drama within the histories of television drama (as a Gothic anthology series dealing with tales of the supernatural and the monstrous, *Mystery and Imagination* lay firmly outside the realist/naturalist paradigm), as well as the more practical difficulties of piecing together other examples of 'early' ITV drama series from haphazardly preserved materials archived by a widespread variety of organisations and companies.

Throughout its five-season run, the individual teleplays of *Mystery and Imagination* shifted between two distinct modes of Gothic representation: the suggestive, restrained ambiguity of the supernatural ghost story, owing much to an earlier broadcast version of the genre (the BBC radio play) in its elaborate sound design (e.g. 'The Open Door' [19 February 1966], d. Joan Kemp-Welch, w. Margaret Oliphant/George F. Kerr) and the excessive, spectacular Gothic drama, having more in common with theatrical and cinematic presentations of the Gothic, but ultimately developing what can be seen as a 'televisual' version of the genre (e.g. 'Dracula', [18 November 1968], d. Patrick Dromgoole, w. Bram Stoker/Charles Graham).

Dromgoole's adaptation is particularly notable for a final sequence in which Dracula (played by Denholm Elliott) is defeated by Van Helsing (Bernard Archard), in a moment described by Peter Haining as 'unlike anything ever seen on television before' (1993, p. 292). During this sequence (shot on videotape, as with other *Mystery and Imagination* episodes), the image is dramatically switched to negative and then a series of close-ups of Dracula's rapidly decomposing body are dissolved together, offering an early version of a 'morphing' technique, until only a pile of dust remains. This moment and others from the series (such as the image of two Ian Holms facing one another, playing the eponymous hero and the monster in 'Frankenstein' [11 November 1968]), offer an accentuated performance of non-naturalistic television drama style, and thus delineate the sense of innovation and *display* which characterised *Mystery and Imagination* (see Wheatley, 2002, for a further discussion of this series).

Helen Wheatley

teen in the 1979–80 season), serial drama became increasingly prevalent and accomplished, with a surge of period drama and adaptations, including *A Family at War* (Granada, 1970–2), *South Riding* (Yorkshire, 1974) and *Edward and Mrs Simpson* (Thames, 1978). These serials can in turn be seen as precursors to the highly exportable 'heritage' television of the 1980s (*Brideshead Revisited* [Granada, 1981] and *Jewel in the Crown* [Granada, 1984]), which exploited the values of 'quality' television (see Brunsdon, 1990), to make them the commercial successes of the decade.

ITV in the 1980s continued to respond to an increase in broadcasting hours and the pressure of competition from the new cable and satellite broadcasters in the UK, buying in soaps from Australia to fill the afternoon schedules such as *Sons and Daughters* (Grundy, 1983–90) and *Home and Away* (Seven Network Australia, 1989–2000), and placing its newest television genre, the audience-based discussion show, in both the mid-morning slot freed by educational broadcasting's move to Channel Four, and in the increased late-night broadcasting slot. This genre is represented by such programmes as *The Time, The Place* (Thames, Anglia, 1987–98) during the day and, in the late-night slot, *Central Weekend* (Central, 1986–). The 1980s also saw the beginning of breakfast television with TV-am's *Good Morning Britain*, which was fronted by David Frost, Michael Parkinson, Robert Kee, Angela Rippon and Anna Ford, and conceived as a more serious, news-led show than the BBC's *Breakfast Time*, launched two weeks earlier in January 1983. However, the programme soon produced disappointing ratings, and was 'rescued' by Australian Kerry Packer, new presenters

(Anne Diamond and Nick Owen) and a 'lighter', more bland presentational style. In fact, the failure of *Good Morning Britain* in the mid-1980s might be seen as indicative of the general misconceptions surrounding ITV programming; while the public, press and regulators expected populist, hackneyed output from the network, a sizeable proportion of what the ITV companies actually produced was challenging and innovative.

Helen Wheatley

RECOMMENDED READING

Haining, Peter (1993), *The Television Late Night Horror Omnibus*, London: Orion.

Potter, Jeremy (1989), *Independent Television in Britain, Volume Three: Politics and Control, 1968–80*, London and Basingstoke: Macmillan.

Potter, Jeremy (1990), *Independent Television in Britain, Volume Four: Companies and Programmes, 1968–80*, London and Basingstoke: Macmillan.

Sendall, Bernard (1982), *Independent Television in Britain, Volume One: Origin and Foundation, 1946–62*, London and Basingstoke: Macmillan.

Sendall, Bernard (1983), *Independent Television in Britain, Volume Two: Expansion and Change, 1958–68*, London and Basingstoke: Macmillan.

Vahimagi, Tise (1996), *British Television*, 2nd edition, Oxford: Oxford University Press

The 'Youth Revolution' and American Television

'The Vast Wasteland.' This phrase, coined by early 1960s FCC Chairman Newton Minow, remains the dominant characterisation of American network programming in the 1960s and 70s. While racial and generational turmoil profoundly challenged the body politic, and movements for social change destabilised the post-war social consensus, TV viewers were treated to a bizarre fantasy world of flying nuns, suburban housewife witches, millionaire Okies in Beverly Hills, talking horses named Ed, bumbling espionage agents talking into their shoes, and other such inanities. Broadcast historian James Baughman argues that 1960s' programming 'meant offering evenings of avoidance' (Baughman, 1985, p. 92).

To an extent this is true. By the early 1960s, the three-network structure was in place. All three targeted middle-class, family audiences. Coming of age in a conformist 1950s of red scares and witch-hunts, CBS, NBC and ABC were generally loath to deal with socially and politically controversial material in entertainment programming. They also viewed the audiences they delivered up to advertisers as an undifferentiated bulk rather than as distinct demographic units. Programming was meant to appeal to mom, pop, the kids, the teens and young adults all more or less equally.

A problem began to develop in the mid-1960s, however. First wave Baby Boomers – young people who had literally grown up with television as the first 'television generation'– were entering their late teens and apparently abandoning the medium. Beginning in 1966 and 1967, all three networks began worrying about the drop-off in young adult and juvenile viewership. CBS in particular worried about its position as video's 'maiden aunt' (Pitman, 1967, p. 25). Increasingly the networks announced their desire to attract a 'youth' audience. However, 'youth' was an amorphous and rather broadly defined category for network executives, advertisers and the Nielsen ratings' people. In the TV-audience business a youth audience comprised the demographic range of eighteen to forty-nine. This rather generous definition of youth hampered the networks in targeting Baby Boomers because they were working with a demographic that, as the 1960s wore on, included two generations whose interests, tastes and ways of interpreting social reality were radically different. The eighteen-to-forty-nine demographic managed to encompass the so-called 'generation gap' of rebellious Boomer youth and their more conservative parents. *TV Guide*, early in 1967, noted, 'the paradox of the networks' consuming passion for attracting young adult viewers is that the TV-ratings race continues to be paced by middle-aged-to-elderly stars' (Doan, 1967, p. 12). Among the networks' biggest stars in this period – all in their fifties and sixties – were Lawrence Welk, Ed Sullivan, Bob Hope, Red Skelton, Jackie Gleason, Lucille Ball, Eddie Albert, Buddy Ebsen and Lorne Greene.

The networks initially attempted to capitalise on elements of the growing youth culture with *Shindig* (ABC, 1964–6) and *Hullabaloo* (NBC, 1965–6), both musical variety shows that showcased current chart-topping recording artists. Both shows provided a very scrubbed down, non-threatening version of youth culture with, in the case of *Hullabaloo*, go-go dancers frugging to musical arrangements that would not have been out of place on the more geriatric *Lawrence Welk Show* (ABC, 1955–71). The show also featured middle-of-the-road and middle-aged guest hosts such as Sammy Davis Jr and Jerry Lewis. Presumably the networks' strategy was to lure the young with pop-rock acts like the Lovin' Spoonful, Sonny and Cher, the

Musical variety and chart-topping artists: *Hullabaloo* (1965–6)

Supremes and occasionally even megastars such as the Rolling Stones and the Beatles while keeping the show's overall environment vapidly unthreatening so as not to discomfort the grownups. *Variety* noted the dilemma that networks encountered when they attempted to entice young viewers: they 'sometimes looked as ridiculous as a matron in a miniskirt and love beads' (Brown, 1969, p. 21).

ABC tried a different strategy to lure young viewers with *The Monkees* (ABC, 1966–8), which featured four wacky, long-haired musicians. The show drew inspiration from the Beatles' films *A Hard Day's Night* and *Help*. Like those films, *The Monkees* was not overly concerned with narrative continuity or logic, relying on frequent blackout sketches and musical numbers. The show's use of a prefabricated musical group put together by a casting call in *Variety* generated some controversy among young people, especially as the actors hired to portray the Monkees increasingly sought legitimation by their generational cohort. While the show may have had authenticity problems with its target audience that increasingly expected its rock troubadours to voice the concerns of the generation, older audiences had problems with the visual style of the show and the proliferation of hippie signifiers like long hair. Some network affiliates so disliked the show and its stars that they refused to broadcast it. A number of production professionals also disliked the show's countercultural 'let it all hang out' style. One director hired to work on the show grumbled, 'If you don't care about your focus or your lighting, and if you're going to let four idiots ad-lib your dialogue, you don't need a director' (Raddatz, 1967, p. 19). The show proved wildly successful, nevertheless, with teens and pre-teens. It provided a showcase for the initially pre-packaged records the band produced, which quickly became chart-toppers. As the series moved into its second (and last) year on ABC's schedule, the Monkees attempted to wrestle themselves away from their bubblegum image and display more signifiers of 'hipness'. They actively pointed out their constructedness, invited counter-culture figures like Frank Zappa and Tim Buckley onto the show, took more control over their music and, in general, tried to show that they were not complicit with a commodity system that had, in fact, created them. Oddly, considering its success, the show did not become a model for youth-oriented programming as the decade went on.

By the mid-1960s, American network television was only one of a range of media institutions attempting to woo young people. The Hollywood film industry, the recording industry, even the advertising industry, increasingly targeted Baby Boomers as highly coveted potential consumers. This attempt to cater to youth was, however, a tricky problem in the 1960s and 70s because the most visible, articulate, photogenic and exciting segment of the youth demographic was increasingly at odds with all the values, mores and institutions of the American social and political order. While the majority of Baby Boomers did not drop out and join the counter-culture or engage in New Left campus activism, it was these youth rebels who typically stood in for the entire generation in media discourse, and it was the youth dissidents that the media industries found themselves enamoured of. Even advertising agencies – next to network television the most establishmentarian of culture industries – tried to embrace the sentiments of the counter-culture (Frank, 1997). Prime-time television found itself performing, at times, a treacherous ideological balancing act as the decade progressed and youth rebellion intensified. How would prime time take note of and package the highly dramatic, colourful, sexy, vibrant and politicised youth culture without subverting traditional middle-class, capitalist, post-war norms? As it turned out, in order to even begin courting the young, television programmes increasingly began tilting more towards the values, political critiques and lifestyles of the rebellious young in the medium's ideological balancing act.

Three shows, *The Smothers Brothers Comedy Hour* (CBS, 1967–9), *The Mod Squad* (ABC, 1968–73) and *Rowan and Martin's Laugh-in* (NBC, 1968–73) are the most notable examples of how American prime time attempted to grapple with the youth revolution. The Smothers Brothers' comedy-variety series (see grey box) proved the most successful at luring Baby Boomer audiences, but also proved the most controversial and contentious for the network. With their anti-war, pro-counter-culture allegiances increasingly clear, the Smothers Brothers battled with network censors and executives over political content in sketches, over the kinds of songs guests affiliated with the anti-war movement could perform, and over questions of 'taste'. The heavy-handed censorship the show endured legitimated it to many of the era's dissenting youth but also ensured its demise by industry forces still intent on appealing to a broader audience.

Another variety series, *Laugh-in*, provided a more successful model for bringing youth movement values and style to prime time without unduly ruffling establishment feathers. The NBC series was indebted to *The Smothers Brothers Comedy Hour* for bringing politically and socially oriented humour to the medium, but diverged from the Smothers' series by proving more adept at playing the ideological and generational balancing act. *Laugh-in*'s hosts were two middle-aged, tuxedoed, Las Vegas-style lounge performers who, unlike the Smothers Brothers, could never be mistaken for youth movement fellow travellers. While Rowan and Martin as stars may have been the picture of middle-of-the-road establishmentarianism, the visual style of *Laugh-in* partook far more of the counter-culture than the Smothers' show ever did. The show abounded in hallucinogenic flashes, zooms, quick cuts, a barrage of psychedelic colours, along with volleys of one-liners that mined the same anti-establishment terrain as the Smothers Brothers' show. But the rapid-fire delivery of anti-war/pro-drug lines (or their presentation scrawled on the body of gyrating, bikini-clad Goldie Hawn) tended to blunt the political implications of the humour. By the time the viewer 'got' the message behind the joke, a number of non-political jokes or blackouts had already whizzed by. *Laugh-in* quickly became the top-rated show in the country by providing popular relevancy, an acknowledgment of youth movement style *and* politics, but also familiar vaudeville hijinks, and grownup hosts to keep the counter-culture material within safe bounds.

Aaron Spelling's police drama, *The Mod Squad*, was another attempt to balance conflicting youth and adult tastes, politics and worldviews. However, in its ideological balancing act, the Spelling production typically tilted notably towards disaffected youth. The show's premise was both ludicrous and brilliant in appealing to the needs of the two generations. Three disaffected youths with links to various elements of the youth movement were recruited into the Los Angeles Police Department as unarmed undercover cops. Linc, Pete and Julie ('one black, one white, one blonde') were never entirely comfortable with their status as police officers. They typically went after villainous adults preying on vulnerable young people. The trio seemed to be constantly reasserting their allegiance to the rebellious youth. When their boss, Captain Greer, encourages them to infiltrate a youth movement paper whose offices have been bombed, Pete angrily responds, 'We don't like the idea of spying on an underground newspaper!' Greer, the benevolent adult who shares their politics, assures the Squad that they can help the paper by infiltrating. When a radical black priest discovers that the Mod Squad was assigned to protect him from an assassination attempt, Julie and Linc are quick to point out that they don't consider him an assignment: 'We've been around because we wanted to': meaning they support his Black Power politics. Because the trio are police officers and therefore work within the institution of law and order, the image of hippie cops could potentially prove comforting to adults. Moral panics about out-of-control youths

rioting in the streets could be allayed by the comforting image of rebellious youth incorporated by the most establishmentarian of dominant institutions.

In 1969 and 1970, when all three networks were casting about for programming models to help them revamp their programming, *The Mod Squad* served as the prototype. The show's balancing act of advocating the politics and perspectives of dissident young people and wrapping it all within the comforting confines of traditional institutions run by benevolent grown-ups would be reworked all over the TV dial in 1970 and 1971. *The Smothers Brothers Comedy Hour* may have been more successful in actually appealing to politicised and counter-culture youth (if commentary in the underground press is any guide), however, *The Mod Squad* was more polysemic (open to a range of possible readings by different audiences). The Smothers' show tended to shut out perspectives and audiences that did not side with its increasingly politicised viewpoints. *The Mod Squad* advocated much the same structure of generational feeling, yet suffered no censorship or network battles. The show provides an example of how American television could incorporate bits and pieces of an oppositional movement and make it broadly palatable.

The 1970–1 so-called 'season of social relevance' brought the youth revolution to prime time in unprecedented strength. The 'hayseed' shows and fantastical sitcoms so popular earlier in the previous decade would all be gone by 1972. However the networks' experimentation with *Mod Squad*-style social relevance was not a big success. A slew of shows placing disaffected young people in traditional institutions, such as *Storefront Lawyers* (CBS, 1970–1) and *The Young Lawyers* (ABC, 1970–1) about idealistic young members of the bar, *The Interns* (CBS, 1970–1) about idealistic young doctors and *The Young Rebels* (ABC, 1970–1) about idealistic, long-haired patriots fighting America's War of Independence were all Nielsen duds. Established network programmes like *Ironside* (NBC, 1967–75) with familiar characters, however, also embraced youth-relevance themes and did quite well in the ratings game. The networks' attempts to lure youth audiences and negotiate youth politics and values would only begin to succeed when programmers turned from drama to comedy. As CBS's great triumvirate of early 1970s' comedies, *All in the Family* (CBS, 1971–9), *The Mary Tyler Moore Show* (CBS, 1970–7), and *M*A*S*H* (CBS, 1972–83) would prove, youth-targeted, socially conscious television flourished when served up with generous helpings of laughter.

In 1970, jazz musician Gil Scott-Heron declared in a musical piece, 'The revolution will not be televised'. In the

THE SMOTHERS BROTHERS COMEDY HOUR (CBS, 1967–9)

When the Smothers Brothers, a folk-singing, comedy duo, joined CBS's prime-time line-up in 1967, *Time* magazine described them as 'hippies with haircuts'. The show was designed to appeal to 1960s youth sensibilities, but was expected to embrace CBS's traditional family audience as well. Initially the variety show seemed to do just that with middle-of-the-road guest performers like George Burns and Carol Burnett, along with counter-culture acts like Buffalo Springfield. Sketches featured mildly political humour, but mostly celebrated consensus over confrontation.

Things changed quickly and *The Smothers Brothers Comedy Hour* has gone down in television studies as one of the most controversial programmes in American broadcast history. It endured heavy-handed network censorship, struggles over political speech in an entertainment environment, questions of acceptance during a period when taste distinctions were rapidly changing, and battles over what role television entertainment could adopt in commenting on contentious current events.

The Smothers Brothers (especially Tom, 'the dumb one') were very sympathetic to the anti-war and pro-counter-culture youth movement. When their show firmly established itself as a Nielsen success in its first year on the air, the brothers and their team of young writers increasingly began pushing the envelope of acceptable variety show material. In their second season premiere on 10 September 1967 they invited legendary folk singer Pete Seeger to perform. Seeger's scheduled rendition of 'Waist Deep in the Big Muddy', an obvious allusion to President Johnson's Vietnam War policy, raised network hackles. Network censors were particularly concerned with the lyric: 'Now every time I read the papers/That old feelin' comes on/We're waist deep in the Big Muddy/And the big fool says to push on.' CBS censored Seeger's appearance. Public outcry eventually forced the network to relent and Seeger appeared singing the anti-war song later in the season. But the battle lines between the network and the Smothers were now drawn.

In order to appeal to counter-culture youth, the show featured a recurring hippie character named Goldie Keefe (both first and last name were current slang for marijuana) who extolled the merits of mind-expanding substances. But because her comedy was so heavily coded, censors had a difficult time policing her material. Comedian David Steinberg was less lucky. His regular 'sermonettes' were often deemed in poor taste and likely to offend the religiously minded. Sketches about the very subject of censorship were also often censored.

Material that commented on the contemporary youth movement came in for the most struggle. Harry Belafonte's 'Don't Stop the Carnival' number, which commented on the recent riots at the Chicago Democratic Convention, was summarily cut. Anti-war folk singer Joan Baez had her comments about her husband, a draft resistance leader, snipped.

The show's censorship woes increased its legitimacy among counter-culture and radical youth even as it lost appeal with more mainstream viewers. Conservative CBS affiliates complained about the show and threatened to pull it. Some viewers argued that the Smothers were nothing but propagandists for the anti-war movement, and the show's ratings plunged.

Finally, in April 1969, CBS threw the show off the air before its season was over. The network argued that the Smothers Brothers had not delivered a preview tape in time for review by network censors. This may well have been the case, but, in fact, *The Smothers Brothers Comedy Hour* was just too hot for prime time, polarising audiences rather than bringing them together. The show played out on television the same generational tensions, political and cultural turmoil, and crisis of authority that also raged in the body politic that characterised the United States in the 1960s.

Aniko Bodroghkozy

The Smothers Brothers Comedy Hour: TV counter-culture?

late 1960s and early 1970s, prime time may not have been awash in revolution, but it was not showcasing the status quo either. The networks found themselves compelled to disseminate often sympathetic representations of anti-war and counter-culture positions because of the industry's need to woo the huge numbers of American youth to its products. Television thus found itself actively participating in the social transformations of this explosive decade.

Aniko Bodroghkozy

RECOMMENDED READING

Bodroghkozy, Aniko (2001), *Groove Tube: Sixties Television and the Youth Rebellion*, Durham, and London: Duke University Press.

Carr, Steven Alan (1992), 'On the Edge of Tastelessness: CBS, the Smothers Brothers, and the Struggle for Control', *Cinema Journal*, vol. 31, no. 4.

Gitlin, Todd (1983), 'The Turn to "Relevance" ', in *Inside Prime Time*, New York: Pantheon.

Spector, Bert (1983), 'A Clash of Cultures: The Smothers Brothers vs. CBS Television', in John E. O'Connor, (ed.) *American History/American Television*, New York: Frederick Ungar.

Spigel, Lynn and Curtin, Michael (eds) (1997), *The Revolution Wasn't Televised: Sixties Television and Social Conflict*, New York: Routledge.

The BBC Adapts to Competition

For a brief period, 1926–54, the BBC had no domestic competition in its sound, or from 1946, in its TV services. For rest of its history the BBC has had to adapt to increasing competition, first from commercial TV, or ITV (1955), and subsequently from illegal pirate radio (1964), legal commercial radio, or ILR (1973), and, in the 1980s and 90s, to commercial cable, satellite and digital TV and radio services. This pattern of competition was conducted within a shifting political and economic framework, which influenced the pace and nature of change. This contribution outlines some of the key changes in the period after 1954, surveys shifts in programming from the 1950s to the 90s, and examines the BBC's position in the competitive environment in the 1990s.

The BBC's purpose since the 1920s was to provide a public service in broadcasting, based on licence fee funding. Under its first Chief Executive and Director-General, John Reith (1922–38), it pursued a policy of mixed programming in its radio services, designed to entertain but also to elevate the tastes of the population. The BBC was very successful, but its mixed programming service met with competition from continental commercial stations, which transmitted music and advertisements to the UK in the 1930s. This, combined with the need to provide morale boosting services in World War II (1939–45) led to the introduction of more streamed radio (three separate and differentiated services) by the end of the 1940s. So, by the time the first ITV station came on stream in September 1955 the BBC had experienced competition. Indeed, as Briggs has shown, the corporation had been preparing for competition in advance of the 1954 Television Act, which authorised a series of regional TV companies, privately owned and funded by 'spot' advertisements, between, and during breaks in, programmes (Briggs, 1979, pp. 937–97). The 1954 Act , by giving ITV companies a separate source of income and requiring that the companies provide a service modelled on BBC standards, in effect established the economic and regulatory context for UK TV until the passage of the 1990 Broadcasting Act.

In an attempt to generate advertising revenue, ITV pursued a strategy of scheduling light entertainment, comedy and game shows. In the third quarter of 1957, according to the BBC's calculations, ITV achieved a 72 per cent share of the viewing public where there was a choice (Briggs, 1995, p. 20). While ITV was winning audiences, by scheduling, in 1957, ten give-away shows in one week (Crisell, 1997, p. 103), its populism was losing the battle with opinion formers. The BBC fought back, developing the populist news magazine programme *Tonight* (1957), drama, like the detective series *Maigret* (1960), and popular music shows like *Juke Box Jury* (1956) and *Six-Five Special* (1956). It also responded to ITV's innovations in news coverage by introducing newscasters.

The aggressive Director-General Hugh Carleton Greene (1960–9) thought the BBC should set itself the target of winning 50 per cent of audience share. He also set out to win government approval for a second channel. Greene prepared the BBC meticulously for the government-appointed Committee on Broadcasting, known after its chair as the Pilkington Committee, which sat from 1960–2. When Pilkington reported in 1962 it was very critical of ITV's populism. Consequently the government awarded a second TV channel to the BBC. BBC2 went on air in 1964. The 1964 Television Act allowed the Independent Television Authority to force ITV companies to transmit serious drama, news and current affairs at peak times. Thus Pilkington had the effect of strengthening the public service element in UK television (Crisell, 1997, p. 112; Curran and Seaton, 1997, p. 195).

The 1960s and 70s was a period in which the BBC and ITV settled into stable competition for audiences but not for revenues. In the 1960s there occurred a creative surge in BBC programme-making, echoing the general liberalis-ation of cultural values in society which developed in those years. The gritty, realist *Z Cars* (1962–78) set new standards for TV cop shows. By 1963 *Z Cars* had audiences of 16.5 million. The *Wednesday Play* strand produced innovative and socially challenging drama, such as *Cathy Come Home* (1966). News and current affairs flourished with peak-time programmes like *Panorama* (1957–). TV satire developed rapidly under the influence of *That Was the Week That Was* (1962–3). It was also a period of challenging comedy, prob-ing generational, *Steptoe and Son* (1962–74), and social issues *Till Death Us Do Part* (1966–74).

During the 1970s there developed a growing body of criticism from broadcasters, the public, trade unionists and academics about the degree to which broadcasting was accountable and represented social diversity in its output. (Briggs, 1995, pp. 993–1004). Simultaneously broadcasters faced problems posed by a period of military conflict in Ireland, exemplified by government criticism of the BBC's *The Question of Ulster* (1972) (Crisell, 1997, p. 184). In addition. this was a period of intense industrial conflict and led to academic criticism of the way the BBC and ITV covered these topics (Beharrell and Philo, 1978).

During the 1970s and 80s the duopoly of the BBC and ITV remained intact. The BBC produced high-quality comedy, *Yes Minister* (1979–82), drama *I, Claudius* (1976) and dramatic serials like the brilliant *Pennies from Heaven* (1978). Its output in peak time included top-rating comedy and light entertainment shows featuring comedians like Morecambe and Wise and Bruce Forsyth. The BBC made a major effort to build audience in the mid-1980s, having been criticised heavily for what emerged as a temporary failure to match ITV. It produced a new soap, *EastEnders* (1985–) and had successes with imports like the US-produced *Dynasty* (1981–9).

In retrospect, viewing share remained fairly constant, with regular, but not dramatic variations. In 1973–4 BBC1 took 43 per cent of audiences, with ITV 49 per cent (Briggs, 1995, p. 960). The arrival of Channel Four in 1982 altered the balance a little, such that in 1987 shares were BBC1, 38 per cent; BBC2, 12 per cent ; ITV, 42 per cent; and Channel Four, 8 per cent. A period of rapid policy development in the 1980s resulted in two major pieces of legislation. The 1990 and the 1996 Broadcasting Acts introduced competi-tion into the commercial sector. From the late 1980s

Yes Minister: serious comedy from the BBC

onwards cable and satellite services and, after 1996, digital TV, dramatically altered the balance of audience share. By 2000 the shares were, BBC1, 27.2 per cent; BBC 2, 10.8 per cent; ITV 29.3 per cent; Channel Four, 10.5 per cent; Channel 5, 5.7 per cent; and cable and satellite 16.6 per cent. Cable and satellite's share had risen from just 4 per cent in 1991, signalling the rapid change in the competitive environment faced by the BBC. (Total of 100.1 per cent for 2000 as given in BARB, 2002a.)

New communications technologies were introduced in a manner which directly challenged the idea that public service broadcasting should be the principle governing broadcasting (O'Malley, 2001a). The Conservative govern-ments of Margaret Thatcher (1979–90) devised policies that called into question the continuance of the BBC. Cable and satellite technologies were introduced as com-mercial competitors with, compared to the BBC and ITV, very few expensive public service programming obli-gations. The government signalled its disapproval of the ethos of public service television by attacking the BBC throughout the 1980s, banning the *Real Lives* (1985) pro-gramme on Ireland, and fostering a climate which led to the withdrawal of a programme on the spy satellite *Zircon* in 1987 (see grey box). Thatcher established the Peacock Committee (1985–6), which judged that, while the BBC should remain licence fee-funded, broadcasting should

ZIRCON

In the 1960s and 70s investigative journalism was well developed in the press and TV. In particular a combination of the cultural and political activism of the 1960s and 70s and the commitment of the BBC and ITV to peak-time current affairs programmes (*Panorama*, *World in Action*) helped foster a widespread perception of 'investigatory journalism as a public interest' (Doig, 1997, p. 194).

During the 1980s, in senior circles in the ruling Conservative Party there existed a view that public service broadcasting, and the BBC in particular, produced anti-Conservative programmes. The government attacked the BBC over its coverage of Ireland, banning the 1985 *Real Lives* programme. It also vigorously assaulted the corporation over its coverage of the UK-backed US bombing raids on Libya in 1986 (O'Malley, 1994).

In March 1986 the respected investigative journalist, Duncan Campbell, was commissioned by BBC Scotland to do a series of six programmes on official secrecy under the title of *The Secret Society*. One of these was on the Zircon spy satellite, a device intended for spying on the Soviet Union. The existence of the satellite had never been officially confirmed. Campbell's work showed that the £500 million projected expenditure had not been approved by the Public Accounts Committee of Parliament, as it should have been under an agreement with the government. In November 1986, Alan Protheroe, the deputy Director-General, viewed all six programmes. As a result of contacts with the Ministry of Defence, Protheroe advised and the Director-General Alasdair Milne agreed, in January 1987, that the programme should not be shown.

Campbell then wrote an account of the programme, which was published in the *New Statesman,* an article that the government tried, unsuccessfully, to ban. A leaked copy of the programme was shown to MPs. Over the next couple of weekends the Special Branch of the police raided Campbell's flat and BBC Scotland, looking for evidence that there had been a breach of official secrecy. The conflict between Milne and the Board of Governors, which had a strong Conservative bias and which had been at odds with him over, among other things, BBC political coverage, was exacerbated by the incident. At this point, coincidentally, Milne was forced to resign as Director-General. the programme was finally shown in September 1988 (Leapman, 1987, pp. 346–50; Milne, 1988, pp. 259–66; O'Malley, 1994, pp. 62–4, 140, 152–6; Barnett and Curry, 1994, pp. 42–4, 266).

The period after 1987 saw the emergence of a politically chastened BBC, where management led by Hussey, determined to avoid clashes with the government, tightened internal controls over news and current affairs production (Barnett and Curry, 1994, pp. 73–95). The commercial forces unleashed by the 1990 and 1996 Broadcasting Acts created a situation by the late 1990s where, in the increasing drive to achieve audience share, current affairs programming was more and more concerned with 'domestic, consumer and ratings-friendly subjects' and less with 'complex political and economic issues' (Barnett and Seymour, 1999, p. 5). These two forces, political pressure combined with a new commercial climate, helped to undermine peak-time current affairs, and signalled to broadcasters that the space for the kind of critical investigative reporting characterised by the *Zircon* programme was less and less available on UK terrestrial TV. In that sense, the controversy over the *Zircon* programme can now be seen as a major staging post in what has been described as more general decline in investigatory reporting in UK journalism in the late twentieth century (Doig, 1997).

Tom O'Malley

move towards a more market-driven system (O'Malley, 1994; Goodwin, 1998).

The effect of these changes was to increase competition, and to force the BBC to adapt. In 1987 Thatcher appointed as BBC chair an ex-employee of the media owner Rupert Murdoch, Marmaduke Hussey. Hussey led the BBC in the 1990s, most of the time with the director-general, John Birt. Between 1986 and 1990 the BBC shed 7,000 jobs. It began to take increasing proportions of its output from independent production companies and implemented an 'internal market' within the BBC. Birt embarked on a strategy of entering the new satellite, Internet and digital arenas, in a mix of licence fee and commercially financed deals

(Crisell, 1997, pp. 234–6). Birt, towards the end of his time as Director-General, in July 1999, looked to the future and envisaged the BBC, not as primarily a public service broadcaster, but as a 'publicly funded body with public purposes' (Birt, 1999).

In 1999–2000 the BBC was, in addition to its national and local radio services, offering the satellite channels BBC Choice, BBC News 24, BBC Knowledge (which became BBC4 in 2002) and BBC Parliament, as well as the BBC Online website. The vast bulk of BBC expenditure in 1999 went on terrestrial TV (62 per cent or £1,451 million out of £2,318 million). Throughout these years the BBC continued to produce high quality comedy programmes, drama, news and current affairs. By the late 1990s the BBC, like ITV , was broadcasting an increasing number of soaps in peak time in response to the competitive environment (BBC, 2000, pp. 6–7; Barnett and Seymour, 1999). It was able to compete well with ITV, so that in 2000 BBC1 and BBC2 had a combined share of 38 per cent compared to ITV's 39.8 per cent (BARB, 2002a).

The BBC adapted to the challenge of ITV in the 1950s by matching it in populist programming and by forcing its competitor, with the help of Pilkington, to up its standards. The period from the mid-1960s to the late 1980s can, in retrospect, be seen as a period of relative institutional creativity and stability. After Peacock (1986) the whole direction of UK broadcasting policy, in line with developments in Europe (Williams, 2001) shifted towards more market-driven services. The BBC underwent radical structural change in the 1990s, a change forced on it by government policy and technological change. It survived institutionally, but at the expense of its audience share and, as some have pointed out, at the expense of making peak-time schedules more populist (Barnett and Seymour, 1999). Throughout all of this the BBC remained a centre of programming excellence, but excellence achieved under increasingly competitive conditions. In short, institutionally the BBC changed in the period after 1954 in response to successive waves of competition and to the changing political, economic and technological landscape.

Tom O'Malley

RECOMMENDED READING

Briggs, Asa (1979), *The History of Broadcasting in the United Kingdom Volume IV: Sound and Vision 1945–1955*, Oxford: Oxford University Press.

Briggs, Asa (1995), *The History of Broadcasting in the United Kingdom Volume V: Competition 1955–1974*, Oxford: Oxford University Press.

Crisell, Andrew (1997), *An Introductory History of British Broadcasting*, London and New York: Routledge.

Curran, James and Seaton, Jean (1997), *Power Without Responsibility: The Press and Broadcasting in Britain*, 5th edition, London and New York: Routledge.

US Networks in the 1970s and 80s

Television programming in the US in the 1970s and 80s was marked by contradiction. During this period the medium produced some of the most highly touted, most socially insightful, most creatively innovative programming to date. At the same time, the industry called upon old stand-bys – the domestic sitcom, the episodic cop show, the easily exploitable thrills of sex and violence – to reach a mass audience long used to the formulaic nature of much commercial television fare. That mass audience remained the highly sought-after target of the 'big three' broadcast networks and their national advertisers; television was still a family medium and prime-time network programming was generally designed to please as many members of that family as possible. However, in keeping with the 1960s' industry's interest in a younger, more demographically specific group of viewers, the 1970s also saw a move towards more narrowly targeted broadcast programming, programming designed to appeal to urban, educated, upwardly mobile eighteen- to forty-nine-year-olds who had grown up with the medium and who were eager to see television that spoke more meaningfully to their own lives. In these waning years of the 'big three' broadcast networks' immense profitability and power, US commercial television programming began to fragment, splitting between social relevance and seeming irrelevance, narrowly targeted 'quality' and mass-marketed mediocrity.

The newest ideas in 1970s' television surfaced early on in the decade, when CBS, eager to improve the ratings at its urban owned and operated stations, overhauled its successful schedule. The network ended the runs of its 'rural' shows by 1971 (labelled as such both for their settings and for their primary audience), including *The Beverly Hillbillies* (CBS, 1962–71), *Green Acres* (CBS, 1965–71), *Petticoat Junction* (CBS, 1963–70), *The Jim Nabors Hour* (CBS, 1969–71) and *Hee Haw* (CBS, 1969–71; later syndicated). In their place, CBS gradually scheduled series designed to appeal to a younger, more affluent, educated and urban audience – the audience served by the owned and operated stations in such cities as New York, Los Angeles and Chicago (Gitlin, 1983, pp. 205–11). Seeking to avoid the content controversies they encountered with *The Smothers Brothers Comedy Hour* (CBS, 1967–9) one of CBS's late-1960s' attempts to appeal to the youth audience, CBS and the other networks initially sought to bring youthful rebellion and social relevance to television in hour-long dramatic series. The 1970–1 season was dubbed 'The Season of Relevance', as such new series as *Storefront Lawyers* (CBS, 1970–1), *The Interns* (CBS, 1970–1), and *Headmaster* (CBS, 1970–1) took up youth-related social issues in lawyer, doctor and high school settings and continuing series such as *The Bold Ones* (NBC, 1969–73), *Bracken's World* (NBC, 1969–70) and *The Mod Squad* (ABC, 1968–73) also attempted to speak to contemporary issues (Bodroghkozy, 2001, pp. 204–8). When many of these attempts failed, CBS quickly turned back to comedy as the more reliable way to reach young viewers. By the start of the 1972–3 season, the network had found three sitcom anchors that spoke to the changing social worlds of the young while not alienating older viewers or the institutions that supported them. *All in the Family* (CBS, 1971–9; a remake of the British series, *Till Death Us Do Part*), *The Mary Tyler Moore Show* (CBS, 1970–7) and *M*A*S*H* (CBS, 1972–83) each dealt with social change in its own way, but all three managed to use their comedic sensibilities to make both young and old, rebels and authority figures,

the objects of good-natured ribbing. *All in the Family*'s Archie was absurdly bigoted, but his liberal son-in-law, Mike 'Meathead' Stivic, was naively idealistic; *The Mary Tyler Moore Show*'s Mary Richards coped with the old-boy-network shenanigans of boss Lou Grant and pompous anchor Ted Baxter while bumbling through her own attempt at life as a single, working woman; and *M*A*S*H*'s unwilling draftee, Corporal Max Klinger, went to ridiculous lengths to be discharged from an army where the hilariously humourless Major Frank Burns wielded his ineffectual authority. These series dealt overtly with social issues of the day: race relations, women's roles, the generation gap, the war in Vietnam (very thinly disguised as the Korean War in *M*A*S*H*). They also featured characters with more depth and relationships with more complexity than had been seen in the sitcom genre before this time (with rare exceptions).

The success of CBS's new sitcoms encouraged the network to schedule spin-off series by the same producers and inspired the other networks to develop similar material. Thus, producer Norman Lear spun off *Maude*

All in the Family: dealing with social change

(CBS, 1972–8), about an outspoken, middle-aged liberal woman, and *The Jeffersons* (CBS, 1975–85), about an upwardly mobile black couple, from *All in the Family*, and *Good Times* (CBS, 1974–9), about a working-class black family trying to make ends meet, from *Maude*. *The Mary Tyler Moore Show*'s production company, MTM, created new series for Mary's friends Rhoda Morgenstern (*Rhoda*, CBS, 1974–8) and Phyllis Lindstrom (*Phyllis*, CBS, 1975–7), each of which depicted the humorous trials of women struggling to make it on their own. CBS's *One Day at a Time* (1975–84) also participated in television's new tales of independent women as its main characters, divorcée Ann Romano and teenage daughters Julie and Barbara, managed jobs, school and relationships in a father-less household. Other producers and other networks also programmed 'relevant' sitcoms that dealt with social change in a lighthearted way, featuring more diverse casts, more controversial subject matter and more young, urban appeal than television comedy had seen in the past. Thus, NBC purchased *Sanford and Son* (1972–7) from producers Norman Lear and Bud Yorkin. Another remake of a British programme (*Steptoe and Son*), *Sanford and Son* made the main characters black and addressed race-related issues on a regular basis. Also on NBC, *Chico and the Man* (1974–8) featured the relationship between young Chicano Chico Rodriguez and his elderly white boss, garage owner Ed Brown. In each of these instances, television audiences encountered an on-screen world with growing racial diversity, expanded roles for women and humorous references to real-world social issues. Relying upon a long-time medium staple – the situation comedy – and seeking increasingly specialised audiences, programme producers and network executives nudged television programming in new directions.

The changes encouraged by the relevant programming appearing on the 'big three' broadcast networks (and especially CBS) during this period were not uncontested. The medium's long-time tendency towards mass appeal and many national advertisers' ongoing interest in reaching the broadest possible audience sustained a programming style and scheduling philosophy that had well served the industry's commercial interests for years. This approach produced programming denigrated at the time and since, programming that drew upon genres such as the sitcom, the cop show and the variety show and audience draws such as sensationalised violence and sex. Led by ABC, the perennially third-place network that would make its mark by counter-programming the explicit social relevance of CBS, this competing approach further introduced contradiction into television programming of the period.

When executive Fred Silverman left CBS to lead ABC Entertainment in 1975 he brought to his new post a faith in the mass audience and their presumably mass taste. This faith led him to support the broadly targeted programming already on the ABC schedule and to cultivate more programming in that vein. While Silverman's reign at CBS had launched the socially relevant, more narrowly targeted sitcom trend, at ABC he sought to develop a comedy 'structure' of kid-friendly characters and jokes, a programming style akin to his efforts as Saturday-morning scheduler at CBS years earlier (Bedell, 1981, pp. 125–6). With his strategy of appealing to his mass audience's common denominator – they had all been kids at one time or another – Silverman made broad, simple comedy and comedy/action/fantasy hybrids the foundations of the ABC schedule. Among the Silverman-supported programming at ABC was producer Garry Marshall's *Happy Days* (1974–84), a family comedy set in Eisenhower-era Milwaukee and pairing all-American teenager Richie Cunningham with best pal Fonzie, a tough-guy greaser with a heart of gold and a magnetic ability to attract female attention. As was the case with the socially relevant sitcoms airing mostly on CBS, ABC took advantage of *Happy Days'* success and signed Marshall to produce spin-off series, first *Laverne and Shirley* (1976–83), about the antics of two 1950s' working-class women, then *Mork & Mindy* (1978–82), about a comedic alien from planet Ork, played by Robin Williams, and his friendship with down-to-earth Mindy McConnell.

Though Marshall's sitcoms had Silverman's valued 'kid' appeal, their humour oftentimes veered into a sexual suggestiveness that helped them attract a wider, more adult audience and that bridged these series with others on the ABC schedule. For example, from the 1977–8 season on, ABC's Tuesday-night line-up began with *Happy Days* and *Laverne and Shirley*, which were followed at 9pm with *Three's Company* (1977–84; a remake of Britain's *Man about the House*), a series founded upon the comic possibilities of the double entendre. Though it matched CBS's relevant series with its contemporary-issue premise – two women and a man platonically sharing an apartment – the programme's humour lay not in the social commentary of an *All in the Family*, nor in the character development of a *Mary Tyler Moore Show*, but in a barrage of physical slapstick, mistaken identity scenarios and ubiquitous sex jokes. The success of *Three's Company* encouraged ABC to develop the controversial daytime drama parody, *Soap*, which ran after *Three's Company* in its first season and depended upon a similar degree of sexual outrageousness.

CHARLIE'S ANGELS

ABC's rise to the number one position after years of third-place ratings was in many ways the major US television industry story of the 1970s. A key programme in helping the network achieve this success was *Charlie's Angels*, a formulaic action/detective series with the unique twist of three women in the lead roles. The glamorously coiffed and costumed Angels worked for the wealthy, mysterious Charlie – a man they never met – and took on a range of cases that required them to adopt undercover identities, identities that frequently necessitated skimpy attire and the application of feminine wiles. After its debut at the start of the 1976–7 television season, the programme quickly acquired a wide audience, regularly reaching 59 per cent of all the television sets in use during its time period. But the series was as controversial as it was popular. It became a target of groups seeking to curb television's perpetuation of sex, as well as drawing the ire of feminists and serving as a source of derision for many. The programme's producers, Aaron Spelling and Leonard Goldberg, openly, even proudly, admitted to the show's exploitative nature and eagerly generated publicity around the Angels' revealing wardrobe and their supposed backstage 'cat-fights'.

The programme's appeal to mass audiences cannot be divorced from these exploitative elements, yet the success of *Charlie's Angels* might be equally attributed to its engagement with issues of women's equality. On one level, the series argued for a liberal feminist, Equal Rights Amendment-style version of women's liberation. Its premise, that the three women have gone to work for the Charles Townsend detective agency because they were so unfulfilled in their exasperating police department jobs as paper-pushers and crossing guards, made the police department's discriminatory practices seem absurd and outdated. Yet, as many critics have pointed out, audiences learned the Angels' backstory through the introduc-

Charlie's Angels: exploitation *and* liberation?

tory credit sequence, narrated by Charlie, who patronisingly referred to them as 'little girls' and paternalistically explained that he 'took them away from all that'. These kinds of contradictions permeated the programme – the Angels transcended conventional gender roles by working in a typically male occupation but at the same time were represented as quintessentially and fundamentally female. Nearly every episode found the Angels taking on undercover guises that took the form of stereotypically feminine roles. Thus, in 'Lady Killer', Jill (Farrah Fawcett-Majors) went undercover as a waitress and centrefold for the *Feline* clubs and magazine. In 'Angel Flight', Kris (Cheryl Ladd) and Kelly (Jaclyn Smith) went undercover as stewardesses-in-training and in 'Pretty Angels All in a Row' they pretended to be beauty pageant contestants. The list is endless, as nearly every episode featured such disguises.

It was in the contradiction between the Angels' more conventionally masculine activities and their reliance upon their femininity that the series most powerfully spoke to the changing gender roles of the 1970s. Ultimately, the programme endorsed the notion of a fundamental difference between men and women. Even while they were 'women acting like men' in their work as detectives, the Angels succeeded in a male-dominated world because they knew how to use their inherent femaleness. This contradictory premise well suited the conflicted feelings of many in the 1970s when it came to men's and women's roles, helping to make the series immensely popular and to make ABC the industry's top-rated network.

Elana Levine

ABC's turn towards sexually suggestive humour in the late 1970s was certainly a strategy for counter-programming CBS's more social issue-oriented fare. Given the sexually tumultuous times within which these series appeared, however, the ABC programmes' reliance on sexual humour was not completely escapist. In fact, the changes in sexual identities and behaviour occasioned by the sexual revolution, the women's liberation movement and the gay rights movement were being regularly addressed – albeit with the giggles and leers of adolescence – on ABC's sexually suggestive comedies in ways they were not being tackled elsewhere in prime time. This preoccupation with sex was also prominent in one of the network's hit action-adventure series, *Charlie's Angels* (1976–81). The three female detectives in this top-rated programme were presented on-screen and off as sex symbols, and weekly episodes showcased their undercover activities in stereotypically feminine – and sexually objectifying – roles. However, ABC was not the only network to use sex appeal to temper the conventionally masculine, action-oriented lead roles being filled by women for the first time during this period. NBC aired *Police Woman* (1974–8), featuring the activities of Sergeant Pepper Anderson, as well as picking up the second season of *The Bionic Woman* (1977–8; the first season aired on ABC). And CBS acquired *The New Adventures of Wonder Woman* (1976–9) after its first season on ABC. Once *Charlie's Angels* and these other action series with women in lead roles proved successful, all three networks clamoured for such fare. The 1978–9 season saw several such imitators quickly fail.

While the sex on 1970s' US television was ultimately rather innocent – this being long before the days of nudity and explicit language in prime time – it generated some significant controversy, particularly from the perspective of organisations such as the National Parent-Teacher Association and the National Federation for Decency. Yet the uproar over television sex was far surpassed by that over television violence (and its links to sex), especially early on in the decade. Citizens' groups (such as the PTA), professional organisations (such as the American Medical Association) and government bodies (such as the US Congress), objected to the excessive amount of violence they were seeing in network television. All three networks were charged with such excesses, as action series such as ABC's *The Streets of San Francisco* (1972–7), *SWAT* (1975–6) and *Starsky and Hutch* (1975–9) were scheduled alongside such programmes as NBC's *Police Story* (1973–7) and *Serpico* (1976–7) and CBS's *Kojak* (1973–8). These episodic cop/detective/action shows attempted to draw the kinds of mass audiences the industry had long sought, though they did so with a heightened quantity of violence in an effort to differentiate 1970s' action series from earlier versions. Thus, despite CBS's move to draw a more narrowly targeted audience with social issue-oriented sitcoms and ABC's affiliations to 'kid appeal' and sex appeal, all three broadcast networks continued to use violent action to programme for a mass audience during the 1970s.

Throughout the 1970s and into the 80s, the 'big three' broadcast networks alternated between long-held strategies for mass-ratings success and newer ideas for attracting more demographically specific audience segments. As cable networks (such as HBO) established themselves, as communication satellites became available for industry use, and as VCR technology approached consumer accessibility, the US broadcast television industry and the programming it offered balanced somewhat precariously between the strongholds of the medium's past and the changes in its future. With programming both socially relevant and seemingly irrelevant, ABC, NBC and CBS delivered audiences both fragmented and mass to advertisers while delivering to those audiences on-screen worlds of sex and violence, drama and humour, reality and fantasy. For the very short time being, the 'big three' broadcast networks could still dominate the commercial television industry and could thus capture the nation's attention with their contradictory mix of programme styles and subjects.

Elana Levine

RECOMMENDED READING

Bedell, Sally (1981), *Up the Tube: Prime-Time TV and the Silverman Years*, New York: The Viking Press.

Bodroghkozy, Aniko (2001), *Groove Tube: Sixties Television and the Youth Rebellion*, Durham and London: Duke University Press.

Douglas, Susan J. (1994), *Where the Girls Are: Growing Up Female with the Mass Media*, New York: Times Books.

PROGRAMMING: NEW VENUES, NEW FORMS

Introduction

The 1980s and 90s ushered in a new era of television, marked by increased commercialisation and competition, new social and cultural norms, and by the globalisation of the media market. The revolution began early in Britain with the introduction of Channel Four, whose redefined hybrid public service/commercial mission produced unique programming and addressed hitherto ignored audiences. Series like *Asian Eye* and *Black on Black* reflected a change in the meaning of 'minority' in Britain, and an innovative film policy underwrote independent productions such as *My Beautiful Laundrette* and *Mona Lisa*, along with new and controversial drama, series, comedy, news, documentary and chat-shows, as well as imports of 'quality' American programmes. Its impact echoed in the US, in the major networks' response to cable and upstart Fox competition by producing a run of highly regarded drama series unsurpassed in US television history. With roots in the live anthology drama of the 1950s, sustained by innovative series such as *Hill Street Blues* in the 1980s, the 'quality drama' dominated schedules in the 1990s in the form of such programmes as *thirtysomething*, *ER*, *Homicide*, *Law & Order* and *China Beach*. Cable television came into its own during this period, producing critically acclaimed first-run programmes like *The Sopranos* and *Six Feet Under*.

Debates over 'quality' became a central feature of the 1990s as the enormous expansion of programme offerings on a plethora of channels called old standards and expectations into question. Anxieties over 'dumbing down' existed side by side with 'quality' discourses, as such programming trends as the perceived decline in serious factual, documentary and public affairs programmes met with the rise of reality shows and 'lifestyle' TV. The 'docusoap' and the makeover show proved highly popular with audiences, injecting a new kind of 'intimacy' and audience participation into network television, along with what some feared as a 'feminisation' of the television schedule in its shift in address from the 'citizen' to the 'consumer'. In the US, the introduction of the new networks Fox, WB and UPN, as well as the rise of original cable programming, challenged the comfortable practices of the former' 'big three' and led to a rise in shows that 'pushed the envelope' of television practice. Fox led the pack with a schedule that blatantly appealed to youth and minorities, with such controversial programmes as *Married . . . with Children*, *The Tracey Ullman Show* (1987) and *The Simpsons*; prime-time soaps like *Beverley Hills , 90210* and *Melrose Place*; so-called reality shows such as *Cops* (1989) and *America's Most Wanted* (1988–); and black-oriented comedies such as *In Living Color* (1990) and *The Sinbad Show* (1993–4).

As satellite and cable channels expanded in both countries, the expansion of specialised programming – films, news, sports – along with an address to niche audiences led to fears that national identities and cultures might be weakened by the new television's globalising influence. In Britain, this has led to a reassessment of what constitutes British television culture, calling into question previous ideas of quality and cultural cohesion. In particular, the dominance of US television in global markets has frequently met with fears of 'cultural imperialism' and 'wall-to-wall *Dallas*', even as audiences clamour for more and as local and national production often receives a stimulus from the introduction of competitive channels and forms. Meantime, the brisk international trade in television programmes and formats has made it increasingly difficult to specify the national or cultural origins of many televisual forms (or to enforce intellectual property rights), most notably the game show and reality genre, and has created new media giants like the UK-based Pearson Group and the Dutch firm Endemol Productions.

Michele Hilmes

Channel Four: Innovation in Form and Content?

Channel Four opened in November 1982 as a unique experiment in television's first era of scarcity before multi-channel and twenty-four-hour broadcasting had arrived in Europe. Broadcasting to England and Scotland (Wales would soon get its own channel), it was charged with providing programmes that were 'innovative in form and content' and distinctive from those offered by the other three channels, and was to find its income, eventually, from advertising. This programming brief, both ambitious and imprecise, has seen three successive phases of implementation, roughly coinciding with the terms of its first three chief executives.

Jeremy Isaacs' tenure from 1982–7 was one of defiance, fizz, bold innovations and heroic failures. It tapped the pent-up creativity of producers drawn from established broadcasters and radicals from the film industry and independent cinema. It also provided, under the banner of liberalism and innovation, a substantial platform for left-wing ideas that were being squeezed out of other media, especially the BBC, by the prevailing orthodoxies of Thatcherism.

It was adventurous enough of Isaacs to establish an hour-long evening news bulletin, supplied by the established agency Independent Television News, in the days before rolling news and CNN. But he went further, reducing the Friday bulletin to half an hour to fit in the subversive *Friday Alternative* (1982), a mixture of critiques of 'dominant' news coverage; campaigns (including one in favour of hanging); and exclusives like the pirated recording of Thatcher's press secretary Bernard Ingham crowing about the sinking of the battleship Belgrano. All of this was wrapped in an innovative use of computer graphics. Elsewhere, an adventurous cultural agenda offered series addressing British Asians (*Asian Eye,* 1993–) and Afro-Caribbeans (*Black on Black*, 1983–5); an unashamed high-cultural arts agenda including *Voices* (1982), a discussion series featuring Susan Sontag and John Berger; and the cinema series *Visions* (1982–5) offering profiles of avant-gardist Michael Snow, animator Jan Svankmajer and features on cinema in China and Africa. *Eleventh Hour* (1982) was a portmanteau slot (a device often used by Channel Four to corral the diverse single offerings of film-makers) offering radical voices from British and world independent cinema like *Handsworth Songs* (1986). Documentaries featured substantial coverage on environmental issues, a twelve-hour series *Vietnam* (a UK/US/France collaboration, 1983) and a serious science series *Equinox*.

An innovative film policy wholly or partially financed movies rather than TV drama, including Frears' *My Beautiful Laundrette* (1985), Greenaway's breakthrough *The Draughtsman's Contract* (1982) and early Neil Jordan films like *Mona Lisa* (1986). Drama series included G. F. Newman's grim indictment of medicine and the National Health Service, *The Nation's Health* (1983). Entertainment included traditional material like the chase/game show *Treasure Hunt* (1983–9) and the word game *Countdown* (1982–) which survived into the twenty-first century still with large audiences for its late afternoon slot. Shrewd buy-ins included the US sitcom *Cheers* (1982–93). Other entertainment was distinctly edgy, including the live *Whatever*

You Want (1982), which proved too routinely obscene for the times, and the innovative music show *The Tube* presented by Jools Holland and Paula Yates. Channel Four also launched its own soap, *Brookside* (1982–), innovative in its location (a modern housing estate in Liverpool) and its mode of production (using real houses rather than sets).

This first phase involved almost daily battles with press derision (it was dubbed 'Channel Snore' to allege that no one was watching, or 'Channel Swore' because of its realistic use of language). It was also the period of the ultimately successful guerrilla war by programme-makers to overturn the regulatory principles of the era of scarcity, especially the idea that individual programmes or series had to be 'balanced' between the prevailing viewpoints in society. Channel Four's contention was that balance could be found across its output rather than within any one instance of it, opening the way for more opinionated and diverse programming. In this sense, Jeremy Isaacs' Channel Four defined many of the terms for British television in the emerging era of availability. It was the crucible in which programme-makers haltingly learned how to address niche or targeted audiences rather than use the universalising forms of address developed for a mass audience.

Isaacs' resignation was typical of his programming strategy: he believed that no feature of Channel Four, not even the successes, should be retained for long. His surprise successor Michael Grade (1987–97) embarked on a policy of consolidation, taking the channel from an audience share of around 5 per cent, to one of 10 to 12 per cent, which it still maintains. Isaacs' eclectic scheduling pattern, based on variety with a few key anchor points like the *7pm News*, was replaced by a more aggressive and familiar strategy of stripping similar programming across the week in key slots. Ten in the evening became the drama slot, more often than not imported US quality series like *St Elsewhere* (1982–9) and *NYPD Blue* (1993–) leavened with occasional UK commissions like *The Camomile Lawn* (1992), *A Very British Coup* (1988) and *GBH* (1991). Where Isaacs had joined the consortium producing the ill-fated euro-soap *Chateauvallon* (1985), Grade banished subtitled material to the very edges of the schedule. Grade's policy succeeded, leaving Channel Four able to support itself from its own revenue, and the owner of a handsome headquarters building designed by Richard Rogers: an asset to tide it through the coming turmoil of intense multichannel competition.

Increasing prosperity saw the end of the necessary cheap commissions like *Opinions*, where an intellectual struggled with reading from autocue for half an hour. Instead the current affairs series *Dispatches* offered committed investigative journalism and the occasional series like *This Food Business* revealed the horrors of Britain's food supply. Documentary strands like *True Stories* and *Cutting Edge* developed a school of politicised personal stories, illustrating the underbelly and less savoury sides of the 'yuppie era' of the late 1980s and early 1990s. With increasing confidence, Channel Four introduced the irreverent *Big Breakfast* into its empty early morning slot, launching Chris Evans into a broadcast genre hitherto dominated by news and soft sofa chat. Personalities became an uneasy addition to the Channel Four repertoire, with the development of such stars as the duo Vic Reeves and Bob Mortimer, of Clive Anderson and Jonathan Ross. Their increasing identification with Channel Four focused attention on two growing problems inherent in the channel's initial conception. The need to work through independent companies meant that they would own (or indeed be owned by) this valuable talent; and the desire to innovate continuously meant that these talents, once established by the channel, would inevitably drift towards the richer competing channels of the BBC or ITV. The logic of Grade's strategy of consolidation was inevitable: stars like Graham Norton were placed on direct, exclusive contract to Channel Four.

Elsewhere, distinctive sitcoms became a feature of the channel, including the long-running *Drop the Dead Donkey*, set in a TV newsroom; *Desmonds*, set in a Brixton barbers' shop; and *Nightingales*, in which three male security guards fought boredom and each other in a surreal limbo. The channel's feature film policy continued, providing much-needed financing for innovative British movies like *The Crying Game* and a series of Ken Loach films including *Raining Stones* and *Riff-Raff*. Increasingly Grade, assisted by his programme controller John Willis, established a market identity for Channel Four. It combined an explicit up market address, exemplified perhaps by the provocative arts journalism of the *Without Walls* series, with an increasing exploration of the post-adolescent, post-pub audience. This led to the scheduling of repeated sitcoms against the complementary early evening news sequences of BBC1 and ITV between 5.45 and 6.45pm, perceived at the time as somehow breaking the unwritten understandings by which public service TV had been run. It also, and more controversially, led to a series of themed evening 'special events' like *Pot Night*, and commissions for the late evening, especially Friday, like *The Word* and *The Girlie Show*. They were intended to present the brash irreverence of the post-feminist 'girl power' generation, and the 'trash culture' of stunts like vomit drinking, but also led to the designation of Michael Grade as Britain's 'pornographer in chief' by a choleric newspaper

Showcasing the 'girl-power' generation: *The Girlie Show*

columnist. Other commentators wondered whether provocation had not replaced innovation as Channel Four's guiding principle. Nevertheless, they vividly illustrated the growing visibility of cultural diversity in Britain in the 1990s.

Grade left Channel Four after ten years, as a secure and distinctive freestanding single broadcast channel within an increasingly competitive market. The channel's independence as a publicly owned commercial channel had been secured by his efforts, but diversification had not been addressed. Michael Jackson, his successor from 1997–2001 brought with him lessons learned from John Birt at the BBC. He conceived of Channel Four as a brand to be exploited in several areas of the fragmenting media landscape of Britain. In his four-year tenure, several subscription and/or digital channels were launched or planned. Two quickly established a place in the marketplace: FilmFour, which exploited Channel Four's own co-financed movies as well as a market for subtitled and cult films not served elsewhere; and E4, devoted to youth-oriented entertainment. Behind E4 lay some controversial business deals, particularly the expensive purchase of all broadcast rights to the US series *ER* and *Friends*. Both established features of Grade's Channel Four, they had hitherto had their first runs on the subscription satellite service of BSkyB. Jackson was now determined to exploit their value to the Channel Four brand into the market for digital services, believing that the essence of Channel Four's identity lay in its programming. Similarly, Jackson bid successfully for the rights to cricket and horse racing in Britain, allowing the possible development of interactive services based around betting. Some of these commercial operations were undertaken by an 'arm's length' company similarly to those operated by the BBC, in order to protect Channel Four's public service operations from cultural contamination and commercial risk.

Jackson's commissioning developed the directions

initiated by Grade, but managed to avoid the worst excesses both of programme content and attacks in the press. Drama series commissions included the arresting *Queer as Folk*, with its matter-of-fact attitude to gay romance, and *Teachers*, which concentrated on their arrested emotional development rather than problems of paedogogy. The impressionist Rory Bremner developed the satirical series *Bremner, Bird and Fortune*, reminiscent of the 1960s' The *That Was the Week That Was*. The uneven late-night topical *The Eleven O'Clock Show* introduced the successful character of Ali G. Comedies were nursed into life in a Friday-night slot hammocked between *Friends* and *Frasier*. They included *Smack the Pony*, featuring three women comedians, and sitcoms *Father Ted*, *Spaced* and *Black Books*, which all developed a distinctive absurdist approach to the genre. Elsewhere, event programming became a distinctive aspect of the channel, from the rescue archaeology of *Time Team* to the highly successful British version of *Big Brother* which ran over successive summers from 2000. *Big Brother* also established Channel Four as an interactive broadcaster, through almost-live web links and the astonishing success of its voting proceedures. On the negative side, arts coverage almost disappeared, being replaced by list programmes like *A Hundred TV Moments from Hell*.

Channel Four was originally conceived in the era of scarcity of British television, as an industrial and programming irritant in an enclosed system of just three channels. It broke that mould, introducing both independent production and programming that was both tendentious and targeted in its address. During its early years, therefore, Channel Four was bringing about the demise of the system that had given birth to it. It enjoyed a brief period of comparative richness within the oligopolistic TV advertising market that existed before the arrival of BSkyB and multi-channel TV as a major force. This allowed it to develop a distinct programming profile, an identifiable brand. Its current gamble is to extend that brand into new broadcasting and electronic markets, where it is a relatively small and undercapitalised player. Mark Thompson arrived from the BBC as the new chief executive in 2002, and faced essentially the same challenge as Jeremy Isaacs twenty years before: how can a commercially funded public service programme provider develop and maintain distinctive and innovative programming in an increasingly competitive environment?

John Ellis

RECOMMENDED READING

Bonner, Paul and Aston, Lesley (2003), *Independent Television in Britain (Volume 6), New Developments in Independent Television, 1981–92*, Basingstoke and New York: Palgrave Macmillan.

Ellis, John (2000), 'Channel Four: From Offer-Led to Demand-Led Television', in *Seeing Things: Television in the Age of Uncertainty*, London: I. B. Tauris, pp.148–61.

Grade, Michael (1999), *It Seemed Like a Good Idea at the Time*, London: Macmillan.

Harvey, Sylvia (2000), 'Channel Four Television: From Annan to Grade', in Edward Buscombe (ed.), *British Television: A Reader*, Oxford: Oxford University Press, pp. 92–117.

Isaacs, Jeremy (1989) *Storm Over Four: A Personal Account*, London: Weidenfeld and Nicholson.

Quality Drama in the US: The New 'Golden Age'?

'Quality TV' has taken on so many different meanings that no two users of the term seem to agree even on the basics (such as which programmes the term references). 'Quality' in the US context could mean non-commercial (anything on PBS), it could mean suitable for children (tame sexual content) or it could mean programming in any TV genre that appeals to a more highbrow, educated audience. 'Quality drama', on the other hand, is a term on whose meaning there is more general agreement. By the 1990s, Robert Thompson was able to argue that, 'quality [drama] has become a genre in itself, complete with its own set of formulaic characteristics' (1996, p. 16). Moreover, it's possible to trace the history of 'quality drama' on US television from its early days in live television of the 1950s to its current incarnation in the HBO 'quality' drama. When HBO advertised shows like *Sex and the City* (1998–) and *The Sopranos* (1999–) with the claim 'it's not TV, it's HBO', they were following a five-decade tradition of distinguishing 'quality TV' from 'regular TV'.

Even before a normative notion of 'everyday television' had solidified, the idea of 'quality drama' existed in the form of the live 'anthology' teleplays of the 1950s. Written by New York playwrights, appealing to an elite audience, and financed by individual corporate sponsors as prestige productions, these live TV dramas carried the cachet of the 'legitimate' theatre. In their minimal use of film techniques as well as the excitement of their live broadcasts these 'single play' dramas exhibited a pattern that would remain important to future generations of quality drama. On the one hand, they defined themselves as quality because they exploited an essential characteristic of their medium: the ability of television to broadcast live in a way films couldn't. On the other hand, their prestige came from an association with a 'higher' form of art, theatre, a form that at this time was widely acknowledged by intellectuals as superior to the film medium as well. Thus when, as sometimes happened, one of these anthology dramas was adapted into a movie, as, for example, *Marty* (1953, 1955), *Days of Wine and Roses* (1958, 1962), *Requiem for a Heavyweight* (1956, 1962), it underwent an odd transformation in cultural prestige. In terms of technical experimentation, live transmission was replaced by slicker and more traditionally filmic shooting styles. But far from signifying an upgrading of the rawness of the often crude live transmission, this turn towards the cinematic was registered as a loss. No matter how prestigious the film version, the television version had come to be seen as higher quality, because of its exploitation of the essence of the medium (liveness) and because it was thus closer to the theatrical. The film adaptations of these teleplays remain obscure, but the live dramas are still admired and studied even in the technically crude kinescope versions of them that remain. The 'golden age of live TV' achieves its aura in both directions: technologically it was experimental, and structurally it was 'theatre' and (like the future HBO) 'not TV'.

By the time MTM Productions was acclaimed as the 'quality' production house of the 1970s, we had a much better idea what the norm was for 'regular TV.' This was the weekly filmed or videotaped series, usually a sitcom or action show, that was formulaic and geared to the lowest common denominator audience in a period when TV ownership by every American was assumed (and the classic network system reigned supreme). In 1981, MTM debuted its breakthrough drama *Hill Street Blues* (NBC, 1981–7), arguably the most transformative and influential television drama ever. Like the anthology dramas, *Hill Street Blues* exploited what were assumed to be the essential characteristics of the television medium. Generically, it 'recombined' the cop show with the soap opera. Technologically, it featured a cinéma vérité *mise en scène*. Narratively, it made use of a large ensemble cast portrayed in quickly intercut multiple storylines that didn't always reach an easy resolution. Resembling the anthology drama's affinity to theatre, *Hill Street Blues* borrowed from (some would say stole from) the independent direct cinema documentary *The Police Tapes* (1978), and its literate dialogue tested the vocabulary of the college-educated viewer. Thus it carried the prestige

The most influential TV drama ever?: *Hill Street Blues*

of higher art forms while redefining the essence of television for a limited but still 'mass' audience.

Hill Street Blues established new norms for quality drama that was not just 'regular TV'. While claiming to appeal to an elite audience, MTM knew the show also had to reach segments of the mass audience so that it could not proceed entirely by reference to more prestigious art forms but had to claim to experiment around television's essential features. In this way, quality drama was redefined for the 1980s and early 1990s, and, as Robert Thompson points out, it became its own genre. In terms of audience, some of the shows in the quality genre became mass-audience successes, such as *Moonlighting* (ABC, 1985–9) and *LA Law* (NBC, 1986–94), while others had a more limited success with elite audiences coveted by advertisers, such as *thirtysomething* (ABC, 1987–91) and *Northern Exposure* (CBS, 1990–5). Quality drama became a uniquely televisual form, its technological and narrative links to the medium more significant than its affinity to cinema or theatre. When quality drama did reference a more prestigious art form, it tended to be 'art cinema'. *thirtysomething*, for example, made numerous references to art cinema while following a soap operatic tendency within the television medium. But the mainstream of quality drama referenced television itself or rummaged through the programme's own history (see grey box on *China Beach*).

The next 'breakthrough' drama, then, would be one which combined 'pure television' with literate but not elite scripts and experimentation which was well within the grasp of a mass audience; namely, *ER* (NBC, 1994–). Although it is said to have taken twenty years (Michael Crichton wrote the original script as a screenplay in 1974) to bring *ER* to the small screen, the show has proven to be an unbeatable top-ten blockbuster while, at least during its

The art cinema sensibility of *Six Feet Under*

earlier seasons, maintaining a claim to 'quality drama'. *ER* was not, however, quality drama in relationship to 'higher' art forms such as theatre and art cinema – at least not directly. Its main narrative innovations – use of a constantly moving Steadicam and rapid pacing – link the show to an exploitation of the TV medium. Even the 'special' episodes which referenced other art forms mediated their quotations through popular film and TV sources. The famous fourth season opening 'live' episode ('Ambush', 25 September 1997) even thematised its reliance on video aesthetics by having as its narrative the portrayal of the ER staff in a video documentary intended for a PBS special. By now, however, the cinéma vérité techniques could refer to *Hill Street* or *Homicide* (NBC, 1993–9) as easily as independent documentary, and the reference to PBS seems to have been tongue in cheek. By then this 'live on tape' look had been exported from *ER* to the numerous 'real ER' video series that followed in its wake.

The witty website <alt.tv.er> posted the following 'candygram' in March 2002: 'MR WELLS STOP YOUR CONSTANT ATTEMPTS AT PLAGARIZING [*sic*] FILMS A NUISANCE STOP WILL BE CONSIDERING LEGAL ACTION STOP SINCERELY J. HUGHES AND A. KUROSAWA STOP'. This jibe no doubt referred to the 13 March 2002 episode 'Secrets and Lies' penned by producer John Wells and referencing the play *Waiting for Godot* (Samuel Beckett, 1948) via the movie *The Breakfast Club* (John Hughes, 1985); and to the 27 September 2001 episode 'Four Corners' which followed the famous Kurosawa film *Rashomon* (1950) in showing the same incidents from the narrative viewpoint of four of the regular characters. But were these really references to modernist theatre and to art cinema? Yes, if one considers them direct references to the film which has come to epitomise the art film and to the theatre play which has come to symbolise theatre of the absurd. But no, if one realises that these 'high art' references had already been mediated through a number of popular film and television intertexts. Writer/ director Edward Zwick had already done a *Rashomon* episode of *thirtysomething*, which he followed up with the film *Courage under Fire* (1996). And the *ER* episode was far

CHINA BEACH (MARCH 1988–JULY 1991, ABC)

For a quality drama critics called a 'masterpiece' and 'TV art' and about which Robert Thompson has written 'an artistic triumph, [*China Beach*] stretched the narrative structure of television more than any TV drama to that date' (1996, pp. 146, 148), *China Beach* is surprisingly little remembered and rarely rebroadcast. The show in its entirety (four seasons) was syndicated only twice on US television, rendering it completely unavailable from 1994 to 2001. *China Beach* could be said to have been entirely typical of quality TV of its period. It was staffed in its final season by the team that went on to create the unmatched first season of *ER* (writer-producer John Wells and director Mimi Leder). The show employed a large ensemble cast and generic mixing. It was a demographic but never a ratings success.

Yet unlike other quality dramas that peaked in their first season, *China Beach*'s greatest hours came after the show had been cancelled as Sasha Torres notes. She writes that '*China Beach* is suspicious of the accuracy, or even the accessibility of popular memory. . . . *China Beach* thus offers the televisual image and televisual narrative in place of popular memory' (1995, p. 151). The final season was thus a *tour-de-force* experiment invoking television's capacity to explore the lives of the ensemble cast after the Vietnam War in a complex time-scheme which mixed events ranging from the China Beach reunion in Youngstown, Ohio, in 1988 back to the show's beginnings in Vietnam in 1967. But this was not a typical 'flashback' structure. In the spirit of historical memory, the episodes moved freely among the events portrayed by the season as a whole, in a sense making the 'text' I am discussing last the season *as a whole* rather than any single episode. Critics who have written on this epic narrative single out the third to last episode entitled 'Rewind' (9 July 1991,written by Carol Flint and John Wells) for analysis (see Torres, 1995; Howell, 1995). Since the memory voyage of the final season could be said to centre around KC's now-grown daughter's search for the 'truth' about her mother (whom she met only once during the fall of Saigon in 1975), this episode would appear to be the most self-reflexive: Karen, the daughter, makes a video about Vietnam in which she interviews most of the major characters who had populated China Beach during the first three seasons.

Yet Karen's search and Karen's video permeate the entire final season, starting with the season opener 'The Big Bang' (teleplay by John Wells, 29 September 1990) in which Boonie (Karen's adoptive father) and his family visit Dr Richard in 1985. Rather than starting with the reunion and flashing back, the season commences with a number of narrative threads to be unravelled in the subsequent fifteen episodes: Karen before she starts her search, Dr Richard already married to another Colleen before the episode in which she is introduced ('Juice', 10 November 1990), and McMurphy for the first time as a mature woman. 'The Big Bang' also introduces the idea of historical memory as photographic and televisual by flashing back to scenes from China Beach evoked by black and white snapshots viewed in 1985. Although some of the episodes focus on a particular set of characters in a particular year, (for example 'You, Babe', the episode in which McMurphy finds herself delivering KC's baby in Saigon in 1967), others roam freely in the manner of memory. Many of the episodes flash back to McMurphy's last days at China Beach, days which haunt McMurphy until we learn in the penultimate episode, 'Through and Through' that she is a victim of post-traumatic stress disorder.

According to Sasha Torres, 'the two-hour final wrap-up episode' Hello Goodbye' (22 July 1991, [teleplay John Wells]), bore as close a generic relation to a made-for-TV movie as to a standard *China Beach* episode (1995, p. 162). However, the finale has the most complex narrative of any episode. Not only does it invoke 'new' footage from Karen's documentary, it creates a new backstory involving the last boy McMurphy treated at China Beach. In addition, the finale 'rewrites' recent episodes from new perspectives. It re-presents a harrowing clip involving eight-year-old Karen's evacuation during the fall of Saigon in 1975 first seen by viewers in '100 Klicks Out' (11 June 1991); then recycled into 'The Always Goodbye' (18 June 1991) as KC's haunted 1975 flashback; now given to us as Karen's 1988 flashback to the same memory. Never has a quality drama played with history and memory and with *our* memory of a television show with such complexity.

Jane Feuer

more indebted to the famous 1985 teen-pic *The Breakfast Club* than to any kind of absurdist theatre. Within the *ER* episode the characters – who are sent by Kerry Weaver to 'sexual harassment training' on a Saturday after some inappropriate sexual behaviour in the *ER*—analogise between their situation and that of *Waiting for Godot* (which Dr Lewis claims never to have understood). But for the *ER* audience the real intertext is clearly the juvenile situation of being sent to 'detention' and thereby encouraged to spill out your guts to fellow 'students', some of whom you scorn and the rest of whom are your current or ex-lovers. There is a televisual aspect to this episode as well because only a show that had lasted for eight seasons could get so much backstory mileage out of two of that show's original characters, Doctors Carter and Lewis.

ER had made many claims to quality status but had never claimed to be 'not TV'. When the tradition of producing original quality drama shifted from the networks to the HBO cable channel, a different and more elitist claim about the nature of quality drama needed to be made to the much smaller pay/cable audience (only 26 million subscribers in 2002) that had to purchase the service which brought them *The Sopranos* and *Six Feet Under* (HBO, 2001–). As David Chase, writer/producer/director of *The Sopranos* has stated in interviews, he does not watch TV and he does not like TV. Rather, he considers himself a film-maker, and at least for its first season tried to make every episode of *The Sopranos* into a little movie (Longworth, 2000, pp. 20–36). Why, then, was *The Sopranos* considered so innovative for television? I believe this judgment was made on the basis of the content of the show and its many affinities to high drama: the moral ambiguity, the dark world portrayed and the language used. In terms of dramaturgy, however, *The Sopranos* has been compared to Greek tragedy and could even be described as 'classical'. It evokes a world of high art for pay/cable audiences who expect to get something more than just TV. Ironically, this makes the new HBO dramas more comparable to the 1950s' 'theatre plays for television' than to the more televisual tradition of quality drama that dominated the networks from *Hill Street Blues* through *ER*. One could say the same of NBC's *West Wing* (NBC, 1999– ; like *ER* and *China Beach*, a John Wells' production although created/written by Aaron Sorkin), whose innovations tend more in the direction of 'literate' drama than bringing out televisual qualities such as serialisation, use of Steadicam, or depth of backstory.

Nowhere is this debt to elite art traditions clearer than in the award-winning HBO 'hit' *Six Feet Under* which rated a *Newsweek* cover story on 18 March 2002. The programme's creator and auteur, Alan Ball, brought the same 'art cinema' sensibility to *Six Feet Under* that had made his film *American Beauty* (1999) the most successful art cinema-to-mainstream Hollywood crossover ever. According to *Newsweek*, Ball 'brings the same idiosyncratic voice to his TV show – satirical, philosophical and disturbing, often all at the same time. . . . it's Chekhov and Beckett, translated into the best Hollywood style' (Peyser, p. 54). One needs to question exactly what it is that makes *West Wing* and the HBO shows so 'new' and 'different' and so 'not TV'. Looking at them in continuity with a long tradition of quality drama on TV reveals a predictable pattern: when definitions of quality can go no further in referencing more elite art forms (usually because of considerations of audience), they tend to turn to innovations that refer to the television medium in particular, often producing quality shows that appeal to more of a mass audience. However, when the opportunity to 'create' for a more select audience re-emerges due to changes in technology and industry economics, we see a return to using as models the same old references to art cinema and to early twentieth- century drama or even to Greek tragedy.

Jane Feuer

RECOMMENDED READING

Thompson, Robert J. (1996), *Television's Second Golden Age: From Hill Street Blues to ER*, Syracuse: Syracuse University Press.

Torres, Sasha (1995), 'War and Remembrance: Televisual Narrative, National Memory, and *China Beach*', *Camera Obscura*, no. 33–4, pp.147–64.

The 1990s: Quality or Dumbing Down?

There are two key points of reference for any consideration of trends in programming on British terrestrial television in the 1990s: the report of the Peacock Committee in 1986 and the subsequent 1988 Government White Paper 'Broadcasting in the '90s: Competition, Choice and Quality', with their emphasis on the market and consumer choice, and the 1990 Broadcasting Act. This required that the BBC, as well as commercial television, source 25 per cent of its programming from independent production companies. The result was increased competition for large audiences and channels scheduling 'head-to-head' (Ellis, 2000, pp. 130–47) as the BBC struggled to justify its licence fee through audience share as well as to continue to offer programmes of distinction. Furthermore, this atmosphere of competition, efficiency and concern with consumer choice produced a reassessment of established notions of public service broadcasting. Tim O'Sullivan has noted, in relation to the search for large audiences and the currency of popular programmes, 'some have suggested that changes in the organisation of British broadcasting in the late 1980s and early 1990s have to be understood as part of a general erosion of the rights of modern British citizens, especially in terms of their access to certain cultural resources, diverse forms of information or entertainment programme services' (1998, p. 198).

Consequently, key debates around British television in the 1990s, in both television studies and in the mass media, centred on discussions of the quality of contemporary British television, and the notion that it had 'dumbed down' (see, for instance, Brunsdon, 1990; Hutton, 2000; Mosley, 2000; Steel, 1999). The 1990s witnessed the loss of ITV's *News at Ten* and *World in Action*, the expansion of 'human interest' stories at the heart of news and current affairs programming and, concomitantly, a perceived decline in serious factual programming, documentary and current affairs television. British terrestrial television in the 1990s developed a nostalgic self-regard, saw the rise of reality formats and the significantly increased presence and importance of the ordinary person on television. Furthermore, the 1990s, claimed Andy Medhurst, were 'the era of Lifestyle TV . . . and the daytime-isation of evening TV' in Britain (1999, p. 26).

Tim O'Sullivan has drawn upon Umberto Eco's use of the term 'Neo-TV' to consider the nostalgic and self-reflexive turn in recent British television. This, he argues,

has been characterised by an inwards- and backwards-looking stance, a 'nostalgia TV' through which television has re-presented its own history to its viewers (and thus their own) through repeats and the use of archive materials. Channel Four's *TV Heaven* series (Illuminations Television, 1992), for instance, was strip-scheduled on Saturday evenings 'with blocks of programmes from yesteryear . . . Episodes from series and serials, single plays, documentaries and other surviving "oddities" were packaged for consumption 20 or 30 years on' (O'Sullivan, 1998, p. 202). It could also be argued that the success in the 1990s of television satire represents another aspect of British television's recent inward-looking turn. For instance, Steve Coogan's *Knowing Me, Knowing You with Alan Partridge* (Talkback for BBC2, 1994) offered an ironic take on the television presenter, and shows based in media scepticism, such as *Have I Got News for You* (Hat Trick Productions for BBC2, 1990–) and Chris Morris's *The Day Today* (Talkback for BBC2, 1994) and *Brass Eye* (Talkback for BBC2, 1997) which lampooned the excessive use of graphics in contemporary television news and current affairs programmes, and duped celebrities and television personalities into giving their name and voice to false news reports in order to reveal the constructed nature of television journalism.

Home video TV: *You've Been Framed*

A second tendency, O'Sullivan argues, was the use of 'out-take' footage in shows such as the long-running and popular *It'll Be Alright on the Night* (LWT for ITV, 1977–), and a third, 'candid video'. From candid camera formats and home video shows like *You've Been Framed* (Granada for ITV, 1990–), which draw upon the increased access to image-making technology such as the camcorder, to new types of documentary format based on the confessional direct address to camera such as BBC2's *Video Diaries* project (Community Programmes Unit, 1990–), which featured reports on aspects of contemporary life in Britain by members of the public, the emphasis in these trends in the 1990s has been one of both 'revelation and intimacy' (O'Sullivan, 1998, p. 199). Whether such programming represented 'dumbed down', cheap, sensationalist television, or on the other hand a commitment to a 'technological determinism that sees the spread of the camcorder as a sign of a vibrant, participatory democracy' (Goodwin, 1993, p. 26), one key consequence of these and other reality television formats, such as the docusoap, has been the presence of the ordinary person on television. This is exemplified both in confessional modes such as *Video Diaries* but also in light entertainment formats such as *Stars in Their Eyes* (Granada for ITV, 1990–) in which members of the public are made over as their favourite singing star and then perform before a live studio audience, as well as the gardening makeover show *Ground Force* (Bazal for the BBC, 1997–) (see grey box).

March 8 1999 saw the end of ITN's *News at Ten* on ITV, which had been broadcast at that time since 1967, and its replacement with two half-hour bulletins: the 6.30pm *Evening News* and 11pm *Nightly News*, enabling the uninterrupted broadcasting (except by commercials) of films and other programming in order that ITV might compete more effectively with the BBC. Due to a drop in viewing figures, it was announced that the news would be moved back to 10pm three nights per week in January 2001, prompting the BBC's move of the *9 o'Clock News* (1971–2000) to 10pm in a head-to-head battle for audiences. In conjunction with the cancellation in 1998 of ITV's flagship documentary programme *World in Action* (Granada, 1963–98), and the BBC's moving of *Panorama* (BBC1, 1953; 1955–) from weekday evening prime time to after 10pm on Sundays at the end of the decade, the move represented a very significant shift in the established schedules of Britain's key broadcasters. These changes crystallised the decade's dominant debates about 'dumbing down', the decline of the BBC's public service provision, the generally perceived decrease in 'serious' prime-time documentary and current affairs (see Hutton,

2000; Ingrams, 1998; Leigh, 1998) and the 'feminisation' of the news with human interest, emotive and sensationalist stories (see Holland, 1998; Langer, 1998; van Zoonen, 1998). These are the lines along which the battle for audience share between the BBC and ITV had developed throughout the 1990s. The BBC repeatedly emphasised their commitment to public service broadcasting exemplifying breadth and quality of provision, in direct contrast to what their 1994–5 *Annual Report* described as ITV's tendency to 'produce, schedule and broadcast programmes to attract large audiences', with a core of 'easily digestible entertainment in well-established formats, abandoning those which are not instant ratings success' (BBC, 1995, p. 7).

Discussion over whether the BBC in fact achieved this commitment in the 1990s has tended to centre on the development of mixed genre 'factual entertainment' formats (also referred to variously as 'infotainment', 'edinfotainment' etc.). In particular, the growth of lifestyle programming – cookery, gardening, home improvements, fashion and consumer issues shows – and the docusoap, such as *Soho Stories* (BBC2, 1997), *Paddington Green* (BBC1, 1998), *The Cruise* (BBC1, 1998) and *Airport* (BBC1, 1998–) attracted attention. These programmes offered 'factual content' in a popular entertainment, dramatic format, and seemed to many to dominate the schedules and replace quality 'serious' or 'hard' documentary or factual prime-time programming in the 1990s. They frequently produced ordinary people as television celebrities and presenters, the rise to fame of 'Maureen' from the docusoap *Driving School* (BBC1, 1997) being a prime instance of this trend. The BBC in their 1997–8 *Annual Report* described the emergence of the docusoap as 'observational documentary . . . revealing new facets of contemporary Britain' (BBC, 1998, p. 100). However, in their use of human interest stories and tragedy to boost ratings these shows were seen as part of a growing trend 'to make all factual programmes tell stories – or rather, little dramatic narratives with some kind of resolution, that always centre on an individual personality' (Cathode, 1996, p. 32).

The BBC's *Annual Report* for 1994–5 situated its development of factual entertainment programming in terms of response to audience demand. 'People and Programmes', the BBC's review of programme strategy in 1995 'underlined the need for the BBC to continue to find inventive ways to cover the leisure pursuits of our audiences' (BBC, 1995, p. 28), leading them into new areas of programming, including the countryside, the internet and computing, travel, food and gardening. The BBC perceived themselves to be broadening their approach to an area in which they had been traditionally strong, with long-running and successful programmes such as *Gardeners' World* (BBC2, 1969–) and *Food and Drink* (BBC2, 1982–). As the report put it, 'the challenges remain to develop leisure programmes that appeal to specialists while drawing casual viewers and to introduce new topics such as personal finance and health' (BBC, 1995, pp. 28–30). At the same time the report commented that the BBC's daytime schedule still lagged behind ITV's in terms of audience share; we might then understand this as the context in which the prime-time schedules were gradually 'daytimed' in the mid- to late 1990s.

BBC1 daytime programming had begun in October 1986, when, for the first time, the schedule ran solidly from 6am into the evening. Later, the *Daytime UK* umbrella (BBC1, 1990–1) was introduced in an attempt to improve the quality of BBC's daytime television provision and to win back the morning TV audience from ITV's long-running and extremely successful magazine programme. *This Morning* (Granada for ITV, 1988–), hosted by married couple Richard Madeley and Judy Finnegan, was initially regionally based and presented, but later moved to London. *Daytime UK* broadcast between *Breakfast News* (BBC1, 1989–) and the *1 o'Clock News* (BBC1, 1986–), jointly hosted and presented from Birmingham and Manchester, and encompassed programmes addressing human stories, issues, personality interviews and popular entertainments such as the discussion programme *Kilroy* (BBC1, 1987–), *Wildlife Gems* (BBC1, 1992–2001) and *Rosemary Conley's Diet and Fitness Club* (BBC1, 1990–1). The *Daytime UK* umbrella was quickly dropped and the main programmes were strengthened as this attempt continued – *Kilroy* continues to be a successful feature in the BBC morning schedule.

As part of the attempt to win back daytime audiences from ITV, the BBC introduced shows such as *Can't Cook, Won't Cook* (Bazal for BBC1, 1995–2000), a cookery competition for those lazy and incompetent in the kitchen; *Style Challenge* (BBC1, 1996–), a personal makeover show; and *Real Rooms* (BBC1, 1997–), a makeover in a real home on a budget. The makeover format powerfully present in the BBC's new daytime schedule in the early 1990s took up popular aspects of daytime magazine programming like *This Morning* and developed entire shows around it, as a way of both improving the daytime schedule and finding new ways to present leisure programming in response to the 'People and Programmes' review. This new presentation of 'original programming which presents factual information in an entertaining way' is highlighted at the beginning of the BBC's 1996–7 *Annual Report* in the language of lifestyle makeover and home improvement television: 'where our morning schedule looked lacklustre, it now gleams' (BBC, 1997, p. 14). The makeover format was moved to prime time on BBC2, and then to BBC1, from the mid-1990s, with home and garden makeover shows *Changing Rooms* (Bazal for the BBC, 1996–) and *Ground Force*. ITV attempted to follow suit with the less successful *Carol Vorderman's Better Homes* (ITV, 1999–). These and other lifestyle and factual entertainment programmes, covering cookery, fashion, crime and docusoaps, came to dominate prime time, the majority made by independent production companies among which Bazal has perhaps been the key player (see Bishop, 1998). They include Delia Smith's *How to Cook* (BBC2, 1998–), *Rick Stein's Fruits of the Sea* (Denham Productions, 1997–2001), *Two Fat Ladies* (BBC2, 1997–9), Jamie Oliver's *The Naked Chef* (Optomen for the BBC, 1999–), *Looking Good* (BBC2, 1997–), *She's Gotta Have It* (Talkback for Channel Four, 1998–), *999 Lifesavers* (BBC Bristol, 1992–), *Police, Camera, Action* (Optomen for ITV, 1994–) (see Hill, 2000; Wheatley in Brunsdon *et al.* 2001) and docusoaps such as *Animal Hospital* (BBC, 1995–), *Children's Hospital* (BBC1, 1993–) and *Vets in Practice* (BBC1, 1996), which, as Johnson (in Brunsdon *et al.*, 2001) argues, also have a makeover structure.

The rise of factual entertainment in prime time has been seen as emblematic of the dumbing down of British television (see, for instance, Hutton 2000) and as an articulation of the erosion of the BBC's public service ethos, perceived as representing a shift in address from citizen to consumer, from 'hard' to 'soft' values in factual programming, and a privileging of entertainment over education and information. A similar discussion was engendered by the natural history documentary *Walking with Dinosaurs* (BBC1, 1999), which, with its combination of science, dazzling graphics and dramatic narrative, became the most popular television science programme ever: was it, though, fact, or speculation and spectacle? (See Steel, 1999, p. 5.) Although an independent advisory panel commented that 'while impressed by the range of output in this genre [they] felt the balance between information and entertainment was not always right, and that opportunities to give more information and practical advice were sometimes missed' (BBC, 1998, p. 13), the BBC have continued to argue that a distinctive public service can also be a popular one.

The pervasiveness of factual entertainment formats and especially lifestyle genres on terrestrial British television in the 1990s is an interesting illustration of both the shifts which took place in broadcasting during that decade as well as the debates and anxieties which surrounded those

MAKEOVER SHOWS

The makeover show was perhaps the most popular and successful format of the prime-time factual entertainment programming that dominated British terrestrial television from the mid-1990s. These are programmes which feature the transformation of a person (e.g. *Style Challenge*), a room or home (e.g. *Changing Rooms*, in which the contestants, with the help of an expert, make over a room in each other's homes in two days), or garden (*Ground Force*, in which a family member and a team of experts make over a garden in the absence of their loved one). The central generic marker of the makeover show is 'the reveal' at the end of the programme, in which the person/room/garden transformed is revealed to the contestant and the audience at home, their reaction visually foregrounded through the use of the close-up. The majority of instances of the makeover show in the 1990s have been on BBC television with independent production company Bazal featuring significantly, although ITV also attempted to work up this format with shows like *Carol Vorderman's Better Homes*.

The rise of the makeover show and the consequent 'daytime-isation' of the prime-time schedules can be traced to the use of the fashion and/or home makeover in daytime magazine programmes, and subsequently in daytime shows such as *Style Challenge* and *Real Rooms*. The makeover has always been a central feature of feminine popular culture, from the transformation structure central to fairytales like 'Cinderella', women's films such as *Now Voyager* (Irving Rapper, 1942) and *Pretty Woman* (Garry Marshall, 1990), to the 'before and after' format common to hair and beauty product advertising and also beloved of fashion and beauty features in women's magazines. The gendered character of the makeover as a genre, then, is partially responsible for the conception of British terrestrial prime-time schedules as increasingly 'feminised' by the growing emphasis on factual entertainment in the 1990s.

Interestingly, in terms of representation, the rise to prominence of the makeover format has opened up traditionally 'feminine' genres, spaces and concerns on television to a new audience of men (fashion and beauty, interior decorating), and vice-versa (DIY and the use of power tools). This occurs despite the fact that the shows often also reinforce traditional divisions of labour – the female presenter of *Changing Rooms*, Carol Smillie, for instance is most frequently seen operating a sewing machine.

Brunsdon (2001, pp. 54–6) has argued that the use of the close-up in the makeover show represents a shift in the visual grammar of the television DIY programme, from an interest in showing the detail of the skill being demonstrated and learned to an emphasis on the reaction of the ordinary person featured in the programme in contemporary instances. This moment highlights the increasing presence and importance of 'the ordinary person' on British television in the 1990s. Its excess of ordinariness is both a source of pleasure and engagement for the audience, exploiting television's potential for intimacy and immediacy in its apparent offer of an authentic moment of genuine emotion (see Moseley, 2000), but also, as Karen Lury (1995) has suggested, serving as a potential source of anxiety and discomfort for the viewer. This dynamic frequently makes the shows rather uncomfortable to watch.

Ground Force : makeover shows go gardening

Rachel Mosele

changes. Yet it might be argued that there is more at stake in these programmes than a simple indication of the extent to which British television culture has 'dumbed down'. Stuart Jefferies, in a book itself indicative of the mood of TV nostalgia prominent in the 1990s, has discussed this mode of television as an instance of 'public service broadcasting in the age of anxiety' (2000, p. 316). More importantly, these are trends in which we can see demonstrated the regendering of television genres and the articulation of changing understandings of the constitution of British identity, society and culture in terms of class, sexuality and ethnicity (see Medhurst, 1999; Brunsdon *et al.*, 2001). Through this democratisation of an old public service discourse (Bondebjerg, 1996) and its attendant shift in understandings of what constitutes the public sphere, we can observe the 'working through' that, as John Ellis has recently argued, opens up possibilities for formulating a new definition of public service broadcasting to serve the new television environment (Ellis, 2000, p. 86).

Rachel Moseley

RECOMMENDED READING

Bondebjerg, Ib (1996), 'Public Discourse/Private Fascination: Hybridisation in "True Life Story" Genres', *Media, Culture and Society*, 18, pp. 27–45.

Brunsdon, Charlotte, Johnson, Catherine, Moseley, Rachel and Wheatley, Helen (2001), 'Factual Entertainment on British Television: The Midlands Television Research Group's "8–9 Project" ', *European Journal of Cultural Studies*, vol. 4, no. 1, pp. 29–62.

Lury, Karen (1995), 'Television Performance: Being, Acting, Corpsing', *New Formations*, 26, pp. 114–27.

Medhurst, Andy (1999), 'Day for Night', *Sight and Sound*, vol. 9, no. 6, pp. 26–7.

Moseley, Rachel (2000), 'Makeover Takeover on British Television', *Screen*, vol. 41, no. 3, pp. 299–314.

O'Sullivan, Tim (1998), 'Nostalgia, Revelation and Intimacy: Tendencies in the Flow of Modern Popular Television', in Christine Geraghty and David Lusted (eds), *The Television Studies Book*, London: Arnold, pp. 198–211.

New US Networks in the 1990s

The emergence of new broadcast networks and cable channels in the United States during the 1980s and 90s hastened the tendency towards market fragmentation begun by the 'big three' during the 1970s. If 'quality' was the mantra uttered by industry executives during the 1970s, the buzzwords in the 1980s and 90s were 'niche marketing', 'brand identities', and 'developing synergies'. The impulses towards pursuing specific demographic groups and lifestyle niches – begun tentatively with the networks' pursuit of the quality audience in the late 1960s and early 1970s – developed into an art form as the 1980s and 90s progressed and a number of new cable and broadcast channels appeared. Fox provided one model for how to do business in a multi-channel universe, using a number of marketing, scheduling and programming techniques that would become standard in both broadcasting and cable in the ensuing years. Cable channels that included MTV, Nickelodeon, BET and Lifetime, as well as two newly formed broadcast 'netlets', WB and UPN, subsequently continued the move towards narrowcasting by targeting particular age and ethnic groups with their shows. As these nascent cable and broadcast entities successfully increased their viewership – often attracting the audiences most valued by advertisers – they

forced NBC, CBS and ABC to reconceptualise their own images and programming strategies.

The development of both cable channels and new networks was a much more gradual process than had been anticipated by either government regulators or the media industries. Although the technological mechanisms were in place for several years, a series of complicated FCC regulations as well as limited resources hindered the development of new cable channels. A turning point came in the mid-1970s when HBO hooked up to the SATCOM I satellite and began airing programming nationwide. Soon after HBO's debut, a number of additional stations appeared, including CBN (Christian Broadcasting Network, launched 1977), USA (1977), Showtime (1978), Nickelodeon (1979), CNN (1980), MTV (1981) and The Nashville Network (1983). At the same time, a select number of local channels including WTBS and WOR connected via satellite to become 'superstations', airing nationally.

In spite of the creation of all these new channels, there was very little original programming available throughout the early and mid-1980s. Instead, cable channels initially relied on sports, old movies and broadcast television reruns (Mullen, 2003, pp. 132–8). The 'fresh' programming available included news, religious sermons, music videos, instructional programming, and public access shows in select localities. Given the limited reach of cable during this time, few networks were willing to fund new shows, and the shows they did fund had very limited budgets and low production values. The Nashville Network was one of the earliest cable networks to generate original programming. Most of its shows, however, were low-cost travelogues (*Country Sportsman*), talent shows (*You Can Be a Star*), musical showcases (*Grand Ole Opry*) and instructional programmes (*The Bassmasters*). Children's and family-oriented programming proved the exception to the low-budget rule. *Fraggle Rock* (HBO, 1983–8), *Faerie Tale Theater* (Showtime, 1982–7), *The New Leave It to Beaver* (Disney, 1985–6) and *The Campbells* (CBN, 1986–9) were among the more ambitious programmes targeted to youth or the family. While this audience proved a viable niche for a number of cable channels, programmers found other niches more elusive. In fact, a number of cable channels had to revamp their schedules or merge with other channels in order to broaden their audience reach. Such was the case with the ARTS Channel and the Entertainment Channel, which joined to form A&E in 1984. In the same year, the Daytime Channel and the Cable Health Network joined to form Lifetime. In both instances, these channels found their narrowcasting strategy to be too narrow for the time (Mullen, 2003, p. 116). In their newly combined forms, however, both networks began funding original series: A&E met with success with the stand-up comedy show, *Evening at the Improv* (1985–95) as well as the long-running documentary series, *Biography* (1987–); Lifetime had an early hit with advice from sexual therapist *Dr Ruth Westheimer* (1984–91).

Even as cable networks continued to struggle to establish themselves during the mid-1980s, a new competitor came along in the form of the Fox network. As the first attempt at a fourth network since DuMont in the 1950s – and one appearing at a time when the 'big three' were struggling to hold onto their audience – many doubted Fox could succeed. However, it benefited from the deep pockets of media mogul Rupert Murdoch, who was ready to sink millions of dollars into creating a fourth broadcast network designed to air original programming (Block, 1991, p. 140). Further, Murdoch was willing to let programmers develop the schedule gradually, with one new evening of prime time being unveiled every six to twelve months. Also, Fox executives felt less pressure because of the decision to schedule programmes for only two hours a night, as opposed to the three prime-time hours scheduled on the other networks.

It was fortunate that Murdoch was prepared to be patient with his new network as Fox got off to a rocky start in both late night and prime time. Fox began its venture into the network business in October 1986 with a five-night-a-week, late-night talk show starring former *Tonight Show* guest host Joan Rivers. Rivers' *The Late Show* proved to be a disaster; ratings remained low and the press attacked the programme as well as the new network. Within eight months, Rivers was out, replaced by a series of rotating guests including Suzanne Somers, Robert Townsend and Arsenio Hall. Fox tried to revamp late night in December 1987 with a comedy/news magazine hybrid, *The Wilton North Report*, but it was pulled after running for less than a month. One last attempt at late night with *The Chevy Chase Show* (1993) became a public relations nightmare. Chase's jokes bombed, the interviews were tedious. Emergency reworking efforts failed, and the show was off the air less than a month after its premiere.

Prime time proved equally bumpy at first, in part because executives lacked a clear vision about the direction the network should take. Programmers relied on a sitcom-heavy schedule during the network's first few years. Among the sitcoms that came and went in Fox's first year in prime time were: *Down and Out in Beverly Hills* (1987), a TV version of the popular motion picture; *Mr President* (1987–8), George C. Scott's return to television after several years in

the role of chief executive; and *Duet* (1987–9), a generic comedy about the lives of two couples. Dramas proved equally troublesome; *Werewolf* (1987–8) failed to attract viewers in spite of its unique promotional gimmick of providing an 800 number for viewers who spotted werewolves in their communities. Meanwhile, Fox's early cancellation of *The Dirty Dozen* (1988, based on the film) led to a very public battle between the network and its production company, MGM.

Although Fox certainly had its share of missteps in its early years, programmers slowly began to develop a clearer sense of what Fox programming should be. They were aided in developing Fox's identity as the 'upstart' network by the success of two of its earliest shows: *Married . . . with Children* (1987–97) and *The Tracey Ullman Show* (1987–90). Each was crucial to the development of Fox as a brand name but in different ways: *Married . . . with Children* helped Fox corner the market on 'alternative sitcoms' – programmes specialising in raunchy humour and testing the boundaries of good taste in both subject matter and dialogue. While NBC celebrated the traditional family and middle-class virtues in *Family Ties* and *The Cosby Show*, several Fox comedies of the late 1980s and early 1990s – led, of course, by *Married . . . with Children* – rejected all such values. Once the Bundy family began to garner media attention and controversy, the sky was the limit for Fox sitcom content. First there was *Women in Prison* (1987–8) about a group of female inmates in a Wisconsin jail, then came *Babes* (1990–1), about three heavy-set sisters living together in New York City, followed by *Woops!* (1992), a comedy about six Midwestern kids living in a post-apocalyptic society.

The Tracey Ullman Show, meanwhile, helped attract critical attention to the network as well as demonstrating to the creative community and the public that Fox could be a haven for quality programming. This comedy-variety show, which featured the multitalented British comedienne, brought Fox its first Emmy nomination. More importantly, it introduced an animated family into American consciousness through a series of shorts placed between Ullman's skits. This family, *The Simpsons* (1989–), proved to be Fox's first bona fide ratings success – even as it garnered praise from critics for its witty satirising of American life and its parodies of popular culture.

The Simpsons and *Married . . . with Children* became two of the signature shows enabling Fox to differentiate itself and its content from CBS, ABC and NBC. These shows also solidified the target demographic for the network – adults aged eighteen to thirty-four. Using this age range as well as its image as the 'alternative network' as the barometer, Fox began to specialise in four specific types of shows. In addition to the sitcoms described above, the network also started generating a large number of reality programmes including *Cops* (1989–), *America's Most Wanted* (1988–) and *Totally Hidden Video* (1989–92). These programmes regularly earned high ratings while offsetting some of the expenses borne by Fox as a start-up enterprise. In an effort to further diversify and explore new niches, Fox produced serialised dramas targeted at teenagers and young adults. Arguing that this was a market currently being overlooked by the other networks, Fox commissioned seasoned producers such as Stephen J. Cannell (*Night Rider, Hunter*) and Aaron Spelling (*Charlie's Angels, The Love Boat*) to develop youth-centred, hour-long dramas. Cannell developed *21 Jump Street* (1987–90), a show about cops who pose undercover as high-school students to fight crime in schools. The show made stars of actors Johnny Depp and Richard Grieco (who got his own short-lived spin-off, *Booker*, 1989–90). Spelling, meanwhile, transferred the successful *Dynasty* formula of sexual temptation and a fascination with the lives of the wealthy into a winning teenage version with *Beverly Hills 90210* (1990–2000). These shows helped spark a 'teen craze' that would overtake television in the 1990s, attracting adolescent viewers to Fox (and later, the WB) even as they turned away from the established networks.

Fox did not just pursue the young adult audience during its early years. In addition to this niche, Fox also sought out African-American viewers. Although the 'big three' had not altogether ignored African-American-centred shows, Fox programmers felt the urban middle- and lower-class, African-American communities were being under-served. NBC's *The Cosby Show* (1984–92) and *The Fresh Prince of Bel-Air* (1990–6), for example, focused on suburban, upper-middle-class African-Americans. Consequently, during the early 1990s Fox aggressively tried to attract what they perceived to be a neglected audience through the airing of such sitcoms as *In Living Color* (1990–4), *Roc* (1991–4), *Martin* (1992–7) and *The Sinbad Show* (1993–4). Fox chose to 'counter-programme' *The Sinbad Show* and *In Living Color* against NBC's 'must-see TV' Thursday-night line-up of *Wings* and *Seinfeld* (Zook, 1999, pp. 3–5).

As the 1980s progressed, a number of cable channels similarly increased their viewership by showing what the traditional broadcast networks did not – or could not. Premium pay cable networks such as Showtime and HBO began airing more original programming, much of which featured explicit language, sexuality and violence that wouldn't get past the networks' Standards and Practices div-

isions. *First and Ten* (HBO, 1984–91*)*, *Russell Simmons' Def Comedy Jam* (HBO, 1992–7) and *The Red Shoe Diaries* (Showtime, 1992–8) all took advantage of their presence on commercial-free, uncensored channels. HBO and Showtime also took on controversial subjects through their made-for-television movies: *And the Band Played on* (HBO, 1993) focused on the AIDS epidemic; *If These Walls Could Talk* (HBO, 1996) dealt with abortion; *Bastard out of Carolina* (Showtime, 1996) depicted child molestation and abuse.

Basic cable networks also slowly raised their output of movies-of-the-week and series programming as the 1990s progressed. A much wider breadth of shows appeared as these cable networks began to acquire more viewers and new corporate owners with deep pockets. As had been the case with Fox, original programming became a means for many cable channels to carve out their market niches and establish clear brand identities with viewers. Nickelodeon invested heavily in new series by the early 1990s, supporting child-oriented sitcoms (*Clarissa Explains It All*, 1991–4), cartoons (*Rugrats*, 1991–4; 1997–), magazine shows (*U to U*, 1994–6), game shows (*Legend of the Hidden Temple*, 1993–5) and dramas (*Fifteen*, 1991–3). These shows enabled Nickelodeon to establish itself as the premier children's programmer. MTV, meanwhile, provided a similar array of programming geared to teenagers: game shows (*Remote Control*, 1987–90), talk shows (*The Jon Stewart Show*, 1993–4), reality programming (*The Real World*, 1992–) and cartoons (*Beavis and Butthead*, 1993–6) all featured youthful characters, fast editing, the latest music and popular culture references in their bid to win over twelve- to twenty-four-year-olds.

USA, in turn, quickly defined itself as a purveyor of B-level genre product with the foreign intrigue programme *Counterstrike* (1990–3), the science-fiction series *Swamp Thing* (1990–3) and the adventure show *Renegade* (1992–7). In addition, it picked up programming rejected by the networks. *Silk Stalkings*, for example, began its life running concurrently on CBS's late-night schedule and on USA. However, even after CBS cancelled the show, USA continued running it for several more years. Such a practice indicated a shift in cable programming strategy initiated in the early 1990s: whereas previously cable channels had predominantly recycled and reconfigured old television product, programmers now began experimenting with re-purposing and multiplexing. These tactics would become even more prevalent as consolidation in the media industries continued. Thus by the late 1990s, USA's investment in the *Law and Order* franchise enabled it to strike a deal with NBC whereby it reran new episodes of *Law and Order: Special Victims Unit* (1999–) within a week of their broad-

MARRIED... WITH CHILDREN
(APRIL 1987–JULY 1997, FOX)

When Ron Leavitt and Michael Moye created one of Fox's first television programmes, they sought to combat the saccharine-sweet sitcom trend sweeping television during the 1980s. The family they created, the Bundys, had little in common with the Keatons (NBC, *Family Ties*, 1982–9) or the Weavers (ABC, *Growing Pains*, 1985–92). And they certainly were 'Not the Cosbys' – the initial working title for *Married... with Children*.

Al (Ed O'Neill) was inadequate as a shoe salesman, a lover and a father. Peggy (Katey Sagal) refused to cook or clean, but she did efficiently spend all of the family's monthly income on clothes, manicures and hairstyling. Semi-literate daughter Kelly's (Christina Applegate) only apparent skill was in the bedroom. And son Bud (David Faustino) couldn't catch a woman – unless she was at least thirty years his senior (or in prison).

If, as Nina Liebman observes, the standard domestic comedy contains 'qualities such as warmth, familial relationships, moral growth and audience inclusiveness' (1997, p. 404), *Married... with Children* subverted all the characteristics of the genre. There seemed to be absolutely no warmth or moral development displayed by the Bundys. Instead, a standard episode involved at least one family member – and often all of them – proving to be incompetent in their respective familial roles: Al's dreams of a peaceful family vacation are destroyed when they end up in an interminable traffic jam (just a few blocks from home). Peg's promise to only spend money on groceries is broken when she purchases a gaudy sculpture for $5,000. Kelly's attempt at monogamy ends when she finds out she's become engaged to a philanderer. Bud risks his life when he skydives at the behest of a girl – only to be dumped when the she falls for the class's instructor.

In place of the tidy moral lessons provided in most domestic-based sitcoms stretching from *Leave It to Beaver* (CBS, 1957–8; ABC, 1958–63) to *Full House* (ABC, 1987–95), *Married... with Children*'s writers concluded each episode showing the Bundy family reaching new personal and moral lows. Thus did it become one of the most irreverent shows to appear on television since *All in the Family*'s (CBS, 1971–9) debut. For eleven seasons, *Married... with Children* regularly and effectively parodied Reagan-era family values as well as network television's traditional construction of the nuclear family. The programme generated this satire predominantly through dialogue, plot and *mise en scène*, while retaining traditional sitcom conventions in its editing and camerawork.

Married... with Children had an impact with critics and viewers almost immediately. Critics generally commended – if not praised – the show's writers for trying to develop some-

Married... with Children: no tidy moral lessons

thing different than that produced by the 'big three'. Viewer response, meanwhile, was split between celebration of the show's distinctiveness and denunciation of its raunchiness. The controversy surrounding the programme peaked in 1989, when suburban mother Terry Rakolta began a letter-writing campaign to forty-five of the show's advertisers, accusing them of 'helping to feed our kids a steady diet of gratuitous sex and violence' (*New York Times*, 2 March 1989, A1). Rakolta's crusade drew heavy media coverage and compelled a number of businesses, including Procter & Gamble and McDonald's, to temporarily halt their sponsorship of the show. More press, however, ultimately brought more viewers: *Married... with Children* subsequently broke into the Nielsen top twenty and experienced an increase in sponsorship (Goldberg, 1989).

The show's cultural and industrial impact continued to resonate long after the Rakolta controversy declined. It was the first in a wave of bawdy blue-collar comedies; *Roseanne* (ABC, 1988–7), *Grace Under Fire* (ABC, 1993–8) and *The Simpsons* (1989–) were just a few of the shows that appeared in the wake of *Married... with Children*'s success. In perhaps the most obvious act of imitation, one of the WB's earliest programmes was the Ron Leavitt-produced *Married... with Children* clone, *Unhappily Ever After* (1995–9). Such attempts to reproduce the Bundys further demonstrate the substantial influence the show had in redefining the domestic comedy of the 1980s and 90s.

Alisa Perren

cast. Such a move provided USA with recent network programming (replete with its high production values) which nonetheless conformed to this specific cable channel's pursuit of Middle America through the airing of genre-oriented product.

If USA was one of the earliest channels to acquire rejected broadcast properties, Fox reversed the trend by reformatting popular cable programmes and bringing them to network viewers. *It's Garry Shandling's Show* (HBO, 1986–90; Fox, 1988–90) re-aired on Fox after Showtime initially aired original episodes; similarly, *Dream on* (HBO, 1990–6; Fox 1995) and *Tales from the Crypt* (HBO, 1989–96; Fox, 1994–5) had short runs on Fox after they ran first on HBO. Although this strategy was used a few times in the 1990s, as the network continued to develop a broader audience than its cable counterparts, newer programmes more frequently flowed from broadcast to cable. In Fox's case, its parent company News Corporation created F/X in 1994 as a means of more fully exploiting Fox-produced programming. Subsequently, F/X became a virtual clearing house for Fox shows, airing *In Living Color*, *Married . . . with Children* and *Beverly Hills 90210* several times a week. The creation of F/X also coincided with a shifting programming strategy on the part of the Fox network. In the mid-1990s, Murdoch encouraged Fox executives to expand the network's reach from its former eighteen- to- thirty-four base to eighteen- to forty-eight-year-olds. This not only motivated a move away from the more narrowly defined niches of teenagers and African-Americans to which Fox had previously catered, but also involved developing more 'mainstream' programming.

Fox's first attempt to expand its audience took place when it outbid CBS for NFL football rights in 1993; this move was followed by *The X-Files'* (1993–2002) high ratings and critical success. The network subsequently attempted to acquire more hour-long suspense shows and science-fiction programmes; *The Visitor* (1997–8), *413 Hope Street* (1997–8) and *Millennium* (1996–9) all represented Fox's effort to reinvent itself as a network catering to young professionals. This proved a tenuous strategy, in part because this market was already being successfully pursued by the self-proclaimed 'quality network', NBC, with such shows as *Homicide: Life on the Street* (1993–9), *The Pretender* (1996–2000) and *Profiler* (1996–2000). Fox's move towards the mainstream thus met with only marginal success, as one series after another bombed and the role of Head of Programming became a game of musical chairs. Thus, the late 1990s marked a tumultuous time for America's fourth network, as the more explicitly niche-oriented programmes of earlier years (*The Simpsons*, *Beverly Hills 90210*, *Married . . . with Children*) continued to bring in some of the highest ratings.

Fox's shifting programming strategy also had broader ramifications in the network landscape. Following Murdoch's mandate to broaden Fox's audience base, a number of top executives departed. Within months, these same executives resurfaced at two newly created netlets, the WB (including head Jamie Kellner) and UPN (including head Lucie Salhany). Both networks, which premiered in 1995, directly modelled their programming on Fox's early years: the WB went young, pursuing twelve- to thirty-four-year-olds, especially females, with such hour-long dramas as *7th Heaven* (1996–), *Dawson's Creek* (1998–) and the Spelling-produced *Charmed* (1998–); UPN, meanwhile, sought the African-American audience seemingly abandoned by Fox. In addition to acquiring the cancelled Fox programme *Between Brothers* (1997–9), UPN picked up a number of additional African-American-centred programmes, including *The Hughleys* (1998–2002) and *Moesha* (1996–2001). The new network also pursued young male viewers with satisfying ratings results via two *Star Trek* iterations, *Voyager* (1995–2001) and *Enterprise* (2001–). Both *Star Trek*s functioned as flagship programmes for UPN.

The exploitation of these *Star Trek* enterprises indicates the direction taken by cable and netlet programming in the late 1990s and early 2000s. As large conglomerates purchased and created network and cable channels, there were increased efforts to develop synergies between television content and other corporate holdings. Thus would Nickelodeon's *Hey Arnold!* afternoon cartoon (1996–) morph into a motion picture in 2002 and the Fox-produced, UPN-based *Buffy the Vampire Slayer* (1997–2002) evolve from a feature-length film into a profitable television series (as well as DVD and video collection) for Twentieth Television. Each of these shows was targeted to an identifiable niche (twentysomething males, children, teen females). These shows reveal how cable and netlet-based, niche-targeted television programmes have become economic drivers in a manner similar to the way that motion picture franchises have driven the entertainment industry since the 1970s. Thus in recent years – accompanying Fin-Syn's repeal, the growth of cable, and the continuing merger and acquisition craze – there has been a transition from the 1980s' cable practices of recycling and reconfiguring old shows to such tactics as re-purposing content, branding networks and synergising programming across divisions within media conglomerates.

Alisa Perren

RECOMMENDED READING

Banks, Jack (1996), *Monopoly Television: MTV's Quest to Control the Music*, Oxford: Westview Press.

Caldwell, John (1995), *Televisuality: Style, Crisis and Authority in American Television*, New Brunswick: Rutgers University Press.

Holt, Jennifer (2003), 'Vertical Vision: Deregulation, Industrial Economy and Prime Time Design', in Mark Jancovich (ed.), *Quality Popular Television: Cult TV, Industry and Fans*, London: BFI.

Turow, Joseph (1997), *Breaking up America: Advertisers and the New Media World*, Chicago: University of Chicago Press.

Satellite and Cable Programmes in the UK

The growth of satellite and cable television provision in the UK from the 1980s onwards plays a significant role in the shifting and reshaping debates about British television culture. Indeed, satellite technology, with its associated technical apparatus has even changed the landscape of television viewing in the UK in a material way with satellite dishes forming external marks on the physical/architectural landscape of the nation. The number of UK homes opting to access satellite and cable broadcasting systems (now also including access to digital formats) has been growing slowly but steadily since the end of the twentieth century. This trend has certain implications for the ways that television viewing will be conceptualised in the twenty-first century, both on the level of 'the national' and also more widely, in terms of the changing relationship between television technologies and television audiences.

To the viewer, one of the key attractions of acquiring satellite or cable television is the ability to receive many more television channels than traditional terrestrial analogue broadcasting permitted. Access to a greater choice of channels including both general and specialist programming has been a major selling point. For instance it becomes possible to receive a wide range of channels e.g. adult-rated channels such as Playboy, Television X, children's channels such as Nickelodeon and Disney Channel, film channels such as Sky MovieMax and TCM, sports channels such as Sky Sports1 and Eurosport and channels with specialist international/overseas programmes such as Asianet. In the British context, the decision to pay extra to become a satel-

lite or cable subscriber and to take that step beyond the general television licence has special meaning. In addition to the regular, and sometimes substantial, financial commitment signed up to by the subscriber, depending on the choice of channel viewing package, the decision to sign up for satellite and cable television can also bring 'moral' dilemmas over subscribers' complicity in eroding social and cultural standards. In particular, many households in Britain have been faced with decisions about whether to acquire (at additional cost to a basic subscription package) additional sports channels in order to ensure the right to view certain events such as regular live coverage of English Premier League football matches, thus perhaps helping to drive major sports events off public channels. In the development of their marketing strategies, such as pay-per-view TV (requiring the payment of a one-off fee usually for a particular high-profile sports or musical event), satellite and cable companies have attempted to target niche or enthusiast audiences in order to exploit as many commercial opportunities as possible. The fact that satellite and cable provision is an obvious business enterprise and free from notions of public service has been blatantly clear from the start. This distinction provides an important framework for understanding the ways that cable and satellite technologies have been perceived in academic discussions.

From the outset, British television has been shaped by a public service ethos and has been considered a matter for regulation. As the heightened debates surrounding the 1990 Broadcasting Act illustrate, real anxieties existed about the proliferation of terrestrial channels. The potential for proliferation was, of course, even greater as satellite and cable systems became more accessible and more widespread in the UK. In addition to concerns about the breakdown of common systems of regulation (e.g. Sky channels observe an 8pm, not a 9pm watershed, the time after which more adult content is allowed to air), one of the main fears articulated was that with increasing access to many more television programmes, 'more might actually equal less' in terms of programme quality. In other words, more repeats and a rise in poor production values may result because of the necessity to make cheap programmes to fill increasing broadcast space. It comes as no surprise that it was also during the 1990s that the British media became progressively more preoccupied with an associated fear linked to proliferation and quality, that of 'dumbing down'. What lies at the core of all these expressions of anxiety, and what is not usually voiced explicitly, is an underlying fear about the nature of television itself, namely that television is too seductive, and that once it starts to proliferate it becomes both excessive and dangerous for the consumer. In discussions of television, there seems to be little notion of self-regulating and discerning viewers but rather discourses of moral panic circulating around the figure of the 'couch potato'. Satellite and cable systems with their promise of multiple channels and fears about dubious quality control encapsulated all these fears about excess and lethargic slavery to television viewing.

Crucially, access to multiple channels by subscription also threatened to destabilise notions of a national viewing culture as it is currently conceived. At the national level, consistent practices such as the 9pm watershed have fashioned both viewing schedules and also viewers' understandings of television. The core channels of British terrestrial television (BBC1 and ITV) have placed British-made programmes at the forefront of the schedule and positioned them as the flagship programmes. For satellite and cable customers, there is the potential for such national specificity in viewing to become displaced. Not only is there the possibility to receive foreign TV channels, but the sheer amount of airtime to be filled when fifty or more channels can be available simultaneously has also increased the amount of imported English-language (e.g. American, Australian etc.) programmes that some British households are now able to receive.

In addition to shifting away from a predominantly nationally specific television service, the multiple, cyclical and repetitious formats employed by satellite and cable programmings are targeted much more towards niche viewing and therefore operate outside traditional patterns. In this way, satellite and cable provision can be seen to move away from the concept of broadcasting to the idea of specialised 'narrowcasting'. Because British television culture has often conceptualised as a public archive of cultural experience, the changing and more individualised viewing experiences made possible by satellite and cable technologies began to be seen as challenging common understandings of television culture and raising concerns about audience fragmentation.

Although satellite and cable television is still in its relative infancy in the UK and its full impact hard to determine, it is already evident that more television has not been as fragmentary and destructive as feared. According to David Gauntlett and Annette Hill's (1999) wide-ranging empirical study *TV Living: Television, Culture and Everyday Life*:

> new channels like Sky One, Sky News, UK Gold and
> movie channels were treated as conventional broadcasters
> (as opposed to special-interest 'narrowcasters') and
> watched by family and households who were as more or
> less united as they ever had been around the TV set.
> (Gauntlett and Hill, 1999, p. 288)

One of the reasons for this is that despite the enormous pleasure that watching television can offer, there are still deep and pervasive cultural suspicions about the activity. Because watching 'too much television' is equated with not having a life, television enjoyment is often tinged with guilt. With this in mind, it is perhaps not that surprising that in the face of increasing programme and channel temptation consumers have not 'given in' but have opted to self-regulate in quite creative ways by exploiting a mixture of VCR recordings and repeated satellite or cable scheduling slots. In these ways, they have chosen to take control of television rather than be controlled by it.

In a similar way, the demise of quality would also seem to have been falsely prophesied (although the criteria and aesthetics will continue to be debated). Flagship texts with high production values remain central to both satellite and cable channel programming and also viewers' own schedules. For satellite and cable viewers in the UK, the emphasis on quality has shifted away from purely British television texts (generally also defined by their heritage connections as well as high production values) and has moved towards more contemporary American programmes such as *ER* (E4) and *Buffy the Vampire Slayer* (Sky One). In addition, opportunities to access 'quality' film texts through channels such as FilmFour and TCM also challenge the notion that satellite and cable viewing equates dumbing down. The configuration of satellite and cable formats provides a web of multiple and parallel channels and the post-modern possibilities for both channel surfing and forming a bricolage of favourite viewing from this web of channels are clear. The availability of this wide range of channels has implications for the ways that we might want to think about television studies in Britain. A close scrutiny of patterns of programming for satellite and cable television seems to indicate that a canon of television

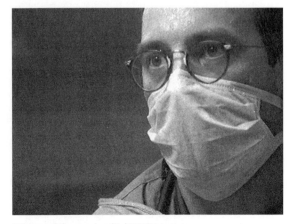

ER: one of the new 'quality' US TV texts

ALL AUSSIE WEEKENDER: SKY ONE DOWN UNDER (SUNDAY 7 NOVEMBER 1999)

The 'All Aussie Weekender' was promoted as a Sky One exclusive for its UK channel and is an example of a new themed programming strategy targeting special interest viewing. The notion of targeted/specialist viewing has been a strong element of satellite and cable television marketing. This particular package capitalised on a significant relationship between Australian and British television and the affection of British viewers for both Australian soap operas and also the actors who play key characters in them. The millennium year made Australia the focus of television screens all over the world because of the high profile Sydney Olympics. The Aussie Weekender viewing package built up to this period of intense television exposure for Australia. It also responded to the fact that Australia has now become a significant tourist/leisure destination for Britain.

The 'weekender' consisted of a Sunday-evening schedule tailored towards Australia and Australian themes, including a Sky One-produced compilation of Australian television's 'greatest moments.' Introduced by the former *Home and Away* actress Isla Fisher, the package consisted of a gala opening of Fox Studios in Sydney presented by former soap star Craig McLachlan and British showbiz personality Tania Bryer, a fast-moving documentary of five young Brits playing hard in an action-packed weekend in Sydney, and two episodes of the American series *The Simpsons* that featured Australian content. Running from 7pm in the evening, these texts were sutured into a programme of viewing by a framework of both visual links and presenter inserts. The visual links employed recognisable signifiers of Australia, such as the Sydney Opera House and the Harbour Bridge, with an upbeat soundtrack dominated by the reverberating drone of the didgeridoo. The presenter links consisted mostly of straightforward exploitations of Australian television iconography chosen for their resonance with the British viewing context, such as Australian actor Dieter Brummer (again formerly of *Home and Away*) standing with Tania Bryer in front of *Home and Away*'s Summer Bay.

One of the links, however, was so excessive as to make it notable. It consisted of Craig McLachlan standing on one of the Fox Studio lots dressed as American-born Australian superstar Mel Gibson in full *Braveheart* costume (including kilt, face-paint and claymore) in order to introduce an episode of *The Simpsons* featuring a storyline based around Mel Gibson. The underlying text of what seems, certainly at first, a highly contrived and rather confusing performance is quite clearly corporate. The links between Australia, Britain and America all come together through the visually absent but structurally central figure of Rupert Murdoch and his business stake in both the American Fox television network and UK satellite station BSkyB. This piece of specific thematic programming, cleverly tailored towards the British satellite and cable market, thus has double signification at the level of the national (Britain/Australia) but reflects the increasingly global nature of corporate connections at work.

Ros Jennings

---

programmes is forming through what is a de facto process of circulation and that, although unspoken, this notion is already evident in the programming of certain satellite and cable channels such as UK Gold and UK Drama.

Although it is still early days, rather than signalling the collapse of British television culture, the growth of satellite and cable provision seems to have modified and extended more established trends, practices and notions. New and diverse viewing cultures and practices are certainly in formation and they are beginning to shape new discourses about both quality and the relationship between television texts and their audiences. However, although satellite and cable television can provide more individualised and specialist opportunities, it would seem that even fan-based or enthusiast viewing still does not always take place in isolation but features as part of a more rounded viewing experience that can include the five main terrestrial channels, VCR recordings and perhaps even Internet use.

Ros Jennings

RECOMMENDED READING

Bignell, Jonathan, Lacey, Stephen and Macmurragh-Kavanagh, Madeleine (eds) (2000) *British Television Drama: Past, Present and Future*, Basingstoke: Palgrave.

Bignell, Jonathan (2000), *Postmodern Media Culture*, Edinburgh: Edinburgh University Press.

Buscombe, Edward (ed.) (2000), *British Television: A Reader*, Oxford and New York: Oxford University Press.

Corner, John (ed.) (1991), *Popular Television in Britain: Studies in Cultural History*, London: BFI.

Corner, John (1999), *Critical Ideas in Television Studies*, Oxford: Clarendon Press.

Gauntlett, David and Hill, Annette (1999), *TV Living: Television, Culture and Everyday Life*, London: Routledge.

Geraghty, Christine and Lusted, David (eds) (1998), *The Television Studies Book*, London: Arnold.

US Television Abroad: Exporting Culture

The international distribution of US television programmes started in the late 1950s just as nation-states around the world began developing national television services. Most of these services were influenced by one of three models that had taken shape during the early days of radio broadcasting: the public service model of the BBC, the commercial model of the US, or the communist model of the Soviet Union (and some combined elements from them). While most nations in Western Europe adopted the BBC model and those in Eastern Europe that of the Soviets, the US networks worked aggressively to encourage commercial television across these boundaries and in other parts of the world. By 1958 commercial television was in operation in twenty-six countries due in large part to the enterprising expansion of US television networks (Barnouw, 1991, p. 230). During the 1950s and 60s the NBC network, for example, was supporting the development of TV services in Saudi Arabia, South Vietnam, West Germany, Wales, Mexico, Lebanon, Sweden, Peru, the Philippines, Argentina, Yugoslavia, Barbados, Jamaica, Kenya, Nigeria and Sierra Leone. Meanwhile, CBS was expanding into India, Greece, Ghana, Liberia, Aden, Gabon, the Ivory Coast, the Congo, Israel, Argentina, Venezuela, Peru and Trinidad. And the ABC network organised an international television network called Worldvision that involved Canada, Guatemala, El Salvador, Honduras, Costa Rica, Panama, Colombia, Venezuela, Ecuador, Argentina, Lebanon, Japan, Australia, Chile and Bermuda (Schiller, 1992, pp. 126–7).

The early priority of most national television services was to provide low-cost local and national news programming, but some sought to develop their own original cultural programming as well. Production costs for such programming were very high, however, and so it was often more cost-efficient for television stations to purchase and air already-existing, syndicated US television series rather than make their own shows. Programmes such as *I Love Lucy* (CBS, 1951–7), *Father Knows Best* (CBS, 1954–5 and 1958–62; NBC, 1955–8), *Bonanza* (NBC, 1959–73), *Cheyenne* (ABC, 1955–63), *Wyatt Earp* (ABC, 1955–61), *Hawaiian Eye* (ABC, 1959–63) and *77 Sunset Strip* (ABC, 1958–64) were among the first US television series to be sold on the international market (Barnouw, 1991, p. 236). In 1965 *Bonanza* was distributed to 60 countries for viewing by 350 million people each week and such programmes

were dubbed into Spanish, Japanese, Portuguese, German, Italian, French and Arabic (Schiller, 1992, p. 126). By cultivating the growth of television stations around the world, US networks NBC, ABC and CBS attempted to guarantee future exhibition outlets for US television series and to assert spheres of influence during a time of Cold War politics. The term 'US television abroad', then, refers not only to programme exports but also to the technical and financial arrangements made during the medium's first decades which resulted in US funding and ownership of foreign broadcast facilities, equipment sales, management service contracts and technical and administrative support.

As commercial US television networks were expanding abroad, so too were those of the US Defense Department. In 1954 the Armed Forces Radio Service (which first emerged in 1942) became the Armed Forces Radio Television Service (AFRTS), and began transmitting US television programmes to combat troops overseas serving in the Korean and later the Vietnam wars. In the late 1960s the AFRTS began using satellites to provide live sports and special events coverage, and by 1982 had developed SATNET a global television network offering US military personnel a 'touch of home'. These services were used extensively during the 1990s by troops serving in wars in the Persian Gulf, Somalia, Bosnia, Croatia, Macedonia and Haiti. By 2002, AFRTS was using two satellites to provide multiple US television services to over 400 outlets in more than 150 countries and to US ships at sea. These and other experiments with satellite broadcasting throughout the 1960s and 70s fostered the growth of the global satellite television industry and companies such as Sky TV, Star TV, Primestar, Direct TV, Dish Networks, Telemundo, Univision, CNN and Al Jazeera emerged in the late 1980s and 90s.

Australian media mogul Rupert Murdoch's company News Corporation became renowned for its use of satellites to extend the reach of US television abroad. In 1989, News Corporation launched Sky TV, a satellite television service offering news, sports and entertainment throughout parts of Western Europe. Sky became a competitor to the well-established BBC as it relayed US television series and sports coverage and movies not otherwise available in the region, prompting the BBC to alter and expand its own programmes and services. Sky's distribution of US television programmes, particularly from the Fox television network (also owned by News Corporation) raised concern about the 'Americanisation' of European television culture. France even introduced a 'Télévision sans Frontières' directive before the European Parliament in 1989 in an effort to place quotas on the amount of US television that could be imported.

After its success in Western Europe, News Corporation started a companion service in Asia. In 1993 Murdoch's company purchased the Hong Kong-based Hutchvision and formed Star TV (Satellite Television Asia Region) to provide programming to the growing English-speaking populations of the Asia/Pacific region. Star TV beamed five twenty-four-hour channels to viewers within the Asiasat 1 footprint, which spanned thirty-eight nations, from Egypt to Japan and from Indonesia to Siberia, targeting a potential audience of 2.7 billion viewers, half the world's population (Man Chan, 1994, p. 114). Four of Star's channels offered English-language programming. BBC World Service Television presented news broadcasts and documentaries, MTV Asia played American and regionally produced music videos, Star Sports featured cricket, badminton and ping-pong matches, as well as the NBA finals, and Star Plus broadcast American and British television sitcoms, dramas, talk shows and movies of the week. The fifth channel featured various Mandarin programmes produced in China, Hong Kong and Taiwan.

Since Murdoch's News Corporation owned America's 20th Century-Fox film studio and television network as well as a storm of syndication rights, the company provided a rich source of programming for the Star Plus channel. Shows such as *Santa Barbara* (NBC, 1984–93), *The Bold and the Beautiful* (CBS, 1987–), *The Simpsons* (Fox, 1990–) *The X-Files* (Fox, 1993–2002), *Beverly Hills 90210* (Fox 1990–2000), *Baywatch* (NBC/syndicated, 1989–2001), *Remington Steele* (NBC, 1982–7) and *LA Law* (NBC, 1986–94) became regular Star TV fare and were being distributed in countries such as China, India, Singapore and Pakistan. Though syndicated American television programmes had been viewed in the Asia/Pacific region for decades, never before had so many American shows reached such enormous audiences. Since Star TV began as a 'free to air' service, anyone in the footprint with a satellite dish and a television set could downlink and view Star TV's five channels. This, of course, generated serious concerns about national sovereignty and political leaders throughout the footprint responded to Star TV's 'cultural invasion from the skies' in a variety of ways (for further discussion, see Kishore, 1994).

China, for example, banned citizens' use of satellite television dishes in 1993 and expedited the development of its state-run cable systems to regulate the content and flow of programming within its borders. By August 1996, China's cable system had 2,000 licensed cable operators and was servicing 40 million subscribers across the country (Chan, 1996). China also eventually legalised satellite reception after it formed its own satellite channels featuring Chinese

LA Law: regular Star TV fare

films, sports, MTV videos and traditional operas in order to counteract foreign signals and supplement its terrestrial television services. In addition, Chinese Central Television created new programme content in a way that acknowledged citizens' interest in foreigners, established in part by Star TV's Western programming. Shows such as *Beijinger in New York* and *Love in New York*, both shot in the US, enabled audiences to watch Chinese immigrants' experiences in the United States. And one show called *Foreign Babes in Beijing* (which could be described as a Chinese *Beverly Hills 90210*) is a dramatic series about the lives of American and European girls who attend school in Beijing. The twenty-part soap opera was so popular it has been rerun five times. In this case, then, US television abroad had the effect of catalysing the expansion of China's broadcasting infrastructure and producers internalised some of the elements and structures of Star TV programming and adapted them to Chinese languages, cultures and tastes. To compete with national broadcast services that offered native language-programming, Star TV since has adopted a strategy of 'global localisation' – it now provides global media services to specific nations or locales, but it tailors programmes to the cultural tastes and linguistic backgrounds of particular audiences with dubbing and subti-

BAYWATCH

Known as 'the most watched TV show in the world', *Baywatch* hit screens in the US in 1989. The series was first conceived in 1980 by veteran Los Angeles county lifeguard Greg Bonnan as a show about 'sand, surf, and sea rescues'. Bonnan worked with producers Doug Schwartz, Michael Berk and Grant Tinker to turn the concept into a two-hour pilot that aired on NBC in April 1989. Pleased with its success, NBC executives bought the show in 1989, but mediocre ratings led to its cancellation after only one season. Just as NBC pulled the plug, *Baywatch* began generating large revenues in Europe. By 1991 Berk and Schwartz used foreign sales revenues to relaunch and syndicate the series independent of the networks, signing with distributor LBS Communications Inc., which later merged with All American Television Inc. Eight seasons of *Baywatch* were produced and sold in markets around the world throughout the 1990s. By 1998 *Baywatch* was seen in 140 countries and in thirty-two languages, from Bolivia to Bangladesh. By the end of the decade, the series was earning $100 million per year, 67 per cent of which was from foreign distribution. At its peak *Baywatch* reached over 1 billion adults worldwide each week.

Baywatch has been described as ready-made for international distribution because its action sequences played on California beaches by attractive characters wearing nothing but skimpy bikinis and briefs, are much easier to translate into multiple languages than the long-winded dialogue and intricate plots found in some soap operas and prime-time dramas. So intrigued were they by *Baywatch*, some international audiences reportedly tuned into the show just to keep track of the latest trends in American culture. Meanwhile, critics in the US blasted the series for presenting nothing more than 'flimsy non-stop T&A', claiming the show circulated ludicrous images of Americans and American lifestyles around the globe. Eric Spitznagel and Brendan Baber, authors of a book entitled *Planet Baywatch*, insist the show promotes an image of Americans as naively obsessed with their bodies, beach life and leisure. They claim *Baywatch* suggests, 'American men and women spend 15 percent of their days running in slow motion along the beach' (Sykes, –).

Despite such criticisms, *Baywatch*'s global popularity catalysed the production of a spin-off called *Baywatch Nights* in 1995 and another called *Baywatch Hawaii* in 1999, both of which were syndicated and now air markets around the world. Both have been broadcast on News Corporation's Star TV in Asia and Sky TV in Europe. In the US *Baywatch* has appeared on cable TV networks such as USA and TNN. Most recently *Baywatch* has become part of a TNN programming strategy to build a brand associated with young adult entertainment. The show plays alongside other hit series such as *Star Trek* and *CSI: Crime Scene Investigation* to lure adults in the eighteen- to forty-nine demographic. Many of the *Baywatch* stars such as David Hasselhoff, Pamela Anderson and Yasmine Bleeth have seen their careers skyrocket as a result of the series' worldwide success. *Baywatch*'s international distribution thus helped establish a global trade route for other syndicated series such as *Knight Rider* and *V.I.P.* featuring these same stars.

Lisa Parks

Baywatch: a weekly billion viewers worldwide at its peak

tles. As a result, the network offers such channels as Star India, Star Taiwan and Star Japan.

In the 1990s and 2000s satellite television services cover most of the globe and US television networks have begun to experiment with digital distribution on the World Wide Web. Most US television programmes are not streamed online, but information about their scheduling, production, cast and crew is available on the web. Some critics understand the international success of recent US television series such as *Baywatch*, *The X-Files*, *Buffy the Vampire Slayer* (WB/UPN 1997–2003) and *Xena: Warrior Princess* (USA, 1995–2001) in relation to the parallel formation of the World Wide Web, which sustains a proliferating number of official and fan websites. These websites not only serve as marketing tools and spaces of impassioned fandom, but in some cases they also facilitate transnational dialogues about the impact of US television abroad.

Lisa Parks

RECOMMENDED READING

Curtin, Michael (1997), 'Dynasty in Drag: Imagining Global TV', in Lynn Spigel and Michael Curtin (eds), *The Revolution Wasn't Televised: Sixties Television and Social Conflict*, New York: Routledge, pp. 245–62.

Herman, Ed, and McChesney, Robert (1998), *Global Media: The Missionaries of Global Capitalism*, London: Cassell.

Miller, Toby, Govil, Nitin, McMurria, John and Maxwell, Richard (eds) (2001), *Global Hollywood*, London: BFI.

Olson, Scott Robert (1999), *Hollywood Planet: Global Media and the Comparative Advantage of Narrative Transparency*, Mahway, NJ and London: Lawrence Erlbaum.

Parks, Lisa (2001), 'As the Earth Spins: NBC's *Wide Wide World* and Live Global Television in the 1950s', *Screen*, vol. 42, no. 4, Winter, pp. 332–49.

Sreberny-Mohammadi, Annabelle, Winseck, Dwayne, McKenna, Jim and Boyd-Barret, Oliver (eds) (1997), *Media in Global Context: A Reader*, London: Arnold.

The Global Television Format Trade

Format is the term used in television industries to describe a set of programme ideas and techniques, already successfully used in one market and subsequently adapted – usually under licence – to produce programmes elsewhere. Many past and present examples of such programme copy-catting come to mind. In radio's heyday, for example, NBC's *What's My Line?* (1952–3) was remade by the BBC. A decade later, the UK's *Till Death Us Do Part* was adapted for US television as *All in the Family* (CBS, 1971–83). By the 1990s, format adaptation had become widespread in many different television genres. Probably the most familiar current in international trade in this area has to do with the migration of a large number of US game show formats – *Wheel of Fortune* (NBC/CBS/syndicated, 1975–), *The Price Is Right* (NBC/ABC/syndicated/CBS, 1956–94), *Card Sharks* (NBC/syndicated/CBS, 1978–89), *Concentration* (NBC/syndicated, 1958–79), *Jeopardy* (NBC/syndicated/

ABC, 1964–90) and many others to different parts of the world over the past fifty years. However, the roots of this particular situation had to do with the emergence of the US syndication market for game show remakes and US producers, with the sole exception of Columbia TriStar, have not pursued an interest in the international licensing of formats in such genres as drama serials and situation comedy. Similarly, the past fifteen years have also seen the migration of the Australian stripped drama serial – itself heavily influenced by earlier UK serials such as *Crossroads* – to Western Europe and the US with such remakes as *Goede Tijden, Slechte Tijden* and *Gute Zeiten Schlechte Zeiten* (both based on *The Restless Years*), *Dangerous Women* and *Hinter Gittern* (*Prisoner: Cell Block H*), *Forbidden Love* and *Skilda Varlder* (*Sons and Daughters*) and *Un Posto Ol Sole* (*Number 96* and *Neighbours*). Even more recently there has been the international licensing of formats in the broad area of infotainment where companies in Western Europe, most especially the UK and the Netherlands, have been particularly active in producing and exporting generically hybrid formats that have variously cross-fertilised such forms as the lifestyle and chat programme, game and quiz show, documentary, sporting competition and music programme (*The Soundmix Show*, *I Do I Do*, *Taxi*, *The Weakest Link*, *Survivor* and others).

Typically, past business arrangements concerning the international adaptation of TV programme formats tended to be informal, *ad hoc* and undertaken on a one-off basis. When fees were paid to the original producer, such as – for example, occurred in the case of the BBC's re-use of the radio format for *What's My Line* – such a reimbursement was in the nature of a somewhat unexpected courtesy payment rather than a pre-set fee. Not surprisingly, there was also a good deal of international borrowing of formats that involved neither authorisation nor the payment of fees. Altogether, from the 1950s onwards, numerous unauthorised, US format adaptations turned up in Brazil, Mexico, the Netherlands and elsewhere in the world.

However, the most significant case of such piracy was the New Zealand remake of the UK game show *Opportunity Knocks*. In 1989, Hughie Green, the UK format originator/producer, brought legal action against the New Zealand Broadcasting Corporation. Charges included infringement of format copyright. Under the Berne Convention, such action had to occur in the jurisdiction where the alleged offence occurred. However, the case was lost in the New Zealand court and a UK appeal to the Privy Council was also dismissed.

Despite this doubt about the legal protectability of television formats, most of the more important producers in

The Price Is Right: the game show is a staple of format trading

the West active in this area now play by rules that assume that formats are indeed protected in law. This formalisation of the trade has occurred over the past twenty years and has broadly coincided with an explosion in the volume of global trade in formats. One main reason for such an increase in this kind of commerce lies in the worldwide expansion of television channels thanks to deregulation, new technologies and the advent of *laissez-faire* economics in public policy. Faced with an ever more desperate struggle for ratings success, TV producers and broadcasters are ever more inclined to adapt an already successful programme format rather than to take a chance on an original (and therefore untested in the marketplace) format. With more potential overseas licensing revenues at stake, format owners are less willing to allow their work to be pirated. Thus, there has been a determined attempt to ensure that players stick to a set of rules in the game of the international adaptation of formats. Several elements are at work here. First, the fact that format trade now occurs at such industry conventions as MIPCOM rather than by overseas producers surreptitiously recording off-air in LA hotel rooms means that at least some parts of the trade are controlled. In addition, TV format owners continue to believe that formats do carry legal protection. Playing the game according to a perceived set of rules helps maintain

business reputations and legitimates access to new formats. Further, format licensing fees tend to be relatively modest, being partly determined by the kind of asking price that might be set for the broadcast rights of an imported version of the same programme. (Of course, such fees are likely to vary from one television market to another, depending on their relative affluence or otherwise, so that owners, producers and broadcasters maintain a general silence concerning licensing fees, including the principles underlying particular rates.) Additionally, to dissuade producers from plagiarising a format off-air, an owner also usually makes available a series of important ancillary elements as part of a format licensing package. These elements can include: titles and other software; set designs, production schedules and so on; scripts; videotapes of on-air episodes; confidential ratings and demographic information; and consultancy services. Thus, it is important not to overestimate the significance of a format as such but to realise that it may be one of the accompanying elements in such a package that may be the catalyst for a trading agreement. Finally, in terms of producers following rules, there is always the threat of legal action such as, for instance, occurred in 1999 when the UK producer of the 'reality' format *Survivor* undertook a lawsuit against Endemol, producer of *Big Brother*, alleging format infringement.

One further sign of the formalisation of exchange in television programme formats has been the recent organisation of a trade association. In 2000, the Format Recognition and Protection Association (FRAPA) was established in London. FRAPA's functions are threefold: first, it has established a system of dispute arbitration between members to avoid legal action which is often unpredictable, costly and usually slow. Second, it acts as an information clearing house for members. Third, in the longer term, it hopes to lobby particular national governments to enact format protection legislation. Not surprisingly, FRAPA has succeeded in signing up the major agencies in the international field of format trade including Endemol, Pearson, Columbia TriStar, King World, Distraction, Mentorn International, Action Time, Hat Trick Productions, Celador and Expand Images.

Harry de Winter, head of Dutch IDtv, believes that the international TV programme format business will ultimately end up in the hands of two or three giants with smaller independent companies being the ones that actually generate most of the new format ideas. Thus, the UK's Pearson Television and Endemol from the Netherlands are likely to be the central agencies in the format trade of the near future.

Pearson Television is an arm of the UK-based Pearson

BIG BROTHER

Endemol's 'jewel in the crown', *Big Brother* was thirty months in development and was the brainchild of co-principal, John de Mol. First broadcast on Veronica in 1999 and an immense ratings success, the programme has been adapted in over eighteen territories in Western Europe, the UK, the US and elsewhere. Meanwhile, even as first adaptations continue, second and third series have also gone on air.

Big Brother's generic family tree includes documentary, soap opera, game shows and television sport. Here, we concentrate on continuities with the latter, especially events such as World Cup soccer. Competition is a major sequencing element in both types of programmes with successive rounds leading to finals and ultimately single winner(s). Both programme types broadcast according to principles of saturation and ubiquity. Their on-air season is short, daily coverage extensive and access is increasingly available through ancillary media including cable, Internet, press and radio.

Like the local version of an Olympic Games, each incarnation of *Big Brother* is a national version of an international diasporic television brand name. The latter's mechanisms include product merchandising, a multiplication of different local spin-off programmes, the possibility of participant celebrityhood and the enhanced commercial value of venues. Again, too, while on air, *Big Brother* also pervades the world

of commerce, coupling with brand names for other commercial products and services. Thus, for example, in Australia, various TV commercials such as those for Pizza Hut were consciously moulded in terms of such elements as camera style and situation in order to obtain closer fit with the programme's content. This kind of linkage was consolidated by other marketing strategies such as product placement and phone line voting.

Each *Big Brother* adaptation constitutes a kind of mega-formatting that warrants the name of franchising. The TV format trade has always had this potential although licensing usually only involves formats and ancillary materials. However, *Big Brother*'s international arrangements have entailed various commercial rights relating to such additional platforms as cable, advertising, radio, telephone, billboards, merchandising and personal management. The parallels with a televised global sporting event are clear. Both conduct a type of business arrangement where a package rather than an individual right is managed, thereby ensuring the generation of profits from a series of additional operations that are not normally licensed but rather exist in the area of publicity. The term franchising relates to the licensing control of such a package of rights. It also relates to the kind of business operation whereby one firm, Endemol or its local subsidiary, grants the rights to distribute the national version of its format across a series of outlets to several local companies

Big Brother (UK, 2003): international TV brand name

including television networks, cable operators and telecommunications organisations. The total package of rights, together with the supporting vehicle that is *Big Brother*, is the product. Like the television marketing of an Olympic Games, the franchising of *Big Brother* involves the buying of a package of services that almost certainly guarantees profitability for the broadcasting network. Endemol has avoided levering the highest possible price from networks competing to broadcast the programme. Instead, like any wise, franchising parent, the company was disposed to strengthen the overall, international commercial reputation of the format and to secure a local licensing fee compatible with such an objective. This franchising makes *Big Brother* unique in the field of international television although with production and distribution finances in flux, it may also be a harbinger of the future.

Albert Moran

media group. Already owner of Thames Production, the company set out to acquire an extensive programme format catalogue in the early 1990s. In 1995, it took over Grundy Worldwide, achieving dominance most especially in the areas of game show and drama serials. Pearson's 1997 acquisition of All American Fremantle International gave it control of the very substantial Mark Goodson library of game shows including such classics as *The Price Is Right*, *Family Feud* (ABC/syndicated/CBS, 1976–93) and *Card Sharks*. Successful Grundy drama formats were already on the air in Australia, the Netherlands and Germany with new adaptations of formats such as *Sons and Daughters* and *Prisoner Cell Block H* appearing more recently in Sweden, Finland, Germany and Greece. In turn, the UK company also acquired additional formats through the takeover of a string of small production companies in the UK, Germany, Italy and South Africa. To concentrate on Spanish markets in the US and in Latin America, Pearson established a production company in Miami in 1999. Altogether, by 2002, the company has over 160 programmes in production in thirty-five different territories with particular production strengths in the UK, Germany, Sweden, the US and Australia. With an extensive format catalogue at its disposal, it was inevitable that Pearson would see strategic market advantage in joining a vertically integrated media group. Since 1997, it has been part of the UK Channel Five broadcasting consortium and in 2000 linked with the German based CTL-Ufa group. Most recently, Pearson has been in discussion with Sony. A takeover or merger here would see further realignment in the global format marketplace because of Sony's ownership of US format major, Columbia TriStar.

The other international format giant, Endemol, was established in 1993 with the merger of two independent Dutch companies, Joop van den Ende Productions and John de Mol Productions. In turn, it was floated as a public company on the Amsterdam stock exchange in 1996 and the capital inflow this has created has led to aggressive global expansion. Endemol now has companies in seventeen different territories in Western and Eastern Europe, the UK, Australia, South Africa, the US and Argentina. Meanwhile, in 2000, it linked with the Telefonia group, the largest supplier of telecommunications and Internet services in the Spanish- and Portuguese-speaking worlds. It now provides content for broadcasting companies as well as for Internet, third-generation mobile telephone and other distribution platforms. The basis of Endemol's remarkable expansion has been its catalogue of TV formats which currently numbers over 400 titles. These include not only some of the older pre-1993 formats belonging, variously, to Joop van den Ende Productions and John de Mol Productions such as *Forgive Me* and *All You Need Is Love* but more recently originated ones, most especially *Big Brother*. Indeed, the latter format has provided the basis for a comprehensive franchising operation involving the systematic exploitation of rights in relation to new distribution platforms that may be a significant clue to future directions in the format business.

Finally, it is important to note that, despite FRAPA's efforts, there are many producers outside the US and Western Europe who refuse to accept any rules. This is particularly the case in the People's Republic of China where the state does not support the notion of intellectual property. Even where intellectual property legislation is in place in territories such as India, the Philippines, Hong Kong and Thailand, a great deal of unauthorised format borrowing goes on, not only between an overseas original and a national clone but also between one regional remake and that in another locality or city. Further compounding this situation is the fact that it is frequently difficult to distinguish between a format infringement and a more general generic imitation. In any case, until some kind of global map of the main currents of the trade exists, it is far from clear just what are the major centres of format origination.

Albert Moran

AUDIENCES

Introduction

Often overlooked in writing the history of television is the role of the audience, the 'great unknown' without whom all is meaningless, but whose presence and predilections can only be guessed at by anxious broadcasters. Far from existing 'naturally' before television summons it into being, the television audience from the beginning has been assembled, constructed, defined, reviled, measured, manipulated and largely taken for granted by television's producers and administrators. Whether invoked as 'the viewing public', a convocation of citizens of a nation sitting before the tube ready to receive instruction and information, or as a vast and vague army of 'consumers' receiving their marching orders from television's advertisers, the television audience remains as often ignored and silenced as it is measured, spoken for and caused to exist.

The essays in this section each look at different ways of 'viewing the viewer', examining various lenses through which the audience has been perceived and understood throughout television's history: from the early years of network formation to the current period of neo-network segmentation; from early fears of the 'mass' and its susceptibility to manipulation and persuasion to notions of a more active, meaning-constructing audience that actively understands and decodes the messages laid out before it; to the history of quantitative audience measurement developed by commercial broadcasting to produce the commodity audience so valuable to advertisers; and to the ways in which audiences have been conceptualised in regulatory discourses, particularly in the recurring controversies over television violence and its effects. Finally, the Internet has opened up the relationship of audiences to television texts in ways that were hardly anticipated – and are only sometimes appreciated – by the industry. In particular, online fan communities have enabled a new kind of active participation, not only in the reception and interpretation of programmes, but in social movements arising out of issue-driven content and in ongoing interactive relationships with programme producers: voiceless no more.

Michele Hilmes

From Network to Neo-Network Audiences

To most of us, the word 'audience' has a rather straightforward meaning. It conjures up the image of a group of people who are watching a speech, performance or public event. Yet in fact, the meaning of audience has changed throughout history and it has most significantly changed over the last hundred years with the introduction of electronic mass communication. As we shall see, television audiences today are very different than they were fifty years ago, but before considering the recent changes in TV audiences, we should detour back to the early years of radio in order to more fully appreciate the transformations that have taken place.

Our common-sense notion of the audience comes from the time when audiences were defined by the fact that they constituted a group of people gathered in one place for the purpose of participating in a specific collective event. Thus, physical co-presence was an important characteristic of the audience experience. Yet, as scholars such as Paddy Scannell (1996), Michele Hilmes (1997) and Roland Marchand (1985) have shown, the advent of radio made possible new audience experiences in which one was listening in on live events, such as sports contests and political speeches, while in the company of absent others. Although some people actually attended these events, others – who normally wouldn't attend – now had the opportunity to listen in from a distance.

Moreover, radio shows that were produced in a studio often had no physical audience present during the performance. Everyone was listening in and performers had to imagine the audiences who might be tuned to their radios at home. Thus, radio dramatically altered the listener's relationship to performative events. Indeed, Heywood Broun wryly noted shortly after the emergence of broadcasting, that one of the key advantages of radio was the fact that one could listen to a sermon, smoke a cigar and throw in a few cuss words all at the same time. One no longer had to worry what others in the audience might think, or even what the preacher of the sermon might think, because one's relationship to them was fundamentally imaginary.

For those who ran broadcast institutions, this posed a peculiar problem: how did they know who was listening? In many countries with public service systems, this was an urgent question because broadcasters had to justify their budgets to public officials, opinion leaders and the audience itself. Countries with commercial broadcasting systems had a similar problem in that they needed to calculate advertising rates to support their businesses. Consequently, broadcasters began to use largely quantitative methods in order to assemble images of the audience that they could use for their own purposes. Critics, scholars and policy-makers also expended a tremendous amount of time talking about the radio audience as they ruminated on ways to regulate and improve broadcasting. They too had to imagine an audience they had never met.

Three key points emerge from this short history. First of all, the radio audience was an *imagined* entity rather than an empirical fact. Whoever made reference to the audience had to create an image of a group that could not be directly perceived; and those who created such images did so for specific reasons. Second, those with the most power to define audiences were politicians, policy-makers and industry personnel. As the radio era progressed, these influential actors increasingly defined the audience as a national audience. This served the purposes of advertisers, commercial networks and public service institutions, but just as importantly, it served the interests of governments, as military conflicts began to escalate on the eve of World War II.

After the war, the emergence of television further consolidated the concept of the national audience that would prevail in industry and policy discourse until approximately 1980. This early period of television might be referred to as the 'classic network era'. In the United States, this classical period existed because the economies of scale of early TV production combined with a government licensing system heavily favoured the development of only three national broadcast services. When television first started, many other media companies, such as Time-Life and Paramount, wanted to establish networks of their own, and indeed the technology was available. But during this early licensing phase, government regulators favoured the existing radio networks and their lobbyists, thereby setting in place an officially sanctioned oligopoly. Yet no major objections were raised at the time because of the widespread presumption that given the heavy cost of developing the new technology, a few large broadcast corporations could best serve the needs of vast national and even international audiences (Baughman, 1985; Boddy, 1990).

As with most oligopoly corporations that are sanc-

tioned by the government, the new television networks tried to legitimise their special status by promoting their services as offering something for everyone, combined with sporadic efforts to provide 'public service' programming, such as documentaries. The 'something for everyone' formula also had practical economic benefits, since at the time companies that purchased TV ads were manufacturers of mass consumer goods. Thus, even though TV audiences of this period were obviously diverse – distinguished by class, race, ethnicity, gender, political preferences, etc. – network executives aspired to represent them as a unified entity in ratings, marketing reports and promotions. Moreover, they characterised the overarching mission of the networks as integrative: pulling people together, uniting various regions, forging ever-larger markets (Balio, 1990; Spigel and Curtin, 1997). Television was conceived as a mass, national medium, which engendered ongoing criticism of network television as a cesspool of homogeneous drivel, or, as FCC Chairman Newton Minow famously described it, a 'vast wasteland'.

The operative principles of the classic network era still exercise a powerful hold on our imaginations, suggesting that power and control over national consciousness reside primarily in the boardrooms of a few major networks. Over the past decade, as we have witnessed the merging of gigantic media firms into huge conglomerates, many critics seem to assume that this concentration of ownership means greater control at the top of the corporate pyramid and an increasing standardisation of cultural products worldwide.

Yet the principles that guide the television industry have undergone significant change over the past twenty years. Transformations in national and global economies have fragmented the marketplace, pressuring the culture industries to reorganise and restrategise. Television advertising is no longer dominated by firms that manufacture products or provide services exclusively for mass markets. Changing market conditions have led companies to target their advertising at particular demographic groups and to disperse their messages throughout a variety of media (D'Acci, 1994; Feuer, Kerr and Vahimagi, 1984; Gitlin, 1983). Furthermore, transnational marketing has become increasingly popular as both advertisers and their ad agencies have sought out new customers around the globe. Finally, public service broadcast systems around the world have faced intense pressure to deregulate. Television has changed so dramatically that we might refer to this most recent period as the 'neo-network era'.

As opposed to the nationally based television corporations that prevailed during the classical network era, the current period is paradoxically characterised by both transnationalisation and fragmentation. New technologies, deregulation and relentless competition have undermined the national frameworks that once shaped the industry. Although mass markets continue to attract corporate attention and blockbuster media products are still a priority, industry discourse about the mass audience no longer refers to one simultaneous exposure to a particular programme, artist, or event, so much as a shared, asynchronous cultural milieu. For example, US TV viewers less frequently experience a major social or cultural event, such as the 1964 pop-rock 'British invasion' when families and friends collectively gathered around the television set at eight o'clock on a Sunday night to watch the Beatles' first television performance in North America. Instead, performers, trends and ideas now achieve prominence in often circuitous and unanticipated ways. Variety show host Ed Sullivan, who was the consummate 1960s' gatekeeper of popular entertainment, has no counterpart in television today.

In part, this is because the culture industries exercise less control over the daily scheduling of popular entertainment; audiences time-shift and channel surf or they pursue a myriad of other entertainment options. As a result, media executives strive instead for broad exposure of their products through multiple circuits of information and expression. They also seek less to homogenise popular culture than to organise and exploit diverse forms of creativity towards profitable ends. Besides their heavily promoted blockbusters, media corporations also cultivate a broad range of products intended for more specific audiences. Flexible corporate frameworks connect mass-market operations with more localised initiatives.

Two strategies are now at work in the culture industries. One focuses on mass cultural forms aimed at broad national or global markets that demand low involvement and are relatively apolitical, such as blockbuster Hollywood films, like *Spiderman*, or broadcast television programmes, like *Frasier* (NBC). Media operations that deal in this arena are cautious about the prospect of intense audience responses either for or against the product they are marketing. By comparison, those products targeted at niche audiences actively pursue intensity. They seek out audiences that are more likely to be highly invested in a particular form of cultural expression. Among industry executives these are referred to as products with 'edge'. Thirty years ago they received little attention, but today product development meetings are peppered with references to attitude and edge, that is, references to products that sharply define the boundaries of their intended audi-

ence. Programmes with edge – ranging from hip hop comedies like *South Central* (Fox), to gender-bending parodies like *Absolutely Fabulous* (Comedy Central), to renegade cop shows like *The Shield* (Fox), to teen horror-comedies like *Buffy the Vampire Slayer* (UPN) – can be marketed on cable, satellite, video cassette or via the new networks recently started by News Corporation, Warner Bros. and Paramount. Such programmes have even found their way onto broadcast TV, as the major networks attempt to respond to the new competitive environment. For example, NBC launched Michael Moore's politically provocative *TV Nation* after an initial run on Fox and ABC ran Ellen DeGeneres' sitcom, *Ellen*, which explicitly revolved around issues of sexual orientation. Although both of these series eventually succumbed to the residual pressures of classical network reasoning, the fact that they survived two seasons on the national broadcast networks highlights the changes that have taken place since the early 1980s.

We are therefore witnessing the organisation of huge media conglomerates around the so-called synergies that exploit these two movements between mass and niche marketing. This is what we refer to as the neo-network era, an era characterised by the multiple and asynchronous distribution of cultural forms, an era that operates according to the logic of what David Harvey (1989) refers to as a 'flexible regime of accumulation.' Rather than a network structure anchored by a three-network oligopoly or a public service monopoly, the neo-network era features elaborate circuits of cultural production, distribution and reception (Curtin, 1997; 1999).

This transformation is not a radical break with the past. Rather, both classic network and niche network tendencies exist side-by-side, and probably will continue to do so for some time. Blockbuster films that appeal to a transnational audience are still the desideratum of major Hollywood studios, but the same conglomerate that may own a major motion picture studio may also own a boutique TV production company, a speciality music label, and a collection of magazines that target very specific market niches. 'As you get narrower in interest,' media executive Mark Edmiston (1997) observes, 'you tend to have more intensity of interest and [the consumer] is more likely to pay the extra money.' What makes a niche product profitable is that it can be marketed to select audiences and sponsoring advertisers at a premium price. The key to success is no longer the ownership and control of a centralised and highly integrated medium-specific empire like the classical networks, but the management of a conglomerate structured around a variety of firms with different audiences and different objectives.

Although the mass market is still attractive, micro markets can be extremely lucrative, a realisation that has engendered an intensive search for narrowly defined and under-served audiences. Race, gender, age and ethnicity have now joined socio-economic status as potentially marketable boundaries of difference. Despite the intensity of interest that these firms may find among a micro audience, a media company's participation in a particular market is not based on a commitment to the material interests or political principles of the audience. Rather these firms simply are following a marketing strategy that they characterise as strictly capitalistic and generally disinterested in content issues.

In the eyes of media executives, a neo-network strategy will ideally present opportunities whereby a micro-market phenomenon may cross over into a mainstream phenomenon, making it potentially exploitable through a greater number of circuits within the media conglomerate. Some hip hop artists' careers obviously followed this trajectory, perhaps best represented by the success of a performer like Will Smith whose rap music career was levered into a hit television series and then into a leading role in one of the highest-grossing films in Hollywood history. But the converse is also true. A product that was originally a mass product can be spun out through a myriad of niche venues, which has been Viacom's strategy behind *Star Trek*, one of its most profitable brands.

Most commonly, media moguls today find themselves chasing after audiences with a plethora of information and entertainment alternatives, resulting in the flood of material crying for attention. Consequently, promotion has become ever more important within the media marketplace where consumers confront a blizzard of options. One of the key strategies to address such confusion in the marketplace is the concept of 'branding'. Companies like

Disney and AOL Time Warner try to develop a collection of products that are linked across media. Disney's films, videos, toys and theme parks are the most obvious example. The look, feel and packaging of Disney products give consumers a fairly good idea of what to anticipate from each item. Pursuing the same strategy, Time-Life magazines—the purveyors of *Time*, *Fortune* and *Entertainment Weekly*—have developed television news magazines on CNN and World Wide Web sites that are tied to the parent print publications, providing an archetypal example of synergistic relations between components of the AOL Time Warner empire. Likewise, MTV (owned by Viacom/Paramount) is moving into feature film production where it will target the same audiences that watch the cable channel. In a neo-network environment characterised by a glut of media products (rather than the artificially imposed restrictions of only three national television channels during the classical network era) conglomerates such as Disney are trying – via the concept of branding – to influence audience awareness of the informational and cultural options available to them. They are also trying to construct various brand images that help advertisers understand the kinds of audiences that their products tend to attract, for example, ABC, Lifetime, ESPN, A&E and Disney Channel are all Disney services that are targeted at different audiences. Thus, images of the audience have changed dramatically during the age of broadcasting, from the imagined national mass audience of the classic network era to the diverse range of audiences that neo-network media conglomerates seek to attract in order to satisfy the needs of various advertisers.

Michael Curtin

RECOMMENDED READING

Curtin, Michael (1999), 'Feminine Desire in the Age of Satellite Television', *Journal of Communication,* vol. 49, no. 2, Spring, pp. 55–70.

D'Acci, Julie (1994), *Defining Women: The Case of* Cagney and Lacey, Chapel Hill: University of North Carolina Press.

Gitlin, Todd (1983), *Inside Prime Time*, New York: Pantheon.

Hilmes, Michele (1997), *Radio Voices: American Broadcasting, 1922–1952*, Minneapolis: University of Minnesota Press.

Ohmann, Richard, Averill, Gage, Curtin, Michael, Shumway, David and Traube, Elizabeth G.(eds) (1997), *Making and Selling Culture*, Hanover: Wesleyan University Press.

Scannell, Paddy (1996), *Radio, Television, and Modern Life: A Phenomenological Approach*, Cambridge: Blackwell.

Spun out through a myriad of niche venues: Viacom's *Star Trek*

From Mass to Meanings

The development of mass media in the twentieth century created a new and, for many, worrisome topography. It was as if the increasingly urban landscape was now composed of living breathing masses: *mass* society and *mass* culture bound together by the power of *mass* communication. Much of the concern about mass communication and culture was directed towards audiences – audiences that were larger, less bound by time and space, less predictable and less knowable than hitherto. As political franchises became more universal and social boundaries less tangible, the power of the mass media to influence public behaviour and opinion became a pressing issue – most notably for political, cultural and economic elites, for whom the mass audience represented a potentially serious challenge.

Raymond Williams has suggested that much of the early concern about mass audiences was based on a deep distrust of the popular or the democratic – whether in culture or in politics – and there was a sense in which the twentieth century 'mass' replaced the 'mobs' of the eighteenth and nineteenth centuries as the *bête noire* of the ruling classes (Williams, 1963). But the rise of a sinister and undemocratic form of mass politics (Hitler in Germany, Mussolini in Italy and Franco in Spain) – a fascism fuelled by the propagandist use of mass media – gave rise to legitimate concerns about the power of mass media to influence audiences.

Indeed, the success of Nazi propaganda cast a long shadow over early audience research. Mass communications scholars at Columbia University in the 1940s and 50s were informed by fears that media could become agents for mass persuasion. Such fears were highlighted by the panic induced by Orson Welles' 1938 radio production of *The War of the Worlds*. The broadcast, written as a series of news reports, inadvertently fooled up to a million Americans, as across the country people spilled out onto the streets in the belief that the United States was in the midst of a Martian invasion.

If such persuasive power was to be understood, it needed to be measured, and the development of sampling and survey methodology in the 1920s and 30s gave researchers the means to turn the mass audience into a more comprehensible form. The habits and attitudes of an audience of millions could, if the correct sampling procedures were adopted, be gauged by interviewing a tiny fraction of the population. Better still, the relationship between what people read, watched or listened to and what they did or thought could be mapped out scientifically with correlations and cross-tabulations. The techniques of social science thereby offered the promise of rendering mass audiences

conceptually manageable and, in theory, less enigmatic (Beniger, 1987). Thus began the *effects* tradition of audience research, in which the power of media over audiences was evaluated by the quantitative tools of social science.

The effects model remains influential – not least in public discussions of media influence, which tend to focus on direct, immediate and usually negative forms of media influence (such as copycat violence). The early effects studies were limited by this rather narrow view of media influence – and in particular by fears of a mass media that could be politically manipulative or create antisocial forms of behaviour. Because the early research suggested that the mass media did *not*, on the whole, generate widespread mimicry or delinquency (see, for example, Lazarsfeld and Katz, 1955), this led many to conclude that the effects of media on society were minimal. Indeed, the search for negative media effects was replaced by a more benign model of media and a more robust conception of the reader, listener or viewer. The birth of 'uses and gratifications' research in the 1950s was, in a well-known phrase, concerned less with what media did to people than with what people did to media.

At its crudest, the uses and gratification approach was also more in keeping with the consumerist ideology promoted by the public relations industry – most visibly in the United States – during the 1950s. The audience were no longer seen as a potentially gullible mass but as distinct groups of consumers motivated by needs and desires that could be met by media, and, of course, by the consumer society advertised in much of that media. The irony of this association between consumer sovereignty and the growth of advertising and public relations was that these industries were propagandist in form, deeply committed to influencing the way audiences thought and behaved. The sovereign consumer was thereby embraced by market research which sought not to inform but to persuade, and to thereby transform audiences into consumers.

At its best, uses and gratifications provided media research with a more sophisticated conception of audiences, who were no longer seen as a homogeneous mass but as members of a complex set of social groups who engaged with media in various ways. This was not necessarily a matter of discounting media influence, but of recognising its complexity. Indeed, research over the next few decades suggested that the notion of 'minimal' media effects was premature. Once it became clear that the content of most media (apart, perhaps, from advertising) was more descriptive than overtly propagandist, researchers understood that the relationship between media and audiences could not be grasped merely by using a simple model of persuasion (one in which ways of thinking or behaving were – or were not – grafted onto a mass public). From the 1960s and 70s, various research traditions began to conceive media as *ideological agencies* in a broad sense, agencies that might gently reinforce social attitudes, or create symbolic or informational frameworks in which certain kinds of ideas become plausible or relevant.

The emergence of 'agenda setting' research in the late 1960s and early 1970s posed the question of media effects in a way that more closely matched the nature of media content to media influence. It began by avoiding the question of how opinions are formed altogether, focusing less on what people thought than on what they thought about. While the distinction between what people think and what they think about was ultimately untenable, since, as McCombs, Danielian and Wanta put it: 'one's store of information shapes one's opinions' (1995, p. 295), it allowed researchers to see whether the news media's general content influenced audience priorities. From the 1970s on, the results of agenda-setting studies have shown repeated instances where the degree of prominence of an issue in the media related directly to the importance people afforded to it, regardless of 'real-world' indicators. So, for example, when media coverage of crime increases while figures suggest no proportional increase in actual crime, public *concern* about crime tends to go up in response to the shift in media content, regardless of the actual risk of crime. At its most dramatic, the agenda-setting phenomenum creates a spiral of concern, in which public figures feel obliged to respond to media agendas, thereby reinforcing that agenda and creating 'moral panics', such as the 'mugging crisis' in 1970s' Britain (Hall *et al.*, 1978), or the anti-drug fears in the late 1980s in the US – both instances where moral panics led to a heavy-handed and enduring institutional response.

During the 1980s and 90s, agenda-setting research began to explore more complex responses to media content. So, for example, Iyengar (1991) looked at how the way in which news stories are told influences the way those stories are understood. Iyengar's research suggests that when stories or events are covered with little consideration of background or explanation (what Iyengar calls an 'episodic frame'), audiences find it difficult to focus on the social causes of those stories or events. This, in turn, creates an ideological climate in which political leaders are not required to address the structural or social causes of social problems.

Another significant approach to media influence to emerge during the 1970s and 80s was cultivation analysis (Signorielli and Morgan, 1990). The 'cultural indicators' project based at the University of Pennsylvania looked at the representational

and symbolic content of prime-time television to explore how dominant representations might inform people's assumptions about the world. The idea of 'cultivation', like agenda-setting, is based on matching a content analysis of media with audience responses, although the scope of cultivation analysis is rather broader. Moreover, while media effects has traditionally been concerned with changes in attitudes or behaviour, cultivation analysis was interested not only in the more long-term ideological forms of media influence, but also in how media might *reinforce* dominant ideas and thus prevent or limit social change. So, for example, the consistent presence of forms of gender stereotyping in the media might suggest a tendency to reinforce traditional gender roles rather than promote a change towards more progressive or feminist ideas about gender equity.

The results of the cultivation studies in the US suggested that the more television people watched, the more likely they were to assume the world around them was, either symbolically or literally, like the television world. So, for example, heavy TV viewers in the US were more likely hold traditional views about gender, more likely to fit self-consciously within a 'mainstream' of political ideas and, in one of the more literal and most obviously misguided forms of cultivation, more likely to see the absence of old people on television as indicative of a more general absence of old people in society (even while there are more old people living longer and healthier lives than ever before). Perhaps most famously, cultivation studies in the US suggested that while it may be unclear whether the predominance of violence on US television created violent behaviour, heavy viewers were, regardless of who they were or where they lived, more likely to see the world as a violent place (referred to the 'mean-world syndrome').

Both agenda-setting and cultivation analysis developed against the backdrop of the survey-based mass communications effects traditions prominent in the United States. In Britain, the emergence of cultural studies during the 1970s provided a different point of departure. Cultural studies fused theoretical developments in semiology, Marxism and structural anthropology in Continental Europe with notions of culture that focused on popular and working-class cultural forms. In so doing, cultural studies saw the study of media as central to understanding the construction of meaning and ideology in contemporary society. Media studies in Britain – and subsequently, elsewhere – was heavily influenced by these developments, and tended to adopt the more qualitative forms of analysis used in semiology and discourse analysis.

The audience research flowing out of this new approach to media studies saw the relationship between media texts

CITIZENS AND CONSUMERS

The concepts of citizenship and consumerism are useful ways of describing various forms of subjectivity. The idea of the citizen dates back to ancient Greece, and is generally associated with participatory forms of democracy. The citizen is seen as someone who takes part in civic life and actively contributes to processes of democratic decision-making. Hence the concept of citizenship became irrelevant in medieval Europe, where political power was disseminated through feudal hierarchies and where public gatherings were merely witnesses or expressions of that power. The nineteenth and twentieth centuries can be seen as periods in which rights of citizenship became the focus of political struggles – struggles that resulted in the extension of citizenship to encompass certain legal political and material rights, and to include people regardless of property, wealth, race or gender.

And yet the increasing power and scope of citizenship in the twentieth century have been overshadowed by the substitution of the notion of citizenship with the more limited idea of the consumer. Unlike the citizen, the consumer's means of expression is limited: while citizens can address every aspect of cultural, social and economic life (operating in what Jürgen Habermas called 'the public sphere'), consumers find expression only in the marketplace. As an ideology, consumerism reduces human activity – whether it involves the search for happiness or solving social problems – to individual acts of consumption. The consumer merely chooses to buy or not to buy.

The history of television is deeply implicated in the battle between citizenship and consumerism. The notion of 'public service broadcasting' is clearly tied to the notion of citizenship: indeed, public service broadcasting seeks to strengthen citizenship by educating people about public affairs and by increasing people's access to a range of cultural forms. Exactly *how* public service broadcasting achieves this is much contested, and this contestation is partly an argument about the nature of citizenship in multicultural societies. Commercial television, on the other hand, addresses viewers as consumers rather than citizens. The increasing presence of television advertising is, in this sense, not ideologically innocent. TV commercials may sell everything from lipstick to lifestyles and use every imaginable strategy to do so, but together they create an insistent drumbeat in which every problem and every desire can be resolved through an act of consumption.

The degree to which television programmes are themselves a commodity depends on how they are paid for. It is often assumed that commercial television raises revenue from advertising to produce programmes for viewers to consume, but in economic terms, it is *TV audiences* who become the commodity being produced and sold, and it is the TV advertiser who pays for access to these audiences. The function of programmes is simply to produce the most attractive and valuable commodity i.e. a large, affluent audience in the right mood to watch a TV commercial. In a commercial system paid for by advertising, the TV viewer is continually constructed as a consumer by the discourse of advertising, even while they are deprived of the limited power accrued to consumers because it is the advertisers rather than the viewers who are paying for the programmes. So, for example, a programme with a large audience of less affluent viewers will be less valuable to advertisers (and hence more likely to be cancelled) than one with a smaller audience of viewers with high levels of disposable income.

The kind of broadcasting we choose thus depends on how we are conceived. As citizens, we can contribute to the debate about the broad content, form and regulation of television through discussion and debate. As consumers, we can make more limited choices – on the level of individual programmes – if we have pay-per-view or subscription television, which allows us to pay for programmes directly. But the most common form of commercial television – paid for by advertisers – promotes the ideology of consumerism while reducing viewers to mere commodities to be bought and sold.

Justin Lewis

and audiences as a complex process of *meaning construction*, using various semiotic codes. Thus, in Stuart Hall's influential model, production of media can be described as 'encoding', while audience reception can be described as 'decoding' (Hall, 1980). This process was not only understood in microscopic terms, but in the context of ideological and representational struggles in society as a whole. A key question for this kind of audience research was therefore the extent to which the meanings produced by interactions between media and audiences contributed to – or resisted – forms of political and cultural hegemony.

The first attempt to test the decoding model empirically was David Morley's study of audience responses to a British current affairs programme, *Nationwide*, published in 1980. Since then, a number of qualitative studies have looked at the complex ways audiences can become inscribed within hegemonic ways of thinking. So, for example, McKinley (1997) looks at the way girls watching *Beverly Hills 90210* are encouraged to adopt anti-feminist positions, while Jhally and Lewis (1992) look at the way audiences of *The*

Beverly Hills 90210: audiences, anti-feminism and ideology

The Ratings System and Its Effects

In common parlance, television ratings tell us which pro-grammes are the most watched and most popular. This suggests that programmes like *Frasier* (NBC, 1993–) or *Witchblade* (TNT, 2001–) or *The Sopranos* (HBO, 1999–) remain on television only as long as the vast majority of viewers want to watch them. However, when we study the history of the ratings industry in the United States, and especially when we analyse the structures of the interlocked markets for television audiences, audience measures and television programmes, we realise that such 'common parl-ance' misrepresents the situation.

Cosby Show find it difficult to understand the role social class plays in racial inequality in the US. Other research – especially on fan culture – has explored the way audiences exploit textual ambiguities to construct progressive or counter-hegemonic meanings. While this research is seen as embracing the notion of 'active audiences' head on, it acknowledges that audiences nonetheless operate 'within rather than outside the ideological framework provided by the program' (Jenkins, 1992, p. 263; see also Lewis, 2001 for a summary of this research).

The strength of this research on 'decoding' or reception is its qualitative depth. It has tended to draw upon detailed analysis of conversations with individuals or small groups, allowing us to glimpse at the way in which the information, ideas and representations used in media inform everyday conversations. Its weakness is that while it gets us much closer to the moments at which meanings are constructed, the small samples generally used in such research limit the degree to which we can draw more general conclusions about the meaning of media in society. The more qualitat-ive audience research informed by cultural studies and the more quantitative 'mass communications' approaches like cultivation and agenda-setting have, historically, tended to follow their own trajectories. Nonetheless, the field has, in recent years, begun to show signs of theoretical and meth-odological crossovers between the use of quantitative frameworks and cultural studies approaches (see for example, Herbst, 1993; Lewis, 2001; and Ruddock, 2001).

Justin Lewis

The unity of demand between advertisers and net-works, plus their shared desire to pay low prices for audi-ence measures, are crucial constraints on the market for audience measures. Because the sale and purchase of audi-ences is a highly routine transaction conducted by rela-tively low-paid employees of advertisers and networks, these corporations have little interest in competing accounts of a show's performance. These concerns dovetail, generating a preference among the buyers of audience measurements for a single seller of those information com-modities. Generally, then, the market for audience measures in the US has been dominated by a single company, starting with the Co-operative Analysis of Broadcasting controlling radio ratings in 1928–9, then the C. E. Hooper Company monopolising radio ratings from 1929–40, and finally by the A. C. Nielsen Company (ACN) whose monopoly extended from radio in the early 1940s into television and the twenty-first century. Rivals to the monopolist emerge only when some sizeable faction of buyers is dissatisfied with the current monopolist.

ACN currently uses two approaches to gather its audi-ence measures: diaries and Peoplemeters. The Peoplemeters figure heavily in ACN's promotions, where claims about their objectivity and scientificity abound. This is typical of ACN, which has always emphasised its use of sophisticated technology in ads but relied on a mixture of diaries and meters. The diaries depend on the willing-ness of respondents to write down information, every fif-teen minutes, about who watches what programme. Generally, ACN uses diaries for information about demo-graphics, while relying on meters for information about programme choices. With the Peoplemeter, both demo-graphic and programme information may be gathered: the meter flashes a reminder light every fifteen minutes so that viewers can push their individual buttons to identify them as watching the programme. No positive reinforcement is provided; Peoplemeter households are expected to report viewing for seven years. Because it is relatively expensive and requires a dedicated phone line to report responses, ACN installs a Peoplemeter only on a household's main television set. Most Peoplemeter households subscribe to cable television. Nationally, 5,000 households are designated as Peoplemeter households. At any particular time, some households may have left the group; others may be reporting unusable responses due to technical breakdowns. The precise number of households reporting usable responses is proprietary information. Despite its promotion of Peoplemeters, ACN continues to use diaries.

When ACN entered ratings production in the late 1930, it used diaries for demographics, Audimeters to determine what radio stations were tuned in, and Recordimeters to report if sets were on or off. Information from diaries and Recordimeters was edited to conform to reports from the Audimeters. Promoted in much the same way as Peoplemeters, Audimeters were installed on radio sets and calibrated to expose a film according to what channel was playing. Recordimeters simply exposed the film from the time the set was turned on, until it was turned off. No rationale for combining these measures was offered. ACN designated 1,200 households for its metered sample.

When CBS and RCA's NBC introduced television after World War II, ACN installed Audimeters on televisions bought by its radio-Audimeter households. This locked television programming to radio programming, reflecting both advertisers' reluctance to abandon radio and CBS and NBC's strategy of broadcasting radio shows on both media. The essential organisation of ACN's households as radio-based persisted into the 1960s, when the House Special Subcommittee on Investigations (HSSI) determined, among other things, that ACN was still using households from its 1936 experimental Audimeter installation in Appleton, Wisconsin. In terms of the interlocked markets for networked programmes, audience measures and audiences, the new medium of television and the old medium of radio were identical. While the HSSI investigation forced some changes in ACN's meters and sample, it had neither an immediate nor a long-term effect on the interlocked markets for audiences, audience measures, and programming that underpin television.

In the television industry, 'ratings' is used both in terms of common parlance and to indicate a specific form of audience measurement. A programme's rating identifies its rank among the shows run during a particular segment of the programming day. The rating is determined by calcu-

lating the percentage of households tuned into the show. Ratings allow comparison between shows that are competing for viewership at a specific time. Ratings are further manipulated to determine the top ten programmes by day part – top ten in prime time, daytime, etc. – as well as to rank the broadcast networks overall. These further manipulations are only as reliable as the original measures, which are themselves questionable.

Ratings are augmented by the two other measurements: 'share' and 'demographics'. Share provides a context for ratings by taking into account the fact that not all households in the ACN sample are using their sets at any one time. Share, then, is the fraction of the total number of households using television (HUT) tuned into a particular show. A programme that is rated number one may have a share that is unacceptable for advertisers and thence to its network if, for example, the share is low because the HUT is spread over too many channels. A programme that is number one in its day part, but with a poor share, may be cancelled despite the good rating.

Ratings and shares are further contextualised by descriptions of the types of people who comprise the audience, called 'demographics' in the trade. Networks also seek demographic information because advertisers divide audiences in terms of age, gender, economic status, race, ethnicity and mode of access (cable, broadcast only). At the time of writing, the most highly prized demographic group is comprised of viewers who are eighteen to thirty-four years old, male, upmarket, white and living in households that subscribe to cable.

To remain on television, programmes must meet advertisers' preferences in terms of ratings, share and demographics. That success is key to network decisions about renewing, reformulating or cancelling a show. From an industrial perspective, television shows are only successful when advertisers get a large chunk of the audiences that they have selected as worthwhile. For a series to be popular with advertisers is not necessarily the same as being popular with the vast majority of viewers.

This subtle, but important, difference is rooted in the three interlocking markets that underpin network television: the markets for audience measures, audiences and programmes. Because networks earn revenues mainly from advertisers, networks' most important market is the one in which networks sell and advertisers buy audiences. The market for audiences influences the way that networks act in the market for programmes: they seek programming that will allow them to satisfy advertisers' demands for particular audiences rather than trying to appeal to everybody who watches television. As noted above, the most highly

THE A. C. NIELSEN COMPANY

The history of television ratings is inextricably intertwined with the A. C. Nielsen Company (ACN). In 1923, Arthur C. Nielsen, Sr founded ACN as an operations consultant for heavy manufacturers. In 1929, the Great Depression left ACN searching for another market niche. That led ACN into information production: its Nielsen Retail Index (NRI) reported the shelf space given to name brand products and their promotional materials by selected retailers. The NRI allowed companies to compare space given to rival brands across retail outlets. ACN traces its interest in radio ratings to the success of its NRI: since manufacturers of name brands were also advertisers, and most bought the NRI, why not develop an index to measure the radio audiences to which they advertised?

One reason not to – unmentioned in ACN's company histories – was that the C. E. Hooper Company (CEH) monopolised radio ratings (see The Ratings System and its Effects). To challenge CEH, ACN crafted a two-pronged strategy. First, ACN sought a means of measuring audiences that would differentiate its ratings from, and make them appear superior to, Hooperatings. Second, ACN sought to combine its retail indices with ratings and with information on the purchases of respondents (so-called 'pantry audits'). That attempt failed, but remains a corporate goal.

ACN located a primitive meter invented by two professors at Massachusetts Institute for Technology. Purchasing the patent, ACN derived the Audimeter and Recordimeter (see The Ratings System and its Effects) and used them, plus diaries, to generate ratings, shares and demographics. ACN promoted the resulting Nielsen Radio Indexes to its NRI clients as well any company interested in radio. ACN's promotional campaign stressed the superiority of modern engineering, embodied in the Audimeter, over CEH's human interviewers. ACN replaced CEH as the ratings monopolist in radio, leaving ACN poised to monopolise national television ratings. Having achieved that by 1950, ACN expanded into international markets.

ACN's monopoly invited scrutiny: from 1963–5, ACN was investigated by Congress. This ultimately forced ACN to update measurement practices, initiate overnight ratings in major cities and submit to oversight by NBC, CBS and ABC via their Committee on National Television Audience Measurement (CONTAM). That submission ensured ACN's monopoly over ratings, despite occasional challenges. Not until the late 1970s did ACN loosen its ties to the networks and expand into cable ratings, when Turner Broadcasting Systems offered to pay ACN to measure its audiences. That deal, tapping advertisers' interest in cable, redefined television as both cable and broadcast shows, and opened the way to ACN's invention of the Peoplemeter. In 1984, ACN was purchased by Dun & Bradstreet (D&B), which owned one of two technologies used to scan prices. D&B tried integrating scanning data with television ratings, but to no avail. In 1996, D&B spun off ACN as an independent company with operations in ratings (television, Internet, radio); in scanning (retail and pantry audits); retail indices; test marketing; and box-office information for films, etc. In 2001, ACN was purchased by VNU N.V., a privately held Dutch company specialising in market information and trade publications, including *Adweek* and *Billboard*.

Eileen R. Meehan

demanded and most expensive audience is comprised of men who are eighteen to thirty-four, white, upmarket and living in cable households. Most prime-time programming is designed with this audience in mind, although some networks will incorporate elements into a programme to expand its appeal. That practice usually targets the sexual partners of these men – upmarket, white women aged eighteen to thirty-four who watch television with their partners. Within that group, advertisers generally place more value on women who work outside the home thirty hours per week than women who work in the home.

These industrial practices have interesting effects. For example, the Lifetime cable network, which has advertised itself as 'television for women' since the 1980s, targets most of its daily schedule to upmarket women who stay at home and its prime-time schedule to heterosexual couples who watch television together and are eighteen to thirty-four years old, white and upmarket. Despite Lifetime's success – it has long been ranked in the top-ten cable networks – Lifetime remains, in industrial parlance, a niche programmer rather like Black Entertainment Television. This contrasts with ESPN's status as a mainstream programmer, despite its concentration on sports. While American culture traditionally defined sports as male activities, not all men are sports fans; not all fans are male; and some fans are selective, rather than generic, viewers of sports. But as long as ESPN targets and delivers men who are eighteen to thirty-four years old, white, upmarket and cable subscribers – regardless of its programming – ESPN is treated as a mainstream programmer attracting 'the audience' and not a specialised programmer attracting the niche audience of sports fans. In industrial terms, television's audience is whatever segment of the population most demanded by advertisers.

This has a significant impact on the market for audience measures. With advertisers and networks focused on 'the audience', their demand for ratings, share and demographics will emphasise that commercially desirable segment. Any interest in commercially defined niche audiences (like people over thirty-four, women, Hispanics, downmarket subscribers to cable, etc.) will vary among advertisers and networks. This sets up market constraints for those companies that want to sell audience measures to networks and advertisers. No ratings company can afford to produce measurements that advertisers and networks do not demand; every ratings company knows which segment is in greatest demand. For example, with advertisers interested in cable as a means of separating bona fide consumers from mere viewers, a ratings company has little incentive to measure the approximately 11 million television households in the United States that do not have access to cable service.

This has an impact on the market for programmes as networks use track records of past success in earning ratings, share and demographics to predict success. Networks look for producers, actors, or celebrities who have a track record of recent successes; for genres that were hot during the last year; and for programme elements that were featured in last season's hits on television or at the box office. This mix-and-match approach has been termed recombinant television (Gitlin, 2001) as new shows are created by combining bits and persons connected to old and successful shows.

However, this approach is no guarantee of success as NBC's situation comedy *Emeril* (NBC, 2001) demonstrates. The workplace situation comedy had the track record of its producer, Linda Bloodworth-Thomason, who had worked on three successful workplace sitcoms (*Designing Women*, CBS, 1986–93; *Rhoda*, CBS, 1974–8; and *M*A*S*H*, CBS, 1972–83). *Emeril*'s star, Emeril Lagasse, had established his first name as a brand through extensive licensing and merchandising deals. Further, *Emeril* built on Lagasse's success on the Food network. The sitcom appeared to be a fictionalised account of what happens off-camera during the taping of Lagasse's *Emeril Live* (Food, 1997–) cooking show, then the centrepiece of the Food network's prime-time schedule. Both Bloodworth-Thomason and Lagasse were known for working with men and women of various racial, ethnic and regional backgrounds, and *Emeril*'s casting built on that. With this track record, *Emeril* should have been a hit. Instead, it was the first series cancelled in autumn 2001, given its terrible performance on audience

measurements. With the failure of new series running from 80–90 per cent for any given season, recombinant designs — and the audience measures upon which they are based – are poor predictors for programme success.

Eileen R. Meehan

RECOMMENDED READING

Meehan, Eileen R. (2002), 'Gendering the Commodity Audience,' in E. R. Meehan and E. Riordan (eds), *Sex and Money: Feminism and Political Economy in Media Studies*, Minneapolis: University of Minnesota Press, pp. 281–99.

Meehan, Eileen R. (2003), 'Why We Don't Count: The Commodity Audience', in Michele Hilmes (ed.), *Connections: A Broadcasting History Reader*, Belmont: Wadsworth.

Mosco, Vincent (1996), *The Political Economy of Communication*, Thousand Oaks: Sage.

The Television Violence Debates

Debates about television violence have been an integral part of the medium's history, particularly in the United States (Cowan, 1979; Rowland, 1983; 1997). From the very beginning, the violence question has been intimately intertwined with television's economics, programming, regulation, social impact and even its technology. With the arguable exception of obscenity, violence and its alleged effects on children have been the premier focal point of public criticism, legislative inquiry, social research, industry defensiveness and press confusion about US television. This has been true, though more sporadically, in most other nations as well. Questions about journalistic fairness and bias also have been major themes of debate, but despite their importance they have not elicited as much officially sponsored academic research and formal political inquiry.

Yet for all its prominence, and the claims of many social science and media reform groups notwithstanding, the violence issue has gone largely unresolved. Behavioural researchers, media critics and politicians have regularly raised it, often in government-sanctioned forums, with highly publicised arguments about the purported scientific evidence of its deleterious social effects, particularly on children (APA, 1993). Their positions have been typically countered by media scholars from other social science disciplines, television executives and constitutional experts who variously provide alternative insights into media and cultural processes, critique the research and point to core free-speech principles (Fowles, 1982; Freedman, 1988; Gitlin, 1994; Newcomb, 1978; Deutsch, 1984).

These countervailing positions, and the powerful economic and political interests behind them, have tended to lead to applied public policy stand-offs. As a result, instead of achieving any significant official action, the primary role of 'television violence' has been to serve as a symbolic object of concern, as a leading cultural issue to be debated, worried over, roundly denounced or defended. The television violence debate has been consumed with concern about the putative negative effects of television on children and society, yet its own chief effect has been as a political device to divert attention from other questions about television structure, purpose and reform.

The issue of violent media content was well rehearsed in the US long before the advent of television. It had been posed at least as early as the turn of the twentieth century, at the time of the rise of the industrialised national mass media, particularly the popular press and film (Comstock, 1883/1967). Virtually all the core arguments and positions that were to characterise the later debates about television were articulated at that time.

Those concerns and the patterns of academic and policy response were shaped in a context of major economic and social transformations in late nineteenth- and early twentieth-century American life (Hofstadter, 1954; Noble, 1958; Wiebe, 1967). The press and film, themselves products of the new industrial order, quickly became popular and powerful vehicles of cultural expression reflecting many of the shifting patterns of power and anxiety in an increasingly complex world. As such they were objects of intense scrutiny and frequent blame (Charters, 1933). However, as unregulated media of communication they were formally beyond direct government sanction.

When television arrived in the mid-twentieth century as the newest popular mass medium, it did not take long for the traditional patterns of debate about violence to reappear. The US was emerging from the Great Depression and World War II. It was beginning to lead the world's next major phase of economic growth, while also becoming embroiled in a widespread social reordering domestically and in related Cold War and Third World struggles for power and freedom globally. In this environment, television, a mysterious, powerful new medium and arbiter of popular culture, became a subject of considerable interest and anxiety.

As with any new medium there were great expectations at the outset, and in certain respects they seemed to be ful-

filled. Elements of commercial television in the early years included such apparent public interest material as live dramatic performances, local children's productions and even college courses. But these few examples and the positive rhetoric celebrating them masked the realities of the new medium's core structure and purpose. Built on the model of the commercial, network-dominated radio industry before it, US television became primarily an industrialised system for distributing popular entertainment programmes and generating large audiences for national and local advertisers. In keeping with its for-profit mandate, and despite its few high-culture and educational efforts, it quickly manifested mass-audience characteristics. Television adopted many of the popular entertainment forms of the pulp press, the dime-store novel, film and commercial radio before it: situation comedies, musical variety reviews, soap operas, Westerns and urban crime and detective series. Many of these had a great deal of violent content, and that fact in combination with television's powerful visual and aural characteristics, and its rapid diffusion and disruptive impact on domestic life, raised widespread popular and critical concern. Violence quickly became the talisman of all the ambivalent anxieties about this intrusive new medium.

Yet, unlike most other media, broadcasting was licensed under a fiduciary standard to serve 'the public interest, convenience and necessity' (Communications Act, 1934), making it subject to regulatory and legislative review. Therefore, in contrast to the treatment of other media, early fears and anxieties led immediately to a regular pattern of public inquiry about television's alleged negative impacts on social behaviour, particularly with regard to violence (see e.g., US House, 1952; US Senate, 1954; 1955; 1961, 1962). Simultaneously, the explosive post-war growth of the US university system and federal funding for applied research of all kinds (Lyons, 1969) helped place social science research at the heart of the public policy debates over violence. But research findings were complex and often contradictory, open to different interpretations from different interests and for different purposes. A continuing stand-off developed, permitting public authorities to indulge in strong criticism of television violence while remaining protected by First Amendment and political considerations from ever taking significant remedial steps.

This primarily symbolic function of the struggle over television violence also reflects a key dilemma of communications policy-making in the US. The broadcast media were regulated for essentially technical reasons (management of the scarce spectrum). The public interest standard might have implied something about content in the minds of many, but in reality FCC regulation turned largely on technical and fiscal matters. Television was part of the private media system, protected by the First Amendment from obtrusive programme regulation. So the Congressional hearings of the 1950s and 60s, under the leadership of Representative Oren Harris (Democrat Arkansas) and Senators Estes Kefauver (Democrat Tennessee) and Thomas Dodd (Democrat Connecticut), remained severely circumscribed by conflicting interests and the constitutionally contradictory status of television content regulation, with very little attention given to the more comprehensive type of structural critique that might have produced actual change.

In the late 1960s the television violence issue heated up considerably and developed a particularly strong presence in public discourse. This was a period of otherwise considerable social and ideological struggle over a powerful set of issues including civil rights, the Vietnam War, consumerism and the environment, all punctuated by a steady parade of peace marches, demonstrations and several summers of urban riots. The media, particularly television, were widely thought to be exacerbating factors in the social unrest. As a result, television violence became a key site for political debate about the changing social order. Congress initiated repeated investigations of television throughout the early and mid-1970s (see e.g., US Senate, 1969; 1971; 1972; 1974), particularly under the leadership of Senator John Pastore (Democrat Rhode Island). To assist in the investigations, Congress authorised a large federal investment in behavioural research under the aegis of the National Science Foundation, the US Surgeon General and the National Institutes of Health and Mental Health (National Commission, 1970; Comstock and Rubinstein, 1972; Surgeon General's Scientific Advisory Committee, 1972; Cater and Strickland, 1975; Skolnick, 1970).

Other players in the debates were the behavioural researchers, child advocates and citizen activists who used the new federal financial support to try to develop a broader scientific platform for their critique. They sought to emulate the emerging medical science case against smoking and the then new Surgeon General's inquiry into the health effects of tobacco (Surgeon General's Advisory Committee, 1964). These reformers were able to mobilise a popular, common-sense acceptance of the behavioural science case and to contribute to the impression that Congress was taking the matter seriously. But their critiques resulted in little else besides government exhortation and industrial promises of closer self-examination, unlike the more definitive steps beginning to be taken by Congress in the case of tobacco. The reformers seldom articulated demands

for major structural or institutional changes in US television, seemingly content to accept the reality of a thoroughly commercial system and its advertising-based programming logic, with little apparent awareness of how limited would be the regulatory and legislative response.

Meanwhile, to protect their ever-growing and increasingly profitable enterprise, broadcast industry leaders introduced oppositional research evidence based on their own studies. They simultaneously issued loud warnings about the First Amendment implications of any formal government action and hinted more quietly about the electoral consequences for those who too effectively might press the violence case to the point of legislation. They sought to avoid any programme restrictions or content regulations and, most importantly, any serious consideration of major structural alternatives to the US system of predominantly private, commercial, network-dominated television.

To do so they continued a pattern of carefully influencing the US academic and communication research discourse about media impact and audience behaviour they had adopted years earlier (Lazarsfeld and Stanton, 1941; 1949), through a programme of their own 'administrative research'. In opposition to the initially dominant stimulus-response or direct-effects models rising out of mid-century behavioural psychology, the networks established their own offices of social research, underwriting academic centres of media research and supporting studies in functionalist sociology that led to more complex 'two-step flow' models (Klapper, 1960; Lazarsfeld and Katz, 1955). Those models proved highly useful in deflecting the negative direct-effects arguments about radio and television content, and they provided a platform upon which to critique the negative impact studies. The critiques focused on the laboratory settings of most of the research, its reliance on correlation statistics and the short-term, weak nature of the impacts found, all suggesting that there were in fact no significant, real-world, long-term causal findings.

The principal architect of the administrative research strategy was Frank Stanton, the social research PhD President of CBS. Over time he and other industry leaders designed a carefully nuanced pattern of response that included a demeanour of polite appreciation for criticism along with largely empty promises to reduce the amount of violent content and underwrite more educational and positive fare, especially for children, without admitting any actual wrongdoing or serious negative social effects. As a result Congress continued to bluster about televised violence without taking any meaningful action.

In one response to the concerns about violence, and also about other alleged shortcomings of commercial tele-

THE V-CHIP

The V-Chip is a fine example of the classic American reaction to intractable political and social problems. It is a 'technological fix' that appears to resolve a complex major issue, giving the appearance of a solution to what is in effect an unresolved and continuingly murky realm.

The debate about television violence had raged for over thirty years, with virtually no Congressional action except a long series of repetitive investigations and hearings. In the mid-1980s proposals began to emerge regarding the use of an electronic monitoring device that could be included in television sets to permit the blocking of violent programmes. The technology was dubbed the 'V(iolence)-Chip' and became a major focus of communications policy debate in the late 1980s and early 1990s (Banta, 1998). If television programmes were coded in some way, perhaps along the lines of the content-rating system in the film industry, the V-Chip could detect them and, if properly programmed by the television set owner, could prevent the display of the coded programme.

There were precedents for this level of intervention by government. Over the years Congress had directly legislated or authorised the FCC to establish broadcast transmission and reception standards in such matters as the allocation of the spectrum, the core NTSC system and colour standards, dual VHF-UHF set reception capacity and closed captioning. The V-Chip could be seen as an extension of that sort of technical requirement, justifiable under the 'public interest' criterion of the Communication Act, because it did not inject the government into programming decisions. It was seen instead as a way of giving parents a new tool to make such decisions themselves for their children.

Initially the television industry resisted the V-Chip and ratings-system concepts. Broadcasters had long been successful in avoiding content regulations of all kinds, and they were not interested in any measures that could be interpreted as breaching those walls. Also there was a danger that this sort of technology inserted in the television set could cultivate in viewers an interest in other uses, such as blocking commercials.

But by the late 1980s and early 1990s the policy situation was changing dramatically enough for broadcasters to reassess their position. It was becoming increasingly clear that in keeping with overarching ideological forces in favour of marketplace solutions to all sorts of late-twentieth century economic and social issues, Congress and successive presidential administrations were steadily deregulating all of telecommunications, including broadcasting, and even beginning to privatise portions of the spectrum. The official goal was to increase competition in telecommunications, and to that end there was every indication that, far from seeking to impose content restrictions, Congress intended to provide maximum economic and content freedoms for the broadcast industry.

With the emergence of new distribution technologies such as cable, satellites and the Internet, broadcasters could no longer be certain that their very form of reaching the public would remain intact. Meanwhile, by the early 1990s the prospect of converting the broadcast system to digital was increasingly likely. In light of all this impending change the broadcasters needed certain protections and guarantees, such as new spectra during the transition to digital, maintenance of must-carry rights on analogue cable, extension of that principle to digital cable, and comparable rights on direct broadcast satellite systems. Given that the V-Chip and ratings system could be seen as not being a means for censorship, the broadcasters found that conceding to their adoption would be a small price to pay for the large economic gains to be had from the new protections. Accordingly, by the mid-1990s the television industry was prepared to develop its own ratings system, in parallel with another being implemented by the cable industry, and it ceased opposition to the V-Chip. The chip was therefore written into the Telecommunications Act of 1996, with the requirement that by the year 2000 all television sets sold in the US would incorporate it.

Meanwhile, the anti-violence movement appeared to have achieved a great victory. After years of avoidance, Congress seemed finally to have accepted the reformers' relentless arguments about the validity of social effects research and the danger to society it evinced. Here was a tangible result that both the reformers and Congress could claim. Yet, as usual with technological fixes in American experience, much else was left unaddressed. For one thing, the research evidence justifying this step remained higly arguable (Teotonio, 2002). For another, it seemed to some to be an attempt to impose 'virtue by machine', and it was not entirely clear that it was constitutional (Polivy, 1997). And as always before, it allowed Congress to appear to have been diligent in reforming broadcasting, while allowing it to continue to support the fundamental economics and programme-planning dynamics of the industry and avoiding serious public policy consideration of any real alternatives.

Willard D. Rowland, Jr

vision, Congress and the Johnson administration created a new public broadcasting enterprise in the late 1960s, built on the older, weak, educational radio and television movement (Carnegie Commission, 1967; Public Broadcasting Act, 1967). But support for public broadcasting remained limited and, although public radio and television grew dramatically in the 1970s and 80s, they never had the funding for the wide variety of non-violent dramatic and entertainment programming common in the schedules of national public service broadcasting systems abroad.

By the 1980s and into the early 1990s, with the rise of cable and satellite television, industry apologists were able to couple oppositional research and First Amendment justifications with utopian predictions of the capacities of newer technologies to provide more choice in the media marketplace and to transcend the limits of broadcast television. They were joined in that approach by many of the media reformers who, while continuing to assail the industry and to point to the findings of behavioural effects research, also came to rely on the promises of the newer broadband, interactive technologies and the hoped-for liberations of the new information society. This approach was in keeping with a longstanding pattern among US social reformers and media critics, who historically have tended to see redeeming features in every new technological innovation (Guimary, 1975; Rowland, 1982).

During this period Congress resumed the pattern of recurring investigations and hearings about television violence. Now the pediatric medical community joined behavioural, psychological and psychiatric researchers in linking television violence to social pathology. Unable to convince policy-makers on the basis of the correlation evidence, and blocked by the constitutional issues, the psychologists and physicians turned the strategy towards epidemiological grounds. They claimed that social health was endangered enough by television violence to trump traditional First Amendment concerns and to require some sort of political response.

But, beginning in the mid-1970s, Congress, with the support of successive presidential administrations and the courts, began to pursue an increasingly widespread programme of economic and social deregulation and privatisation. This federal policy regime was mapped directly onto the electronic media. In a steady series of Justice Department and federal court actions, formal legislation (e.g., Cable Communications Policy Act, 1984; Telecommunications Act, 1996) and regulatory agency rulings, the telephone and cable television industries were deregulated, broadcast licence periods were extended, the Fairness Doctrine was eliminated, media cross-ownership

rules were relaxed, and portions of the spectrum were auctioned off to private owners.

In this environment the prospects for serious content regulation of US television eroded even further. In the early 1980s, residual sub-government forces from the Surgeon General's period kept the violence issue alive through a continuing series of grant programmes, reports and publicity campaigns (US House, 1981; National Institute of Mental Health, 1982). Throughout the 1980s and into the early 1990s another cycle of television violence hearings ran its course, led principally by Senator Paul Simon (Democrat Illinois) and Representative Edward Markey (Democrat Massachusetts) (see e.g., US House, 1983; 1988; 1992; US Senate, 1984; 1987). New self-regulatory measures and anti-trust exemptions were proposed, including programme content rating systems and the V-Chip, an electronic programme-blocking device to be installed in television sets (grey box). For its compliance in this measure, the industry received substantial benefits in the form of digital spectrum frequencies and protection from new media competition.

By the mid-1990s it appeared that much of the media content debate was shifting from violence on television to indecency on the Internet. The anti-violence and reform communities were able to claim an applied public policy success in the V-Chip, and Congress also could claim to have finally legislated something about television violence.

Yet in that very appearance of a reformist victory the old pattern of an essentially symbolic, avoidance process persisted. In the major piece of communications legislation during the period and the most seeping media law since 1934 (the Telecommunications Act of 1996), there was no support for reform or structural change in broadcasting. No efforts were made to strengthen public and community broadcasting. With much fanfare and self-congratulation Congress inserted, and President Clinton signed, a provision banning indecency on the Internet. But, as the congressional leadership and lawyer President knew it would be, that section was quickly struck down by the courts, because of its patent unconstitutionality.

As a result of this continuingly cynical approach to communications policy-making and the further triumph of a simplistic marketplace ideology, broadcasting and all of telecommunications, including the newer interactive technologies, continued to be ever more privatised during the turn into the new century. There were no policy efforts to provide alternatives to the underlying economic logic of commercial service and national programming.

Meanwhile, few of the reformers, journalists and academic participants in the long drama of the television violence debates had come to understand the reality and effects of its recurrent, cyclical process, and how they, in fact, had helped perpetuate it. Fewer still had mounted the sort of structural critique of US television's essentially commercial character that might lead to any substantial institutional alternative to the conditions that were the cause of so much violence-laden content and other programming shortcomings in the first place.

Willard D. Rowland, Jr

RECOMMENDED READING

Cowan, Geoffrey (1979), *See No Evil: The Backstage Battle over Sex and Violence on Television*, New York: Simon & Schuster.

Fowles, Jib (1982), *Television Viewers vs. Media Snobs: What TV Does for People*, New York: Stein & Day.

Freedman, Jonathan (1988), 'Television violence and aggression: what the evidence shows', in Stuart Oskamp (ed.), *Television as a Social Issue*, Newbury Park: Sage.

Gitlin, Todd (1994), 'Imagebusters: the hollow crusade against TV violence', *American Prospect*, 16, Winter, pp. 42–9, excerpted in the *Utne Reader*, May/June 1994, pp. 92–3.

Rowland, Willard D., Jr (1983), *The Politics of TV Violence: Policy Uses of Communication Research*, Beverly Hills: Sage.

Rowland, Willard D., Jr (1997), 'Television Violence Redux: The Continuing Mythology of Effects', in Martin Barker and Julian Petley (eds), *Ill Effects: The Media/Violence Debate*, London: Routledge.

Audiences and the Internet

The impact of the Internet on television audiences has been profound. The Internet has greatly expanded the number and variety of fan communities surrounding television programmes, enabled more direct contact and dialogue between television producers and consumers, made television audiences more available to corporations as merchandising targets and made their fan activity more subject to corporate policing.

The most significant site of television audience activity on the Internet has been the programme website, especially the 'home page', an online extension of a television network or programme that provides scheduling information and promotional material, and offers opportunities for viewer feedback and communication. Home pages for news networks like CNN or the BBC contain frequent news updates, links, and polls, while home pages for narrative programmes provide episode guides, star/character biographies, merchandising and programme-specific advice and information.

Officially licensed home pages and unofficial fan websites proliferated in the early 1990s, and were developed by both producers and viewers. Some of the first fan sites were devoted to supporting the fledgling series *The X-Files* (Fox, 1993–2002), which was under threat of cancellation in its first season. Programme producers took note of these sites and developed an official website for the show to both encourage fans and convince network executives of the demographic value of *The X-Files*' audience, a move widely seen as saving the show (Seiter, 1999, p. 119). Universal provided an official home page, the 'Netforum', for *Xena: Warrior Princess* (syndicated, 1995–2001) fans soon after the show's premiere, and they developed it into one of the largest fan communities in the world. By the mid-1990s, home pages had become standard practice for networks eager to promote their product (and related merchandise) to viewers, while unofficial fan websites multiplied around specific programmes, particularly science-fiction and fantasy genres.

The most attractive and novel aspect of such sites was their interactive capability, the 'bulletin boards' or 'posting boards' where viewers could provide feedback to the network or producers and talk to each other about news issues or narrative developments. The instant nature of the web revolutionised television viewing the way the telegraph's 'lightning lines' had revolutionised news gathering, erasing time and geographical distances. Fan communities that had before taken months or years to develop appeared literally overnight and grew exponentially within weeks. The television experience changed significantly for many viewers, who were now able to continue their textual engagement after the programme's end by logging on to a programme website and analysing the episode with other fans. This kind of 'participatory spectatorship' provided viewers with additional reading strategies and enlarged the possible meanings of the text (Murray, 1999, p. 223; Jenkins, 1992, p. 23).

Such 'textual poaching' was familiar to many of the earliest Internet television fans, who were also active producers of 'fanzines', bound collections of fan fiction, art and comment devoted to particular programmes (Jenkins, 1992). Zines were amateur, non-profit publications, very popular and well known within their fan communities but considered 'underground' and largely invisible to the gen-

eral public. Fanzines primarily developed around programmes with science-fiction or fantasy content like *Star
Trek* (NBC, 1966–9) and *Doctor Who* (BBC, 1963–89) and
fans often gathered at conventions held in large cities where
they could meet each other (and sometimes the show's personnel), and purchase fan-related memorabilia.

Early Internet fan-sites replicated the practices of
fanzines but moved these fan communities above ground.
Their new public accessibility and visibility permitted the
emergence of diverse and multiple fan-sites, made subcul-
tural reading practices more widely available, and connected viewers much more easily across lines of age, region,
race, education, class, gender, sexuality and nation. For the
archivist and the academic as well as the fan, the current
web makes accessible a degree of information and a variety
of points of view that is unprecedented. A popular site like
Roswell's <crashdown.com> for example, contains numerous discussion 'threads' to suit the various interests of the
Roswell (WB/UPN 1999–2002) community, among them
threads for African-American fans, for those interested in
homoerotic relationships and for those devoted to dwelling
on the details of a particular relationship. Smaller websites
might devote themselves to specific aspects of a programme,
like a star or a romantic coupling or a philosophical or political question ('Is Xena a Christ figure?' 'Is Buffy a feminist?'); they might document and catalogue a producer's
thoughts or a character's lines, or provide an archive of the
material that was edited out of a script before it aired. Some
websites offer opportunities for discussion of several programmes and/or provide detailed episode synopses or critiques, like <televisionwithoutpity.com>. Still others are
devoted to 'spoilers', inside information or speculation
regarding upcoming plots (indeed, the rapid spread of
information online has resulted in much greater studio
secrecy). One of the most popular television sites,
<jumptheshark.com>, invites television viewers to debate
the moment at which a particular programme 'jumped the
shark', or peaked and started to go downhill. All of these
sites share sophisticated reading strategies that acknowledge various kinds of 'subtext' and promote alternative
readings among fans, who are encouraged by the community to think of themselves as active producers of meaning as well as textual consumers.

Internet communication has also made it easier for television fans to organise in support of their favourite programmes. Teenage fans of the ABC teen drama *My
So-Called Life* (ABC, 1994–5) led one of the first Internet
campaigns to save a show during its first and only season.
The fans (who called themselves 'Lifers') pooled money
and took out advertisements on behalf of the programme

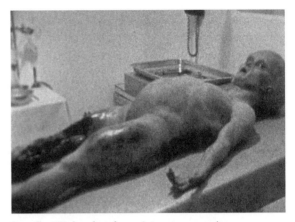

Roswell: a TV show but also an Internet community

in *Variety* and the *Hollywood Reporter*, developed several
campaign sites on the World Wide Web, and filled *My So
Called Life*'s home page with thousands of protests (the
show was cancelled, but its teen viewers were rewarded by
repeated viewings on MTV) (Murray, 1999). Fans of the
alien teen drama *Roswell* had more success in 2000 when
they bombarded WB network executives with 6,000 bottles
of tabasco sauce (a topping favoured by the programme's
alien characters) to show their support for the show when
it was threatened with cancellation. One of the largest and
most organised online fan communities, *Roswell* fans saved
their show from cancellation twice, doubling their efforts
in 2001 to successfully get the programme picked up by
another network (UPN) when the WB cancelled it. Given
the strength and investment of these communities in their
texts, it is not surprising that some of the most popular
television programmes worldwide since the dawn of the
Internet have been those with the strongest international
Internet fan bases – shows like *The X-Files*, *Xena*, and *Buffy
the Vampire Slayer* (WB/UPN, 1997–2002).

The availability of immediate audience feedback has
also significantly altered the relationship between the
industry and the audience, and both cable and network
producers have developed a variety of ways of promoting
television–Internet interaction. Producers and writers of
many television shows prowl Internet posting boards
(announced or unannounced) after programme airings to
chart viewer reactions, and producers have often cited such
feedback as having a significant impact on their development of characters and storylines. MTV's *Total Request Live*
(MTV, 1998–) is built around fan online requests for and
comments about their favourite videos, while E!
Entertainment Television's awards show broadcasts allow
viewers to rate the attire of the nominees online as they're
entering the theatre. Some cable networks combine

XENA AND BUFFY FANS

Certain television programs like *Xena: Warrior Princess* (syndicated, 1995–2001) and *Buffy the Vampire Slayer* (WB/UPN, 1997–2002) have developed huge worldwide Internet fan followings. While part of the reason for their sustained popularity is the intense international marketing of the programmes by parent corporations MCA/Universal and Fox, *Xena* and *Buffy* developed their fan followings before their parent corporations jumped on the bandwagon. Indeed, the specific nature of these fan communities points to the new kinds of opportunities Internet fandom has provided for television audiences.

Both *Xena* and *Buffy* are fantasy/adventure texts with empowered female characters in leading roles and strong lesbian subtexts, which helps explain the programmes' popularity among women, teenagers and gay/lesbian audiences. Their intense online fan following suggests the particular significance of Internet fandom for these groups, who may have access to computers but may not have as much access to supportive organisations or other means of making their voices heard in the media. Many *Xena* and *Buffy* fans have noted online their own sense of alienation and isolation before becoming members of the fan community.

Teenagers in particular view these fan communities as safe spaces for exploring questions of social and sexual identity. Because of the broad age range of *Xena* and *Buffy* fans, sites become places where older fans not only train 'newbies' in the kinds of reading practices and 'slash' (queer) fiction techniques used by community members, but also provide advice and support teens may not be able to find elsewhere.

Significantly, *Xena* and *Buffy* fan communities do not just exist online. Fans have met and become friends, and there are many instances where fans have moved countries or continents to be together, formed life-long partnerships and had children. Because the communities are so large and far-reaching, many hold yearly events where fans meet and socialise. *Buffy* fans, for example, hold annual posting board parties, which fans attend from around the world.

Such inclusive communities might not have been possible had the producers and writers of *Xena* and *Buffy* not been so actively supportive of the fans and their 'subtextual' readings. *Xena*'s staffers began posting on the show's bulletin board within a few weeks of its premiere and engaged in lengthy e-mail conversations with fans they contacted there. *Xena*'s star Lucy Lawless publicly expressed gratitude to her lesbian fans, and producers made sure to keep the lesbian subtext alive in the programme's narrative. In a similar way, *Buffy*'s producer Joss Whedon advised fans to 'bring your own subtext' when watching the show, and he and other show personnel still routinely check in with fans online to get their feedback. The core fans and producers of *Buffy* have developed affectionate bonds and even working relationships: fans have had characters named after them, worked as assistants to production staffers and, in one case, a former fan has become a staff writer for *Buffy*'s spin-off, *Angel* (WB, 1999–). Such relationships have made these fans feel more a part of the production as well as the reception end of the text, and the respect the producers show towards them has inspired fierce loyalties and attracted more fans to the programmes.

Allison McCracken

Internet chat and episode text directly like Oxygen, which airs reruns of *Xena* with live web comment running along the bottom of the screen. The bigger networks are not shying away from interactive possibilities either, in some cases even permitting the online audience to determine content. With its ratings sagging, for example, *Two Guys and a Girl* (ABC, 1998–2001) invited audiences to choose which character in the programme they wanted to be pregnant, and then aired the viewer-chosen ending along with the others during its final episode.

Most major network promotions, however, tempt Internet viewers with the promise of additional material from the programme if they log on, underlining the privileged and more valued status of the Internet viewer to broadcasters. In one instance, ABC's fictional character Drew Carey rigged up his house with a video camera that broadcast images over the World Wide Web. The simul-

taneous web version of the programme added gags and cameo appearances that the viewers at home did not see, and tallied a record 1.9 million hits for a website event. In some cases, the differences between the broadcast text and the Internet text are more substantial and significantly reduce the possible meanings available to broadcast audiences. Internet viewers of CBS's reality programme *Big Brother* (CBS, 2000–1), for example, were able to see footage of important events that were cut out of the programme when it was packaged for broadcast, thus leading to very different readings of the programme by the two audiences. In similar ways, news programmes have often placed more complex or controversial material online rather than broadcast it, making such news inaccessible to people without Internet access and thus sharpening the digital divide.

While television audiences with Internet access are valuable commodities to corporations, there has been substantial corporate backlash against some television fan activity. Both 20th Century-Fox and Viacom have been particularly aggressive about shutting down fan-sites that they decide infringe on their programme copyrights. These 'cease and desist' orders have been targeted at fan-sites for *The Simpsons* (Fox, 1990–), *Millennium* (Fox, 1996–9), *The X-Files*, *Star Trek* and *Buffy the Vampire Slayer*, and primarily involve sites that have script catalogues or large quantities of sound or video bytes. Television fans have also been cited for using the Internet to exchange videotapes of programmes and for downloading programmes broadcast in other countries but delayed in the US (such as *Buffy*'s 'Graduation Day' episode in 1999). The policing of television fans on the Internet suggests that although the net has made television audiences more visible and in some ways more vulnerable, they have also become more actively resistant, more unified and more sophisticated because of it.

Allison McCracken

RECOMMENDED READING

Jenkins, Henry (1992), *Textual Poachers: Television Fans and Participatory Culture*, New York: Routledge.

Katz, John, 'Voices from the Hellmouth', <www.slashdot.org>, accessed 26 April 1999.

Murray, Susan (1999), 'Saving Our So-Called Lives: Girl Fandom, Adolescent Subjectivity, and *My So-Called Life*', in Marsha Kinder (ed.), *Kids' Media Culture*, Durham: Duke University Press.

Seiter, Ellen (1999), *Television and New Media Audiences*, Oxford: Oxford University Press.

Silver, Diane, 'The History of *Xena* Fan Fiction on the Net', <www.whoosh.org/issue25/lunacy1.html>.

List of Illustrations

Whilst considerable effort has been made to correctly identify the copyright holders, this has not been possible in all cases. We apologise for any apparent negligence and any omissions or corrections brought to our attention will be remedied in any future editions.

Technologies: Lord Reith, © Hulton Deutsch Collection; *The Archers*, BBC; **Institutions: From Origins to Stability:** *The Likely Lads*, BBC; *Up the Junction*, BBC; *Dragnet*, Mark VII Ltd ; *The Bionic Woman*, Harve Bennett Productions/Universal TV; **Institutions: Conflict and Change:** *Brookside*, Mersey Television; *Shoah*, Films Adelph/Historia Films; *The Sopranos*, Brad Grey Television/Brillstein-Grey Entertainment/Chase Films/HBO/Sammax Inc./Soprano Productions; *Dawson's Creek*, Outerbank Entertainment/Columbia TriStar Television/Columbia TriStar Domestic Television/Granville Productions/ Procter & Gamble Productions/Sony Pictures Television; **Programming: 1950s–80s:** *Susannah and a Suicide*, ; *Father Knows Best*, ABC/CBS/NBC/Rodney-Young Productions/Screen Gems Television; *The $64,000 Question*, CBS Television/ Entertainment Productions Inc.; *Highway Patrol*, ZIV Television Programs Inc.; *Rawhide*, CBS Television/MGM Television; *Hullabaloo*, Hullabaloo Enterprises/NBC; *The Smothers Brothers Comedy Hour*, American Broadcasting Company/CBS Television/Comedic Productions Inc./Ilson/Chambers Productions; *Yes Minister*, BBC; *All in the Family*, Bud Yorkin Productions/CBS Television/Norman Lear/Tandem Productions; *Charlie's Angels*, Spelling-Goldberg Productions; **Programming: New Venues, New Forms:** *The Girlie Show*, Rapido TV; *Hill Street Blues*, MTM Enterprises Inc./NBC; *You've Been Framed*, Action Time/Granada Television; *Ground Force*, Bazal Productions; *Married … with Children*, Columbia Pictures Television/ELP Communications/Embassy Television; *ER*, Constant c Productions/Amblin Entertainment/Warner Bros. Television/Amblin Television; *LA Law*, 20th Century Fox Television; *Baywatch*, The Baywatch Company/Tower 12 Productions/Tower 18 Production Company; *The Price is Right*, ABC//Mark Goodson-Bill Todman Productions/NBC; *Big Brother*, Bazal Productions; **Audiences:** *Star Trek*, Paramount Network Television Productions/Paramount Television; *Beverly Hills 90210*, Spelling Television/Torand Productions, Inc.; *Roswell*, 20th Century Fox Television/Jason Katims Productions/Regency Television

BIBLIOGRAPHY

Introduction

Ang, Ien (1985), *Watching Dallas: Soap Opera and the Melodramatic Imagination*, New York: Methuen.

Branston, Gill (1998), 'Histories of British Television', in Christine Geraghty and David Lusted (eds), *The Television Studies Book*, London: Arnold.

Camporesi, Valeria (2000), *Mass Culture and National Traditions: The BBC and American Broadcasting, 1922–1954*, Fucecchio, Italy: European Press Academic Publishing.

Collins, Richard (1999), 'The European Union Audiovisual Policies of the UK and France', in Michael Scriven and Monia Lecomte (eds) *Television Broadcasting in Contemporary France and Britain*, New York: Berghann.

Hendy, David (2000), *Radio in the Global Age*, Cambridge and Malden: Polity.

Hilmes, Michele (1997), *Radio Voices: American Broadcasting 1922–1952*, Minneapolis and London: University of Minnesota Press.

Hilmes, Michele (2003), 'British Quality, American Chaos: Historical Dualisms and What They Leave out', *Radio Journal: International Studies in Broadcast and Audio Media*, vol. 1, no. 1.

Lacey, Kate (2002), 'Radio in the Great Depression: Promotional Culture, Public Service, and Propaganda', in Michele Hilmes and Jason Loviglio (eds), *The Radio Reader*, New York: Routledge.

Miller, Jeffrey (2000), *Something Completely Different: British Television and American Culture*, Minneapolis: University of Minnesota Press.

Scannell, Paddy and Cardiff, David (1986), 'Good Luck War Workers! Class, Politics and Entertainment in Wartime Broadcasting', in Tony Bennett, Colin Mercer and Janet Woolacott (eds), *Popular Culture and Social Relations*, Milton Keynes and Philadelphia: Open University Press.

Scannell, Paddy and Cardiff, David (1991) *A Social History of British Broadcasting Volume 1: 1922–1939, Serving the Nation*, Oxford and Cambridge: Blackwell.

Scriven, Michael and Lecomte, Monia (eds) (1999), *Television Broadcasting in Contemporary France and Britain*, New York: Berghann Books.

Smith, Anthony (ed.) (1998), *Television: An International History*, 2nd edition, Oxford and New York: Oxford University Press.

Strinati, Dominic (1992) 'The Taste of America: Americanization and Popular Culture in Britain', in Dominic Strinati and Stephen Wagg (eds), *Come On Down? Popular Media Culture in Post-War Britain*, London: Routledge.

Vipond, Mary (1992), *Listening in: The First Decade of Canadian Broadcasting, 1922–1932*, Montreal: McGill-Queen's University Press.

Technologies

Austin, Bruce A. (1990), 'Home Video: The Second-Run "Theater" of the 1990s', in Tino Balio (ed.), *Hollywood in the Age of Television*, Boston: Unwin Hyman.

BBC (1936), *BBC Annual 1936*, London: BBC.

Berners-Lee, Tim (1999), *Weaving the Web: The Original Design and Ultimate Destiny of the World Wide Web By its Inventor*, New York: HarperBusiness.

Boddy, William (1990), *Fifties Television: The Industry and Its Critics*, Urbana: University of Illinois Press.

Briggs, Asa (1961), *The History of Broadcasting in the United Kingdom: Vol II The Golden Age of Wireless*, Oxford: Oxford University Press.

Briggs, Asa (1995), *The History of Broadcasting in the United Kingdom*, five volumes, Oxford: Oxford University Press.

Collins, Richard (1990), *Culture, Communication, & National Identity*, Toronto: University of Toronto Press.

Collins, Richard and Murroni, Cristina (1996), *New Media, New Policies*, Cambridge: Polity.

Crisell, Andrew (1994), *Understanding Radio*, London and New York: Routledge.

Crisell, Andrew (1997), *An Introductory History of British Broadcasting*, London and New York: Routledge.

Derry, Mark (ed.) (1994), *Flame Wars: The Discourse of Cyberculture*, Durham: Duke University Press.

Douglas, Susan (1999), *Listening in: Radio and the American Imagination*, New York and Toronto: Random House.

Economist, The (2001), 'Outgrowing Auntie', 18 August.

Fink, D. G. (1945), 'Television Broadcast Practice in America – 1927 to 1944' *Proceedings of the Institute of Electrical Engin-eers*, vol. 99, Part III in G. Shiers (ed.) (1977), *The Tech-nological Development of Television*, New York: Arno.

Garratt, G. R. M. and Mumford, A. H. (1952), 'A History of Television', *Proceedings of the Institute of Electrical Engineers*, vol. 99, Part IIIA in G. Shiers (ed.) (1977), *The Technological Development of Television*, New York: Arno.

Gibas, H. (1936), 'Television in Germany', *Proceedings of the Institute of Radio Engineers*, vol. 24, in G. Shiers (ed.) (1977), *The Technological Development of Television*, New York: Arno.

Griffiths, Richard T. (2001), 'From ARPANET to World Wide Web', *History of the Internet, Internet for Historians (and just about everyone else)*, Universiteit Leiden, 4 October, <www.let.leidenuniv.nl/history/ivh/frame_theorie.html>, accessed 30 January 2002.

Hafner, Katie and Lynon, Matthew (1996), *Where Wizards Stay up Late: The Origins of the Internet*, New York: Simon & Schuster.

Harries, Dan (ed.) (2002), *The New Media Book*, London: BFI.

Hendy, David (2000), *Radio in the Global Age*, Cambridge and Malden: Polity.

Hilmes, Michele (1997), *Radio Voices: American Broadcasting, 1922–1952*, Minneapolis and London: University of Minnesota Press.

Hilmes, Michele and Loviglio, Jason (eds) (2002), *Radio Reader: Essays in the Cultural History of Radio*, New York and London: Routledge.

Hollins, T. (1984), *Beyond Broadcasting: Into the Cable Age*, London: BFI.

Hubbel, R. W. (1942), *4000 Years of Television*, New York: Putnam.

Humphreys, Peter J. (1996), *Mass Media and Media Policy in Western Europe*, Manchester: Manchester University Press.

Jensen, A. G. (1954), 'The Evolution of Modern Television', *Journal of the SMPTE*, vol. 64, p. 174 in G. Shiers (ed.) (1997), *The Technological Development of Television*, New York: Arno.

Kristula, Dave, 'The History of the Internet', March 1997, updated August 2001, <www.davesite.com/webstation/net-history.shtml>.

McChesney, Robert. (1999), 'The Internet and US Communication Policy-Making in Historical and Critical Perspective', *Journal of Communications*, vol. 46, no. 1, Winter, pp. 98–124.

Naughton, John (2000), *A Brief History of the Future: From Radio Days to Internet Years in a Lifetime*, Woodstock: The Overlook Press.

Negrine, Ralph (1994), *Politics and the Mass Media in Britain*, 2nd edition, London: Routledge.

Parsons, Patrick R. and Frieden, Robert M. (1998), *The Cable and Satellite Television Industries*, Boston: Allyn and Bacon.

Plummer, James (2002), 'Consumers, Digital Technology, and Copyrights', *Consumers' Research Magazine*, vol. 85, no. 9, pp. 34–5.

Robins, Kevin and Webster, Frank (1999), *Times of the Technoculture: From the Information Society to the Virtual Life*, New York: Routledge.

Rutherford, Paul (1990), *When Television Was Young: Primetime Canada, 1952–1967*, Toronto: University of Toronto Press.

Scannell, Paddy (1990), 'Public Service Broadcasting: The History of a Concept', in Andrew Goodwin and Garry Whannel (eds), *Understanding Television*, London and New York: Routledge. Also published in Edward Buscombe (ed.) (2000), *British Television: A Reader*, Oxford and New York: Oxford University Press.

Scannell, Paddy and Cardiff, David (1991), *A Social History of British Broadcasting: Volume 1: 1922–1939 Serving the Nation*, Oxford and Cambridge: Blackwell.

Schrage, Michael (1983), 'Big Computer Network Split by Pentagon', *Washington Post*, 4 October, Tuesday, final edition, D7.

Shiers, G. (ed.) (1977), *The Technological Development of Television*, New York: Arno.

Spar, Deborah L. (2001), *Ruling the Waves: Cycles of Discovery, Chaos, and Wealth from the Compass to the Internet*, New York: Harcourt.

Stone, Allucquere Rosanne (1995), *The War of Desire and Technology at the Close of the Mechanical Age*, Cambridge: The MIT Press.

Turkle, Sherry (1995), *Life on the Screen: Identity in the Age of the Internet*, New York: Simon & Schuster.

Ubois, Jeff (1989), 'Old ARPANETs Never Die; They Just Migrate to DRI', *Network World*, 24 July, 1.

Uricchio, William (1990), 'Introduction to the History of German Television', *Historical Journal of Film, Radio and Television*, vol. 10, no. 2.

Vaidhyanathan, Siva (2001), *Copyrights and Copywrongs: The Rise of Intellectual Property and How It Threatens Creativity*, New York: New York University Press.

Waldrop, F. C. and Borkin, J. (1938), *Television: A Struggle for Power*, New York: William Morrow.

Winston, Brian (1998), *Media, Technology and Society*, London: Routledge.

Zakon, Robert Hobbes, 'Hobbes' Internet Timeline v5.2', <www.zakon.org/robert/internet/timeline>, accessed 17 March 2001.

ONLINE RESOURCES

'Digital Packet-Switching', Inventors, MIT website: <www.web.mit.edu/invent/www/inventorsA-H/Baran. html, accessed 1 February 2002.

'Internet Protocols, (TCP/IP)', *The Lemelson-MIT Awards: Invention Dimension*, <www.web.mit.edu/invent/www /inventorsA-H/cerf.html>.

'On Distributed Communications' Series, RAND web page: <www.rand.org/publications/RM/baran.list.html>, accessed 1 February 2002.

Institutions: From Origins to Stability

Alvey, M. (2000), 'The Independents: Rethinking the Television Studio System', in H. Newcomb (ed.), *Television: The Critical View*, New York: Oxford University Press.

Anderson, Christopher (1994), *Hollywood TV: The Studio System in the Fifties*, Austin: University of Texas Press.

Balio, Tino (ed.) (1990), *Hollywood in the Age of Television*, Boston: Unwin Hyman.

Baughman, James L. (1985), *Television's Guardians: The FCC and the Politics of Programming, 1958–1967*, Knoxville: University of Tennessee Press.

BBC (1949), *BBC Year Book 1949*, London: BBC.

Benjamin, Louise (2001), Freedom of the Air and the Public Interest, Carbondale: Southern Illinois University Press.

Bensman, Marvin R. (1976), 'Regulation of Broadcasting by the Department of Commerce, 1921–1927', in Lawrence W. Lichty and Malachi C. Topping (eds), *American Broadcasting: A Source Book on the History of Radio and Television*, New York: Hastings House.

Boddy, William (1990a), *Fifties Television: The Industry and Its Critics*, Urbana: University of Illinois Press.

Boddy, William (1990b), 'The Seven Dwarfs & the Money Grubbers: The Public Relations Crisis of US Television in the Late 1950s', in P. Mellencamp (ed.), *Logics of Television*, Bloomington: Indiana University Press, pp. 98–116.

Briggs, Asa (1961), *The Birth of Broadcasting, The History of Broadcasting in the United Kingdom, Volume 1*, London: Oxford University Press.

Briggs, Asa (1979), *The History of Broadcasting in the United Kingdom – Volume IV: Sound and Vision 1945–1955*, Oxford: Oxford University Press.

Brunsdon, Charlotte (1996), *Screen Tastes*, London: Routledge.

Burns, Tom (1977), *The BBC: Public Institution and Private World*, London and New York: Macmillan.

Buscombe, Edward (ed.) (2000), *British Television: A Reader*, Oxford and New York: Oxford University Press.

Chaney, David (1983), 'A Symbolic Mirror of Ourselves: Civic Ritual in Mass Society', *Media, Culture and Society*, vol. 5, no. 2.

Clayton, Ian, Harding, Colin and Lewis, Brian (eds) (1995), *Opening the Box: The Popular Experience of Television*, Bradford: Yorkshire Arts/National Museum of Photography, Film and Television.

Cohen, Lizabeth (1990), *Making a New Deal: Industrial Workers in Chicago, 1919–1939*, New York: Cambridge.

Corner, John (ed.) (1991), *Popular Television in Britain: Studies in Cultural History*, London: BFI.

Corner, John (1995), *Television Form and Public Address*, London: Arnold.

Crisell, Andrew (1997), *An Introductory History of British Broadcasting*, London and New York: Routledge.

Curran, James and Seaton, Jean (1988), *Power without Responsibility: The Press and Broadcasting in Britain*, London: Routledge.

Curran, James and Seaton, Jean (1991), *Power without Responsibility: The Press and Broadcasting in Britain*, 4th edition, London: Routledge.

Curran, James and Seaton, Jean (1997), *Power without Responsibility: The Press and Broadcasting in Britain*, 5th edition, London and New York: Routledge.

Curtin, Michael (1995), *Redeeming the Wasteland: Television Documentary and Cold War Politics*, New Brunswick: Rutgers University Press.

Davies, John (1994), *Broadcasting and the BBC in Wales*, Cardiff: University of Wales Press.

Doll, Bob (1996), *Sparks out of the Plowed Ground: The History of America's Small Town Radio Stations*, Long Beach: Streamline Press.

Freedman, Des (1999), 'How Her Majesty's Opposition Grew to Like Commercial Television: The Labour Party and the Origins of ITV', *Media History*, vol. 5, no. 1, pp. 19–32.

Geddes, Keith (1991), *The Setmakers: A History of the Radio and Television Industry*, London: BREMA.

Gitlin, Todd (1983), *Inside Prime Time*, New York: Pantheon.

Goldie, Grace Wyndham (1977), *Facing the Nation: Television and Politics 1936–76*, London: Bodley Head.

Goodman, David (2001), 'The American System', paper presented at the American Studies Association Conference, Washington, DC.

Goodman, Mark and Gring, Mark (2000), 'The Radio Act of 1927: Progressive Ideology, Epistemology, and Praxis', *Rhetoric and Public Affairs*, vol. 3, no. 3, pp. 397–418.

Gorham, Maurice (1952), *Broadcasting and Television: Since 1900*, London: Andrew Dakers.

Greene, Hugh (1969), *The Third Floor Front: A View of Broadcasting in the Sixties*, London: Bodley Head.

Halper, Donna (2002), *Invisible Stars: A Social History of Women in American Broadcasting*, Boston: Sharpe.

Hilmes, Michele (1997), *Radio Voices: American Broadcasting 1922–1952*, Minneapolis and London: University of Minnesota Press.

Lucas, Rowland (1981), *The Voice of a Nation*, Llandysul: Gomer.

MacCabe, Colin and Stewart, Olivia (eds) (1986), *The BBC and Public Service Broadcasting*, Manchester: Manchester University Press.

Mander, Mary S. (1984), 'The Public Debate about Broadcasting in the Twenties: An Interpretive History', *Journal of Broadcasting*, vol. 28, no. 2.

McChesney, Robert W. (1994), *Telecommunications, Mass Media, and Democracy*, New York: Oxford.

Medhurst, Jamie (1988), 'The Mass Media in Twentieth-Century Wales', in Philip Henry Jones and Eiluned Rees (eds), *A Nation and Its Books: A History of the Book in Wales*, Aberystwyth: National Library of Wales.

Miall, Leonard (1994), *Inside the BBC: British Broadcasting Characters*, London: Weidenfeld and Nicholson.

Mittell, Jason (2002), 'The Great Saturday Morning Excile: Scheduling Cartoons on Television's Periphery in the 1960s', in C. Stabile and M. Harrison (eds), *Television Animation: A Reader in Popular Culture*, New York: Routledge.

Paulu, Burton (1961), *British Broadcasting in Transition*, London: Macmillan.

Potter, Jeremy (1989), *Independent Television in Britain. Volume Three: Politics and Control, 1968–80*, London and Basingstoke: Macmillan.

Reith, John (1924), *Broadcast over Britain*, London: Hodder & Stoughton.

Reith, John (1949), *Into the Wind*, London: Hodder & Stoughton.

Report of the Committee on Broadcasting 1960, Cmnd 1819 (1962), London: HMSO [Pilkington].

Report of the Committee on Broadcasting Coverage, Cmnd 5774 (1974), London: HMSO [Crawford].

Report of the Committee on the Future of Broadcasting (1977), London: HMSO [Annan].

Report of the Committee on the Future of Broadcasting, Cmnd 6753 (1977), London: HMSO [Annan].

Roberts, Graham and Taylor, Philip (eds) (2001), *The Historian, Television and Television History*, Luton: University of Luton Press.

Sales, Roger (1986), 'An Introduction to Broadcasting History', in David Punter (ed.), *Introduction to Contemporary Cultural Studies*, London and New York: Longman.

Sarno, Edward F. Jr (1976), 'The National Radio Conferences', in Lawrence W. Lichty and Malachi C. Topping (eds), *American Broadcasting*, New York: Hastings House.

Scannell, Paddy (1990), 'Public Service Broadcasting: The History of a Concept', in Andrew Goodwin and Garry Whannel (eds), *Understanding Television*, London and New York: Routledge. Also published in Edward Buscombe (ed.) (2000), *British Television: A Reader*, Oxford and New York: Oxford University Press.

Scannell, Paddy and Cardiff, David (1986), 'Good Luck War Workers! Class, Politics and Entertainment in Wartime Broadcasting', in Tony Bennett, Colin Mercer and Janet Woolacott (eds), *Popular Culture and Social Relations*, Milton Keynes and Philadelphia: Open University Press.

Scannell, Paddy and Cardiff, David (1991), *A Social History of British Broadcasting: Volume 1 1922–1939 Serving the Nation*, Oxford and Cambridge: Blackwell.

Schwoch, James (1994), 'A Failed Vision: The Mutual Television Networks', *Velvet Light Trap*, 33, Spring.

Sendall, Bernard (1982) *Independent Television in Britain: Volume I – Origin and Foundation 1946–1962*, London: Macmillan.

Sendall, Bernard (1983), *Independent Television in Britain: Volume II – Expansion and Change, 1958–1968*, London: Macmillan.

Silvey, Robert (1974), *Who's Listening? The Story of BBC Audience Research*, London: Allen & Unwin.

Spigel, Lynn and Curtin, Michael (eds) (1997), *The Revolution Wasn't Televised: Sixties Television and Social Conflict*, New York: Routledge.

Sterling, Christopher H. and Kitross, John M. (1990), *Stay Tuned: A Concise History of American Broadcasting*, 2nd edition, Belmont: Wadsworth. Third edition (2001), New York: Lawrence Erlbaum.

Stuart, Charles (ed.) (1975), *The Reith Diaries*, London: Collins.

Thompson, R. J. (1996), *Television's Second Golden Age: From Hill Street Blues to ER*, New York: Continuum.

Tracey, Michael (2000), 'The BBC and the General Strike: May 1926', in Edward Buscombe (ed.) (2000), *British Television: A Reader*, Oxford and New York: Oxford University Press; originally published in Michael Tracey (1977), *The Production of Political Television*, London: Routledge & Kegan Paul.

Vaillant, Derek (2002), 'Sounds of Whiteness: Local Radio, Racial Formation, and Public Culture in Chicago, 1921–1935', *American Quarterly*, vol. 54, no. 1, pp. 25–40.

Weymouth, Tony and Lamizet, Bernard (1996), *Markets & Myths: Forces for Change in European Media*, London and New York: Longman.

Wheen, Francis (1985), *Television: A History by Francis Wheen*, London: Century Publishing.

Williams, Kevin (1998), *Get Me a Murder a Day! The History of Mass Communication in Britain*, London and New York: Arnold.

Williams, Raymond (1966), *Communications*, London: Pelican Books.

Williams, Raymond (1974), *Television: Technology and Cultural Form*, London: Fontana.

Winston, Brian (1990), 'How Are Media Born?', in John Downing and Annabelle Sreberny-Mohammadi (eds), *Questioning the Media*, London: Sage.

Institutions: Conflict and Change

Advisory Committee on Public Interest Obligations of Digital Television (1998), *Charting the Digital Broadcasting Future*, Washington, DC at <www.ntia.doc.gov/pubintadv com.piacreport.htm>.

BARB (Broadcasters Audience Research Board) (2002a), *Television Ownership in Private Domestic Households 1956–2001*, at<www.barb.co.uk/TVFACTS.cfm?fullstory =true&newsid=13&flag=tvfacts>, accessed 11 February 2002.

BARB (2002b), *Cable and Satellite Development 1992–2001*, at <www.barb.co.uk/TVFACTS.cfm?fullstory=true&newsid= 10&flag=tvfacts>, accessed 11 February 2002.

BARB (2002c), Annual % Shares of Viewing (Individuals) (1981–2000), at <www.barb.co.uk/TVFACTS.cfm?full story=true&newsid=11&flag=tvfacts>, accessed 11 February 2002.

Barnett, Steven and Seymour, Emily (1999), 'A shrinking iceberg travelling south . . .' *Changing Trends in British Television: A Case Study of Drama and Current Affairs*, London: University of Westminster.

Barnett, Steven, Seymour, Emily and Gaber, Ivor (2000), *From Callaghan to Kosovo: Changing Trends in British Television News 1975–1999*, London: University of Westminster.

Baughman, James L. (1992), *The Republic of Mass Culture*, Baltimore, London: Johns Hopkins University Press.

Blanchard, Simon and Morley, David (eds) (1982), *What's This Channel Four?*, London: Comedia.

Boyle, Deirdre (1997), *Subject to Change: Guerrilla Television Revisited*, Oxford: Oxford University Press.

Briggs, Asa and Burke, Peter (2002), *A Social History of the Media. From Gutenberg to the Internet*, Cambridge: Polity.

Brinson, Susan L. (1998), 'Frieda Hennock: FCC Activist and the Campaign for Educational Television 1948–1951', *Historical Journal of Film, Radio and Television*, vol. 18, no. 3.

Brown, Duncan H. (1994), 'The Academy's Response to the Call for a Marketplace Approach', *Critical Studies in Mass Communication*, vol. 11, no. 3.

Channel Four Television (1988), *Report and Accounts for the Year Ended 31 March 1988*, London: Channel Four.

Croteau, David and Hoynes, William (2001), *The Business of Media: Corporate Media and the Public Interest*, Thousand Oaks: Pine Forge Press.

Curran, James and Seaton, Jean (1997), *Power Without Responsibility: The Press and Broadcasting in Britain*, 5th edition, London and New York: Routledge.

DCMS (1999), *The Future Funding of the BBC*, London: Department of Culture, Media and Sport.

Docherty, David, Morrison, David E. and Tracey, Michael (1988), *Keeping Faith? Channel Four and Its Audience*, London: John Libbey,

Engelman, Ralph (1996), *Public Television and Radio in America: A Political History*, Thousand Oaks: Sage.

Enzensberger, Hans Magnus (1974), *The Consciousness Industry*, New York: Seabury Press.

EPC (1993), *EPC Position Paper on the Impact of New Technology: The Emergence of a Multimedia Industry in Europe*, London: European Publisher's Council.

Fowler, Mark S. and Brenner, Daniel L. (1982), 'A Marketplace Approach to Broadcast Regulation', *Texas Law Review*, vol. 60.

Goodwin, Peter (1998), *Telvision under the Tories: Broadcasting Policy 1979–1997*, London: BFI.

Grade, Michael (1999), *It Seemed Like a Good Idea at the Time*, London: Macmillan.

Harvey, Sylvia (1994), 'Channel Four Television: From Annan to Grade' in Stuart Hood (ed.), *Behind the Screens. British Broadcasting in the 1990s*, London: Lawrence and Wishart; reprinted in Edward Buscombe (ed.) (2000), *British Television: A Reader*, Oxford and New York: Oxford University Press.

Hilmes, Michele (2001), *Only Connect: A Cultural History of Broadcasting in the United States*, Belmont: Wadsworth.

Hollins, Timothy (1984), *Beyond Broadcasting: Into the Cable Age*, London: BFI.

Home Office (1977), *Report of the Committee on the Future of Broadcasting*, London: HMSO [Annan].

Independent Television Commission (ITC) (2001), *ITC Annual Report and Accounts 2000*, London: ITC.

Independent Television Commission (ITC) (1999), *Annual Report, 1998*, London: ITC.

Independent Television Commission (ITC) (2000), *Annual Report, 1999*, London: ITC.

Independent Television Commission (ITC) (2001a), *ITC Notes. No 14. Satellite Television*, at <www.itc.org.uk>, July, accessed 11 February 2002.

Independent Television Commission (ITC) (2001b), *ITC Notes. No 15. Cable Television*, at <www.itc.org.uk>, July, accessed 11 February 2002.

Independent Television Commission (ITC) (2001c), *Annual Report, 2000*, at <www.itc.org.uk>, accessed 11 February 2002.

Independent Television Commission (ITC) (2002), *Television Audience Share Figures* (Twenty-first Quarterly Report to 31 December 2001, twelve-month figures), London: ITC.

Isaacs, Jeremy (1989), *Storm over Four: A Personal Account*, London: Weidenfeld and Nicholson.

Lambert, Stephen (1982), *Channel Four: Television with a Difference?*, London: BFI.

Ledbetter, James (1997), *Made Possible by . . .: The Death of Public Broadcasting in the United States*, New York and London: Verso.

Marcus, Daniel (ed.) (1991), *ROAR! The Paper Tiger Guide to Media Activism*, New York: Paper Tiger Television and Wexner Center for the Arts.

National Cable Television Association (2002), at <www.ncta.@.com>.

News Corporation (2002), at <www.newscorp.com>, accessed 13 February 2002.

O'Malley, Tom (1994), *Closedown? The BBC and Government Broadcasting Policy 1979–1992*, London: Pluto Press.

O'Malley, Tom (2001a), 'The Decline of Public service Broadcasting in the UK 1979–2000', in Michael Bromley (ed.) (2001), *No News Is Bad News. Radio, Television and the Public*, Harlow: Longman; pp. 28–45.

O'Malley, Tom (2001b), *Communications Revolution: Who Benefits?*, London: CPBF.

Parsons, Patrick R. and Frieden, Robert M. (1998), *The Cable and Satellite Television Industries*, Boston: Allyn and Bacon.

Pegg, Mark (1983), *Broadcasting and Society 1918–1939*, London: Croom Helm.

Shamberg, Michael and Raindance Corporation (1971), *Guerrilla Television*, New York: Holt, Rinehart and Winston.

Shawcross, W. (1993), *Murdoch*, London: Pan Books.

Shivers, Jube and Morris, Dwight (1996), 'They Wanted Congress to See Telecom Their Way', *Los Angeles Times*, 1 February, D2.

Stein, Laura (2001), 'Access Television and Grassroots Political Communication in the United States', in John Downing, *Radical Media: Rebellious Communication and Social Movements*, Thousand Oaks: Sage.

Sterling, Christopher H. and Kitross, John Michael (2001), *Stay Tuned: A History of American Broadcasting*, 3rd edition, New York: Lawrence Erlbaum.

Streeter, Thomas (1997), 'The Cable Fable Revisited: Discourse, Policy, and the Making of Cable Television', *Critical Studies in Mass Communication*, vol. 4, no. 2.

Tomos, Angharad ((1982), 'Realising a Dream', in Simon Blanchard and David Morley (eds), *What's This Channel Four? An Alternative Report*, London: Comedia.

Walker, James and Ferguson, Douglas (1998), *The Broadcast Television Industry*, Boston: Allyn and Bacon.

Zook, Kristal Brent (1999), *Color by Fox: The Fox Network and the Revolution in Black Television*, New York: Oxford University Press.

Programming: From 1950s–1980s

Anderson, Christopher (1997), 'I Love Lucy', in Horace Newcomb (ed.), *The Encyclopaedia of Television*, Chicago: Fitzroy Dearborn.

Bakewell, Joan, and Garnham, Nicholas (1970), *The New Priesthood: British Television Today*, Harmondsworth: Allen Lane/Penguin.

Barnett, Steven and Curry, Andrew (1994), *The Battle for the BBC*, London: Aurum Press.

Barnouw, Erik (1975), *Tube of Plenty: The Evolution of American Television*, New York and Oxford: Oxford University Press.

Barr, Charles (1997), ' "They Think It's All Over": The Dramatic Legacy of Live Television', in J. Hill and M. McLoone (eds), *Big Picture, Small Screen: The Relations between Film and Television*, Luton: University of Luton Press/John Libbey.

Baughman, James L. (1985), *Television's Guardians: The FCC and the Politics of Programming, 1958–1967*, Knoxville: University of Tennessee Press.

BBC (2000), *Annual Report and Accounts 1999/2000*, London: BBC.

Bedell, Sally (1981), *Up the Tube: Prime-Time TV and the Silverman Years*, New York: The Viking Press.

Beharrell, Peter and Philo, Greg (eds) (1978), *Trade Unions and the Media*, London: Macmillan.

Birt, John (1999), *The Prize and the Price. The Social, Political and Cultural Consequences of the Digital Age*, London: BBC; *New Statesman* Media Lecture.

Boddy, William (1986), 'The Shining Centre of the Home', in P. Drummond and R. Patterson (eds), *Television in Transition*, London: BFI.

Boddy, William (1993), *Fifties Television: The Industry and Its Critics*, Urbana and Chicago: University of Illinois Press.

Bodroghkozy, Aniko (2001), *Groove Tube: Sixties Television and the Youth Rebellion*, Durham and London: Duke University Press.

Briggs, Asa (1979), *The History of Broadcasting in the United Kingdom. Volume IV: Sound and Vision 1945–1955*, Oxford: Oxford University Press.

Briggs, Asa (1985), *The BBC. The First Fifty Years*, Oxford: Oxford University Press.

Briggs, Asa (1995), *The History of Broadcasting in the United Kingdom. Volume V: Competition 1955–1974*, Oxford: Oxford University Press.

Brown, Les (1969), 'TV's Old Math for New Myth: Wooing of Youth Proves a Fizzle', *Variety*, 31 December, p. 21.

Brunsdon, Charlotte (1990), 'Problems with Quality', *Screen*, vol. 31, no. 1, pp. 67–90.

Caldwell, John (1995), *Televisuality: Style, Crisis, and Authority in American Television*, New Brunswick: Rutgers University Press.

Carr, Steven Alan (1992), 'On the Edge of Tastelessness: CBS, the Smothers Brothers, and the Struggle for Control', *Cinema Journal*, vol. 31, no. 4.

Caughie, John (2000), *Television Drama: Realism, Modernism and British Culture*, Oxford: Oxford University Press.

Corner, John (ed.) (1991), *Popular Television in Britain: Studies in Cultural History*, London: BFI.

Crisell, Andrew (1997), *An Introductory History of British Broadcasting*, London and New York: Routledge.

Curran, James, and Seaton, Jean (1988), *Power without Responsibility: The Press and Broadcasting in Britain: Studies in Cultural History*, London and New York: Routledge.

Curran, James and Seaton, Jean (1997), *Power without Responsibility*, 5th edition, London: Routledge.

Doan, Richard (1967), 'The Doan Report', *TV Guide*, 25 March, p. 12.

Doig, Alan (1997), 'The Decline of Investigatory Journalism', in Michael Bromley and Tom O'Malley (eds), *A Journalism Reader*, London: Routledge, pp. 189–213.

Douglas, Susan J. (1994), *Where the Girls Are: Growing up Female with the Mass Media*, New York: Times Books.

Forman, Denis (1997), *Persona Granada: Some Memories of Sidney Bernstein and the Early Days of Independent Television*, London: Andre Deutsch.

Frank, Thomas (1997), *The Conquest of Cool: Business Culture, Counterculture, and the Rise of Hip Consumerism*, Chicago: University of Chicago Press.

Gitlin, Todd (1983), *Inside Prime Time*, New York: Pantheon.

Goodwin, Peter (1998), *Television under the Tories: Broadcasting Policy 1979–1997*, London: BFI.

Hollins, Timothy (1984), *Beyond Broadcasting: Into the Cable Age*, London: BFI.

Jacobs, Jason (1997), 'Gerald Cock', in H. Newcomb (ed.), The Encyclopaedia of Television, Chicago: Fitzroy Dearborn.

Jacobs, Jason (2000), *The Intimate Screen: Early British Television Drama*, Oxford: Oxford University Press.

Jowett, Garth (1994), 'Dangling the Dream? The Presentation of Television to the American Public, 1928–1952' *Historical Journal of Film, Radio and Television*, vol. 4, no. 2.

Kennedy-Martin, Troy (1964), 'Nats Go Home: First Statement of a New Drama for Television', *Encore*, 48, March–April, pp. 21–33.

Leapman, Michael (1987), *The Last Days of the Beeb*, revised edition, London: Coronet.

Marc, David (1997), *Comic Visions: Television Comedy and American Culture*, 2nd edition, Oxford: Blackwell.

Marschall, R. (1986), *History of Television*, London: Bison Books.

Milne, Alasdair (1988), *The Memoirs of a British Broadcaster*, London: Coronet.

Miner, Worthington (1985), *Worthington Miner, interviewed by Franklin Schaffner*, Metuchen and London: The Directors Guild.

News Corporation (2002), at <www.newscorp.com>, accessed 13 February 2002.

Norden, Denis (ed.) (1985), *Coming to You Live!: Behind-the-screen Memories of Forties and Fifties Television*, London: Methuen.

Norman, Bruce (1984), *Here's Looking at You*, London: BBC and Royal Television Society.

O'Malley, Tom (1994), *Closedown? The BBC and Government Broadcasting Policy 1979–1992*, London: Pluto Press.

Pegg, Mark (1983), *Broadcasting and Society 1918–1939*, London: Croom Helm.

Pitman, Jack (1967), 'Demon Demographics Key to CBS Massive Surgery on Winning Sked: Out to Slough Geriatric Stigma', *Variety*, 1 March, p. 25.

Potter, Jeremy (1989), *Independent Television in Britain, Volume Three: Politics and Control, 1968–80*, London and Basingstoke: Macmillan.

Potter, Jeremy (1990), *Independent Television in Britain, Volume Four: Companies and Programmes, 1968–80*, London and Basingstoke: Macmillan.

Raddatz, Leslie (1967), 'More Fun Than . . . a Barrel of the Originals', *TV Guide*, 28 January, p. 19

Scannell, Paddy (1996), *Radio, Television, and Modern Life: A Phenomenological Approach*, Cambridge: Blackwell.

Sendall, Bernard (1982), *Independent Television in Britain, Volume One: Origin and Foundation, 1946–62*, London and Basingstoke: Macmillan.

Sendall, Bernard (1983), *Independent Television in Britain, Volume Two: Expansion and Change, 1958–68*, London and Basingstoke: Macmillan.

Shawcross, W. (1993), *Murdoch*, London: Pan Books.

Spector, Bert (1983), 'A Clash of Cultures: The Smothers Brothers vs. CBS Television', in John E. O'Connor (ed.), *American History/American Television*, New York: Frederick Ungar.

Spigel, Lynn and Curtin, Michael (eds) (1997), *The Revolution Wasn't Televised: Sixties Television and Social Conflict*, New York: Routledge.

Sturcken, Frank (1990), *Live Television: The Golden Age of 1946–1958 in New York*, Jefferson: McFarland.

Thumim, Janet (ed.) (2002), *Small Screens, Big Ideas: Television in the 1950s*, London: I. B. Tauris.

Vahimagi, Tise (ed.) (1994), *British Television: An Illustrated Guide*, Oxford: Oxford University Press.

Wheatley, Helen (2002), '*Mystery and Imagination*: Anatomy of a Gothic Anthology Series', in Janet Thumim (ed.), *Small Screens, Big Ideas: Television in the 1950s*, London: I. B. Tauris, pp. 165–80.

Williams, K. (2001), 'Demise or Renewal? The Dilemma of Public Service Television in Western Europe', in Michael Bromley (ed.) (2001), *No News is Bad News. Radio, Television and the Public*, Harlow: Longman, pp. 9–27.

Programming: New Venues, New Forms

Banks, Jack (1996), *Monopoly Television: MTV's Quest to Control the Music*, Oxford: Westview Press.

Barnouw, Eric (1991), *Tube of Plenty*, Oxford: Oxford University Press.

Barth, Steve (1998), 'Exporting Fantasy', *World Trade Magazine*, March, at <www.global-insight.com/wt9803a.htm>, accessed on 2 May 2002.

Baywatch Database, at <members.tripod.com/~baywatchun>, accessed on 1 July 2002.

Baywatch Website, Official, at <www.baywatch.com>, accessed on 2 May 2002.

BBC (1995), *Annual Report and Accounts 1994–1995*, London: BBC.

BBC (1997), *Annual Report and Accounts 1996–1997*, London: BBC.

BBC (1998), *Annual Report and Accounts 1997–1998*, London: BBC.

Bignell, Jonathan (2000), *Postmodern Media Culture*, Edinburgh: Edinburgh University Press.

Bignell, Jonathan, Lacey, Stephen and Macmurragh-Kavanagh, Madeleine (eds) (2000), *British Television Drama: Past, Present and Future*, Basingstoke: Palgrave.

Bishop, Louise (1998), 'A Life of Leisure', *The Journal of the Royal Television Society*, April, pp. 22–3.

Block, Alex Ben (1991), *Outfoxed: The Inside Story of America's Fourth Television Network*, New York: St Martin's Press.

Boddy, William (1994), 'US Television Abroad: Market Power and National Introspection', *Quarterly Review of Film & Video*, vol. 15, no. 2, pp. 45–55.

Bondebjerg, Ib (1996), 'Public Discourse/Private Fascination: Hybridisation in "True Life Story" genres', *Media, Culture and Society*, 18; pp. 27–45.

Bonnan, Gregory L. and Lewis, Brad Alan, (2000), *Baywatch: Rescued from Prime Time*, Beverly Hills: New Millennium Press.

Bonner, Paul and Aston, Lesley (1998), *Independent Television in Britain, Volume 5: ITV and the IBA 1981–1999: The Old Relationship Changes*, Basingstoke: Macmillan.

Bonner, Paul and Aston, Lesley (2003), *Independent Television in Britain, Volume 6: New Developments in Independent Television, 1981–92*, Basingstoke and New York: Palgrave Macmillan.

Brunsdon, Charlotte (1990), 'Problems with Quality', *Screen*, vol. 31, no. 1, pp. 67–90.

Brunsdon, Charlotte, Johnson, Catherine, Moseley, Rachel and Wheatley, Helen (2001), 'Factual Entertainment on British Television: The Midlands Television Research Group's "8–9 Project" ', *European Journal of Cultural Studies*, vol. 4, no. 1, pp. 29–62.

Brunt, R. (1985), 'What's My Line?', in L. Masterman (ed.), *Television Mythologies*, London: Comedia, pp. 21–8

Buscombe, Edward (ed.) 2000, *British Television: A Reader*, Oxford and New York: Oxford University Press.

Caldwell, John (1995), *Televisuality: Style, Crisis and Authority in American Television*, New Brunswick: Rutgers University Press.

Cathode, Ray (1996), 'The Box', *Sight and Sound*, vol. 6, no. 10, pp. 32–3.

Chan, Christine (1996), 'Foreign Filmmakers Cash in on Cable', *South China Morning Post*, 8 August, p. 7.

China Beach Episode Guide (1992), compiled and copyright by Jerry Boyajian, expanded from an episode guide started by Christoper Kribs and Jerry Boyajian. At <www.danadelany.com/chinabch.txt>.

Coles, Gail (2000), 'Docusoap: Actuality and the Serial Format', in Bruce Carson and Margaret Llewellyn-Jones (eds), *Frames and Fictions on TV: The Politics of Identity within Drama*, Exeter: Intellect, pp. 27–39.

Cooper-Chen, A. (1994), *Games in the Global Village: A 50-Nation Study*, Bowling Green: Bowling Green University Popular Press.

Corner, John (ed.) (1991), *Popular Television in Britain: Studies in Cultural History*, London: BFI.

Corner, John (1996), 'Mediating the Ordinary: The "Access" Idea and Television Form', in John Corner and Sylvia Harvey (eds), *Television Times: A Reader*, London, New York and Sydney: Arnold.

Corner, John (1999), *Critical Ideas in Television Studies*, Oxford: Clarendon Press.

Curtin, Michael (1997), 'Dynasty in Drag: Imagining Global TV', in Lynn Spigel and Michael Curtin (eds), *The Revolution Wasn't Televised: Sixties Television and Social Conflict*, New York: Routledge.

Davies, J. (1983), 'Sale of the Century – Sign of the Decade', *Australian Journal of Screen Theory*, no. 13/4, pp. 19–33.

Dovey, Jon (2000), *Freakshow: First Person Media and Factual Television*, London: Pluto.

Ellis, John (2000), *Seeing Things: Television in the Age of Uncertainty*, London: I. B. Tauris.

Ellis, John (2001), 'The Infotainment Debate', in Glen Creeber (ed.), *The Television Genre Book*, London: BFI, pp. 118–122.

Fiddy, D. (1997), 'Format Sales, International', in H. Newcomb (ed.), *The Encyclopaedia of Television*, Chicago: Fitzroy Dearborn, pp. 623–4.

Gauntlett, David and Hill, Annette (1999), *TV Living: Television, Culture and Everyday Life*, London: Routledge.

Geraghty, Christine and Lusted, David (eds) (1998), *The Television Studies Book*, London: Arnold.

Gibson, Janine (1999), 'Fast food TV threatens quality', *The Guardian*, 25 October, p. 3.

Gillespie, M. (1995), 'Sacred Serials, Devotional Viewing and Domestic Worship: A Case Study in the Interpretation of Two TV versions of The Mahabharata in a Hindu Family in South London', in Robert C. Allen (ed.) (1995), *To Be Continued: Soap Operas Around the World*, London and New York: Routledge, pp. 354–80.

Goldberg, Robert (1989), 'Television: Offended? Don't Watch!', *The Wall Street Journal*, 31 July, section 1, p. 8.

Goodwin, Andrew (1993), 'Riding with Ambulances: Television and Its Uses', *Sight and Sound*, vol. 3, no. 1, pp. 26–8.

Hartley, John (1998), 'Democratainment: Television and Cultural Citizenship', in John Hartley (ed.), *Uses of Television*, London and New York: Routledge, pp. 154–65.

Harvey, Sylvia (2000), 'Channel Four Television: From Annan to Grade', in Edward Buscombe (ed.), *British Television: A Reader*, Oxford: Oxford University Press.

Heinderyckx, F. (1993), 'Television News Programmes in Western Europe', *European Journal of Communication*, vol. 8, no. 4, December, pp. 425–50.

Herman, Edward S. and McChesney, Robert (1998), *Global Media: The Missionaries of Global Capitalism*, London: Cassell.

Hill, Annette (2000), 'Crime and Crisis: British Reality TV in Action', in Edward Buscombe (ed.) (2000), *British Television: A Reader*, Oxford and New York: Oxford University Press, pp. 218–34.

Hill, Annette and Calcutt, Ian, 'Vampire Hunters: The Scheduling and Reception of *Buffy the Vampire Slayer* and *Angel* in the UK' in *Intensities: the journal of cult media*, <www.cult-media.com/issue1/Ahill.htm>.

Holland, Patricia (1998), 'The Politics of the Smile: "Soft News" and the Sexualisation of the Popular Press', in Cynthia Carter, Gill Branston and Stuart Allan (eds), *News, Gender and Power*, London and New York: Routledge, pp. 17–32.

Hollins, Timothy (1984), *Beyond Broadcasting: Into the Cable Age*, London: BFI.

Holt, Jennifer (2003), 'Vertical Vision: Deregulation, Industrial Economy and Prime Time Design', in Mark Jancovich (ed.), *Quality Popular Television: Cult TV, Industry and Fans*, London: BFI.

Hood, Stuart (1994), *Behind the Screens: the Structure of British Broadcasting in the 1990s*, London: Lawrence and Wishart.

Howell, Amanda (1995), 'Reproducing the Past: Popular History and Family Melodrama on *China Beach*', *Camera Obscura*, May, 35, pp. 159–84.

Hutton, Will (2000), 'How *The Naked Chef* Killed *Panorama*: Actually, Don't Blame Jamie Oliver. Blame Instead the BBC Bosses Who Are Delighted to See the Back of Television News Journalism', *The Observer*, 8 October, p. 30.

Ingrams, Richard (1998), 'Not My Fault, Guv, Said the Bearded Controller, It's All Down to That BR', *The Observer*, 22 November, p. 31.

Isaacs, Jeremy (1989), *Storm over Four: A Personal Account*, London: Weidenfeld and Nicholson.

Jefferies, Stuart (2000), *Mrs Slocombe's Pussy: Growing up in front of the Telly*, London: Flamingo.

Kishore, Krishna (1994), 'The Advent of STAR TV in India: Emerging Policy Issues', *Media Asia*, vol. 21, no. 2.

Kreutzner, G. and Seiten, E. (1995), 'Not all "Soaps" Are Created Equal: Towards a Cross-Cultural Criticism of Television Serials', in Robert C. Allen (ed.) (1995), *To Be Continued*, London and New York: Routledge, pp. 234–55.

Langer, John (1998), *Tabloid Television: Popular Journalism and the 'Other News'*, London: Routledge.

Leigh, David (1998), 'World Inaction', *The Guardian*, 9 December, p. 22.

Leibman, Nina C. (1997), 'Comedy, Domestic Settings', H. Newcomb (ed.), *The Encyclopaedia of Television*, Chicago: Fitzroy Dearborn.

Longworth, James L., Jr (2000), *TV Creators: Conversations with America's Top Producers of Television Drama*, Syracuse: Syracuse University Press.

Lury, Karen (1995), 'Television Performance: Being, Acting, Corpsing', *New Formations*, 26, pp. 114–27.

Man Chan, Joseph (1994), 'National Responses and Accessibility to Star TV in Asia', *Journal of Communication*, vol. 44, no. 3, Summer, p. 114.

Medhurst, Andy (1999), 'Day for Night', *Sight and Sound*, vol. 9, no. 6, pp. 26–7.

Miller, Toby, Govil, Nitin, McMurria, John and Maxwell, Richard (eds) (2001), *Global Hollywood*, London: BFI.

Moran, Albert (1997), *Copycat TV: Globalisation, Program Formats and Cultural Identity*, Luton: University of Luton Press.

Moseley, Rachel (2000), 'Makeover Takeover on British Television', *Screen*, vol. 41, no. 3, pp. 299–314.

Mosley, Ivo (2000), *Dumbing Down: Culture, Politics and the Mass Media*, Thorverton: Imprint Academic.

Mullen, Megan (2003), *The Revolution Now in Sight: A History of Cable Television Programming in the United States*, Austin: University of Texas Press.

Olson, Scott Robert (1999), *Hollywood Planet: Global Media and the Comparative Advantage of Narrative Transparency*, Mahway and London: Lawrence Erlbaum.

O'Sullivan, Tim (1998), 'Nostalgia, Revelation and Intimacy: Tendencies in the Flow of Modern Popular Television', in Christine Geraghty and David Lusted (eds), *The Television Studies Book*, London: Arnold, pp. 198–211.

Parks, Lisa (2001), 'As the Earth Spins: NBC's *Wide Wide World* and Live Global Television in the 1950s', *Screen*, vol. 42, no. 4, Winter, pp. 332–49.

Parks, Lisa and Kumar, Shanti (eds) (2002), *Planet TV: A Global Television Reader*, New York: New York University Press.

Peyser, Marc (2002), 'Six Feet under Our Skin', *Newsweek*, vol. 139, no. 11, 18 March, p. 52.

Schiller, Herbert I. (1992), *Mass Communications and American Empire*, 2nd edition, Boulder: Westview Press.

Skovmand, Michael (1992), 'Barbarous TV International: Syndicated Wheels of Fortune', in Michael Skovmand and Kim Christian Schroeder (eds), *Media Cultures: Reappraising Transnational Media*, London: Routledge, pp. 84–103.

Sreberny-Mohammadi, Annabelle, Winseck, Dwayne, McKenna, Jim and Boyd-Barret, Oliver (eds) (1997), *Media in Global Context: A Reader*, London: Arnold.

Steel, Mark (1999), 'Yes, Even I know My Triceratops from My Stegosaurus', *The Independent* (*The Tuesday Review*), 12 October, p. 5.

Strange, Nikki (1998), 'Perform, Educate, Entertain: Ingredients of the Cookery Programme Genre', in Christine Geraghty and David Lusted (eds), *The Television Studies Book*, London: Arnold, pp. 301–12.

Sykes, Pam, 'Is David Hasselhoff Really the Antichrist', at <www.home.intekom/intekom/newlookalive/alive/webmis tress–980520.stm>.

Talbot, Paul (2002), personal telephone interview by Lisa
    Fotheringham, 20 April.

'The Media Business: A Mother Is Heard as Sponsors
    Abandon a TV Hit', *New York Times*, 2 March 1989, A1.

Thompson, Robert J. (1996), *Television's Second Golden Age:
    From Hill Street Blues to ER*, New York: Continuum.

Torres, Sasha (1995), 'War and Remembrance: Televisual
    Narrative, National Memory, and *China Beach*', *Camera
    Obscura*, no. 33–4, pp. 147–64.

Turow, Joseph (1997), *Breaking up America: Advertisers and
    the New Media World*, Chicago: University of Chicago
    Press.

van Manen, J. R. (1994), *Televise Formats: en iden naar
    Netherlands recht*, Amsterdam: Otto Cranwinckle
    Untgever.

van Zoonen, Liesbet (1998), 'One of the Girls?: The Changing
    Gender of Journalism', in Cynthia Carter, Gill Branston
    and Stuart Allan (eds), *News, Gender and Power*, London
    and New York: Routledge, pp. 33–46.

Whannel, Garry (1982), '*It's a Knockout*: Constructing
    Communities', *Block*, no. 6, pp. 37–45

Whannel, Garry (1992), 'The price is right but the moments
    are sticky: Television, quiz and game shows, and popular
    culture', in D. Strinati and S. Wagg (eds), *Come on Down?:
    Popular Media Culture in Post-War Britain*, London and
    New York: Routledge pp. 179–201

Zook, Kristal Brent (1999), *Color by Fox: The Fox Network
    and the Revolution in Black Television*, New York: Oxford
    University Press.

Audiences

APA (1993), *Violence and Youth: Psychology's Response*,
    volume 1, Summary Report, Washington, DC: American
    Psychological Association.

Balio, Tino (ed.) (1990), *Hollywood in the Age of Television*,
    Boston: Unwin Hyman.

Banta, Mary Ann (1998), 'The V(Violence)-Chip Story', in
    Ray Elden Heibert (ed.), *Impact of Mass Media: Current
    Issues*, 4th edition, New York: Longman.

Baughman, James L. (1985), *Television's Guardians: The FCC
    and the Politics of Programming, 1958–1967*, Knoxville:
    University of Tennessee Press.

Beniger, J. R. (1987), 'Toward an Old New Paradigm. The
    Half-Century Flirtation with Mass Society', *Public Opinion
    Quarterly*, 51, pp. 46–66.

Boddy, William (1990), *Fifties Television: The Industry and Its
    Critics*, Urbana: University of Illinois Press.

Cable Communications Policy Act of 1984, P.L. 98–549,
    30 October.

Carnegie Commission on Public Television (1967), *Public
    Television: A Program for Action*, New York: Bantam
    Books.

Cater, Douglass and Strickland, Stephen (1975), *TV Violence
    and the Child: The Evolution and Fate of the Surgeon
    General's Report*, New York: Russell Sage Foundation.

Charters, W. W. (1933), *Motion Pictures and Youth: A
    Summary*, New York: Macmillan.

Communications Act of 1934, P.L. 73–416, 19 June.

Comstock, Anthony (1883/1967), *Traps for the Young*, edited
    by Robert Bremner, Cambridge: Harvard University Press.

Comstock, George A. and Rubinstein, Eli A. (eds) (1972),
    Television and Social Behavior: Reports and Papers,
    volumes 1–5, Washington, DC: Department of Health,
    Education and Welfare.

Cowan, Geoffrey (1979), *See No Evil: The Backstage Battle
    over Sex and Violence on Television*, New York: Simon &
    Schuster.

Curtin, Michael (1997), 'On Edge: Culture Industries in the
    Neo-Network Era', in Richard Ohmann, Gage Averill,
    Michael Curtin, David Shumway and Elizabeth G. Traube
    (eds), *Making and Selling Culture*, Hanover: Wesleyan
    University Press.

Curtin, Michael (1999), 'Feminine Desire in the Age of
    Satellite Television', *Journal of Communication*, vol. 49, no.
    2, Spring, pp. 55–70.

D'Acci, Julie (1994), *Defining Women: The Case of Cagney
    and Lacey*, Chapel Hill: University of North Carolina
    Press.

Deutsch, Benjamin P. (1984), 'Wile E. Coyote, ACME
    Explosives and the First Amendment: The Unconstitut-
    ionality of Regulating Violence on Television', *60 Brooklyn
    Law Review 1101*.

Edmiston, Mark (1997), interview in Richard Ohmann, Gage
    Averill, Michael Curtin, David Shumway and Elizabeth
    G. Traube (eds), *Making and Selling Culture*, Hanover:
    Wesleyan University Press.

Feuer, Jane, Kerr, Paul and Vahimagi, Tise (1984), *MTM:
    'Quality Television'*, London: BFI.

Fowles, Jib (1982), *Television Viewers vs. Media Snobs: What
    TV Does for People*, New York: Stein & Day.

Freedman, Jonathan (1988), 'Television Violence and
    Aggression: What the Evidence Shows', in Stuart Oskamp
    (ed.), *Television as a Social Issue*, Newbury Park: Sage.

Gitlin, Todd (1983, 2001), *Inside Prime Time*, New York:
    Pantheon.

Gitlin, Todd (1994), 'Imagebusters: The Hollow Crusade Against TV violence', *American Prospect*, 16, Winter, pp. 42–9, excerpted in the *Utne Reader*, May/June, pp. 92–3.

Guimary, Donald L. (1975), *Citizens' Groups and Broadcasting*, New York: Praeger.

Hall, Stuart (1980), 'Encoding/Decoding', in S. Hall (ed.) *Culture, Media, Language: Working Papers in Cultural Studies, 1972–79*, London: Hutchinson.

Hall, Stuart, Critcher, C., Jefferson, T., Clarke, J. and Roberts, B. (1978), *Policing the Crisis: Mugging, the State and Law and Order*, London: Macmillan.

Harvey, David (1989), *The Condition of Postmodernity: An Enquiry into the Origins of Cultural Change*, Oxford: Blackwell.

Herbst, Susan (1993) *Numbered Voices: How Opinion Polling Has Shaped American Politics*, Chicago: University of Chicago Press.

Hilmes, Michele (1997), *Radio Voices: American Broadcasting, 1922–1952*, Minneapolis: University of Minnesota Press.

Hofstadter, Richard (1954), *The Age of Reform*, New York: Alfred A. Knopf.

Iyengar, S. (1991), *Is Anyone Responsible?*, Chicago: University of Chicago Press.

Jenkins, Henry (1992), *Textual Poachers: Television Fans and Participatory Culture*, New York: Routledge.

Jhally, Sot and Lewis, Justin (1992), *Enlightened Racism: The Cosby Show, Audiences, and the Myth of the American Dream*, Boulder: Westview Press.

Katz, John, 'Voices from the Hellmouth', <www.slash.org>, accessed 26 April 1999.

Klapper, Joseph T. (1960), *The Effects of Mass Communication*, New York: Free Press.

Lazarsfeld, Paul F. and Katz, Elihu (1955), *Personal Influence*, Glencoe: Free Press.

Lazarsfeld, Paul F. and Stanton, Frank N. (eds) (1941), *Radio Research*, New York: Duell, Sloane & Pearce.

Lazarsfeld, Paul F. and Stanton, Frank N. (eds) (1949), *Communications Research, 1948–1949*, New York: Harper & Brothers.

Lewis, Justin (2001), *Constructing Public Opinion: How Elites Do What They Like and Why We Seem to go along with It*, New York: Columbia University Press.

Lyons, Gene M. (1969), *The Uneasy Partnership*, New York: Russell Sage Foundation.

Marchand, Roland (1985), *Advertising the American Dream: Making Way for Modernity, 1920–1940*, Berkeley: University of California Press.

McCombs, M., Danielian J. and Wanta, W. (1995), 'Issues in the News and the Public Agenda', in C. Salmon, C. and T. Glasser, (eds), *Public Opinion and the Communication of Consent*, New York: Guilford Press.

McKinley, E. G. (1997), Beverly Hills, 90210*: Television, Gender, and Identity*, Philadelphia: University of Pennsylvania Press,

Meehan, Eileen R. (2002), 'Gendering the Commodity Audience', in E. R. Meehan and E. Riordan (eds), *Sex and Money: Feminism and Political Economy in Media Studies*, Minneapolis: University of Minnesota Press.

Meehan, Eileen R. (forthcoming), 'Why We Don't Count: The Commodity Audience', in Michele Hilmes (ed.), *Connections: A Broadcasting History Reader*, Belmont: Wadsworth.

Morley, David (1980), *The Nationwide Audience*, London: BFI.

Mosco, Vincent (1996), *The Political Economy of Communication*, Thousand Oaks: Sage.

Murray, Susan (1999), 'Saving Our So-Called Lives: Girl Fandom, Adolescent Subjectivity, and *My So-Called Life*', in Marsha Kinder (ed.), *Kids' Media Culture*, Durham: Duke University Press.

National Commission on the Causes and Prevention of Violence (1970), *To Establish Justice, To Insure Domestic Tranquility*, New York: Praeger.

National Institute of Mental Health (1982), *Television and Behavior: Ten Years of Scientific Progress and Implications for the Eighties*, volumes 1–2, Washington, DC: Department of Health and Human Services.

Newcomb, Horace (1978), 'Assessing the Violence Profile of Gerbner and Gross: A Humanistic Critique and Suggestion', *Communication Research*, July, vol. 5, no. 3, pp. 264–83.

Noble, David W. (1958), *The Paradox of Aggressive Thought*, Minneapolis: University of Minnesota Press.

Ohmann, Richard, Averill, Gage, Curtin, Michael, Shumway, David and Traube, Elizabeth G. (eds) (1997), *Making and Selling Culture*, Hanover: Wesleyan University Press.

Polivy, Denise R. (1997), 'Virtue by Machine: A First Amended Analysis of the V-Chip Provisions of the Telecommunications Act of 1996', 26.

Public Broadcasting Act of 1967, Connecticut Law Review 1749. , P.L. 90–129, 7 November.

Rowland, Willard D., Jr (1982), 'The Illusion of Fulfillment: The Broadcast Reform Movement', *Journalism Monographs*, December, no. 79.

Rowland, Willard D., Jr (1983), *The Politics of TV Violence: Policy Uses of Communication Research*, Beverly Hills: Sage.

Rowland, Willard D., Jr (1997), 'Television Violence Redux: The Continuing Mythology of Effects', in Martin Barker and Julian Petley (eds), *Ill Effects: The Media/Violence Debate*, London: Routledge.

Ruddock, A. (2001), *Understanding Audiences: Theory and Method*, London: Sage.

Seiter, Ellen (1999), *Television and New Media Audiences*, Oxford: Oxford University Press.

Signorielli, N. and Morgan, M. (1990), *Cultivation Analysis*, Beverly Hills: Sage.

Silver, Diane, 'The History of *Xena* Fan Fiction on the Net', <www.whoosh.org/issue25/lunacy1.html>.

Skolnick, Jerome H. (1970), 'The Violence Commission: Internal Politics and Public Policy', in I. L. Horowitz (ed.), *The Use and Abuse of Social Science*, New Brunswick: Transaction.

Spigel, Lynn and Curtin, Michael (eds) (1997), *The Revolution Wasn't Televised: Sixties Television and Social Conflict*, New York: Routledge.

Surgeon General's Advisory Committee of the Public Health Service (1964), *The 1964 Report on Smoking and Health*, Washington, DC: Government Printing Office.

Surgeon General's Scientific Advisory Committee on Television and Social Behaviour (1972), *Television and Growing up: The Impact of Televised Violence*, Washington, DC: Government Printing Office.

Telecommunications Act of 1996, P.L. 104, 8 February.

Television Program Improvement Act of 1990, P.L. 101–650, 5 December.

Teotonio, Isabel (2002), 'TV Violence Study Gets Second Viewing', *Toronto Star*, 14 April.

US House (1952), Committee on Interstate and Foreign Commerce, Federal Communications Commission Subcommittee, *Investigation of Radio and Television Programming*, Hearings (82, 2), June, September, December.

US House (1981), Committee on Energy and Commerce, Subcommittee on Telecommunications, Consumer Protection, and Finance, *Social/Behavioral Effects of Violence on Television*, Hearing (97, 1), 21 October.

US House (1983), Committee on the Judiciary: Subcommittee on Crime, *Crime and Violence in the Media*; Hearing (98, 1), 13 April.

US House (1988), Committee on the Judiciary: Subcommittee on Monopolies and Commercial Law, *Television Violence Act of 1988*, Hearing (100, 2), 5 October.

US House (1992), Committee on the Judiciary: Subcommittee on Crime and Criminal Justice, *Violence on Television*, Hearing (102, 2), 15 December.

US Senate (1954), Committee on the Judiciary, Subcommittee to Investigate Juvenile Delinquency, *Juvenile Delinquency (Television Programs)*, Hearings (83, 2), June, October.

US Senate (1955), *Television Programs*, Hearings (84, 1), April.

US Senate (1961, 1962), Investigation of Juvenile Delinquency in the United States, Part 10, *Effects on Young People of Violence and Crime Portrayed on Television*, Hearings (87: 1, 2), June, July, January, May.

US Senate (1969), Committee on Commerce: Subcommittee on Communications, *Federal Communications Commission Policy Matters and Television Programming*, Hearings, parts 1–2 (91, 1), March.

US Senate (1971), *Scientific Advisory Committee on TV and Social Behavior*, Hearing (92, 1), 28 September.

US Senate (1972), *Surgeon General's Report by the Scientific Advisory Committee on Television and Social Behavior*, Hearings (92, 2), 21–4 March.

US Senate (1974), *Violence on Television*, Hearings (93, 2), 3–5 April.

US Senate (1984), Committee on the Judiciary: Subcommittee on Juvenile Justice, *Media Violence*, Hearing (98, 2), October.

US Senate (1987), Committee on the Judiciary: Subcommittee on Antitrust, Monopolies and Business Rights, *Television Violence Antitrust Exemption*, Hearing (100, 1) 25 June.

Wiebe, Robert (1967), *The Search for Order, 1877–1920*, New York: Hill & Wang.

Williams, Raymond (1963), *Culture and Society*, New York: Columbia University.

Index

Page numbers in **bold** type denote detailed treatment in a 'grey box' study; Page numbers in *italic* denote illustrations (may be textual material on same page); *t* = table/diagram